Inventing

the American Woman

Inventing the American Woman

An Inclusive History

Fourth Edition
Volume 2: Since 1877

GLENDA RILEY
Alexander M. Bracken
Professor of History Emeritus
Ball State University

Harlan Davidson, Inc.
Wheeling, Illinois 60090-6000

Library of Congress Cataloging-in-Publication Data

Riley, Glenda, 1938-
    Inventing the American woman : an inclusive history / Glenda Riley. — 4th ed.
        p. cm.
    Includes bibliographical references and index.
    ISBN-13: 978-0-88295-250-5 (v. 1 : alk. paper)
    ISBN-13: 978-0-88295-251-2 (v. 2 : alk. paper)
    1. Women—United States—History. 2. Sex role—United States—History. I. Title.
    HQ1410.R55 2007
    305.40973—dc22
                                    2006030395

Cover photos: Details from Library of Congress advertising and theatrical posters. Front: "The Black Patti, Mme. M. Sissieretta Jones," LC-USZC4-5164; Back, left to right: "Stage Women's War Relief," LC-USZC4-1342; "Asian woman in shorts, cape, and hat," card #var1994001539/PP; "The Pocahontas Chewing Tobacco," LC-USZC2-671.
Cover design: Chris Calvetti, c2itgraphics

Contents

Volume 2: From 1877

Introduction
Gender Expectations
across Cultures

Since the first edition of *Inventing the American Woman* appeared in 1986, the study of women's history—a fascinating subject that scholars had ignored for far too long—has entered the curriculums of most American high schools, colleges, and universities. The overwhelmingly positive response to that first edition and subsequent ones further demonstrates the tremendous and sustained thirst that Americans have for knowledge concerning the historical experiences of their women. Like its predecessors, this fourth edition of *"Inventing"* (the nickname by which many loyal users refer to the book) presents an overview of the history of women in the United States. Intended for use as a core textbook for courses in women's history or as a supplement to any U.S. survey text, *Inventing* combines factual knowledge with a thesis meant to provoke discussion and further thought. More specifically, this two-volume work tracks the evolution of gender expectations and social constructs concerning the essence of womanhood that have played, and continue to play, a critical role in directing and shaping the behaviors, responses, and dissatisfactions of American women.

American Indians were the first peoples to establish gender expectations in the land we know today as the United States, yet when European settlers reached America they disregarded or rejected Native peoples' ideas regarding women. The newcomers established their own beliefs, which soon became dominant and reflected the thinking of a society that argued for the acceptance of certain enduring "truths" regarding women. A "real" American woman supposedly was, among other things, a devoted mother, a domestic individual who labored most happily and productively within her own home, an unusually virtuous person who remained aloof from the corruption of politics, and a weak-minded, physically inferior being in need of guidance from wiser and stronger people, namely men. Once established as principles, these tenets helped shape a series of intricate images and prescriptions that defined and limited women's roles. In other words, people invented an ideal American woman.

On one hand, one might deem this model of womanhood as harmless. Generally, white middle- and upper-class women best fulfilled its mandates. In turn, it rewarded and honored them. If they remained domestic and unassertive, such women could anticipate the approval of family members, friends, and clergy. In many cases, such women felt grateful, even revered; they gained satisfaction from meeting their society's expectations of women. For other groups of women, especially Native Americans, African Americans, Spanish-speakers, and Asians, as well as poor whites and those employed outside the home, this model simply appeared irrelevant.

On the other hand, one should not underestimate the power of this model as a form of social control, for it provided a comfortable substitute for careful thought. People generally found it easier to believe that both women and men had a well-defined "place" than to consider the complexities of human society and personality. Such thinking also helped maintain an economic system based on the usually greater physical strength of men, who for centuries had performed the heavy labor involved in hunting, farming, and manufacturing, while women often remained behind to bear and raise children and perform lighter tasks. And these ideas reinforced a political system in which men made more of the public decisions and women more of the private, or domestic, ones. Gender expectations and social constructs also kept in force power imbalances. Gradually, prevailing beliefs regarding women translated into policies and legislation regulating families, schools, churches, politics, and the workplace. Too often, these codes robbed all women of the opportunity to cultivate their talents and deprived the developing nation of women's nondomestic skills and labor. Such constraints narrowed the range of women's formal education and socially acceptable literature, delimiting opportunities and expansion of the mind. They also encouraged the development of impractical, sensuous, and physically restrictive women's clothing and tended to relegate women's pastimes to things trivial. Consequently, during the 1600s, 1700s, and early 1800s, thousands of women of different social classes and racial backgrounds resisted, refusing to fit into the mold of the idealized American woman.

These dissidents typically drew on women's culture, such as female networks, to help them endure the system or reform it. At the same time, such forces as early industrialization, urbanization, and national expansion not only tested customary prescriptions but demonstrated their unsuitability to a modernizing society. By the mid-1800s, the model of the ideal American woman sustained open attack. Women's participation in women's rights activism, reformism, religious revivalism, and paid employment helped erode it.

During the late nineteenth century and well into the twentieth, such other developments as Progressivism, world wars, the quest for civil rights, contemporary feminism, and the emergence of double-income families forced many Americans to rethink their beliefs, to recast their ideas in ways that better fit the reality experienced by all kinds of women living in the United States, including professionals, poor single mothers, lesbians, full-time homemakers, divorcees, and those of color. To this day, Americans struggle with, and redefine, expectations of women and societal constructs affecting them—and increasingly those affecting men as well. Understanding the historical development of both the nation and its women is essential to these undertakings.

Therefore, this book considers women and the changes they experienced during various eras of American history. To assist the reader, each chapter ends with several learning aids. One of these is a checklist of names, terms, phrases, and dates. Also included are several issues to think about and discuss. Finally, a selected bibliography provides the interested reader with additional information, varied interpretations, and methodological perspectives regarding women's issues and themes.

About terminology: a special attempt has been made in this text to respect sensitivities regarding the labels and language that carry significance in discussing such issues as racism, sexism, ageism, and classism. Some of the relevant style choices and definitions observed include referring to so-called minorities as peoples of color. References to African Americans and blacks are interchangeable. In accordance with present usage, peoples of Spanish-heritage are called Hispanics, or Chicanos/Chicanas for Mexican Americans. Uppercase Native Americans is used interchangeably with American Indians or, where unmistakable, Indians. Except where hyphens are truly necessary to avoid misreading, this text also prefers not to hyphenate groups of people, even when such compounds as African American and Asian American are used as adjectives.

Such choices in terminology and style remain an especially important effort in a book that braves generalizations regarding the complex historical experience of so many people—in this case, more than half the people of the United States. This fourth edition also eliminates a number of examples of women's achievements. Fortunately, women's history has reached such a stage of development and degree of public acceptance that it is no longer necessary to offer long lists of women's names and instances of their accomplishments to "prove" that women indeed participated in such historical events as wars, migrations, politics, or literary and artistic movements. Consequently, the fourth edition of *Inventing* contains fewer names but further examination of women-related issues and transitions.

This edition has additional features. It has been restructured and reedited to make it more accessible to readers. And, in keeping with American society's growing awareness of the importance of multiculturalism, it includes enhanced discussions of women of color, that is, Native American, African American, Hispanic, and Asian women. Similarly, women's relationship to nature and participation in the conservation movement is more thoroughly covered, as is women's involvement in sports and the military. Throughout, the results of new scholarship have been incorporated and suggested reading lists updated. Because women's history is one of the most energetic and prolific areas of historical investigation, the reader will not only profit from exploring the many books and articles listed herein, but by keeping an eye out for recent publications.

Clearly, this book is about more than the past and present of American women. By implication, it is also about their collective future, one that will witness the emergence of a long overdue development—a reinvented, and far more inclusive, model of American womanhood.

Chapter Six

"Reordering Woman's Sphere": The Gilded Age and Progressive Era, 1878 to 1914

The years between the end of Reconstruction in 1877 and the beginning of World War I in 1914 encompassed two contradictory trends: materialism and reformism. After the Civil War, many Americans had tired of hearing about the nation's ills and what they should be doing to remedy them. They wanted to be left alone, free to run their farms or businesses or seek their fortunes in the American West.

At the same time, wealthy capitalists and entrepreneurs hoped to expand their holdings into unheard-of fortunes. While such names as "Carnegie" and "Rockefeller" became synonymous with fabulous success and affluence, even the average American hoped that through hard work she or he might achieve prosperity. Yet for all its glamour and achievement, the period between 1878 and 1890 was dubbed the Gilded Age after the title of a Mark Twain novel of the day. As the name implies, these years offered more style than substance. At first glance, the era may have shone like gold, but further inspection revealed base metal under the surface. Although unprecedented economic expansion characterized the Gilded Age, so did growing discontent among farmers and workers.

The year 1890 marked a turning point. The newly founded Populist (People's) party demanded drastic changes in numerous areas of American life. Between 1893 and 1897, the worst economic depression in American history (up to that point) caused people to rethink their values. During the mid- and late-1890s, Americans began to recognize that hard work did not guarantee success. Despite their best efforts, many could not escape hardship and poverty.

Another round of reformism seemed to be the answer, and during the 1890s and early 1900s, the so-called Progressive Era, government welfare and social justice programs were effected to try to redress the inequities of the lopsided economic structure. As the nation turned from the excesses of the Gilded Age to the realities of Progressive Era reform, women both implemented change and benefited from it. Women, especially those of the white and black middle- and upper-classes, used their energy and will to revise a spectrum of ideas, including those regarding gender.

The Gilded Age, 1878 to 1890

Industrialization

Four major developments characterized the period that bridged the Reconstruction and Progressive Eras: industrialization, urbanization, immigration, and agrarian discontent. The first of these, industrialization, affected American women in a number of ways. The proliferation and availability of technological devices and convenience goods altered the nature of women's work within the home. Such products as ready-made clothing and baked goods freed many women from much domestic drudgery.

At the same time, the rapid expansion of the industrial work force opened a growing number of employment opportunities to native white and immigrant women. As a result of mass production and the assembly line, jobs once done by skilled male workers could now be performed by anyone willing to work for low wages.

With wages thus suppressed, the marginal earnings that many working men brought home forced a great number of wives to take paid employment to supplement the household income. In immigrant families, daughters were expected to contribute to the family budget as well. Finally, an increasing number of single women, many of them migrants from rural areas, needed to support themselves.

Despite women's entry into the labor force, old ideas held sway. Women found themselves segregated in "women's" jobs that required minimal training and got little respect. In the textile industry, for example, men served as managers and such skilled operatives as fabric cutters, whereas women worked as machine operators, trimmers, and finishers. In bakeries, men held the position of baker and women that of packer. In breweries, men labored as brewers and women as bottle washers.

Women had little choice but to throng to industries that would employ them—textile, garment, tobacco, printing, and food processing. Unfortunately, the availability of women workers ensured that all working women would remain pigeonholed and poorly paid. Typically, unskilled women earned considerably less than unskilled men. Even skilled women earned only about one-half the wage commanded by their skilled male counterparts.

The nature of female labor had definitely changed. Although "mill girls" at such textile centers as Lowell, Massachusetts, had enjoyed a degree of independence, this was no longer true for most women workers. Nor was the money brought in by rural women engaged in piecework in their homes any longer a bonus for rural families. Because of the huge migration to cities, urban women competed with each other for jobs, thus keeping all women's wages low. At the same time, women's earnings became a crucial part of working-class families' struggle to survive. Whether single or married, rural or urban, working women had to contribute to the money their families needed.

For women in rural areas, teaching offered employment, especially for young, single women. The schoolhouse also allowed women to escape some of the drudgery of farm work. Although female teachers often helped with farm chores during their offtime, as well as stoking the schoolhouse stove and cleaning classrooms, they usually felt they were better off than women who worked full time on family farms.

In cities, the employment opportunities for white women typically entailed office and sales work, once the province of white men. In this area, employers discriminated against women of color, as well as immigrant women, preferring to hire native-born white women to work in shops and offices. White women also replaced men as telegraph and telephone operators. In 1870, nineteen thousand women held office jobs. By 1890, this figure jumped to seventy-five thousand. Because office work had become female-dominated, the pay remained low and the hours long.

A growing number of women sought to remedy their situation by organizing Working Girls' Clubs. During the 1880s, several such groups appeared in New York City, the members of which addressed practical issues including wages, insurance, employment bureaus, and lunch programs. These organizations never gained the clout held by labor unions, however.

Meanwhile, a number of women joined men's labor organizations. After 1881, when the Knights of Labor opened membership to women, female workers joined all-male assemblies and organized female assemblies. Black women workers participated by founding assemblies of laundresses, chambermaids, and housekeepers. The Knights chartered 130 locals that enrolled men and women, as well as approximately 270 gender-segregated "ladies' locals." By 1887, the Knights counted sixty-five thousand women among its members.

The Knights of Labor attracted women by blending the "domestic" values of fairness, cooperation, and social service with labor activism. The Knights supported equal pay for equal work, woman suffrage, and temperance. In addition, the Knights established a women's department. Paid female organizers lectured about the benefits of joining the Knights, inspected factories, and organized labor assemblies. During the late 1880s, the Knights fell into decline after several unsuccessful strikes and abandoned much of its women-oriented agenda.

Beginning in 1881, white women were eligible to join the newly organized American Federation of Labor (AFL), although it was not until 1888 that AFL president Samuel Gompers urged the active recruitment of women workers. Nonetheless, women soon found union dues too high to be spared from their limited wages. Also, the reception female inductees received from male members was decidedly cool. In 1891, hoping to bring more female workers into the AFL, union officials created the office of National Organizer for Women.

Despite these changes, resistance to women working outside the home remained strong. Most male workers clung to the long-standing ideology of women as wives and mothers. They failed to recognize that economic necessity propelled women into the labor force. Also, many men feared that women's need to accept low wages would devalue their own earning power.

The situation of working women of color was even more discouraging. Black women earned only one-half the pay of white women. In the South, black women worked predominantly in tenant farming and sharecropping, whereas black women prisoners were hired out as convict labor in fields and on road-building crews. In addition, all women of color faced double jeopardy—discrimination based on gender as well as race. The belief that people of color were best suited for menial labor confined black women to such jobs as laundry workers, scrubwomen, cooks, cannery workers, field hands, crop pickers, and tobacco strippers.

Only a small number of women of color held factory employment. In 1890, census figures indicated that only 2.76 percent of the 975,530 nonwhite women employed worked in manufacturing, whereas 30.83 percent worked as servants, and 15.9 percent worked as laundresses. Nor were women of color often hired to work in offices or retail establishments.

At the same time that factory and menial labor offered dismal conditions and meager wages, the professions opened slightly to women, white and of color. In part, this occurred because earlier women had prepared the way. In addition, after the trauma of Civil War and Reconstruction abated, the need for professionals, notably teachers and nurses, increased. Centers of reformism like Boston and Philadelphia seemed anxious to put new racial and gender principles into practice.

As a result, white and black women of the middle- and upper-classes continued to swell the ranks of professionals. In cities, where school enrollments were high and teachers in great demand, the number of women teachers grew rapidly. Similarly, in urban areas, where hospitals and clinics were concentrated, many women entered nursing.

Women also became doctors. By 1880 the number of women doctors had grown to 2,312. White and black women attended such interracial institutions as the New England Female Medical College in Boston, the

Women's Medical College of Pennsylvania, and Howard University's medical school in Washington, D.C.

Women were less successful in the field of law during the Gilded Age. Although a number of women entered law school, most of them had difficulty establishing a successful practice. Law was still a male-dominated profession, and few male attorneys welcomed the idea of having female colleagues. Also, unlike in education and medicine, it was difficult to argue that a link existed between women's traditional domestic duties and the practice of law. In short, those women who did become lawyers did so against considerable odds.

Among white women attorneys, Belva Ann Lockwood stands out. In 1879, she became the first woman to practice law before the U.S. Supreme Court. Throughout her career, Lockwood used her position to defend women and to lobby for such women-related reforms as property rights and suffrage. In 1884 and again in 1888, she drew attention to woman suffrage by running on the National Equal Rights party ticket for the presidency of the United States. In 1884, Lockwood won more than 4,000 votes in six states. She was less successful in 1888. Despite the support of many women—who wore banners bearing her name, their daughters' donning "Lockwood" caps—Lockwood simply could not compete with male candidates. She spent her later years campaigning for woman suffrage and world peace.

Among black women attorneys, Mary Ann Shadd Cary provides a remarkable example. In 1883, at the age of sixty-three, this teacher and former abolitionist received a law degree from Howard University. Whether she practiced law is unclear, but her moving speeches, extensive writing, and ability to undertake law training later in life made Cary an extraordinary role model for other African American women.

Overall, by 1890 nearly 4 million women worked for wages outside their homes. Stated another way, approximately one out of every seven women held paid employment. The overwhelming number of these women were single (never married). Slightly over 14 percent were married, and nearly 18 percent were divorced or widowed. These statistics suggest that although some women worked because they wanted to, many others did so out of economic necessity. The entry of women into the paid labor force was a trend unlikely to disappear. Instead, employed women were a force that would demand due respect.

Urbanization

The second major trend of the Gilded Age, urbanization, deeply influenced women's lives. During the 1870s and 1880s, cities became marketplaces and manufacturing hubs, changes that created an upheaval in American ideas and values. During these decades, America's urban population grew far more rapidly than its rural population. New York City and Chicago served as magnets, drawing Americans from rural areas and non-Americans from abroad.

The cities of the 1880s were crowded, noisy, yet strangely isolating. Although neighborhoods in which people knew one another existed, it was possible for urban women to remain anonymous amidst the clamoring throngs. Many new arrivals had left their families back on the farm or in small towns, free of parental control for perhaps the first time in their lives. As a result, more women than ever before chose to earn a living on the stage or through prostitution. A number became confidence artists, people who supported themselves through deceit and fraud. Although confidence women had appeared shortly after the Civil War, their numbers increased during the Gilded Age. Such women had mastered blackmail and other such scams. Some were petty pickpockets and shoplifters. Others passed themselves off as heiresses in need of a temporary loan. Typically, these women played to societal expectations of women. While acting helpless and innocent, they adroitly relieved trusting souls of their wallets or savings.

Without doubt, the opportunities presented by city life were rife with problems. For instance, theaters needed women as actresses and dancers, but many of these positions demanded the wearing of scanty attire. Also, huge department stores offered an unimaginable array of goods, as well as the opportunity for even middle-class women to shoplift. Most "respectable" Victorian women were outraged at what they saw around them. Large concentrations of reform-minded women in urban populations found themselves face to face with a huge number of social ills.

Middle- to upper-class white women felt the effects of urbanization in other ways as well. The rise of consumer culture, especially women's sections of the new department stores, introduced clothing and housewares in bold designs and startling colors like Venetian green and brick red. Similarly, the dressmaking and millinery shop in every city and town still offered custom production, ensuring that women with money could have whatever they wanted.

The relaxation of social mores also allowed female fashion to take new directions. In their leisure time, working girls donned dashing bonnets and clingy skirts intended to attract men's attention. For afternoon wear, middle-class women adopted loose tea gowns worn over uncorseted bodies. Even women who wore conventional dress, including corsets and floor-length skirts, might add puffed sleeves or unusual collars to express their individuality.

Urbanization also affected family size. Large families, which provided sorely needed hands on the farm, were expensive and inefficient in the city, so urban women tended to reject traditional thinking regarding large families. During the late 1870s and 1880s, a variety of women supported the concept of Voluntary Motherhood. These women included suffragists, moral reformers, and women who desired freedom from continual pregnancies and childcare. A number of men also wanted fewer children so they could better support and educate those they did have.

Because the Comstock Law of 1873 outlawed the mailing and advertising of birth-control devices under the guise of obscenity, women had to rely on other means to avoid pregnancy. Preventive measures included abstinence from sexual relations, male continence (the avoidance of ejaculation), and *coitus interruptus* (withdrawal just before ejaculation). Occasionally, urban women obtained rubber condoms and pessaries (female prophylactics). Sometimes, subtle advertising that avoided the term *birth control* attracted women. The manufacturers of the Gem Pessary, for example, claimed that their product would prevent and cure "uterine disease." Women who knew how to read between the lines realized that they could used the Gem Pessary to avoid pregnancy. As always, truly desperate women resorted to illegal or self-inflicted abortion.

In reaction to these attempts to limit family size, Americans who feared women's control over childbirth launched a crusade against planned parenthood and abortion. These people were afraid that birth-control measures would lead to medical complications for mothers and infants, as well as cause a general decrease in the U.S. population. Leaders of the American Medical Association and the Young Men's Christian Association (YMCA) initiated national anti–birth-control programs. Yet family size continued to decline, especially among native-born, middle-class, and well-educated urban white women. During the 1880s, these women bore an average of two to three children. Even in the face of warnings and dire threats, women placed importance on avoiding unwanted pregnancies.

Among women of color and immigrant women, a different pattern developed. Black women's rate of fertility, which had begun to decline somewhat even before the Civil War, continued to drop during the 1880s, though at a slower rate than did that of white women. First-generation immigrant women appeared the most hesitant to embrace the idea of Voluntary Motherhood. Instead, they clung to traditional ideas of family size and limited roles for women. Second-generation immigrant women were much more likely to accept beliefs regarding the limitation of pregnancies.

Meanwhile, customary thinking regarding marriage changed. Urban women, native-born white and black, divorced their spouses at higher rates than did rural women. They obtained divorces in greater numbers than did urban men. They also adopted such catchall grounds as "cruelty." In other words, urban women contributed heavily to the nation's rising divorce rate, as well as to a newly relaxed attitude toward such proceedings.

Opposition to the rising divorce rate, and to women's willingness to pursue divorce, proved swift and vocal. When the New England Divorce Reform League, organized in 1881, became the National Divorce Reform League in 1885, it initiated the first divorce reform movement in the United States. League officials especially lobbied Congress, asking legislators to fund a statistical study of U.S. marriage and divorce.

When in 1889 the U.S. Census Bureau released its first report regarding divorce, it confirmed the fears of many Americans. Not only was the divorce rate rising, but people in states with restrictive laws, such as New York and South Carolina, sometimes took advantage of permissive laws in such areas as South Dakota and Oklahoma Territory by temporarily migrating there to get divorces. The study also indicated that American marriages failed at the rate of one in every thirteen to fifteen. Women obtained two-thirds of divorces and men one-third. Despite Victorians' emphasis on romance, love, and family, the U.S. divorce rate increased at a rate of approximately 30 percent every five years and held the record as the highest in the world.

The National Divorce Reform League crusaded for uniform divorce laws in every U.S. state and territory. The League hoped this provision would at least halt so-called migratory divorces. Congress, however, maintained that divorce legislation fell under states' rights rather than federal power. In addition, numerous women's rights leaders opposed uniform divorce laws. Elizabeth Cady Stanton explained that liberal divorce laws were "for oppressed wives . . . what Canada was for Southern slaves." In 1913, the Divorce Reform League collapsed. Americans continued to seek migratory divorces, especially in the newest center of liberal divorce, Reno, Nevada.

Urban women put growing pressure on other American conventions, namely education. Because education was crucial to women's advancement, a number of middle- and upper-class white women insisted that urban institutions of higher education admit them. By 1879, Columbia College in New York City permitted women to enroll in selected courses and, in 1889, established Barnard College for women. Barnard utilized Columbia's professors, library, and course standards; nine women graduated in its first class with an education equivalent to that of male students at Columbia. Meanwhile, in 1888 Hunter College of the City University became the first U.S. college to provide free education for white women and women of color.

Urban women addressed other issues as well. Because of their numbers and proximity, they could gather informally or hold conventions to discuss social problems and possible solutions. Usually these women considered urban ills, but on other occasions their concerns broadened. It was in cities, for example, that organized groups of white middle- and upper-class women confronted the dire situation of American Indians. Meetings not only raised painful questions but inspired individuals to take action.

One reformer was Helen Hunt Jackson of Massachusetts. After the death of her first husband in 1863, she earned her living as a writer. In 1875, she remarried and moved to Colorado Springs, Colorado. Through living in the West, Jackson developed sympathy for American Indians. After attending meetings in eastern cities and hearing Ponca leader Standing Bear speak (through an interpreter) in Boston in 1879, Jackson wrote about Native American rights. In 1881, Jackson's *A Century of Dishonor* revealed the cruelty and corruption of U.S. government relations with Indians. Three years later, Jackson's romantic novel *Ramona* achieved best-seller status. Although most who purchased *Ramona* wanted to enjoy its theme of tragic love, all who read it absorbed pro-Indian messages. Reaction to the novel led to public complaints on behalf of American Indians. Jackson died in 1885, but *Ramona* was reprinted more than three hundred times and made into several film versions.

At the same time, to save her people from the ravages of white hypocrisy, a Paiute chief from Nevada, Sarah Winnemucca, traveled to American cities in the East and West. In 1880 in Washington, D.C., Winnemucca met with President Rutherford B. Hayes and Secretary of the Interior Carl Schurz. Although the men promised Winnemucca land for her people, the orders were never carried out. Despite this disappointment, Winnemucca continued her crusade. As a public lecturer appearing in beautiful Native attire, she attracted large audiences. She also wrote the stirring *Life Among the Paiutes: Their Wrongs and Claims* (1883), which alerted the nation to the cause of poverty-stricken American Indians.

Cities of the 1880s proved to be a cauldron of ferment for change. Not only were groups of women living near one another, but they became more aware of their own and others' needs. Therefore, in circular fashion, the Gilded Age spawned huge cities, which became centers of reform.

Immigration

The third trend of the Gilded Age, immigration, further altered women's situations. The massive wave of immigration of the late 1870s and the 1880s added thousands of women of varied backgrounds and cultures to the U.S. population. Some of this immigration was family-based, but much of it was not. For instance, although German and Scandinavian women and men immigrated at approximately equal rates, the majority of both groups were single. Jewish men and women came to the United States in similar numbers; married couples and families among them outnumbered single people. Irish women, especially single ones, migrated at higher rates than did Irish men after the potato famine of 1846; they continued to do so during the 1880s and 1890s, the last great decade of Irish immigration.

During the Gilded Age, the ethnic background of the immigrants broadened. Although the largest immigration originated in northern and western Europe, the United States also drew peoples from southern and eastern Europe, Asia, and Latin America, especially Mexico. Among these groups, Italian, Greek, and Chinese male immigrants vastly outnumbered females. Among Spanish-speaking peoples, women arrived in relatively equal proportion to men.

Each immigrant group influenced American life, culture, and the economy in its own way. Among the Irish, for example, most women, whether single or married, took paid employment in positions ranging from factory operatives to domestics. In addition, Irish women took part in reform causes. Irish women Religious, including the Sisters of Mercy, the Presentation Sisters, and the so-called gray nuns, fanned out over the northern and western United States. They established schools and hospitals, as well as providing social services to immigrant and working women.

Beginning in 1880 the Irish immigrant Mary Harris "Mother" Jones became, in her words, "Totally engrossed in the labor movement." Originally a dressmaker, Jones moved to Chicago after losing her husband and four children to a yellow fever epidemic in Memphis, Tennessee. Four years later, the great Chicago fire of 1871 destroyed Jones's dressmaking business. Jones, who had been attending meetings of the Knights of Labor, turned to labor organizing. She used Socialist rhetoric to organize workers in the coal mining, western (ore) mining, and southern cotton industries—and to stir up strikes. A fearless crusader, Mother Jones participated in all the fiery labor confrontations of the era. Although she developed ideological eccentricities that annoyed everyone from Socialists to industrial managers, she was instrumental in founding the Social Democratic party and the Industrial Workers of the World (IWW). Tramping through mining camps, this small, white-haired woman wielded her umbrella like a sword, becoming an American legend.

Agrarian Discontent

The fourth trend, agrarian discontent affected women, black and white, during the Gilded Age. Beginning in 1884, five years of agricultural prosperity collapsed. Farm prices declined. When the drought of 1887 further complicated matters, farmers founded the Farmers' Union, the Farmers' Mutual Benefit Association, the Texas State Alliance, and the National Colored Farmers' Alliance. Out of these came two regional groups, the Southern Alliance and the National Farmers' Alliance of the Northwest.

Women were not expected to take activist positions in these organizations. Yet thousands of rural women, especially white women, did just that, contributing to the Southern Alliance and the National Farmers' Alliance in whatever ways they could. They formed women's auxiliaries, which urged the inclusion of women's programs in the groups' agendas. They were present at meetings, demonstrations, and protests. Like male farmers, these women wanted federal legislation to break up corporate monopolies and control inflation. They added their own planks to the Alliance platform, notably woman suffrage.

One female activist was Luna E. Kellie of Nebraska. When the Farmers' Alliance unit first organized in her neighborhood during the late 1870s, Kellie had little interest in the group or its proceedings. "Politics was the furthest thing from my mind then," she said. By the time her family had grown to include eleven children, Kellie served as an editor, speaker, secretary, and bookkeeper for the Alliance. She edited the Populist newspaper, *Prairie Home*, on her dining-room table. She even wrote several Populist songs.

Another active and vocal woman was Annie La Porte Diggs. During 1882, she and her husband published the *Kansas Liberal*, which supported the Farmers' Alliance. Later, as associate editor of a Topeka newspaper called the *Alliance Advocate*, Diggs built a reputation as a spokesperson for agricultural reform. Diggs was also an energetic politician, taking the speaker's platform when the Populist party formed in Kansas in 1890.

Reform during the Progressive Era, 1890 to 1914

Women and Social Ills

In 1890 unrest seemed to hang over the United States like a dark cloud. Three years later, the Panic of 1893 (an economic depression) reduced Americans to poverty and despair. In 1894, populist leader Jacob Coxey led a march on Washington, D.C. By the time he reached the nation's capitol, Coxey's Army, as Coxey's jobless followers were called, numbered about five hundred people, including women, who demanded that the federal government provide much-needed relief. Their protest inspired similar "armies" of the jobless to become "living petitions" to Congress.

Out of such events was born the Progressive Era, and the word *reform* was once again heralded across the land. Meaningful transformations must occur, people said, in industry, business, education, government, race relations, the family, and women's roles. In the face of poverty, labor violence, urban slums, and spreading disease, numerous Americans gave up their fascination with the pursuit of wealth and the creation of gigantic corporations. Instead, they turned to "trust-busting" and a concern for workers' as well as consumers' rights.

During the 1890s and early 1900s, young, educated, white, middle- to upper-class Americans formed the vanguard of the Progressive movement. Because they had visibility and access to the political system, they became the voice of dissatisfied people all over the nation. They spoke for the poor, the ill, and those of color. Their ranks included a huge number of women who, although disenfranchised, spoke, wrote, lobbied, and protested to advance their causes.

In response to the excesses of the Gilded Age, thousands of Progressive women stood poised and ready to support various reforms. Again mostly white and middle-class, these women had the time and education to lead reform movements. In addition, they were fed up with the limitations on their private lives, including restrictive laws concerning birth control and divorce. Charged with a pent-up energy, these determined women set out to mend, heal, and improve American society.

Of course, women had long participated in reform movements, notably abolitionism, temperance, and women's rights. Now they joined voluntary reform associations in greater numbers than ever before. They brought their own reform ideas with them and advocated existing causes, notably improved education for women.

Educational Changes

During the 1890s and early 1900s, a growing number of white middle- and upper-class women attended Barnard, Bryn Mawr, Mount Holyoke, Radcliffe, Smith, Vassar, and Wellesley. True to educational theory of the day, which claimed that too much education might weaken women mentally and physically, women's colleges tried to educate young women without damaging their health or femininity. Because a favorable climate of opinion existed for women pursuing botany and other scientific fields, faculty members developed their expertise and offered a growing number of courses to female students.

These schools produced many successful women, but the question of whether to perpetuate old beliefs or break with them remained unanswered. Under the presidency of M. Carey Thomas between 1894 and 1922, Bryn Mawr, a Quaker women's college, took the lead in challenging Americans' concepts of domesticity. Thomas, who held a Ph.D. degree, believed that women had the capability to achieve serious scholarship. She disdained learned women who sacrificed careers for "suffocating" marriages. In 1913, Thomas wrote that women "May have spent half a lifetime in fitting themselves for their chosen work and then may be asked to choose between it and marriage." She added, "No one can estimate the number of women who remain unmarried in revolt before such a horrible alternative." To Thomas, marriages could be happy only if the partners were equally involved in home and careers.

Thomas herself chose not to marry. Instead, she established a long-term romantic relationship with a female partner. Other women made similar choices. Actress Charlotte Cushman, lived, worked, and traveled with a female sculptor for twenty years. At the time, people sometimes referred to such relationships as "Boston Marriages." Because most of these female couples hedged in their personal lives with great privacy, it is unknown if their liaisons were lesbian in nature.

Ultimately, women's colleges failed to resolve the question of how women could combine career and family, or if they should attempt to do so. In 1910, approximately 5 percent of college-age Americans, of whom 40 percent were female, attended college. Also in 1910, 67 percent of Bryn Mawr graduates married, as compared with only 45 percent before 1900. These later Bryn Mawr graduates bore a larger number of children than their predecessors, and fewer of them entered graduate schools and professions. A decade after her 1900 graduation, a Radcliffe College graduate described the dilemma of a college-trained woman: "I hang in a void midway between two spheres. A professional career puts me beyond reach of the average woman's duties and pleasures, but the conventional limitations of the female lot put me beyond reach of the average man's duties and pleasures."

At the same time, many coeducational colleges and universities faced their own problems. After 1900, the percentage of women in their student bodies rose to 50. In a knee-jerk reaction to what was perceived as the feminization of higher education, these schools limited female admissions and developed programs to attract more male students. In other words, they established quotas for women. These schools also channeled female students to normal schools (teacher-training) or home economics departments. Along with many other Americans, the administrators of higher education feared that college-trained women would reject marriage and motherhood, at the expense of the nation as a whole.

Similarly, at the large research universities that emerged during the 1890s and early 1900s, female students faced restricted opportunities. After 1900, however, female enrollments, especially in the social sciences, climbed dramatically at schools like the University of Chicago and New York's Columbia University. As the number of women faculty members increased, so did the number of research projects on gender differences. At Chicago, a graduate student in psychology pioneered intelligence tests of undergraduates, which showed that men and women students differed only slightly in intellect. At Columbia, another psychology graduate student confirmed that male and female intellectual capabilities were indeed similar. Meanwhile, several studies of human sexuality refuted long-held myths regarding women's "natural" inhibitions.

Though often overlooked, during the 1890s and early 1900s black women's education also took tremendous strides forward. Relatively few black women received higher education before 1890, but soon thereafter a growing number of them sought advanced training, especially as teachers. By 1900, 13,524 black women taught school, as opposed to 7,734 black men. By 1910, 22,547 of the nation's 29,772 black teachers were female.

These women attended such integrated schools as Oberlin in Ohio and such all-black schools as Wilberforce University, also in Ohio. Black schools often diverged from their white counterparts in curriculum. Anxious to meet the practical needs of the African American community rather than provide a rigorous, classical education, black women's schools offered training as homemakers and teachers. By World War I, nearly one hundred black colleges and universities admitted women. Of these, Scotia Academy, Spelman, and Bennett accepted only black women.

An outstanding example of black woman teachers was Maria Louise Baldwin of Cambridge, Massachusetts. Beginning in 1887, she taught at the interracial Agassiz Grammar School. Two years later, Baldwin received appointment as principal, a post she held for more than thirty years. She continued her own education by taking classes at Harvard University and Boston University. An inspiring lecturer, Baldwin spoke against racial prejudice and for greater tolerance.

Women's Sports

During this time, colleges and universities began to offer women the chance to take part in athletics. In the 1880s, tennis became the most popular sport for college women. During the 1890s, after Smith College's sponsorship of basketball for women, basketball challenged tennis for the top spot. By the mid-1890s, college athletic associations sponsored women's competitions in aquatics, field hockey, rowing, track and field, and winter sports. Golf achieved popularity among women because it seemed well suited to their supposedly delicate, genteel nature.

Next came the bicycle craze. Female biking enthusiasts explained that they rode attired in simple, modest suits composed of a tweed skirt and jacket, a straw hat, and walking shoes with gaiters (to keep their skirts down). Women were also drawn to the excitement surrounding the automobile. Between 1905 and 1909, one young woman reigned as an auto-racing champion. Another earned the distinction of being the first woman to drive across the United States.

Baseball also attracted female players. The game started at Vassar College in Poughkeepsie, New York, in 1866. By the 1890s and early 1900s, a number of white and black women had exchanged feminine passivity for ability on the diamond. By the early 1900s, women had amateur, semiprofessional, and professional teams, including the Chicago Ladies and the Bloomer Girls of Texas. Players wore—what else?—bloomers. During the early 1890s, these women's teams played exhibition games against men's teams. Although women players received publicity, they did not have the opportunity to jump to a female major league, for none existed.

At the turn of the century, Louise Pound was an outstanding example of a woman who thrived on scholarship *and* sports. In 1900, Pound earned a Ph.D. at the University of Heidelberg. She gained attention for her prowess in lawn tennis during the 1890s and in golf between 1900 and 1927. She later remarked that she had long played golf without a set of matched clubs: "Most women at that time would use their husbands' clubs cut off. When I got a set of matched clubs . . . I cut six strokes off my game." Pound became a humanities professor at the University of Nebraska, where she supported a women's basketball program and organized a female military company replete with 1880-model Springfield rifles.

Continuing Modification in Family Practices

According to prescriptive literature of the time—guide books and etiquette manuals—wives and mothers were to foster harmonious relations within the family. They were to provide their children and husbands with moral examples, solace and support, and practical instruction. Obviously, this advice did not differ from that given American women before the Civil War. What had changed was women's ability and willingness to follow such counsel.

Most women worked—at home, on farms, in family businesses, or in factories. Now, even white middle- and upper-class women found themselves in a time crunch. Because Victorian homes featured a different room for every function, such as sewing and music, as well as separate bedrooms for each member of the family, so-called women of leisure had to employ a small army of servants if they hoped to keep their household clean and orderly. Supervising these servants demanded continuous attention. In 1900, an essayist in *Harper's Bazaar* warned women to spend more time at home and less in club and reform activities: "We American women all take our 'public works' too seriously, toil and strive too unremittingly, give too little heed to the trivial round of home life, which we expect to maintain itself unaided."

Statistics suggest that women of all backgrounds ignored such advice and continued to assert their independence and individuality. During the 1890s and early 1900s, approximately 10 percent of women chose not to marry. Once married, women had fewer children. In 1900, birth rates showed a drop to 3.5 children per mother, a sharp contrast to the 7 or 8 children per mother a hundred years earlier.

As mothers, women expected more civility to exist in their homes. Many supported groups like the Massachusetts Society for the Prevention of Cruelty to Children and the Society for the Prevention of Child Cruelty, which defended battered children. They also joined the National Parent-Teacher Association, founded in 1897, which served as a child-advocate in the nation's schools.

When their marriages failed to meet their rising expectations, women sought divorces. Despite a few plateaus along the way, the American divorce rate in 1900 continued its upward swing. The 1900 rate indicated that one in twelve marriages ended in divorce. Ten years later, nearly one out of nine marriages dissolved. Women still obtained nearly two-thirds of divorces and men one-third. Unlike their mothers and grandmothers, growing numbers of women were willing to face the social stigma of divorce, and they were better able to find means of financial support other than that provided by their former husbands.

Women's Club Movement

Education and family practices were basic elements of women's reform. Beyond this, women's priorities splintered. The age, ethnicity, gender, race, religion, and social class of the individual affected her thinking concerning reform. Women held different beliefs about which reforms should take priority, when they should be implemented, and how they should be accomplished.

Many white, middle- and upper-class women chose to work for reform through their long-established, and increasingly politicized, women's clubs. By 1890, the women's club movement had grown to such proportions that individual clubs joined into a national association. Called the General Federation of Women's Clubs (GFWC), it encompassed two hundred clubs and twenty thousand members.

White clubwomen focused on cultural and literary activities, as well as improving social conditions within their own communities. They concentrated on opening new jobs and careers for women, and achieving woman suffrage. In other words, club members devoted their energies to "municipal housekeeping." Women believed they had special talents and moral responsibilities compelling them to solve civic problems. As one commentator explained in 1912: "Woman has a special function—her power to make, of any place in which she may happen to live, a home for all those who come there. Women must now learn to make of their cities great community homes for all the people."

Soon, the philosophy of the women's club movement verged on feminism, or "domestic feminism" as it is sometimes called, meaning the enlargement of women's interests and sphere through reform activities. By providing a basis for women's organized volunteerism and legitimizing women's participation in civic affairs, the club movement helped white women enter the public arena so long dominated by men. In 1914, these clubs formally endorsed woman suffrage. Although clubwomen did not yet demand equality, they made it clear that women's proper place was no longer restricted to the home.

Club ideologies reached huge numbers of women, well beyond native-born, white, Protestant women. For instance, Jewish women developed a club movement. During the 1880s, short-lived Jewish agricultural communities throughout the United States had declared gender equality as one of their goals. During the 1890s, urban Jewish women took a different tack. They attempted to change society and advance themselves by organizing self-help groups. The National Council of Jewish Women, founded in 1893 in New York City, offered a variety of social services. Jewish women also organized local synagogue sisterhoods and staged demonstrations to address local problems, including anti-Semitism. In 1902, Jewish women picketed against sharp rises in the price of kosher meats. Lasting almost a month, the kosher-meat protests confirmed Jewish women's growing militancy.

After 1900, many additional Jewish women's groups organized on behalf of the Zionist movement, which hoped to establish a Jewish homeland in Palestine. These women had a dream, perhaps best described by Emma Lazarus, whose poem "The New Colossus" was inscribed in 1903 on the Statue of Liberty's pedestal. Lazarus's poem called for freedom from oppression. Lazarus's essays in popular journals championed Jewish nationalism. In 1912, women's support for Jewish nationalism culminated in the founding of Hadassah, the Jewish women's Zionist group dedicated to funding medical and other services in Palestine.

By no means, however, did the women's club movement encompass all types of women. White clubwomen had not added racial discrimination to their list of potential reforms, nor did they recruit black members. Although the General Federation of Women's Clubs admitted black women's clubs, it did so only as segregated local chapters.

Rather than pressuring white women's clubs for admittance, black women developed a separate yet strong club movement. Members were largely middle- and upper-class women interested in pursuing educational, philanthropic, and welfare activities. Instead of adopting white clubwomen's priorities, black women focused on improving the lives of African Americans. In 1895, a convention established the National Federation of Afro-American Women. Like its rival association, the Colored Women's League, the group dedicated itself to initiating social and race-oriented reforms.

In 1896, the National Association of Colored Women (NACW) formed. Its mission, to help other African Americans even as they bettered their own situations, was stated in its motto: Lifting as We Climb. NACW provided a network for black women's clubs by bringing together thirty-six clubs, including the National Federation of Afro-American Women and the Colored Woman's League. Mary Church Terrell served as the organization's first president. Although from a privileged background, Terrell had taken a job teaching. She also spoke, wrote, and lobbied on behalf of black women's rights. As a speaker, Terrell reached groups of black and white women regarding racial progress, lynching, black history, and black women and men who passed themselves off as whites.

During the early 1900s, black clubwomen remained segregated. One African American woman living in Cheyenne, Wyoming, explained that black women of her acquaintance had little desire to join white women's clubs, noting that black women were content as members of the Searchlight Club, founded in 1904 by African American women. She maintained that widespread prejudice kept the two groups of women segregated, adding that white and black women valued reform ideas very differently. White women could afford to worry about such environmental issues as saving trees, but black women had to fight just to get the garbage collected in their neighborhoods.

Although race-related reforms received first priority, black clubs of the Progressive Era, much like their white counterparts, added woman suffrage to their list of causes. One prominent black woman argued that black women needed the vote to secure a fair share of public school funds for black schools. Another reasoned that black women could use suffrage to further social reform. Consequently, black women's groups supported women's right to vote through lectures and writings.

Generally, such women's clubs activities and reform programs revised the traditional image of women as helpless and passive creatures. Women's influence on community problems, social structures, and power bases proved that women were effective organizers and managers who could motivate government to deliver crucial services to a highly industrialized, urbanized, and complicated nation.

Yet the effect of clubwomen's activities on the old view of American women proved somewhat limited. Too often, clubwomen cast themselves in the role of moral keepers. Like women of the pre–Civil War era, reformers and clubwomen of the 1890s and early 1900s emphasized their womanly virtue. By characterizing themselves as a unique group vested with special attributes, they isolated themselves from men rather than embracing them as colleagues in reform endeavors.

Settlement Houses

By the 1890s, urbanization and massive immigration had created cities filled with tenements, crime, disease, and despair. By 1900, six American cities numbered more than a half-million people; three of them contained more than a million people. In all six cities, officials seemed unable to address the proliferating social problems.

White women reformers sprang to the rescue. They attacked urban issues of importance to women. For one, in a "Social Purity" crusade, they assailed prostitution. Ignoring the economic needs that drove women to practice it, the reformers branded prostitution a "social evil." Making prostitution a criminal offense, however, only created new problems. Even with the 1910 passage of the White-Slave Traffic Act (Mann Act), which forbid transporting a woman across state lines for immoral purposes, prostitution continued to thrive. The streetwalker replaced the brothel, whereas pimps and crime syndicates took over the organizing and marketing of prostitutes.

Other women reformers, notably Jane Addams, believed that something more fundamental was needed. Born in Illinois in 1860, Addams graduated from Rockford College. In 1883, she left medical school due to poor health. While recuperating in Europe, she observed a number of social experiments, mostly in England. Enthused about settlement houses located in slums to provide immediate aid to the poor, immigrant, and other disadvantaged people, Addams returned to Chicago. In 1889, she and her friend Ellen Starr established Hull House. In her 1910 autobiography, *Twenty Years at Hull-House*, Addams explained that the two women had intended "To provide a center for a higher civic and social life; to institute and maintain educational and philanthropic enterprises, and to investigate and improve the conditions in the industrial districts of Chicago."

The founders of Hull House, and those of the approximately fifty other American settlement houses patterned on its model, were influenced by the social sciences while in college. In establishing settlement houses, they wrought a revolution in social service. Reformers now lived among the people they served, experiencing and understanding their problems, instead of just reading and writing about them. As a result, settlement house leaders designed for their clients a range of programs, including job training, childcare, youth clubs, and health education. They combatted urban blight by pressuring city governments for better garbage collection, public health programs, and the establishment of branch libraries and museums. They fought poverty by crusading for the eight-hour day and the minimum wage. And they advocated welfare programs, unemployment compensation, and an early form of social security.

In addition to helping the urban poor, settlement houses proved instrumental to the careers of the women who ran them. Settlement houses served as training schools for women activists, giving them experience in local politics and the attainment of power. Florence Kelley was a leading reformer who came out of a settlement-house background. A graduate of Cornell University, Kelley began her social-reform career in 1891 at Hull House.

Kelley's reports exposing the horrid working conditions of women and children in Chicago's poor neighborhoods led to the passage of an 1893 Illinois law limiting working hours for women and forbidding child labor. In 1894, Kelley graduated from Northwestern University's school of law and gained admission to the bar. Beginning in 1899, Kelley served for thirty-two years as the head of the National Consumers League and remained an outspoken opponent of child labor.

Similarly, the Henry Street Settlement House on New York City's East Side produced many female reformers. Lillian Wald, a settlement worker on Henry Street during the 1890s and one of the first public health nurses, became a leader of the child-welfare movement. In 1904, Wald joined Florence Kelley and others in founding the National Child Labor Committee. In 1912, Wald and Kelley convinced the U.S. Department of Commerce and Labor to establish a Children's Bureau.

Kelley and Wald were only two of the many self-styled female social workers involved in the settlement house movement of the 1890s and early 1900s. In addition to training female reformers, settlement houses became centers of support for woman suffrage. Settlement workers fell short of their goals because they lacked political influence; they recognized the importance of gaining the vote. Thwarted in their efforts to ease what Addams described as "unsanitary housing, poisonous sewage, contaminated water, infant mortality, adulterated food, smoke-laden air, juvenile crime, and unwholesome crowding," these women added the suffrage message to their speeches, articles, and petitions. How could women, they argued, fully exercise their moral obligations to American society without political participation and power?

Meanwhile, Mary E. Richmond became influential in the charity organization movement and helped professionalize it. Beginning in 1889, she facilitated the transformation of charitable efforts into a valid profession. During her early career, she played leadership roles in several groups and in 1909 took an executive position with the new Russell Sage Foundation in New York City. In 1922, she wrote her most important book, *What is Social Case Work?* She helped promote the organization of schools to train social workers, taught workers herself, and designed curricula.

Temperance

Temperance was another long-held goal of female reformers. Women who blamed alcoholism for the disruption of American family life and for hindering the advancement of the working classes flocked to the temperance movement. During the 1890s, the Women's Christian Temperance Union (WCTU) became the largest women's organization yet. By the turn of the century, it counted more than 176,000 members, with chapters in every state and county in the United States.

Because the WCTU owned newspapers, office buildings, temperance hotels, and other related businesses, it provided a training ground for female leaders, business executives, speakers, and writers. Under the aggressive leadership of Frances Willard, the WCTU added woman suffrage to its multifaceted program.

As president of the WCTU between 1879 and 1898, Willard maintained that women's political influence was crucial to the achievement of temperance goals. Willard's slogan—"Do Everything"—supported alcohol-free restaurants as well as a huge range of other endeavors. These included boys' clubs for orphans, industrial schools for girls, homes for alcoholic women, and paid temperance organizers. The WCTU supported woman suffrage speakers, the dispersion of suffrage literature, and the gathering of names on suffrage petitions.

Willard recognized that women's influence lay in unity. Unlike other reformers who overlooked women of color, immigrant women, and regional women, Willard urged the WCTU to reach across racial, ethnic, class, and regional lines. Willard not only attracted women of many backgrounds and persuasions to temperance but to woman suffrage as well.

After Willard's death in 1898, the WCTU backed off from its strong suffrage stance. WCTU leaders worried that people might construe their support of woman suffrage as feminism, which was considered a "radical" cause at the turn of the century. Outside of the WCTU, however, many temperance proponents continued to advocate woman suffrage.

Environmental Conservation

Historians and lay people alike have overlooked women's participation in the emerging conservation movement. Yet it was a woman who founded environmental science. Beginning in 1873, Ellen Swallow Richards, holder of a chemistry degree from Massachusetts Institute of Technology and a professor of "sanitary chemistry," worked to bring domestic science (home economics) and new ideas of ecology together to form environmental science. In 1892, when Richards announced the new science in Boston, she received less than one page of coverage in the *Boston Globe*. Photographs of the fashions worn by female guests at Richards's lecture dominated the report; the word *environment* did not even appear in it. Although Richards argued, "To secure and maintain a safe environment there must be inculcated habits of using the material things in daily life in such a way as to promote and not to diminish health," only today is she recognized as the founder of ecology.

Thousands of other women who supported the conservation of the environment are similarly overlooked. From sportswomen and clubwomen to nature writers and artists, women devoted millions of hours to saving America's natural environment. In practice, women saw landscapes as one of their special causes. Just as they felt obligated to clean up their communities, women believed they had stewardship over natural vistas as well.

The story of Mary Ann Dyer Goodnight illuminates the ways in which women's efforts faded into the background. Beginning in 1877, Goodnight was a rancher's wife living on an isolated ranch in the vast Texas Panhandle. Rather than complaining, Goodnight turned to nature for comfort and purpose. She helped all creatures in need, especially the orphaned American bison (buffalo) calves that she raised herself. Goodnight crusaded against what she called the "needless slaughtering" of buffalo. Gradually, her calves grew up and formed a considerable herd, yet her name is not attached to it. The animals that Mary Ann Goodnight preserved flourished over time to become the centerpiece species of the Charles Goodnight Buffalo and Catalo Park.

Yet women persevered. As one told the General Federation of Women's Clubs convention in 1912, "If we do not follow the . . . most modern discoveries of how to conserve and propagate and renew wherever possible those resources which Nature in her providence has given Man for his use but not abuse, the time will come when the world will not be able to support life."

Young women also participated in the salvation of the outdoors, notably through Juliette Gordon Low's Girl Scouts of America, founded in 1912. American girls, who frequently resisted playing the role of "proper" young ladies, thronged to the Girl Scouts. By 1919, there were Girl Scouts in every state except Utah.

Girl Scout leaders taught domestic and outdoor skills to members, which included girls of color and from poor families. Using female volunteers, the Girl Scouts reached millions of young women with such messages as the benefits of outdoors exercise and the wisdom of preserving the environment. Girl Scouts troops learned elements of natural history, went on organized hikes, and attended girls' camps.

Racial Issues

During the Progressive Era, the continuing existence of antimiscegenation laws—those forbidding inter-racial marriage—indicates that few white Americans, female or male, wanted mixing of races. In 1906, twelve southern states, eleven western states, and two northern states prohibited black/white marriages. In the supposedly egalitarian West, four states barred marriage between whites and "Mongolians," that is, Asians. Besides these western states, three southern states banned white/Asians unions.

White women were aware of some of the problems facing black Americans. Yet white women seemed unable or unwilling to act to redress the injustices reported daily by the media. For one thing, white women found it difficult to free themselves from long-standing racial prejudices. For another, many feared endangering their own reforms by adding racial issues to the mix.

Black women, however, were quite willing to seize the initiative, especially regarding the lynching of African Americans. Between 1882 and 1900, white mobs lynched more than one thousand southern black men and women. The peak came in 1892, the year in which a black newspaper editor in Memphis, Tennessee, Ida Bell Wells-Barnett, organized a national antilynching crusade. Born in 1862, the daughter of former slaves and the eldest of eight children, sixteen-year-old Ida taught school to support her brothers and sisters after her parents died in a yellow fever epidemic. Soon, she wrote articles about issues concerning African Americans. In 1889, she purchased an interest in the *Free Speech and Headlight* in Memphis. Later she became the newspaper's editor.

In 1892, three successful black grocery-store managers were charged with conspiracy against a competing white store. Protests, arrests, and a riot followed, the violence culminating with the three black men being taken from the county jail and shot and hanged. Although Wells-Barnett had assumed, like most white and black Americans, that whites lynched black men accused of raping white women, she now undertook a thorough investigation of the phenomenon. She concluded that lynching was used against black men, and some women, who had achieved financial independence or in some other way threatened white dominance.

When Wells-Barnett launched editorial attacks on lynching, she infuriated the white community in Memphis. At one point, she suggested that some white women initiated relationships with black men. She believed, "Four-fifths of the cases of so-called assault of white women by black men would be called adultery" if both parties were of the same race. Wells-Barnett advised Memphis blacks to save money so they could leave the city and settle elsewhere. She herself left Memphis to travel and speak against lynching and for black suffrage.

Wells-Barnett helped organize black female and reform organizations. Her pleas to black women to defend their race from violence led to the founding in 1892 of the Women's Loyal Union in New York. Years later, in 1909, she helped organize the National Association for the Advancement of Colored People (NAACP). When she broke with the NAACP, she launched a number of black woman suffrage organizations. Like white women, she recognized that black women would advance little without the right to vote. Her career also demonstrated the tie between religious beliefs and the struggle for social justice.

Undoubtedly, lynching and black suffrage were momentous issues during the 1890s and early 1900s. So, too, was public health among African Americans. Black clubwomen, who numbered less than 5,000 during the late 1890s, fought high mortality rates in black communities through health education and medical care. Black middle-class women not only improved and lengthened the lives of poor blacks, but, much like white women, they imposed their social class values in the process. For black women it was a necessity to "lift" the standards of the lower classes. White Americans only saw one class of blacks, and treated all of them accordingly. In 1904, one black clubwoman explained, "The status of the race is fixed by the impoverished conditions of the majority and not by the noble achievements of the ever increasing few." Another agreed that middle-class black women had to "Go down among the lowly, the illiterate and even the vicious, to whom they are bound by the ties of race and sex, and put forth every possible effort to reclaim them."

Black clubwomen attacked a range of other race-related problems; the black women's club movement in Indiana during the 1890s and early 1900s provides a case study of the national pattern. Although black women in Indiana were few in number, they created numerous benevolent organizations. Two of the earliest were the Sisters of Charity (1874) and the Alpha Home Association (1883), which helped elderly African Americans suffering from illness and poverty. Increasing black migration to Indiana and the growth of urban social problems stimulated the organization of additional clubs and societies. In 1903, the Woman's Improvement Club (WIC) organized in Indianapolis. Committed at first to the self-improvement of its members, the WIC soon turned its attention to eliminating tuberculosis among black Americans. Some years later, in 1911, the Thursday Coterie formed to rescue young black Indiana women from the grips of prostitution.

Woman Suffrage

Clearly, the characteristic that all female reformers shared was a growing sense of political impotence. Without the right to vote and hold office, women had few ways to influence legislators and politicians. Before the Civil War, female abolitionists and temperance leaders had come to the same conclusion. After the war, suffragists renewed their campaign, but with limited gains. By 1890, new generations of women recognized the need for suffrage. The liberal thrust of the Progressive Era encouraged women to think in terms of expanded rights, notably their own right as American citizens to vote.

In 1890, the suffrage movement entered a renewal phase. The National Woman Suffrage Association and the American Woman Suffrage Association united into the National American Woman Suffrage Association (NAWSA). Elizabeth Cady Stanton served as the organization's first president. Many suffragists, however, feared that Stanton's extreme views—for example, those in favor of easy divorce—would turn public sentiment against the NAWSA and its goals. To make the situation worse, Stanton was hard at work on her controversial *Woman's Bible*, intended to reveal religion's role in the oppression of women. In 1892, the NAWSA elected Susan B. Anthony to replace Stanton.

During the 1890s and early 1900s, the NAWSA sought support state by state. Leaders argued that women voters would "clean up" politics, making it more humane and democratic. In California, state suffrage groups upheld Progressive goals. They emphasized that women sought political power to enhance the public good. They also argued that early-twentieth-century women lived in an increasingly public world, working, socializing, and participating in organizations outside their homes. American women had a right to enter political aspects of public life and they needed to do so to protect themselves. For instance, women workers should have the right to influence labor legislation, whereas women reformers should have the right to vote out of office those politicians who thwarted solutions to society's ills.

In 1911, California voters approved woman suffrage. Because of California's sizable population, this was a crucial victory for woman suffrage nationwide. The California suffrage campaign revealed the power network that women had developed. Women who worked for wages had not only increased in number, but had organized in their fields. These workers were well aware of the benefits that woman suffrage offered. Women who had gained influence in such fields as law and journalism advocated suffrage as well.

In the meantime, opposition to woman suffrage continued to strengthen. Naturally, antisuffragists disagreed with all of suffragists' claims. "Antis," who included women and men, maintained that involvement in politics would contaminate women, thereby corrupting everything from homes and families to schools and other public institutions. If men remained in charge politically, women could contribute female purity and virtue to American society. In 1910, antis had been alarmed when Washington state adopted woman suffrage. After the California decision in 1911, they formed a national organization called the National Association Opposed to the Further Extension of Suffrage to Women, which soon boasted a membership larger than that of the NAWSA.

Between 1904 and 1915, newly elected NAWSA president Anna Howard Shaw dealt with opposition by staying in the middle of the road, trying to offend no one. The daughter of an English reformer, Shaw was an ordained minister, an M.D., and an ardent suffragist. Although she was a powerful speaker, she lacked administrative abilities and antagonized male voters, who, of course, would have to approve woman suffrage. Under her leadership, the NAWSA rejected militancy, relying instead on the education of women and state suffrage campaigns to advance its cause. It also replaced the argument that women had a right to vote with the declaration that women needed the vote to become more effective reformers and caretakers.

Race and Woman Suffrage

Suffrage appeared to be a white woman's crusade. Certainly, recruiting American Indian women into the ranks was never an issue, although suffrage leaders were quick to use Indian imagery when it suited their purpose. They pointed to Indian women, especially Iroquois, as having power within their tribes. Although white society widely regarded Indian men as "savages," these men had long ago recognized the equality of men and women. Suffragists implied that if Indian men could act in a fair way, supposedly "civilized" white men could do so as well.

Neither did the NAWSA do much to reach out to Hispanic women, many of whom, such as Haitian and Puerto Rican female migrants in Florida, had not yet achieved citizenship and could not have voted even if American women had secured that right. Others were indeed American citizens, as well as avid supporters of suffrage.

In 1913, when Quaker suffragist Alice Paul founded a suffrage group called the Congressional Union (CU), she wanted to recruit Hispanas as members. In 1915, when Paul broke with the NAWSA and founded the National Woman's party, she sent organizers to such states as New Mexico. Nevertheless, white suffragists generally left Spanish-heritage women on their own in the fight for suffrage and the right to hold political office.

Regarding black women, white suffrage leaders vacillated, sometimes assuring black women of their support and other times siding with white supremacists. The NAWSA believed that many white male voters would reject woman suffrage if it also enfranchised black women. To avoid provoking hostility, the NAWSA all but stopped recruiting black members. One exception was Adelia Hunt Logan of Alabama. A member of the National Association of Colored Women and the NAWSA, Logan wrote in 1905 one of the most comprehensive arguments in support of woman suffrage, insisting that, "Government of the people for the people and by the people is but partially realized so long as woman has no vote." Logan encouraged black southern women to realize that they too deserved the right to vote.

Typically during the Progressive years, black women formed separate suffrage associations, the Tuskegee Woman's Club of Alabama and the Colored Woman's Suffrage Club of Los Angeles being two of them. Unlike their white counterparts, black woman suffragists developed comprehensive programs. They saw woman suffrage as a gender *and* a racial issue, arguing that they needed the vote for themselves as female citizens as well as to uplift and liberate all African Americans. In the view of many black reformers and suffragists, black female women activists had to fight for women's rights and black rights at the same time.

The "New Woman"

During the 1890s, it appeared that American women—at least white women of the middle- and upper-classes—had reached a new pinnacle. In 1893, the World's Columbian Exposition not only featured women's art and other work, but included three buildings designed by and for women. Outside the Exposition gates, Buffalo Bill Cody's Wild West Show drew thousands of men, women, and children to its tents, where they watched women shoot, rope, and ride broncos. Of these, Annie Oakley claimed center stage. By becoming a better shooter than most men, Oakley won the hearts of millions. She also helped open what she called "arenic sports" to thousands of other women performers.

Americans labeled women who acted differently than their mothers as "new women," the essence of which Charles Dana Gibson captured in his drawings of modern women for *Life* magazine during the 1890s. The "Gibson Girl" was a healthy, sensual, and rebellious young woman. Dressed in a simple shirtwaist and skirt, or in a one-piece bathing suit, the provocative Gibson Girl appeared on magazine covers, in advertisements, and in prints hung on the walls of homes and public places.

These "new women" were white, college-educated, single, and self-supporting. They, and sometimes married women as well, cycled, skated, played golf and lawn tennis, and took up hunting and match shooting. Others loosened their corsets or, like Alice Roosevelt, smoked in public. When President Theodore Roosevelt was criticized for his daughter's behavior, he responded that he could do one of two things—be President or control Alice.

Yet other "new women" took to the air. For the first time, in 1911, a woman obtained a pilot's license, soon becoming the first woman to fly across the English Channel. Other female pilots followed and set other aviation records. Female "barnstorming" pilots looped their planes, stood on airplane wings during flight, and did other stunts.

During the early 1900s and 1910s, "new women" dared to extend their social behavior. Without escorts or chaperones, young women (mostly those employed outside the home) strutted around amusement parks, such as New York's Coney Island, or picnic grounds, beaches and dance halls that dotted every major city. Young women now met men in public restaurants and bars, allowing them to buy them drinks, and casually chatting and dancing with them. In 1912, the dance craze promoted such risqué frolics as the bunny hug, the turkey trot, and the tango. Two years later, the Massachusetts Vice Commission reported that a significant number of young women let themselves be picked up by men with whom they had sexual relations. In response, female reformers enlarged the "Social Purity" crusade against prostitution to restrict the activities of "disorderly" white women. Everything from special police forces to detention centers were used to curb these "delinquent" women.

What, many Americans wondered, would become of these "new women"?

Employed Women during the Progressive Era, 1890 to 1914

Continuing Problems

While mainstream America seemed upset over the "new women" phenomenon, it represented a small portion of American women. Millions of other women lived more mundane lives, working for wages outside their homes while doing their best to care for themselves and their families. These included immigrants, women of color, and native-born poor whites. Driven by economic necessity, during the 1890s such women entered the U.S. labor force in growing numbers.

Despite their prevalence in the work force, women experienced little improvement in working conditions or the length of the workday. In 1893, a report by Helen Campbell entitled *Women Wage-Earners* described the horrific conditions the Massachusetts Bureau of Labor had discovered: "Employees packed 'like sardines in a box'; thirty-five persons, for example, in a small attic without ventilation of any kind." Campbell added, "There are no conveniences for women; and men and women use the same closets [bathrooms], wash-basins, and drinking cups. . . . In another case, a water-closet in the center of the room filled it with a sickening stench."

The 1893 report also detailed health hazards faced by women workers. Lung and bronchial diseases affected women who handled dust-laden feathers, fur, and cotton. Caustic soda ate at soap workers' hands, which became raw and bleeding by the end of each workday. Because they inhaled particles of phosphorus, match workers' jaws often grew cancerous. Button and pin workers jammed and caught their fingers in machinery; after the first three incidents, they had to treat these injuries at their own expense.

While factory workers of all kinds were in peril, homeworkers also suffered. In eastern cities, women, especially new immigrants and mothers with small children, produced artificial flowers or hand-rolled cigars on kitchen tables in overcrowded tenement apartments. In Florida, many Cuban and Puerto Rican women were pieceworkers. In Texas, Mexican American women worked in their home for wages, as did Asian American women in Washington state. In the inland industrial centers of Chicago and Indianapolis, black women comprised the majority of women who worked at home.

In all cases, these women were paid by the number of pieces they produced. Because six, or even seven, days of labor from dawn to dusk resulted in less than a living wage, these women recruited their children to boost their production. A woman might nurse an infant at her breast, as she and her other children worked with inadequate light, sanitation, and ventilation (essential when working with glue, varnish, or paint). Nor did they take necessary rest breaks from their labors. Because these women and children worked at their drudgery behind tenement walls, their situation remained invisible to Progressive reformers.

In spite of the dangers and hardships involved, by 1900 more women worked for wages than ever before. Five million women, or one out of every five, held paid employment outside their homes. Put another way, four times as many women as in 1870 now worked in industry. Of those, three out of four were under the age of twenty-five. Nearly 75 percent of them were single, white urban dwellers. Although most worked in the manufacture of textiles, shoes, hats, gloves, stockings, and collars, a smaller number labored in such "heavy" industries as tobacco production, canning, bookbinding, meat packing, and laundries.

Other women worked in sales, especially in the large department stores that played a key role in the new urban consumerism. In 1899, an investigator for the Chicago Consumers' League posed as a department store clerk. Her report disclosed that "shopgirls" received $2.00 to $3.00 a week, supplemented by a sales commission of 5 percent. Shopgirls' total wages averaged $3.00 to $5.00 per week, or about $.06 to $.10 per hour. In addition, managers expected female clerks to stand constantly without rest breaks, to take only a thirty-minute lunch period, and to protect the store's goods from shoplifters. The investigator added that by afternoon many clerks limped, making sales "under positive physical agony."

Other employed women worked as office clerks. Although in 1870 men had composed 97.5 percent of clerical laborers, by 1890 women constituted 17 percent of the clerical work force. The newly invented typewriter eased women's entry into office work. Indeed, typing soon became known as "women's work." By 1910, women constituted 80.6 percent of all stenographers and typists. Women also dominated clerical work because of the belief that women's "feminine" qualities, including manual dexterity, attention to minor details, and talent as caretakers, suited them to it. By World War I, women composed 50 percent of all clerical workers.

Yet other working women toiled as housekeepers, maids, nursemaids, and dressmakers. Largely immigrants and women of color, domestic servants left their jobs when better employment came along. In 1910, servants accounted for 31 percent of all employed women. The following year, a government study discovered that women even preferred commercial laundry work over domestic service; an African American woman and an Irish woman who worked in laundries explained that they had more time to themselves and received better pay. Avoiding work as a domestic was also a good way to avoid sexual harassment. In 1911 an African American cook said that she lost her domestic service job when she refused to let her employer's husband hug and kiss her.

Insurgency and Protest

During the 1890s and early 1900s, a new wave of reform-minded journalists hailed as "muckrakers" exposed the conditions that working women and children endured. Investigatory bodies learned that women tolerated dangerous working conditions because they had to support themselves and help their families. For similar reasons, garment workers endured grueling conditions in sweatshops, as garment factories were known, as well as tyrannical bosses, called "sweaters."

Gradually, reformers began to ask penetrating questions. Did the economic system lie at the base of America's industrial troubles? Would economic reforms solve most of women's problems? Writer and speaker Charlotte Perkins Gilman thought so. In her most important work, *Women and Economics*, published in 1898, and in articles and speeches presented well into the 1900s, Gilman called for a "reordering of woman's sphere."

Gilman believed that women's economic dependence on men destroyed the female personality. She argued that independent women made happier and more effective wives, mothers, and individuals. Of course, she said, women must have access to efficient and professional services, including communal kitchens and day-care centers. She wrote, "This is the true line of advance, making a legitimate human business of housework; having it done by experts instead of by amateurs; making it a particular social industry instead of a general feminine function."

To explore further feminist and social-justice issues, in 1909 Gilman created a journal called *The Forerunner*, which included articles, fiction, and editorials. In it, Gilman supported economic reform, woman suffrage, and world peace. Most Americans who read Gilman's work or listened to her speeches found her ideas radical. In 1916, she gave up editing the journal and lived quietly, distancing herself from organized movements of the time.

Meanwhile, Socialist women leaders demanded their own brand of change. During the socialist women's movement, which peaked between 1870 and World War I, Tejana (Mexican Texan woman) Lucy González Parsons wrote for such journals as the *Socialist* and the *Labor Defender*. She also crusaded for a suffrage plank in the Socialist labor platform. In her well-known article "Cause of Sex Slavery," Parsons blamed the capitalist system for women's exploitation. Much like Gilman, Parsons argued, "It is woman's economical dependence which makes her enslavement to man possible."

Other Socialist women expanded these arguments. Russian-born Emma Goldman criss-crossed the nation lecturing on anarchism and women's rights. In 1893, Goldman was jailed in New York City for encouraging unemployed workers to riot. After her release, Goldman went on lecture tours of Europe and the United States. From 1906 to 1917, Goldman edited the radical monthly, *Mother Earth*. She supported "free love," meaning that two people could live together without the permission of church or state, and advocated birth control, which led to another short stay in jail.

Meanwhile, Kate Richards O'Hare, an avowed feminist, championed such issues as woman suffrage and maternity benefits for working women. In 1910, O'Hare made an unsuccessful run for Congress on the Socialist ticket. Two years later, she and her husband edited a socialist journal in St. Louis. O'Hare was a lecturer and writer who spread Socialist and feminist messages across the nation, especially to the Great Plains states.

From muckrakers to Socialists, female labor agitators were not in short supply. They participated in labor reform, forcing middle-class Americans to recognize the peril of working people, including women. These reformers revealed issues, such as sexual harassment in sweatshops, that were not considered topics of polite conversation at the time. They also proposed a wide range of solutions. These were often considered too radical to be workable, but such suggestions forced people to think about and discuss possible reforms. Labor reformers also kept issues alive and in the public eye. Never did they allow an important issue to fade into the background, undiscussed and unconsidered.

Labor Reform

Between 1910 and 1915 alone, more than half a million non-English-speaking women under the age of thirty who needed assistance entered the United States. Originating in southern and eastern Europe, including Italy, Lithuania, Poland, Russia, Yugoslavia, and even Syria, as well as in Mexico and other Spanish-speaking nations, immigrant women lacked knowledge of American language and culture. Because their families expected them to help out financially, these women took jobs, thus becoming targets of exploitation by employers and others eager to benefit from their desperation and ignorance.

Often victimized by unusually low wages, long hours, doing piecework at home, seduction into prostitution, unwanted pregnancies, grinding poverty, and lack of welfare services, immigrant women turned to such organizations as the Immigrant Protective League of Chicago. This and other similar groups assisted new arrivals to obtain employment, housing, and health care. They protected immigrant women from falling, or being lured, into prostitution, even if the income from prostitution would have helped their families survive homelessness, malnutrition, and starvation.

A number of white female reformers were anxious to help working-class women. The National Women's Trade Union League (NWTUL) brought working women together with well-to-do women reformers. Once workers had voiced their grievances, reformers created programs providing health care and assisting immigrant women. The NWTUL organized women into unions or helped them to gain membership in male-dominated unions. The NWTUL supported strikes and lobbied the federal government to conduct investigations and pass prolabor legislation. Unsurprisingly, members of the NWTUL also worked for woman suffrage. Through its journal, *Life and Labor*, published between 1911 and 1921, the NWTUL informed the public about the situation of employed women.

Despite its efforts, the NWTUL had a mixed record. Its leaders never resolved divisions between laborers and reformers, a communication gap that resulted from differences in social class, race, ethnicity, education, and age. Nevertheless, the NWTUL made some significant contributions to labor reform. It not only provided direct aid programs, but it trained rank-and-file women to organize other female workers and push for reforms in the workplace.

Obviously, labor reform was a complicated matter, bringing results slowly. To their credit, most women workers did not sit and wait for others to help them; they learned how to organize and campaign for themselves. And as they learned English and adjusted to life in the United States, immigrant women became active in reform and relief efforts. Some founded ethnic women's organizations, the largest of which was the Polish Women's Alliance. Established in 1898, the group dedicated itself to the education of Polish women. In 1910, Finnish domestics established a group that pooled their funds to rent communal apartments. This venture turned into a self-help cooperative known as the Finnish Women's Cooperative Home, which counted four hundred shareholders and housed more than forty women.

Immigrant women also "Americanized" themselves. In many cases, young employed women provided a link between the outside world and their traditional mothers at home. In this process of acculturation, silent films of the era helped immensely. Even women who could not understand English could follow the new silent movies shown in urban areas. These films attracted large immigrant and working-class audiences and introduced immigrant women to American clothing styles, behavior, and values.

Strikes and Violence

Not satisfied with relief offered by reformers and self-help groups, many women believed that reform of working conditions would come only through unionization. Around 1900, Cuban women workers in the cigar-making industry in Tampa, Florida, organized the Cuban union "La Resistencia." About the same time, other Hispanas helped found the Industrial Workers of the World (IWW) and joined the International Labor Defense (ILD), which assisted laborers and dissidents.

By the early 1900s, the number of working women was so great and their condition so desperate, that the time for unionization had arrived. In 1907 Elizabeth Cady Stanton's daughter, Harriet, helped organize what became the Equality League of Self-Supporting Women. Two years later, the International Ladies' Garment Workers' Union, run by men, hired its first female organizer.

Besides organizing unions, speaking, writing, and lobbying, women picketed and went on strike. One example was the 1898 strike of glove workers protesting new assembly-line techniques and speed-ups. Later, in 1905, some eight thousand laundry workers in Troy, New York, resisted new regulations and the use of machines to replace human workers. And in 1909, twenty thousand shirtwaist workers surged out the doors of factories in New York and Philadelphia to launch the largest women's strike in American history.

Unfortunately, none of these efforts brought much in the way of reform. Then tragedy struck. In 1911, a fire at the Triangle Shirtwaist Factory, which occupied two floors high up in a New York City building, showed the public in graphic detail what bad conditions could mean for working girls. Even though leaders of the 1909 shirtwaist workers' strike had demanded the installation of fire escapes and sprinkler systems, none were in place. As flames ripped through the lofts, igniting bolt after bolt of fabric, terrified women, some with their clothes afire, rushed to the doors only to find them locked; this, it was later learned, was standard practice to prevent workers from walking out with goods. As a result, 146 women perished, either directly in flames or as the result of leaping, in desperation, out of windows ten stories high. One labor leader later proclaimed at a mass meeting, "This is not the first time that girls have been burned alive in the city. . . . Every year thousands of us are maimed."

Despite a public outcry over the Triangle Shirtwaist fire and a mammoth strike of textile workers in 1912 in Lawrence, Massachusetts, employers continued to ignore safety and health measures for their workers. They stopped protests and strikes by using the courts, public opinion, police, blacklists, fines, and dismissal. Women found it difficult to combat such techniques through unionization. Furthermore, long hours on the job and home responsibilities kept women from attending union meetings. Women's low wages kept them from paying union dues. Too, the behavior of hostile male union members frightened women. In 1913 a mere 6 percent of women workers belonged to unions, up only 3 percent from 1900.

Protective Legislation

Reformers concluded that protective labor laws would provide a partial answer to the problems working women faced. A national minimum wage and shorter workdays topped their list of goals. They also hoped for state legislation guaranteeing safe working conditions, reduced health hazards, and compensation for workplace accidents. In the 1908 case *Muller* v. *Oregon*, the U.S. Supreme Court agreed that women's child-bearing abilities and physical weakness deserved protective labor laws.

Reformers quickly rallied to the cause of protective legislation. By 1912, the NWTUL changed its emphasis from organization to legislation. Also in 1912, Massachusetts passed the first minimum-wage law to protect women and children. Strangely, labor unions opposed this legislation. Union leaders believed that unions, not the government, were the best protectors of workers, male and female. A few women's groups also resisted "women-only" legislation. One female leader explained, "Welfare legislation will protect women to the vanishing point." She added that protective legislation identified women workers as a distinct group, emphasizing their physical weakness and child-bearing capabilities. She argued that women had to fight on equal grounds with male workers.

Professional Women

During the Progressive Era, working women rejected the advice to stay home and raise their families. Instead, thousands sought training that suited their talents.

Women willingly entered professions associated with female roles, including midwifery, nursing, teaching, and library and social work. Because these professions had become female-dominated, a constant demand existed for trained women; because pay remained low, men seldom challenged women for jobs. In 1890, women composed approximately 35 percent of all professional people but only 15 percent of the total employed. During the 1890s and early 1900s, women made up a higher proportion of the professions than of the general work force.

In 1900, nearly 9,000 women held physicians' licenses. At the same time, female midwives delivered the majority of babies of immigrants, rural, and southern women. Midwives earned credentials in European or American schools or learned by serving apprenticeships. As late as 1910, midwives were so trusted and preferred over male physicians that they attended approximately 50 percent of all births.

The medical professions also attracted African American women, but their path to a successful medical career was even more difficult. Nevertheless, after the first black trained nurse graduated from the New England Hospital for Women and Children in 1879, hundreds of other black women entered nursing. When denied jobs in white hospitals, the Army Nurse Corps, and the Red Cross, black nurses took jobs within the African American community or worked as private nurses. In 1908, when the American Nurses' Association denied black nurses membership, they formed the National Association of Colored Graduate Nurses.

By 1890, 155 black female physicians lived and worked in the United States. This number rose to 160 by 1900. In 1901, a black female physician in Greenville, South Carolina, drew attention to the odds she faced. She lamented, "There are a great many forces operating against the success of the Negro. These, however, I hope someday will be overcome." The publication *American Men of Science* listed 149 women physicians in 1906, and 204 women in 1910; those named held inferior positions and were denied membership in most professional scientific societies.

Despite prejudice, women not only persevered but produced significant work. Gradually, professional societies like the National Academy of Sciences admitted women to membership. Geologist Florence Bascom, a researcher and professor at Bryn Mawr College, was the first female member of the Geological Society of America. In 1896, Bascom joined the U.S. Geological Survey as its first woman member. Bascom spent her summers searching mountain terrain on horseback or in a buggy, and her winters teaching and writing scientific reports on her summertime discoveries.

Whatever profession they chose, women usually received lower wages than men employed in the same areas. The discrepancy in teachers' pay illustrates this point. In 1890, men teachers averaged $33.00 a week and women $13.00. In 1900, men earned $34.00 and women $14.00. In 1910, men received $36.00 and women $17.00.

In spite of women's efforts, a number of areas stayed closed to them. The ministry, for example, remained a male-dominated field. One of the few women to succeed in it was Mary Baker Eddy who, during the 1870s, founded the Christian Science Church. Eddy achieved overwhelming success because she capitalized on attributes long considered womanly—spirituality and intuition. When she died in 1910, she left a huge, permanent, and wealthy religious institution behind her.

The field of law also dampened women's resolve. Although a number of women graduated from law schools around the turn of the century, they were excluded from courtroom practice. Some left law for academic life or other careers. By 1910, there were only fifteen hundred women attorneys in the United States, most of whom worked for governmental agencies, legal journals, and women's organizations.

Women in the Arts

Because Americans associated art and literature with women's supposed cultural sensibilities, a growing number of women entered these fields. By 1910, women accounted for 45.2 percent of artists and art teachers. At least two of these women became world-class artists whose reputations live on today. Cecilia Beaux, a painter in New York during the early 1900s, gained acclaim for her portraits of famous women. Mary Cassatt, the most distinguished woman artist of the age, achieved renown for both her impressionist paintings and her printmaking.

Women also drew cartoons, comic strips, and illustrated journals and novels. After attending the Philadelphia School of Design for Women and becoming self-supporting at age fifteen, Alice Barber Stephens achieved popularity as an illustrator. Stephens's work appeared in the *Ladies Home Journal* and a number of books.

In the field of literature, women exhibited energy and creativity. In 1892, Frances Ellen Watkins Harper published *Iola Leroy, Shadows Uplifted*, recognized as the first novel by an African American woman. Yet other women contributed to an emerging writing style known as regionalism.

In addition, some women succeeded in journalism. Elizabeth Cochrane Seaman worked until 1895 as a famous *New York World* reporter known as Nellie Bly. During the 1880s, she had pioneered investigative and "stunt" journalism. In 1889, she traveled around the world in seventy-two days, eight less than Jules Verne's fictional hero in *Around the World in Eighty Days*. By the early 1890s, Nellie Bly was the most celebrated journalist in the United States. The daredevil reporter and feminist continued to write and went on several successful lecture tours, inspiring other women to adopt her modern attitudes.

As the American theater drew bigger audiences, women achieved prominence on the stage. Because women typically composed the majority of theater audiences, especially at matinee performances, actresses played to their audiences by addressing women's issues. On and off the stage, one leading lady supported women's clubs, suffrage, and feminism. Another used her status as a cult figure to advocate assistance for working women and emancipation for women.

Despite women's desire for advancement and willingness to work hard, it was obvious that the American economic and social system could only stretch so far at one time. Consequently, professional women came around to the support of woman suffrage in he hope that political power would effect further changes.

The New South during the Progressive Era, 1890 to 1914

Reform

The post-Reconstruction, or "New," South was increasingly industrialized and urbanized. The region experienced many problems, some old, some new, but all demanding solutions. As elsewhere, women reformers came to the fore. Although southern ideas of chivalry and women's proper place lived on well after the Civil War, a number of middle- and upper-class white women created a southern women's movement.

In growing numbers, women joined all types of clubs including church missionary societies, WCTU chapters, school reform associations, and woman suffrage organizations. During the 1890s, women also joined patriotic societies like Colonial Dames, Daughters of the American Revolution, and United Daughters of the Confederacy, all intent on preserving and celebrating events of the past.

The "Black Problem"

During and after Reconstruction, renewed racial prejudice swept over the South. African Americans were now restricted by the concept of Jim Crow. Originally a little man who sang, danced, and jumped about in all-black minstrel shows, a favorite entertainment of the era for white audiences, Jim Crow came to symbolize limits, legal and extralegal, placed on black Americans by white southerners determined to preserve the separation of races in southern society. Especially after the Supreme Court ruled in 1896 in *Plessy* v. *Ferguson* that public facilities could be "separate but equal," signs reading "whites only" and "colored only" appeared over water fountains, rest room doors, and vending machines. Black people were prohibited from entering amusement parks, public swimming pools, and zoos. As if Jim Crow did not humiliate black women enough, the Mammy image, so popular in books and theater, continued to deride them as little more than buxom domestics with just enough sense in their heads to follow orders.

In the face of all this, southern black women, especially those of the middle- and upper- classes, found ways to assert themselves and improve their situation. For one thing, African American parents who could afford it—and many who could not—saw to it that their daughters got the best education possible. Families recognized that without education, black women were doomed to lives of hard labor in someone else's field or kitchen. They also instilled in black girls the confidence to believe in themselves, to fight whatever obstacles lay in their path.

Community organizations helped as well. Through such settlement houses as the Locust Street Settlement House in Hampton, Virginia, black girls could study academic subjects, cooking and canning, childcare, and poultry raising. Black women graduates of teacher-training schools, colleges, and professional programs created other social settlements, where they performed what they called "race uplift work."

In addition, black southerners turned to other organizations for support. Black churches provided social centers and sources of inspiration. In addition, during the 1890s and early 1900s black women's clubs formed in southern communities. For white women, clubs were important in bringing about change; for black women, clubs were crucial. In such cities as Savannah and New Orleans, where welfare institutions excluded African Americans, black women's clubs established kindergartens, day-care centers, orphanages, schools, and health care programs.

In Macon County, Alabama, members of the Tuskegee Women's Club dedicated themselves to helping workers on local plantations. Because sanitation consisted of outdoor toilets and water came from open wells, the health of field workers was constantly at risk. In response, the clubwomen established a social center, much like the settlement houses of Chicago and New York, in which they taught field workers the principles of nutrition and hygiene.

Gradually, local clubs throughout the South multiplied and joined in statewide federations. In Mississippi in 1903, for example, local clubs created the Mississippi State Federation of Colored Women's Clubs to coordinate the efforts of clubwomen throughout the state. Largely college-educated and upwardly mobile, these women provided homes for black working women, established libraries, and operated camps and recreation centers for young people. They also assisted the hearing- and sight-impaired, the physically and mentally challenged, and the tubercular.

Other black women believed that drinking alcoholic beverages limited African Americans' progress. Even before the white-dominated WCTU came to the South, black women had formed temperance groups through black churches, which advocated temperance, tougher penalties for rapists, and legislation to protect black men and women against lynching. Some of these groups allied with the white-dominated WCTU, but those in Arkansas, Georgia, North Carolina, Tennessee, and Texas remained autonomous.

Employed Women

While many southern white women continued to work in agriculture, others took jobs in offices, stores, and factories. As early as 1890, slightly more than two out of five southern textile workers were female. As elsewhere, female reformers tried to improve the lives of working women. In 1891, for example, a noted female journalist and educational crusader helped found the Normal and Industrial School for Women (now the University of North Carolina at Greensboro). Southern women also made inroads into the professions. As in the North, a growing number of women entered nursing and teaching.

Generally, however, black women found the southern labor market restrictive. The usual opportunities open to them—sharecropping, field work, and domestic labor—required long hours and paid meager wages. Black women learned that white employers expected them to be obedient and submissive in their presence. Other industrial jobs were closed to black women. As one government report stated, "The southern industrial workplace was highly segregated and the lines of segregation were remarkably persistent through good times and bad." White women workers in the cotton mills of the New South did not want to labor alongside women of color. Nor did their white employers wish to hire blacks. In this sense, even the horrific Civil War and the long period of federally guided Reconstruction had failed to change things.

Some rural southern black women migrated to cities in the South as well as the North. This was an expensive undertaking, and many black women were upset when they discovered that urban areas, South and North, offered little more rights or jobs than had their home areas. Nor did they understand the culture of northern cities. Having heard word of bad experiences but lacking the money to leave, the majority of southern black women stayed put.

The New West during the Progressive Era, 1890 to 1914

Reform

Like the New South, the New West was industrializing. The New West also experienced tremendous growth in such urban centers as Denver and San Francisco. Immigration from nations ranging from European to Asian was on the rise. As a result, the New West also had its share of social problems—some old, some new.

In response, western women, especially those of the white middle- and upper-classes, dedicated themselves to reform. Top priority was the solution to the so-called farm problem. Mary Elizabeth Lease, a speaker for the Farmers' Alliance and the Populist party during the 1890s, shocked Kansans, Missourians, and far westerners alike with blunt speeches supporting the free coinage of silver and other Populist proposals. Lease was tireless: in

1890 alone, she gave at least 160 speeches in Kansas. With a powerful voice and emotional temperament, Lease agitated audiences and kept the spirit of protest alive among farmers.

Another very different type of reform-minded women were women Religious (Catholic nuns or sisters), who were prevalent in the West. One order in particular worked in Colorado mining camps. In Central City, Denver, Georgetown, and others, the Sisters of St. Joseph of Carondelet (CSJs) established schools, medical clinics, and welfare institutions. As strong, independent women free from the demands of marriage and child rearing, women Religious financed and administered schools and clinics of their own founding. Clearly, they resisted the views of male clergy who thought women were unsuited for such activities. In spite of the anti-Catholic sentiment so widespread in the West during the late 1800s and early 1900s, the CSJs saved from disaster more than one poor, homeless child and nursed more than one injured miner back to health. Indeed, the order provided social services unusual for the early mining frontier.

Unsurprisingly, a huge number of western women campaigned for woman suffrage. Like their eastern and southern counterparts, female reformers in the West felt hampered by their lack of political participation. Woman suffrage campaigns popped up everywhere, from the most remote counties to the biggest cities.

In the Pacific Northwest, the efforts of Abigail Scott Duniway and her suffrage newspaper, *The New Northwest*, played an important role in the passage of woman suffrage. Duniway, an Oregon pioneer, realized that woman suffrage was attainable only through the votes of men. She often admonished eastern and southern women that they must convince men, "That we are inspired by the same patriotic motives that induce them to prize" the vote. Although Washington territory gave women the vote as early as 1883 and Idaho did so in 1896, there is no evidence that—contrary to the arguments of "Antis"—a widespread revolution in gender expectations or women's rights was underway.

Employed Women

By 1890, 13 percent of western women worked outside the home, as compared to 17 percent nationally. Among these were native-born women, white and of color, as well as thousands of immigrants. Irish women, for example, settled throughout the West. During the copper-mining boom of the early 1900s, Irish immigrants formed the largest ethnic group in Anaconda, Montana, where an Irish-born immigrant founded the Anaconda Smelting Works. Irish women in the town worked as domestics in boardinghouses, as cooks in mining camps, and as clerks in company stores and offices.

For most women in the West, employment opportunities varied. Census figures reveal that women worked in agriculture, from managing their own farms and ranches to hiring themselves out as day laborers. In addition, white women living in western cities took jobs in manufacturing, office work, and sales. Because of the relative scarcity of women in the West, many women worked as prostitutes. Yet others took the government up on its offer of homestead land, filing claims and providing a model for other ambitious women who wondered if they had the mettle to make it on western farms and ranches.

Relative to their northern and southern counterparts, western women were well represented in the professions, with 14 percent employed in professional areas, as opposed to 8 percent nationally. Ella L. Knowles, for example, passed the Montana bar examination in 1889 with distinction, becoming the state's first female attorney. Knowles practiced law in Helena, participated in the People's (Populist) party, and, after 1890, campaigned for woman suffrage.

The "Indian Problem"

By 1900, the number of American Indians in the United States had reached an all-time low. The conditions in which they lived were appalling; reservation-based Indians endured disease, malnutrition, and grinding poverty. White Americans were not only aware of the Indians' situation but some had formed groups to help them. These reformers disagreed, however, about just how to "help" the Indians. Many reformers and missionaries recognized the need to supply indigent Native groups with food and medicine; some even came around to understanding the importance of preserving Indian culture. At the same time, agents from the U.S. Bureau of Indian Affairs (BIA) and field matrons (dorm mothers or superintendents) still preached abandonment of Native culture and the assimilation of Indian peoples into American society.

For its part, the BIA established off-reservation boarding schools, notably Carlisle Indian School in Pennsylvania, that literally cut Indian children off from their families, tribemembers, and traditional lifeways. At Carlisle, administrators cut Indian children's hair short, dressed them in white-style clothing, taught them English, and forbade them to speak Native languages or otherwise practice their culture. To help students adopt white ways faster, school administrators even separated sisters and brothers, and during vacations, students lived with white families instead of their own.

Even missionaries sympathetic to Indians' desire to remain Indians agreed that Native Americans must assimilate into the mainstream culture. As might be expected, the majority of Indian peoples resisted becoming pseudo-whites. Even those Indians who wanted to learn white ways hoped to retain some of their Native customs and language. As a result, students at schools like Carlisle found ways to cling to their Indian identities, speaking in their native tongue behind teachers' backs and otherwise outsmarting them.

The U.S. Congress adopted legislation and policies to acculturate American Indians, many of which effected Native women. The Dawes Severalty Act of 1887 provided for the dissolving of Indian tribes. Each male head of household would claim a portion of tribal land as his own, a concept of land ownership contrary to Indian beliefs. He and his family would then live on said parcels, separate from former tribemembers. In 1900, the U.S. government set up a program to try to teach Sioux men in the Dakotas to farm; each man would receive a plot of land, tools, stock, and cash annuities. But Sioux men did not want to be farmers; they preferred their traditional roles as hunters and warriors. In addition, this plan robbed Sioux women of their traditional roles as agriculturalists and eroded their political and economic power within their tribes.

Sioux women adapted by producing textiles and other commodities for sale in the off-reservation marketplace. They cleverly combined techniques of quillwork and beading with "white" skills including quilting, crocheting, and lacemaking. They earned small incomes over which they exercised full control. They also continued to leave unsatisfactory marriages at will, a practice that appalled white missionaries and teachers. Other Indian women married soldiers, agents, traders, and other non-Indian men.

Yet others became reformers. The five LaFlesche sisters, Omaha Indians, provide an excellent example. Of the five, Susan became known as the first Indian woman to receive an M.D. Her sister, Susette LaFlesche, was the most visible Indian woman of her day. Susette lectured and wrote on behalf of Indian rights. During the 1890s, she and her husband settled in Lincoln, Nebraska, where they edited a Populist newspaper, the *Independent*. Susette LaFlesche maintained that Indians must receive full American citizenship, after which they could take charge of their futures. She spent the rest of her life as an advocate for Omahas in particular and American Indians in general.

Hispanic Women

Like American Indians, Hispanics also felt pressure to assimilate. Although Hispanics resented their colonization by white Americans and preferred to retain their culture, white officials viewed Hispanic separatism as a threat to white dominance. During the 1880s and early 1900s, waves of immigration from Mexico swelled the Hispanic population. U.S. federal and state authorities believed that these immigrants should adopt American language, ways, and customs.

Throughout the Southwest, white bureaucrats attempted to squash Hispanic culture. They discouraged traditional Mexican celebrations such as Cinco de Mayo, urging Mexican Americans to celebrate instead such American holidays such as the Fourth of July. In addition, Spanish-speakers were forced to speak only English in public schools. A Cerro Gordo, New Mexico, woman recalled, "Most of us [children] knew only Spanish and we had no way to understand."

Hispanas (Hispanic women) turned for assistance to the Catholic Church, Protestant churches, reform groups, and settlement houses. In El Paso, Texas, the Women's Charity Association, founded in 1903, worked to improve public health and sanitary facilities. In other Texas cities such as El Paso, Houston, and San Antonio, Hispanas volunteered their services but were not given administrative positions in charity organizations.

Hispanas also sought support from kin networks. Even in urban areas, kinship structures remained intact. In urban *barrios* (ethnic enclaves, or ghettos), Hispanic kin systems revived and strengthened with the arrival of each new wave of immigration from Mexico. Hispanas turned to other women—relatives, godmothers, and *compadres* (close friends)—to teach them English and help them cope with life. Kin networks also provided medical care, childcare, food and supplies, and assistance during floods, fires, and epidemics.

Spanish-heritage women developed their own brand of feminism. During the early 1900s, Mexico's Partido Liberal Mexicano (PLM), a political party that, among other things, called for the advancement of women, influenced women on both sides of the border. In the United States, PLM programs opposed lynching of Hispanics, promoted educational opportunities, and supported equal pay for male and female workers.

The Mexican Revolution of 1910, a conflict in which thousands of women fought, further spurred the feminist movement among Hispanas in the United States. In 1911, representatives from *mutualistas* (mutual aid societies) from all over Texas met in Laredo to attend the *Congreso Mutualista*. The delegates discussed civil rights, better education, and combating violence against *Tejanos* (Mexican Texans). Meanwhile, women formed the *Lega Femenil Mexicanista* to address gender- and family-related issues.

African American Women

African American women in the West also proved to be strong and adaptable. Although examples are numerous, one of the most colorful and legendary was that of Mary Fields. Based in Cascade, Montana, Fields became a stagecoach driver known as "Stagecoach Mary." Standing six feet tall, Fields weighed in at two hundred pounds, smoked cigars, and favored a .38 Smith and Wesson for personal protection.

In other cases, black women joined forces to fight common grievances. In Kansas, black women organized clubs as early as the 1880s and 1890s. In 1900, these clubs combined into a statewide federation. For women interested in achieving Victorian ideals of womanhood, club meetings and annual conventions emphasized art, needlework, and domestic science. To assist black communities, the Kansas federation provided homes for the elderly, orphans, and homeless. It also established scholarship funds and helped unwed mothers. The federation motto proclaimed that its members were "rowing, not drifting."

Farther west, Colorado had a smaller black population. In 1900, 4,473 African American men lived in Colorado, as well as 4,097 African American women. Put another way, Colorado contained 1,620 black people for every 100,000 whites. In Denver in 1900, black people comprised 2.9 percent of the population. Of these, 2,042 were women.

Black women faced discrimination. Even though a number of Denver's black women were teachers, most worked as domestic servants, cooks, boardinghouse keepers, factory workers, and clerks. Black women received lower wages than did men and were barred from men's unions. As elsewhere, vigorous black clubwomen in Denver fought discriminatory practices and held drives to motivate black male voters. They also raised money to help African American orphans, the homeless, and the poverty stricken, filling a void in social services for black westerners.

Asian Women

Asian women migrated to many parts of the West. In 1892, Liang May Seen, the first Chinese woman to settle in Minneapolis, arrived with her husband. White female members of the Presbyterian Mission Home in San Francisco had rescued her from forced servitude as a prostitute. Missionary women had sheltered her for three years, then helped her find a husband. Liang May Seen and her husband worked hard, but they learned that Minneapolis was not free of racial prejudice and violence.

Still, she was one of the fortunate ones. Other Asian women faced prejudice and exclusion laws that blocked the establishment of Asian families in the United States. Chinese Exclusion Acts, renewed in 1882, 1892, and 1902 and written permanently into federal law in 1917, limited the number of Chinese immigrants. This policy resulted in split families, meaning that a mother and several children lived in China, while a father and one or two children lived in the United States.

Beginning in 1910, immigration officials detained at San Francisco's Angel Island Immigrant Station those Chinese women who had obtained permission to immigrate. These women spent anywhere from a few weeks to a few years enduring physical examinations, answering questions about their family backgrounds, and waiting for officials to cross-check their information. Once released, most joined their husbands. Some went to rural areas like Monterey County, California, where they worked in the fields. Other Chinese women settled in San Francisco and Los Angeles, and some went on to Chicago, Detroit, Philadelphia, and New York City.

Among Chinese women, a few immigrated as professionals. In 1896, Dr. Kong Tai Heong became the first woman to practice medicine in Hawaii. She had trained at the Canton Medical School in China before moving to Hawaii with her husband, Dr. Li Khai Fai. After the couple founded Honolulu's first Chinese hospital, in 1910 Dr. Kong and her husband entered private practice. She soon achieved renown as a fine obstetrician in Honolulu's Chinese community.

For most Chinese women, however, life in the American West was difficult, at best. Journalist Edith Maud Eaton, the daughter of a Chinese mother and English father who wrote under the name Sui Sin Far, disclosed the reality of Chinese women's lives in the United States. Twenty-three of her stories appeared in popular journals and the anthology *Mrs. Spring Fragrance* (1912). Besides living in neglected, segregated housing where they cooked on wood-burning stoves, sewed by the light of kerosene lamps, and carried their own water, these women struggled daily with anti-Chinese prejudice. Even women of the middle- and upper- classes, who lived isolated lives as wives of merchants and entrepreneurs in Chinatowns, could not avoid bigotry.

At the same time, other Chinese women fought injustice in their own communities. In San Francisco, Shanghai native Mary Tape exposed discriminatory policies against Asians. As a young immigrant, Mary had lived for five years at the Ladies' Relief Society near San Francisco's Chinatown. She later taught herself painting, photography, and telegraphy. When the San Francisco schools denied Mary and Joseph Tape's daughter Mamie admission, Mary sued the Board of Education. The court supported Tape, but the school board circumvented the ruling by establishing a separate Chinese school. Mary wrote the head of the board: "May you . . . never be persecuted like the way you have persecuted little Mamie Tape . . . [who] will never attend any of the Chinese schools of your making!"

The Protestant church, especially Lutherans, reached out to Asian women. Besides converting Asian women to Christianity, Protestant women's and missionary groups provided schools for Asian women and children. These offered everything from English-language instruction to classes in industrial skills. Church groups also established shelters for homeless women and orphans.

Chinese women took from white female missionaries what they found useful, but they also coped by relying on themselves. After the turn of the twentieth century, Chinese women formed their own organizations. They also turned to Chinese clan and district associations, which located paid work for Chinese women, extended credit, assisted the aged and infirm, and maintained Chinese cemeteries.

Japanese women also migrated to the United States. The first known female immigrants from Japan to Oregon arrived in 1880. The majority of Japanese women migrated after 1900. The first-generation Japanese migrants, the *Issei*, were quiet, hardworking, and devoted to conserving Japanese customs. The majority of Issei women arrived married. Because Japanese men returned home to marry or sent for women they had known before leaving Japan, many women immigrated as brides. Alternatively, a Japanese man might agree to marry a "picture bride," a wife he had selected through the custom of arranged marriage. Although thousands of Japanese women entered the United States as picture brides, they were not always happy with their lot. Many discovered that their husbands were older and poorer than they had represented themselves.

Filipinos also immigrated during these years. Although the United States had obtained the Philippines as a result of the Spanish-American War in 1898, Filipino women did not come to America until around 1907. Largely farm workers, these women settled in California's Imperial Valley, Hawaii, and Washington State. Although they were Catholic and educated, Filipino women endured the same prejudice directed at other Asian women. Because white people could not distinguish different Asian peoples, they treated all Asians alike. Like other Asian women, Filipino women turned to their communities, churches, and to women's clubs to learn English, improve their living conditions, and further their education.

Interracial Relationships

As in other regions of the United States, in the West women were not always segregated by race and ethnicity. Western women worked in each other's homes, copied each other's clothing styles, and traded childcare tips and recipes. White women adopted bits of fashionable elegance from clothing worn by women of color, and white women visited urban areas known as Old Mexico, Chinatown, and Little Tokyo. In turn, women of color imitated white women's fashions, tastes, and beliefs.

Occasionally, women married men of other cultures and races. In most parts of the West, interracial marriages were illegal. Member of white and Hispanic upper classes favored these laws. Leaders feared interracial "mixing" because intermarriage caused the transfer of money and property. An 1890 court case revealed the problems that could occur. The wealth of a Hispanic widower who married a young Pueblo Indian woman went to her children after his death rather than to his children from a previous marriage.

The man's earlier children sued, charging that their father's marriage to the Indian woman was, by law, null and void.

Because it was difficult to determine who was Indian, Hispanic, white, black, or Asian, western jurisdictions tightened laws against intermixing by establishing legal definitions of race. An Indian might be designated as a "full blood," "half blood," or "quarter blood," with his or her legal rights differing accordingly. Were Hispanics white or of color? Many nineteenth-century Hispanics preferred to be thought of as white. Could they, then, marry Anglo-Europeans? Did mulattos count as whites or as African Americans? To what race did a person with a Mexican mother and an Asian father belong?

Officials constructed racial identification to meet particular situations. A woman who overlooked a man's racial background at the time of marriage later charged him in a divorce court with having "black" blood in his veins. Apparently, race was a troublesome issue even in the supposedly democratic and egalitarian West of the late nineteenth- and early twentieth-century.

Overall, the Gilded Age and Progressive Era wrought momentous changes in the lives of American women. Women's cultures grew strong and adaptive. Individual women proved themselves determined and effective political organizers and business managers. Meanwhile, Victorianism and the concept of separate spheres showed signs of decay. Some women were now well educated and achievement oriented. The 1914 edition of *Who's Who* included the names of 9,000 women.

Unfortunately, women's arguments had built-in limitations. They maintained that women played a special part in society because of their morality and ability to "keep house" in their homes and communities. And as the twentieth century began, divisions among women were still in place: women remained divided along class, racial, and other lines.

Perhaps the most important change for women was their realization that they must have political participation. Woman suffrage became paramount. Women savored their gains, yet they expected to achieve more in the immediate future.

Study Guide

Checklist of important names, terms, phrases, and dates in Chapter 6. Think about what or who each was and why she, he, or it was significant.

Gilded Age
Progressive Era
Working Girls' Clubs
Knights of Labor
American Federation of Labor (AFL)
Belva Ann Lockwood
Mary Ann Shadd Cary
confidence women
consumer culture
Voluntary Motherhood
National Divorce Reform League
Helen Hunt Jackson
Sarah Winnemucca
Irish women Religious
Mary Harris "Mother" Jones
Southern Alliance
National Farmers' Alliance
Luna E. Kellie
Annie La Porte Diggs
Populist (People's) party
M. Carey Thomas
"Boston Marriages"
General Federation of Women's Clubs (GFWC)
"domestic feminism"
National Council of Jewish Women
National Association of Colored Women (NACW)
"Social Purity" crusade
Jane Addams
Hull House
Women's Christian Temperance Union (WCTU)
Frances Willard

Ida Wells-Barnett
National American Woman Suffrage Association (NAWSA)
Adelia Hunt Logan
"New Woman"
"Gibson Girl"
homeworkers
typewriter
Charlotte Perkins Gilman
Lucy González Parsons
Kate Richards O'Hare
National Women's Trade Union League (NWTUL)
Triangle Shirtwaist Factory fire
protective labor legislation
midwives
National Association of Colored Graduate Nurses
Florence Bascom
Mary Baker Eddy
Alice Barber Stevens
Frances Ellen Watkins Harper
Jim Crow
Plessy v. *Ferguson*
"Mammy" image
Mary Elizabeth Lease
Abigail Scott Duniway
Carlisle Indian School
Susette LaFlesche
Chinese Exclusion Acts
Angel Island Immigration Station
Edith Maud Eaton (a.k.a. Sui Sin Far)
interracial marriages

Chapter 6 issues to think about and discuss

- How could the unionization of women have helped union men during the Gilded Age?
- What kinds of things do the increase of women as prostitutes, confidence women, and theater performers tell us about women's lives during the Gilded Age?
- What factors pushed the divorce rate upward during the Gilded Age?
- During the Gilded Age, immigrants found conditions in the United States far better than in their former homes. Yet such immigrants as "Mother" Jones criticized working conditions in the United States and wanted to change them. This seems contradictory. Is it?

- In what ways did the emerging "farm problem" of the Gilded Age affect farm women?
- Why did educational and sports reforms for women seem to go hand in hand?
- For what reasons did different ethnic and racial women form separate clubs? What were the advantages and disadvantages of such segregation?
- Was (is) prostitution a moral issue or an economic one? Was (is) alcoholism a moral issue or a health one?
- What factors made labor and factory reforms come about so slowly?
- If you were very rich and very wise, how would you have solved racial problems in the New South during the Progressive Era? In the New West?
- Why did western territories and states approve woman suffrage before northeastern and southern states?
- What factors motivate reformers? In what ways is reformism a "career"?
- If you were a reformer in the contemporary United States, what problems would you attack and what solutions would you suggest?

Suggestions for Further Reading

The Gilded Age, 1878 to 1890

Abelson, Elaine, *When Ladies Go A-Thieving: Middle-Class Shoplifters in the Victorian Department Store* (New York: Oxford University Press, 1989).

Anglin, Mary K., *Women, Power, and Dissent in the Hills of Carolina* (Champaign-Urbana: University of Illinois Press, 2002).

Blanchard, Mary, "Boundaries and the Victorian Body: Aesthetic Fashion in Gilded Age America," *American Historical Review* 100 (February 1995): 21–50.

Canfield, Gae Whitney, *Sarah Winnemucca of the North Paiutes* (Norman: University of Oklahoma Press, 1983).

Coburn, Carol K., and Martha Smith, *Spirited Lives: How Nuns Shaped Catholic Culture and American Life, 1836–1920* (Chapel Hill: University of North Carolina Press, 1999).

DeGrave, Kathleen, *Swindler, Spy, Rebel: The Confidence Woman in Nineteenth-Century America* (Columbia: University of Missouri Press, 1995).

Dublin, Thomas, *Transforming Women's Work: New England Lives in the Industrial Revolution* (Ithaca, NY: Cornell University Press, 1994).

Gamber, Wendy, *The Millinery and Dressmaking Trades, 1860–1930* (Urbana: University of Illinois Press, 1997).

Hunter, Jane H., *How Young Ladies Became Girls: The Victorian Origins of American Girlhood* (New Haven: Yale University Press, 2002).

Mathes, Valerie Sherer, *The Indian Reform Letters of Helen Hunt Jackson, 1879–1885* (Norman: University of Oklahoma Press, 1998).

Peffer, George A., *If They Don't Bring Their Women Here: Chinese Female Immigration before Exclusion* (Champaign: University of Illinois Press, 1999).

Turbin, Carole, *Working Women of Collar City: Gender, Class, and Community in Troy, New York, 1864–86* (Urbana: University of Illinois Press, 1992).

Wilson, Elizabeth, *The Sphinx in the City: Urban Life, the Control of Disorder, and Women* (Berkeley: University of California Press, 1992).

Wilson, Margaret Gibbons, *The American Woman in Transition: The Urban Influence, 1870–1920* (Westport, CT: Greenwood Press, 1979).

Reform during the Progressive Era, 1890 to 1914

Baker, Paula, "The Domestication of Politics: Women and American Political Society, 1780–1920," *American Historical Review* 89 (June 1984): 620–47.

Barker-Benfield, G. J., *The Horrors of the Half-Known Life: Male Attitudes Toward Women and Sexuality in Nineteenth-Century America* (New York: Harper and Row, 1976).

Berlage, Gai Ingham, *Women in Baseball: The Forgotten History* (Westport, CT: Praeger, 1994).

Berrol, Selma, "When Uptown Met Downtown: Julia Richman's Work in the Jewish Community of New York, 1880–1912," *American Jewish History* 70 (September 1980): 35–51.

Blair, Karen J., *The Clubwoman as Feminist: True Womanhood Redefined, 1868–1914* (New York: Holmes & Meier Publishers, Inc., 1980).

Bordin, Ruth, *Women and Temperance: The Quest for Power and Liberty, 1873–1900* (Philadelphia: Temple University Press, 1981).

———, *Frances Willard: A Biography* (Chapel Hill: University of North Carolina Press, 1986).

Brady, Marilyn Dell, "Kansas Federation of Colored Women's Clubs, 1900–1930," *Kansas History* 9 (Spring 1986): 19–31.

Brodie, Janet Farrell, *Contraception and Abortion in Nineteenth-Century America* (Ithaca, NY: Cornell University Press, 1994).

Cash, Floris Barnett, *African American Women and Social Action: The Clubwomen and Volunteerism from Jim Crow to the New Deal, 1896–1936* (Westport, CT: Greenwood Press, 2001).

Clapp, Elizabeth J., *Mothers of All Children: Women Reformers and the Rise of Juvenile Courts in Progressive Era America* (University Park: Pennsylvania State University Press, 1998).

Collier-Thomas, Bettye, "The Impact of Black Women in Education: An Historical Overview," *Journal of Negro Education* 51 (Summer 1982): 173–80.

Connolly, Mark Thomas, *The Response to Prostitution in the Progressive Era* (Chapel Hill: University of North Carolina Press, 1980).

Cookingham, Mary E., "Combining Marriage, Motherhood, and Jobs before World War II: Women College Graduates, Classes of 1905–1935," *Journal of Family History* 9 (Summer 1984): 178–95.

Cooper, Patricia A., *Once a Cigar Maker: Men, Women, and Work Culture in American Cigar Factories, 1900–1919* (Urbana: University of Illinois Press, 1987).

Cox, Karen L., *Dixie's Daughters: The United Daughters of the Confederacy and the Preservation of Confederate Culture* (Gainsville: University Press of Florida, 2004).

Davies, Margery W., *Woman's Place Is at the Typewriter: Office Work and Office Workers, 1870–1930* (Philadelphia: Temple University Press, 1982).

Degler, Carl N., "What Ought To Be and What Was: Women's Sexuality in the Nineteenth Century," *American Historical Review* 79 (December 1974): 1467–90.

D'Emilio, John, and Estelle B. Freedman, *Intimate Matters: A History of Sexuality in America* (New York: Harper and Row, 1988).

Durst, Anne, "'Of Women, By Women, and For Women': The Day Nursery Movement in the Progressive Era United State," *Journal of Social History* 39 (Fall 2005): 141–59.

Eisenberg, Ellen, "The Limits of Gender Equality in 19th Century American Jewish Colonies," *Communal Societies* 13 (1993): 71–83.

Epstein, Barbara Leslie, *The Politics of Domesticity: Women, Evangelism, and Temperance in Nineteenth-Century America* (Middletown, CT: Wesleyan University Press, 1981).

Fitzpatrick, Ellen, *Endless Crusade: Women Social Scientists and Progressive Reform* (New York: Oxford University Press, 1990).

Frankel, Noralee, and Nancy S. Dye, eds., *Gender, Class, Race and Reform in the Progressive Era* (Lexington: University Press of Kentucky, 1992).

Gere, Anne Ruggles, *Intimate Practices: Literacy and Cultural Work in U.S. Women's Clubs, 1880–1920* (Champaign: University of Illinois Press, 1997).

Gordon, Linda, "Family Violence, Feminism, and Social Control," *Feminist Studies* 12 (Fall 1986): 453–78.

———, *Gender and Higher Education in the Progressive Era* (New Haven, CT: Yale University Press, 1990).

———, *Heroes of Their Own Lives: The Politics and History of Family Violence, Boston, 1880–1960* (New York: Viking Press, 1988).

Gordon, Lynn D., "The Gibson Girl Goes to College: Popular Culture and Women's Higher Education in the Progressive Era, 1890–1920," *American Quarterly* 39 (Summer 1987): 211–30.

Griswold, Robert L., *Family and Divorce in California 1850–1890: Victorian Illusions and Everyday Realities* (Albany: State University of New York Press, 1982).

———, "Law, Sex, Cruelty, and Divorce in Victorian America, 1840–1900," *American Quarterly* 38 (Winter 1986): 721–45.

Grossberg, Michael, *Governing the Hearth: Law and Family in Nineteenth-Century America* (Chapel Hill: University of North Carolina Press, 1985).

Gullett, Gayle, *Becoming Citizens: The Emergence and Development of the California Women's Movement, 1880–1911* (Urbana: University of Illinois Press, 2000).

Guy-Sheftall, Beverly, *Daughters of Sorrow: Attitudes Toward Black Women, 1880–1920* (Brooklyn: Carlson Publishing, 1990).

Haller, Jr., John S., "From Maidenhood to Menopause: Sex Education for Women in Victorian America," 71–85, in *Procreation or Pleasure? Sexual Attitudes in American History,* edited by Thomas L. Altherr (Malabar, FL: Robert J. Krieger Publishing Company, 1983).

Hewitt, Nancy A., and Suzanne Lebsock, eds., *Visible Women: New Essays on American Activism* (Urbana: University of Illinois Press, 1993).

Higginbotham, Evelyn Brooks, *Righteous Discontent: The Women's Movement in the Black Baptist Church, 1880–1920* (Cambridge, MA: Harvard University Press, 1993).

Hine, Darlene Clark, *When the Truth is Told: A History of Black Women's Culture and Community in Indiana, 1875–1950* (Indianapolis: National Council of Negro Women, 1981).

Hyman, Paula E., "Immigrant Women and Consumer Protest: The New York City Kosher Meat Boycott of 1902," *American Jewish History* 70 (September 1980): 91–105.

Jones, Beverly W., "Mary Church Terrell and the National Association of Colored Women, 1896 to 1901," *Journal of Negro History* 67 (Spring 1982): 20–33.

Knight, Louise W., *Citizen: Jane Addams and the Struggle for Democracy* (Chicago: University of Chicago Press, 2005).

Landsman, Gail H., "The 'Other' as Political Symbol: Images of Indians in the Woman Suffrage Movement," *Ethnohistory* 39 (Summer 1992): 247–84.

Leach, William R., "Transformation in a Culture of Consumption: Women and Department Stores, 1890–1925," *Journal of American History* 71 (September 1984): 319–42.

Leavitt, Judith Walzer, *Brought to Bed: Childbearing in America, 1750 to 1960* (New York: Oxford University Press, 1986).

Levin, Miriam R., *Defining Women's Scientific Enterprise: Mount Holyoke Faculty and the Rise of American Science* (Biddeford, ME.: University Press of New England, 2005).

Lystra, Karen, *Searching the Heart: Women, Men, and Romantic Love in Nineteenth-Century America* (New York: Oxford University Press, 1989).

MacKell, Jan, *Brothels, Bordellos, and Bad Girls: Prostitution in Colorado, 1860–1930* (Albuquerque: University of New Mexico Press, 2004).

Marilley, Suzanne M., "Frances Willard and the Feminism of Fear," *Feminist Studies* 19 (Spring 1993): 123–46.

Mathes, Valerie Sherer, *Helen Hunt Jackson and Her Indian Reform Legacy* (Austin: University of Texas Press, 1990).

Matthews, Glenna, *Just a Housewife: The Rise and Fall of Domesticity in the United States* (New York: Oxford University Press, 1987).

Matthews, Jean V., *The Rise of the New Woman: The Women's Movement in America, 1875–1930* (Chicago: Ivan R. Dee Publisher, 2004).

May, Elaine Tyler, "The Pressure to Provide: Class, Consumerism, and Divorce in Urban America, 1880–1920," 154–68, in *The American Family in Social-Historical Perspective,* edited by Michael Gordon (New York: St. Martin's Press, 1983).

McCarthy, Kathleen D., *Women's Culture: American Philanthropy and Art, 1830–1930* (Chicago: University of Chicago Press, 1993).

Mintz, Steven, *A Prison of Expectations: The Family in Victorian Culture* (New York: New York University Press, 1983).

Mintz, Steven, and Susan Kellogg, *Domestic Revolutions: A Social History of American Family Life* (New York: Free Press, 1988).

Mohr, James C., *Abortion in America: The Origins and Evolution of National Policy, 1800–1900* (New York: Oxford University Press, 1978).

Monoson, S. Sara, "The Lady and the Tiger: Women's Electoral Activism in New York City Before Suffrage," *Journal of Women's History* 2 (Fall 1990): 100–35.

Montgomery, Rebecca S., *The Politics of Education in the New South: Women and Reform in Georgia, 1890–1930* (Baton Rouge: Louisiana State University Press, 2005).

Morantz-Sanchez, Regina, *Conduct Unbecoming a Woman: Medicine on Trial in Turn-of-the-Century Brooklyn* (New York: Oxford University Press, 1999).

Muncy, Robyn, *Creating a Female Dominion in American Reform, 1890–1935* (New York: Oxford University Press, 1994).

Murdock, Catherine Gilbert, *Domesticating Drink: Women, Men, and Alcohol in America, 1870–1940* (Baltimore: Johns Hopkins Press, 2001).

Parsons, Elaine Frantz, *Manhood Lost: Fallen Drunkards and Redeeming Women in the Nineteenth-Century United States* (Baltimore: Johns Hopkins University Press, 2003).

Patterson, Martha H., *Beyond the Gibson Girl: Reimagining the American New Woman, 1895–1915* (Champaign-Urbana: University of Illinois Press, 2005).

Pleck, Elizabeth H., *Domestic Tyranny: The Making of Social Policy Against Family Violence from Colonial Times to the Present* (New York: Oxford University Press, 1987).

Riggs, Marcia Y., and Barbara Holmes, eds., *Can I Get a Witness? Prophetic Religious Voices of African American Women* (Chicago: Orbis Books, 1997).

Rogow, Faith, *"Gone to Another Meeting": The National Council of Jewish Women, 1893–1993* (Tuscaloosa: University of Alabama Press, 1993).

Rosenberg, Rosalind, *Beyond Separate Spheres: Intellectual Roots of Modern Feminism* (New Haven, CT: Yale University Press, 1982).

Rothman, David J., and Sheila M. Rothman, eds., *On Their Own: The Poor in Modern America* (Reading, MA: Addison-Wesley Publishing Company, 1972).

Rothman, Ellen K., *Hands and Hearts: A History of Courtship in America* (New York: Basic Books, 1987).

Ruray, John L., *Education and Women's Work: Female Schooling and the Division of Labor in Urban America, 1870–1930* (Albany: State University of New York Press, 1991).

Scott, Anne Firor, *Making the Invisible Woman Visible* (Urbana: University of Illinois Press, 1984).

———, *Natural Allies: Women's Associations in American History* (Urbana: University of Illinois Press, 1991).

Sicherman, Barbara, "Reading and Ambition: M. Carey Thomas and Female Heroism," *American Quarterly* 45 (March 1993): 73–103.

Sklar, Kathryn Kish, "Hull House in the 1890s: A Community of Women Reformers," *Signs* 10 (Summer 1985): 658–77.

———, *Florence Kelley and the Rise of Women's Political Culture, 1830–1900* (New Haven, CT: Yale University Press, 1995).

Smith, Susan L., *Sick and Tired of Being Sick and Tired: Black Women's Health Activism in America, 1890–1950* (Philadelphia: University of Pennsylvania Press, 1995).

Smith-Rosenberg, Carroll, "The Female World of Love and Ritual: Relations between Women in Nineteenth Century America," *Signs* 1 (August 1975): 1–29.

Solomon, Barbara Miller, *In the Company of Educated Women: A History of Women and Higher Education in America* (New Haven, CT: Yale University Press, 1985).

Sterling, Dorothy, ed., *We Are Your Sisters: Black Women in the Nineteenth Century* (New York: W. W. Norton & Company, 1984).

Strong, Bryan, "Ideas of the Early Sex Education Movement in America, 1890–1920," 127–44, in *Procreation or Pleasure? Sexual Attitudes in American History,* edited by Thomas L. Altherr (Malabar, FL: Robert J. Krieger Publishing Company, 1983).

Tax, Meredith, *Rising of the Women: Feminist Solidarity and Class Conflict, 1880–1917* (Champaign-Urbana: University of Illinois Press, reprint 2001).

Terborg-Penn, Rosalyn, "Nineteenth Century Black Women and Woman Suffrage," *Potomac Review* 7 (Spring/Summer 1977): 13–24.

Thurner, Manuela, "'Better Citizens Without the Ballot': American Antisuffrage Women and Their Rationale During the Progressive Era," *Journal of Women's History* 5 (Spring 1993): 33–60.

Toll, William, "A Quiet Revolution: Jewish Women's Clubs and the Widening Female Sphere, 1870–1920," *American Jewish Archives* 41 (Spring/Summer 1989): 7–26.

Wein, Roberta, "Women's Colleges and Domesticity, 1875–1918," *History of Education Quarterly* 15 (Spring 1974): 31–47.

Wheeler, Leigh Ann, *Against Obscenity: Reform and the Politics of Womanhood in America, 1873–1935* (Baltimore: Johns Hopkins University Press, 2004).

Yost, Nellie Snyder, "Nebraska's Scholarly Athlete: Louise Pound, 1872–1958," *Nebraska History* 64 (Winter 1983): 476–90.

Zach, Kim K., *Hidden From History: The Lives of Eight American Women Scientists* (Greensboro, NC: Avisson Press, Inc., 2002).

Employed Women during the Progressive Era, 1890 to 1914

Aron, Cindy S., *Ladies and Gentlemen of the Civil Service: Middle Class Workers in Victorian America* (New York: Oxford University Press, 1987).

Banta, Martha, *Imaging American Women: Idea and Ideals in Cultural History* (New York: Columbia University Press, 1987).

Basen, Neil K., "Kate Richards O'Hare: The 'First Lady' of American Socialism, 1901–1917," *Labor History* 21 (Spring 1980): 165–99.

Berch, Bettina, *The Endless Day: The Political Economy of Women and Work* (New York: Harcourt Brace Jovanovich, Inc., 1982).

Blocker, Jack S., Jr., "Separate Paths: Suffragists and the Women's Temperance Crusade," *Signs* 10 (Spring 1985): 460–76.

Boris, Eileen, *Home to Work: Motherhood and the Politics of Industrial Homework in the United States* (New York: Cambridge University Press, 1994).

Brownlee, W. Elliot. "Household Values, Women's Work, and Economic Growth, 1800–1930," *Journal of Economic History* 39 (March 1979): 199–209.

Buhle, Mari Jo, *Women and American Socialism, 1870–1920* (Urbana: University of Illinois Press, 1983).

Dewhurst, C. Kurt, Betty McDowell, and Marsha MacDowell, *Artists in Aprons: Folk Art by American Women* (New York: E. P. Dutton, 1979).

Drachman, Virginia G.,"Female Solidarity and Professional Success: The Dilemma of Women Doctors in Late Nineteenth-Century America," *Journal of Social History* 15 (Summer 1982): 607–19.

DuBois, Ellen Carol, "Working Women, Class Relations, and Suffrage Militance: Harriot Stanton Blatch and the New York Woman Suffrage Movement, 1894–1909," *Journal of American History* 74 (June 1987): 34–58.

Dye, Nancy Schrom, "Creating a Feminist Alliance: Sisterhood and Class Conflict in the New York Women's Trade Union League, 1903–1914," *Feminist Studies* 2 (1975): 24–38.

———,"Feminism or Unionism? The New York Women's Trade Union League and the Labor Movement," *Feminist Studies* 3 (1976): 111–25.

Eisenstein, Sarah, *Give Us Bread but Give Us Roses: Working Women's Consciousness in the United States, 1890 to the First World War* (London: Routledge, 1983).

Ewen, Elizabeth. "City Lights: Immigrant Women and the Rise of the Movies," *Signs* 5 (Spring 1980): 545–65.

Folbre, Nancy, "The Unproductive Housewife: Her Evolution in Nineteenth-Century Economic Thought," *Signs* 16 (Spring 1991): 463–84.

Gamber, Wendy, "A Precarious Independence: Milliners and Dressmakers in Boston, 1860–1890," *Journal of Women's History* 4 (Spring 1992): 60–88.

Gilfoyle, Timothy J., *City of Eros: New York City, Prostitution, and the Commercialization of Sex, 1790–1920* (New York: W. W. Norton & Co., 1992).

Golden, Claudia, "The Work and Wages of Single Women, 1870 to 1920," *Journal of Economic History* 40 (March 1980): 81–88.

Harris, Ann Sutherland, and Linda Nochlin, *Women Artists, 1550–1950* (New York: Alfred A. Knopf, 1979).

Hayden, Dolores. "Charlotte Perkins Gilman and the Kitchenless House," *Radical History Review* 21 (Fall 1979): 225–47.

Hine, Darlene Clark, "From Hospital to College: Black Nurse Leaders and the Rise of Collegiate Nursing Schools," *Journal of Negro Education* 51 (Summer 1982): 222–37.

Jacoby, Robin Miller, "The Women's Trade Union League and American Feminism," *Feminist Studies* 3 (1976): 126–40.

Katzman, David M., *Seven Days a Week: Women and Domestic Service in Industrializing America* (Urbana: University of Illinois Press, 1981).

Kenneally, James J., "Women and Trade Unions, 1870–1920: The Quandary of the Reformer," *Labor History* 14 (Winter 1973): 42–55.

Kennedy, Susan Estabrook, *If All We Did Was to Weep at Home: A History of White Working Class Women in America* (Bloomington: Indiana University Press, 1979).

Kerber, Linda, and Jane DeHart-Mathews, eds., *Women's America: Refocusing the Past* (New York: Oxford University Press, 2d ed., 1987), Part IIB.

Kessler-Harris, Alice, *Out to Work: A History of Wage-Earning Women in the United States* (New York: Oxford University Press, 1982).

Kirby, Diane, "Class, Gender, and the Perils of Philanthropy: The Story of Life and Labor and Labor Reform in the Women's Trade Union League," *Journal of Women's History* 4 (Fall 1992): 36–51.

Kleinberg, Susan J.,"Technology and Women's Work: The Lives of Working Class Women in Pittsburgh, 1870–1900," *Labor History* 17 (Winter 1976): 58–72.

Kroeger, Brooke, *Nellie Bly: Daredevil, Reporter, Feminist* (New York: Times Books, 1994).

Kwolek-Folland, Angel, *Engendering Business: Men and Women in the Corporate Office, 1870–1930* (Baltimore: Johns Hopkins University Press, 1994).

Lane, Ann J., *To Herland and Beyond: The Life and Work of Charlotte Perkins Gilman* (New York: Pantheon, 1990).

Levine, Susan, *Labor's True Woman: Carpet Weavers, Industrialization, and Labor Reform in the Gilded Age* (Philadelphia: Temple University Press, 1984).

Litoff, Judy Barrett, *American Midwives: 1860 to the Present* (Westport, CT: Greenwood Press, 1978).

Melosh, Barbara, *"The Physician's Hand": Nurses and Nursing in the Twentieth Century* (Philadelphia: Temple University Press, 1982).

Miller, Sally M., *From Prairie to Prison: The Life of Social Activist Kate Richards O'Hare* (Columbia: University of Missouri Press, 1993).

Morton, Marian J., *Emma Goldman and the American Left: "Nowhere at Home"* (New York: Twayne, 1992).

Murolo, Priscilla, *The Common Ground of Womanhood: Class, Gender, and Working Girls' Clubs, 1884–1928* (Champaign: University of Illinois Press, 1997).

Murphy, Maureen, "Charlotte Grace O'Brien and the Mission of Our Lady of the Rosary for the Protection of Irish Immigrant Girls," *Mid-America* 74 (October 1992): 253–70.

Odem, Mary E., *Delinquent Daughters: Protecting and Policing Adolescent Female Sexuality in the United States, 1885–1920* (Chapel Hill: University of North Carolina Press, 1994).

Peiss, Kathy, *Cheap Amusements: Working Women and Leisure in Turn-of-the-Century New York* (Philadelphia: Temple University Press, 1986).

Pratt, Norma Fain, "Culture and Radical Politics: Yiddish Women Writers in America, 1890–1940," 131–52, in *Decades of Discontent: The Women's Movement, 1920–1940,* edited by Joan M. Jensen and Lois Scharf (Westport, CT: Greenwood Press, 1983).

Reitano, Joanne, "Working Girls Unite," *American Quarterly* 36 (Spring 1984): 112–34.

Rosen, Ruth, *The Lost Sisterhood: Prostitution in America, 1900–1918* (Baltimore: Johns Hopkins University Press, 1982).

Rossiter, Margaret W., "Women Scientists in America before 1920," *American Scientist* 62 (May/June 1974): 312–23.

Scharnhorst, Gary, *Charlotte Perkins Gilman: A Biography* (Metuchen, NJ: Scarecrow Press, 1985).

Schwantes, Carlos A., "Western Women in Coxey's Army in 1894," *Arizona and the West* 26 (Spring 1984): 5–20.

Seller, Maxine Schwartz, ed., *Immigrant Women* (Philadelphia: Temple University Press, 1981).

Shaw, Stephanie J., *What a Woman Ought to Be and to Do: Black Professional Women Workers during the Jim Crow Era* (Chicago: University of Chicago Press, 1996).

Sheppard, Alice. "There Were Ladies Present: American Women Cartoonists and Comic Artists in the Early Twentieth Century," *Journal of American Culture* 7 (Fall 1984): 38–48.

Sklar, Kathryn Kish, *Florence Kelley and the Nation's Work: The Rise of Women's Political Culture, 1830–1900* (New Haven, CT: Yale University Press, 1995).

Tamura, Eileen H., *Americanization, Acculturation, and Ethnic Identity* (Urbana: University of Illinois Press, 1994).

Towne, Marion K., "Charlotte Gilman in California," *Pacific Historian* 28 (Spring 1984): 5–17.

Waldstreicher, David, "Radicalism, Religion, Jewishness: The Case of Emma Goldman," *American Jewish History* 80 (Autumn 1990): 74–92.

Walsh, Mary Roth, *"Doctors Wanted—No Women Need Apply": Sexual Barriers in the Medical Profession, 1835–1975* (New Haven, CT: Yale University Press, 1977).

The New South during the Progressive Era, 1890 to 1914

Alexander, Adele Logan, *Ambiguous Lives, Free Women of Color in Rural Georgia, 1789–1879* (Fayetteville: University of Arkansas Press, 1991).

Appleton, Thomas H., Jr., And Angela Boswell, eds. *Searching for Their Places: Women in the South Across Four Centuries* (Columbia: University of Missouri Press, 2003).

Boime, Albert, *The Art of Exclusion: Representing Blacks in the Nineteenth Century* (Washington, DC: Smithsonian Institution Press, 1989).

Censer, Jane Turner, *The Reconstruction of White Southern Womanhood, 1865–1895* (Baton Rouge: Louisiana State University Press, 2003).

Clinton, Catherine, ed., *Half Sisters of History: Southern Women and the American Past* (Durham, NC: Duke University Press, 1994).

Giddings, Paula, *When and Where I Enter . . . The Impact of Black Women on Race and Sex in America* (New York: William Morrow & Co., 1984).

Gilmore, Glenda, *Gender and Jim Crow: Women and the Politics of White Supremacy in North Carolina, 1896–1920* (Washington, DC: Smithsonian Institution Press, 1993).

Letoudis, II, James L., "School Reform in the New South: The Woman's Association for the Betterment of Public School Houses in North Carolina, 1902–1919," *Journal of American History* 69 (March 1983): 886–909.

Mandle, Jay R., *Not Slave, Not Free: The African American Experience since the Civil War* (Durham, NC: Duke University Press, 1993).

Neverdon-Morton, Cynthia, "The Black Woman's Struggle for Equality in the South, 1895–1940," 43–57, in *The Afro-American Woman: Struggles and Images,* edited by Sharon Harley and Rosalyn Terborg-Penn (Port Washington, NY: Kennikat Press, 1978).

O'Donnell, Margaret G., "Charlotte Perkins Gilman's Economic Interpretation of the Role of Women at the Turn of the Century," *Social Science Quarterly* 69 (March 1988): 177–92.

Patton, Phil, "Mammy: Her Life and Times," *American Heritage* 44 (September 1993): 78–87.

Thurber, Cheryl, "The Development of the Mammy Image and Mythology," 87–108, in *Southern Women: Histories and Identities,* edited by Virginia Bernhard, Betty Brandon, Elizabeth Fox-Genovese, and Theda Perdue (Columbia: University of Missouri Press, 1992).

The New West during the Progressive Era, 1890 to 1914

Albers, Patricia, "Sioux Women in Transition: A Study of Their Changing Status in a Domestic and Capitalist Sector of Production," 175–234, in *The Hidden Half: Studies of Plains Indian Women,* edited by Patricia Albers and Beatrice Medicine (Washington, DC: University Press of America, 1983).

Azuma, Eiichiro, "A History of Oregon's Issei, 1880–1952," *Oregon Historical Society* 94 (Winter 1993–94): 315–67.

Bargo, Michael, "Women's Occupations in the West in 1870," *Journal of the West* 32 (January 1993): 30–45.

Beesley, David, "From Chinese to Chinese American: Chinese Women and Families in a Sierra Nevada Town," *California History* 67 (September 1988): 168–79.

Chan, Sucheng, "Chinese Livelihood in Rural California: The Impact of Economic Change, 1860–1880," *Pacific Historical Review* 53 (August 1984): 273–307.

Coburn, Carol K., and Martha Smith, "'Pray for your Wanders': Women Religious on the Colorado Mining Frontier, 1877–1917," *Frontiers* 15 (1995): 27–52.

Deutsch, Sarah, "Women and Intercultural Relations: The Case of Hispanic New Mexico and Colorado," *Signs* 12 (Summer 1987): 719–39.

———, *No Separate Refuge: Culture, Class, and Gender on an Anglo-Hispanic Frontier in the American Southwest, 1880–1940* (New York: Oxford University Press, 1989).

Diffendal, Anne P., "The LaFlesche Sisters: Victorian Reformers in the Omaha Tribe," *Journal of the West* 33 (January 1994): 37–44.

Emmerich, Lisa E., "'Right in the Midst of My Own People': American Women and the Field Matron Program," *American Indian Quarterly* 15 (Spring 1991): 201–16.

———, "Marguerite LaFlesche Diddock: Office of Indian Affairs Field Matron," *Journal of the Great Plains Quarterly* 13 (Summer 1993): 162–71.

Garceau, Dee, "Single Women Homesteaders and the Meanings of Independence: Places on the Map, Places in the Mind," *Frontiers* 15 (1995): 1–26.

García, Mario T., "The Chicana in American History: The Mexican Women of El Paso, 1880–1920: A Case Study," *Pacific Historical Review* 49 (May 1980): 315–38.

———, *Desert Immigrants: The Mexicans of El Paso, 1880–1920* (New Haven, CT: Yale University Press, 1981).

González, Deena J., *Refusing the Favor: The Spanish-Mexican Women of Santa Fe, 1820–1880* (New York: Oxford University Press, 1999).

Harris, Katherine, "Homesteading in Northeastern Colorado, 1873–1920: Sex Roles and Women's Experience," *Frontiers* 7 (1984): 43–49.

von Hassell, Malve, "Issei Women: Silences and Fields of Power," *Feminist Studies* 19 (Fall 1993): 549–69.

Hodes, Martha, ed., *Sex, Love, Race: Crossing Boundaries in North American History* (New York: New York University Press, 1999).

Ichioka, Yuji, "Amerika Nadeshiko: Japanese Immigrant Women in the United States, 1900–1924," *Pacific Historical Review* 49 (May 1980): 339–57.

James, Caroline, *Nez Perce Women in Transition, 1877–1990* (Moscow: University of Idaho Press, 1996).

Jameson, Elizabeth, "Women as Workers, Women as Civilizers: True Womanhood in the American West," *Frontiers* 7 (1984): 1–8.

———, *All That Glitters: Class, Conflict, and Community in Cripple Creek* (Champaign: University of Illinois Press, 1998).

Jeffrey, Julie Roy, "'There is Some Splendid Scenery': Women's Responses to the Great Plains Landscape," *Great Plains Quarterly* 8 (Spring 1988): 69–78,

Jordan, Teresa, *Cowgirls: Women of the American West* (New York: Anchor Press, 1982).

Kasper, Shirl, *Annie Oakley* (Norman: University of Oklahoma Press, 1992).

Lang, William L., "The Nearly Forgotten Blacks on Last Chance Gulch, 1900–1912," *Pacific Northwest Quarterly* 70 (April 1979): 50–57.

LeCompte, Mary Lou, *Cowgirls of the Rodeo: Pioneer Professional Athletes* (Urbana: University of Illinois Press, 1994).

Lindgren, H. Elaine, *Land in Her Own Name: Women as Homesteaders in North Dakota* (Fargo: North Dakota Institute for Regional Studies, 1991).

Lomawaima, K. Tsianina, "Domesticity in the Federal Indian Schools: The Power of Authority over Mind and Body," *American Ethnologist* 20 (May 1993): 227–40,

Marín, Christine N., *The Chicano Experience in Arizona* (Tempe: University Libraries, Arizona State University, 1991).

Mason, Sarah, "Liang May Seen and the Early Chinese Community in Minneapolis," *Minnesota History* 54 (Spring 1995): 223–33.

Mercier, Laurie K., "We Are Women Irish: Gender, Class, Religious, and Ethnic Identity in Anaconda, Montana," *Montana the Magazine of Western History* 44 (Winter 1994): 28–41.

Moore, Jesse T., Jr., "Seeking a New Life: Blacks in Post–Civil War Colorado," *Journal of Negro History* 78 (Summer 1993): 166–87.

Moynihan, Ruth B., Susan Armitage, and Christiane Fischer Dichamp, eds., *So Much to be Done: Women Settlers on the Mining and Ranching Frontier* (Lincoln: University of Nebraska Press, 1990).

Murphy, Mary, "The Private Lives of Public Women: Prostitution in Butte, Montana, 1878–1917," *Frontiers* 7 (1984): 30–35.

Pascoe, Peggy, "Gender Systems in Conflict: The Marriages of Mission-Educated Chinese American Women, 1847–1939," *Journal of Social History* 2 (June 1989): 631–52.

———, *Relations of Rescue: The Search for Female Moral Authority in the American West, 1874–1939* (New York: Oxford University Press, 1990).

Peterson, Susan, and Courtney Vaughn-Roberson, *Women with Vision: The Presentation Sisters of South Dakota, 1880–1985* (Urbana: University of Illinois Press, 1988).

Petrik, Paula, *"No Step Backward": Women and Family on the Rocky Mountain Mining Frontier, Helena, Montana, 1865–1900* (Helena: Montana Historical Society Press, 1987).

———, "'If She Be Content': The Development of Montana Divorce Law, 1876–1907," *Western Historical Quarterly* 23 (July 1987): 261–92.

Riley, Glenda, *The Female Frontier: A Comparative View of Women on the Prairie and the Plains* (Lawrence: University Press of Kansas, 1988).

———, *The Life and Legacy of Annie Oakley* (Norman: University of Oklahoma Press, 1994).

Roeder, Richard B., "Crossing the Gender Line: Ella L, Knowles, Montana's First Woman Lawyer," *Montana the Magazine of Western History* 32 (Summer 1982): 64–75.

Shoemaker, Nancy, ed., *Negotiators of Change: Historical Perspectives on Native American Women* (New York: Routledge, 1995).

Stefanco, Carolyn, "Networking on the Frontier: The Colorado Women's Suffrage Movement," *Frontiers* 7 (1984): 43–49.

Sunoo, Sonia S., "Korean Women Pioneers of the Pacific Northwest," *Oregon Historical Quarterly* 79 (March 1978): 50–63.

Szasz, Margaret Connell, ed., *Between Indian and White Worlds: The Cultural Broker* (Norman: University of Oklahoma Press, 1994).

Tong, Benson, *Susan LaFlesche Picotte, M.D.: Omaha Indian Leader and Reformer* (Norman: University of Oklahoma Press, 1999).

Trennert, Robert A., "Educating Indian Girls and Women at Nonreservation Boarding Schools, 1878–1920," *Western Historical Quarterly* 13 (July 1982): 271–90.

Underwood, Kathleen, *Town Building on the Colorado Frontier* (Albuquerque: University of New Mexico Press, 1987).

Wegars, Priscilla, "'Inmates of Body Houses': Prostitution in Moscow, Idaho, 1885–1910," *Idaho Yesterdays* 33 (Spring 1989): 25–38.

Yung, Judy, "The Social Awakening of Chinese American Women as Reported in Chung Sai Yat Po, 1900–1911," 195–207, in *Unequal Sisters: A Multicultural Reader in U.S. Women's History,* edited by Vicki L, Ruiz and Ellen Carol DuBois (New York: Routledge, 2d ed., 1994).

Chapter Seven

The "New Woman": World War I and the "Roaring Twenties," 1914 to 1929

*I*n response to the outbreak of World War I in Europe in 1914, President Woodrow Wilson called for U.S. neutrality. Despite Wilson's efforts to keep the United States out of combat, in April of 1917 Congress declared war against Germany. For American women, the war years and those that followed seemed to offer unparalleled opportunities. Among other things, the nation's mobilization for and the prosecution of the conflict drew huge numbers of women out of their homes and into paid employment.

During the postwar years, women made additional gains, the Progressive spirit helping to underwrite the final push for woman suffrage. The exuberant mood of the 1920s further encouraged women, including some of color, to express themselves as independent, sexual, and political beings.

For women, then, the 1920s appeared to extend tremendous liberation. Among white women and those of color, protest and change became bywords. Yet, in retrospect, a strong theme of continuity marked the decade, for when the "Roaring Twenties" came to an abrupt end in 1929 with the most disastrous stock-market crash in the nation's history, many of the changes in women's attitudes and lifestyles proved more superficial than substantial.

Women during World War I, 1914-1918

United States Neutrality

The years of neutrality, 1914 to 1917, kept Americans in suspense. Would the United States enter the war that raged in Europe, or would it manage to hold itself aloof? While indecision hovered over the nation, women pursued reform. In 1915, for example, the Women's City Club of New York organized to improve housing, education, and health. Its members also educated women on the responsibilities of the voter in anticipation of the granting of woman suffrage, which they believed imminent.

Nevertheless, women could not shut out news of the European conflict, and war-related issues grabbed their attention. A significant number of white women opposed the very concept of war and campaigned for world peace. Because these women believed in their moral responsibility to bring order to a chaotic world, they organized such groups as the Women's Peace Party (WPP). Founded in 1915 and led by Jane Addams and other well-known reformers, the WPP dedicated itself to promoting pacifism and feminism. Addams and others denounced the "man-made" war in Europe, calling for mediation and an international agreement on arms limitation. In their speeches and writings, WPP leaders maintained that woman suffrage and women's participation in government would stop this and future wars. To them, war represented the failure of male leaders. They argued that, in the place of men, the "mother half of humanity" should govern the United States.

Even as women spoke on behalf of peace, they found their right to criticize American policies curbed by popular sentiment and, during the war, federal law (the Espionage and Sedition Acts of 1917 and 1918). In this uncertain time, many Americans believed that antiwar advocates should keep their views to themselves. Thus, during the World War I years civil liberties became a major issue in the United States. Women, especially those involved in the peace movement, adopted the cause of protecting Americans' constitutional rights, helping to found the National Civil Liberties Bureau and the American Liberty Defense Union. Women were also instrumental in organizing the Non-Conscription League and League for the Amnesty of Political Prisoners to aid women and men opposed to war and men who refused to serve in the military because war violated their personal beliefs.

The United States Enters the War

Despite opposition, the United States entered the war in 1917. Almost immediately, with patriotism overruling politics, the Women's Peace Party halted its criticism of the male leaders who had declared war. Party leaders supported pacifism, however, claiming that World War I would be the last war in human history. To this end, WPP leaders spoke and wrote to inform Americans about the "causes and cures" of war. They also intensified their demands for the "further humanizing of governments by the extension of the franchise to women."

Suffrage leaders urged women to support World War I. Like American women during all previous conflicts, female reformers proved themselves patriotic and loyal. For the first time, however, women did not put their causes aside entirely during wartime. They believed their involvement in the war effort might help bring about women's goals. Suffrage leaders, therefore, advised women to undertake war-related work, including heavy factory labor.

In addition, the Wilson administration called on women to support the war effort. As in earlier wars, women had to send their husbands and sons to the front, as well as maintain families, farms, and businesses in the absence of their male relatives. More specifically, the Department of Labor told women that, as homemakers, they had the opportunity to help the nation conserve food and other war-related resources. In response to government-sponsored pamphlets and radio broadcasts, women created "meatless," "wheatless," and "butterless" meals to conserve on vital foodstuffs needed by the military. They knitted their own socks and sweaters to save machine-made fabrics for uniforms. And when women fashioned short skirts, raising hemlines to save cloth for the war effort, no one seemed to object.

In every part of the nation, women massed behind the war, and whether or not they believed in it, thousands of women volunteered their services. They joined drives to sell the Liberty Bonds and War Savings Stamps that helped the government finance the war. Women sold war bonds in club meetings, shops, and on the streets. Others helped the Red Cross provide medical supplies and services to the military. Yet others worked with government agencies or with one of women's wartime voluntary associations. These female volunteers had the chance, for the first time in American history, to wear Red Cross or other uniforms that marked them as people of influence and skill. Thousands more had the unprecedented opportunity to serve at the military front.

African American Women in War Relief

The mid-1910s was not a hopeful period for black Americans. The racial prejudice of the era affronted black people at every level of society. White women's groups excluded African Americans, and President Wilson ordered the establishment of segregated restrooms and restaurants in government buildings. Meanwhile, Congress had under consideration such measures as separating people of various races on public transportation and prohibiting black people from holding military commissions. The most popular motion picture of the day, *Birth of a Nation* (1915), reinforced stereotypes of black men as would-be rapists of white women.

Given this situation, black women could either sit out the war or seize the opportunities it presented them. They chose the latter. For one thing, black women joined the groups that wanted them, notably the National War Work Councils of the Young Men's and Young Women's Christian Association and the Salvation Army. Through these organizations, black women helped establish hostess-house programs to assist black servicemen. They mobilized and trained black women to enter wartime jobs and war-relief work.

Black women were also energetic in forming their own associations. They too conserved resources, sponsored bond drives, and provided war supplies. As early as the fall of 1917, northern black women founded in New York City the Circle for Negro War Relief. This was a parallel organization to the white-dominated Red Cross. In Atlanta, southern black women established the Atlanta Colored Women's War Council, which supported Patriotic Leagues for young black women, established food conservation programs, and launched a "suppression of liquor campaign."

This segregation upset some white women who felt that Americans should work together on behalf of the war. Throughout the South, white members of such groups as the Committee on Women's Defense Work exerted pressure on local groups and governments to integrate black women into war efforts. The situation changed very little, however. One investigator reported, "Government employment bureaus here recognize in every colored girl who applies for work only a potential scrub woman, no matter how educated and refined the girl may be."

According to a survey of southern black women, they preferred to work through semi-independent, statewide organizations that were separate from white women's groups. Black women believed they could achieve more if they set their own goals and elected their own leaders. Certainly, if black women had entered white women's organizations, they would have had far less influence than they did in their own groups. The decision turned out to be a wise one. War work opened new avenues to black women and gave them the chance to attack the caste system of the South. Lugenia Burns Hope, a black Atlantan, worked for civil rights in her city and nationwide. Hope, one of the most effective social reformers in the South, argued that the participation of black Americans in the war effort must result in a broadening of their rights.

Historians have noted that the presence and valor of black men in the military during World War I eased racial misunderstanding and prejudice in America. One could make a similar statement regarding black women on the homefront. Like their mothers and grandmothers, these women trained themselves and others to become skilled organizers and fund-raisers. They learned the ins and outs of dealing with city governments, as well as how to function in segregated settings. Their efforts not only boosted their self-esteem but led to a broadened understanding of black women on the part of white women.

Even before the war's end, many white southern women recognized that black women's participation on the homefront might help bring about racial reform. A white female leader in Mississippi pointed out the implications of black women's war work when she stated, "I am vitally interested in this, and can see its far reaching effect—not alone now—but after the war, when we will need trained hands and brains, for the great work awaiting."

Women in War-Related Industries

Early in 1917, one expert pointed out that the United States at war could not supply enough soldiers and industrial workers. According to him, every man at the front required twenty workers at home producing weapons, munitions, and other war supplies. Although this seemed a place to call on women, it was unlikely. In June of 1917, *World's Work* predicted that women would not put on "trousers or an unbecoming uniform and try to do something that a man can do better."

Few people understood, however, the consequences of a world war fought, unlike previous conflicts, on an extensive front and with technologically enhanced ordnance and weapons. Also, this war would not be fought by volunteers; because of the Selective Service Act of 1917, men could now be drafted for military service. When the first draft was held on 20 July 1917, it called 1,347,000 men away from home. Yet throughout the summer of 1917, the Department of Labor repeatedly announced that no additional female laborers would be needed, that plenty of male workers existed to fill the jobs created by war industries.

This statement was overly optimistic. When the supply of male workers proved inadequate, employers filled positions with experienced female workers, then with unemployed and unskilled women. During the fall of 1917, the United States Employment Service recognized that thousands of women would have to work in war industries. The agency launched a governmental campaign to recruit women workers, noting that sacrifice was only necessary for "the duration." After the war, women could return to their former activities.

As they always had in times of war and national emergency, women came out of their homes to do the jobs and provide the services the nation needed. A survey of more than five hundred factories revealed that the first draft caused the number of working women to jump from 14,402 in early 1917 to 19,783 in late 1917. After the second draft, the number reached 23,190.

By the winter of 1917–18, it was clear that women would have to take over jobs thought of as "men's" work. A publication of the Young Women's Christian Association (YWCA) declared, "Avenues of work heretofore unthought of" for women had multiplied greatly. Journals and magazines reported women working in dirigible factories, machine shops, steel mills, oil refineries, railway yards, chemical plants, automobile factories, and iron and steel mills. In addition, newspaper headlines announcing "Steel Mills

Want Women" and "Women Print Liberty Bonds in U.S. Bureau of Engraving" became commonplace. A report from Idaho observed, "Women are being employed in considerable numbers in the lumber mills. . . . They wear overalls, do a man's work and receive a man's wages." By early 1918, women unloaded heavy freight, carried huge shells and steel parts, painted steel tanks, and operated welding equipment, all with proficiency.

Women's expectations for better employment opportunities and higher wages rose during the war years. Four hundred thousand women joined the labor force for the first time. Over the course of World War I, eight million employed women switched to better jobs. Earning ratios between women and men narrowed somewhat and bars against married women disappeared in certain occupations.

To protect their jobs, women joined trade unions and engaged in militancy to protest unfair treatment. Middle-class reformers, referred to as "allies," helped working women by lobbying federal and state legislatures for women's right to join or organize labor unions. These so-called allies also fought for equal pay provisions and laws regulating working conditions. The National Women's Trade Union League (NWTUL) proved especially supportive of working women's goals. In the process of helping these blue-collar women, NWTUL members also educated them on feminist issues.

Prejudice against Female War Workers

Because men generally proved unreceptive to female coworkers, white women working in industry and agriculture often confronted gender prejudice in the workplace. Union leaders worried that female laborers would lower wages and dilute the value of craft skills. Moreover, the traditional idea of women as wives and mothers persisted. Many men believed that women who had to work should be limited to certain "female" occupations and that women who did not have to work should stay home. Such traditional thinking was borne out by state and county governments that paid mothers a subsidy to stay home with their children rather than reporting to work. In 1911, Kansas City, Missouri, enacted the first mothers' pension law. By 1919, thirty-nine states had followed. This forerunner of today's Aid to Dependent Children program also offered assistance to widowed mothers, and occasionally to divorced and deserted women as well.

Men staged protests and strikes to resist the hiring of women. They also utilized protective legislation to block women from certain jobs. They might claim a job required the moving of materials heavier than women were "allowed" to lift. Male workers who belonged to unions either barred women outright or admitted them only grudgingly. Afraid of losing their jobs to women, union men cooperated with women workers only in gender-segregated situations. For instance, male laundry drivers in Kansas City encouraged female laundresses to strike for better wages and working conditions, whereas male telephone installers and repairers urged the unionization of female telephone operators.

Discriminatory attitudes and practices affected nearly every industry and business. Even the federal government failed to free itself from gender prejudice. In 1917, the U.S. Civil Service Commission released an employment announcement for male stenographers in federal agencies. When a women's committee filed a complaint, departmental officials trivialized the matter or denied the existence of discriminatory practices. As one official explained, "Certain positions in the public service cannot be filled by women" because women could not tolerate the "strain" involved.

Gradually, the situation changed. Some businesses reconciled traditional attitudes toward women with the reality of wartime America. The Wells Fargo Express Company, for example, initially welcomed women largely in gender-specific jobs, including agents, cashiers, stenographers, telephone operators, accountants, and auditors. In March 1918, a special edition of the Wells Fargo Messenger devoted to "Women in the Express" revealed new attitudes. One author described a female "Wells Fargo man" who efficiently ran a Montana office, and two women investigators who were "shattering the theory" that investigation was a male-only task. Some pages later, the same edition of the *Messenger* stated that women performed men's jobs so effectively that "Man is fairly certain to have to make a good showing to get the job back again."

Also in 1918, suffrage leader and social reformer Harriet Stanton Blatch stated in *Mobilizing Woman-Power* that, despite resistance, "American women have begun to go over the top." Blatch was enthusiastic about women's "quick wits and deft fingers." Women also had "muscles," which they used "vigorously at three dollars a day." According to her, women had "opened up every line of service" and did every type of job. "When men go a-warring," Blatch wrote, "women go to work."

For African American women, the situation was more complicated. They continued to experience double jeopardy, that is, gender and race prejudice. Consequently, wartime demands for labor opened only a limited number of industrial and government jobs to black women and others of color. Nonetheless, black women were quick to fill such openings, even though they had to work in segregated or "colored" sections separate from white workers.

Because many black women living in the rural South believed that cities might offer them more opportunities, a significant number of them moved, becoming part of the "great migration" that started in 1910 and saw thousands of southern blacks resettle in the North. Those women of color who moved northward in hopes of locating better jobs were usually disappointed. Many of them had to take the same kinds of domestic jobs they had held in the South. One Florida woman assured a Chicago employment agency that she could perform "any kind of housework, laundress, nurse, good cook who has cooked for northern people." Similarly, a Mississippian described herself as a "willing working woman" who could serve as a cook or domestic. To their dismay, some migrants discovered that even in domestic service, urban areas were unable or unwilling to absorb them.

National War Labor Board

President Woodrow Wilson recognized the difficulties that war mobilization created for the nation. To address this massive undertaking, in April 1918 he established the National War Labor Board (NWLB), which he asked to pay special attention to female laborers, and equal pay. At that time, women workers received one-half to two-thirds the wages earned by men for the same work. The belief that women worked for supplemental funds or "pin money" rationalized this disparity. Yet the introduction of 1.5 million women into war industries contradicted the old pin-money argument. Many women now worked because they provided the primary or sole support of their families.

While the NWLB adopted equal pay for equal work in principle, in practice the Board had to deal with numerous people, ranging from employers to lobbyists, who still viewed women primarily as "mothers of the race"—meaning they should stay home. Consequently, the NWLB set a standard for women's wages to be three-fourths of the men's standard rate.

By the time hostilities ended on 11 November 1918, the NWLB had a mixed record. On one hand, the Board gained shorter workdays for women and established women's right to join labor unions. On the other hand, it had failed to devise a consistent policy on working women or to establish the equality of women in industry and business. The board also neglected to plan for demobilization and the difficulties women in the labor force faced as male veterans returned home expecting to reclaim their jobs.

Women in Wartime Agriculture

During the war the nation's farms, like industry, faced a shortage of male workers. Although American women had participated in farming as wives and daughters and as migratory workers, in 1917 most Americans believed that heavy farm labor was beyond women. To interest more women in agricultural labor and convince farm employers that women were capable of farm work, such groups as the New York Woman's Suffrage Party and the New York City Mayor's Committee of Women on National Defense organized agricultural training camps for women. Divided into work squads, female recruits were trained in agricultural skills and then bussed to nearby farms.

In February 1918, the federal government established the Women's Land Army (WLA), which brought together the Women's National Farm and Garden Association, the Garden Clubs of America, the Women's Committee of the Council of National Defense, and a number of women's colleges that raised funds and recruited women as agricultural workers. The WLA eventually included twenty thousand women (primarily white) who traveled the Midwest and the Great Plains to work on farms.

In a publication called the *Farmerette*, the WLA described various farm jobs, including hours and wages. The *Farmerette* also served as a directory of training camps and available scholarships. By this time, thirty-four women's colleges had established agricultural training programs for which numerous women's clubs offered scholarships. Dressed in bloomer uniforms, WLA "graduates" worked in squads in dairying, livestock and poultry care, and fruit picking. They also did such field work as planting, weeding, hoeing, mowing, and operating harvesters. These women believed in the WLA slogan, "The Woman with the Hoe Must Defend the Man with the Musket."

As a result of WLA efforts, women farm workers gained acceptance. They demonstrated women's capacity for demanding physical labor. By late 1918, farmers who had once refused to hire women now paid them substantial wages. By 1919, the WLA had not only overcome the skepticism of farmers, but had opened new employment opportunities for women. The women themselves seemed pleased with the experiment. In 1919, a woman who shocked wheat and cultivated corn wrote: "Some life! Its great, don't think I shall come back to Omaha until after corn-picking is over."

Women in the Military

During World War I, white women had the extraordinary opportunity to serve in the U.S. military. Although women had participated in earlier wars and even fought on the front lines, they could now become official members of the armed services. The U.S. government welcomed white women as drivers, nurses, communications experts, and supply personnel. For the first time, women donned military uniforms, which helped change the public image of women from passive to assertive. As members of the Women's Motor Corps, women drove trucks and ambulances; male officers found themselves depending on the female drivers assigned to them.

Women also entered the United States Army Nurse Corps (ANC), the first women's service to achieve recognition as a corps. Since its founding in 1901, ANC's high requirements and low pay had hampered its growth. In 1917, ANC reorganized and offered enlistees better pay, although benefits were not tendered and a nurse's rank approximated that of a cadet. Despite the drawbacks, during the war female nurses joined ANC by the thousands.

The Navy Nurse Corps (NNC), founded in 1908, supplied additional nurses to the American Expeditionary Forces in Europe. One military nurse recalled that the work was demanding and sometimes appalling. She cared for "gassed men on stretchers, a writhing travesty of manhood, reeking of mud and green bandages, their yellowed faces gasping for air."

The navy and the marines offered women the rank of yeoman. Although U.S. law excluded women from service in the military, officials found a way around the restriction. Women served primarily as telephone operators and clerks. Although navy and marine personnel ranked the women very high, in 1925 Congress passed the Naval Reserve Act, which corrected the existing loophole. Not until World War II would women have another opportunity to challenge the military's all-male stance.

Return to a Peacetime Economy

Like the National War Labor Board, during the war most Americans had ignored issues of demobilization, especially that of women workers. They assumed that the traditional image of the American woman as passive, docile, and homebound would have relevance in the postwar United States. They thought that working women would give up their independence and high wages to make way for the men who returned from military service. In fact, they assumed, women would probably be relieved to go back to their homes and domestic lives. People accepted these ideas because they wanted to, or because they were so close to the situation that they had difficulty understanding the changes the war had brought about in the nation's women.

Because of such fuzzy thinking, most Americans failed to anticipate the problems of demobilization. In relieving women of their wartime jobs, employers, government officials, and policymakers used outdated arguments to soften the blow. They assured women that they were needed far more in their homes than in their jobs. Women workers, they reasoned, must return home in order to repopulate the United States and help it remain a stalwart of democracy.

Despite this rhetoric, working women resisted the surrendering of their high-paying jobs to veterans. Indeed, more than half of them voiced their preference to continue working. They indicated that they expected to earn equitable wages. Women of color who held industrial jobs balked at the idea of returning to domestic and other menial employment.

Women protested and went on strike, yet beginning in late 1918 heavy industries phased out women workers. According to census data, during the postwar years women lost their jobs at a rapid rate in steel, chemicals, electrical goods, airplanes, and automobiles. Female employment remained high in such women-employing sectors as tobacco, leather, and food processing, which absorbed additional women laid off by wartime industry. The number of white women in the clerical sector, including telephone and telegraph operators, clerks, bookkeepers, stenographers, secretaries, and sales personnel continued to grow.

Before long, the labor force resembled its prewar profile. Women had left, or been pushed out of, high-paying jobs that had given them a large measure of autonomy. They either resumed domestic life or stayed in the work force in lesser jobs. A huge number of women who continued to work had no choice, for their veterans never came back from the front, and they had to support themselves.

Woman Suffrage Triumphant

Carrie Chapman Catt and the "Winning Plan"

During World War I, woman suffrage leaders mounted their final campaign. Women's determination to enter the political realm was a logical outcome of the Progressive Era, in which political power seemed to offer solutions to all problems. Women had long believed that their admission to the public sphere would allow them to reform the workplace, schools and colleges, and the family structure. They intensified their argument that it was "expedient" to give women the vote so they could clean up society more effectively than in the past. Now they added the argument that women's extraordinary efforts during the war had proven them deserving of the vote.

At the same time, the National American Woman Suffrage Association (NAWSA) underwent an organizational overhaul. National leaders encouraged the proliferation of state and local suffrage associations. The NAWSA also experimented with open-air meetings, silent pickets, leaflet campaigns, and suffrage parades. In 1915, the NAWSA members persuaded suffrage organizer Carrie Chapman Catt to resume the presidency of the organization. Catt had served as the NAWSA president between 1900 and 1904, when her husband's illness forced her to resign. After her husband died, Catt was active in the New York suffrage movement. Her ingenuity and organizational skills brought her to the attention of the NAWSA leadership, who all but drafted her for the presidency.

Catt took over a divided organization with no defined program, but she arrived ready to capitalize on women's, as well as men's, growing interest in woman suffrage. Women could vote in eleven states, and the issue of adopting woman suffrage on the national level seemed to fill the air. Newspapers frequently discussed the issue and public opinion on it appeared positive.

Now Catt drew on her years of experience working with the Woman Suffrage Party of New York City and her own political savvy to devise her "Winning Plan." She intended to have the NAWSA fight for woman suffrage on the federal and state levels simultaneously. A $2 million anonymous gift encouraged her to think in terms of setting a date: her goal was to gain a suffrage amendment to the U.S. Constitution by December 1920.

The campaign on behalf of woman suffrage intensified when President Wilson declared the war as one "to save democracy," for women contended that the United States itself had not yet achieved democracy. Where is our democracy at home, they cried, when we, American citizens, cannot even vote or hold office in our own country?

The NAWSA hired female organizers to travel from state to state to form suffrage associations. One organizer explained that when she joined the NAWSA Congressional Committee she learned about file cases that held "531 portfolios, 96 for the Senate and 435 for the House." These provided "all the known data about a senator or representative," from sketches of a legislator's life to "facts supplied by our members in the state about his personal, political, business and religious affiliations" to "his stand on woman suffrage." From these and other source materials, the NAWSA headquarters in the nation's capital directed to its workers a steady flow of information to help them put pressure on each state's senators and representatives.

State suffrage groups became highly sophisticated in their organization. Using dynamic and politically wise techniques, Massachusetts suffragists attempted to move their state from the antisuffrage to the prosuffrage side of the congressional aisle. Working in concert, the Massachusetts Woman Suffrage Association, the College Equal Suffrage League, and the Boston Equal Suffrage Association for Good Government utilized a string of open-air meetings, touring speakers, leaflets, petitions, and "Votes for Women" buttons in its campaign.

Many western states also developed highly effective suffrage clubs. While the West had long proved more receptive to woman suffrage than other regions, in some parts of the West strong opposition remained. In South Dakota, for example, suffragists faced an antisuffrage component of conservative German immigrants who, along with liquor interests, feared that once enfranchised, women would vote for prohibition. Beginning in 1910, the South Dakota Universal Franchise League copied the NAWSA in style and tactics. This move resulted in the enfranchisement of South Dakota women in November 1918 and the state's support of a federal amendment to the U.S. Constitution.

In the South, progress came more slowly. Women worked long and hard to bring about the passage of woman suffrage, but many southern men disliked the idea of voting alongside women, especially black women. Many southerners believed in the legitimacy of states' rights, meaning that individual states, rather than the federal government, should decide whether to grant women the right to vote. Although the NAWSA groups in the South worked on behalf of the Nineteenth Amendment to the federal constitution, they often undercut their own efforts by making the compromise statement that suffrage should come from states rather than from the federal government.

Regardless of region, opponents of woman suffrage raised other complaints as well. Antisuffragists, or "antis" as they were known, still maintained the tired argument that women should wield their influence in the home rather than in politics. A major antisuffrage organization was the National Association Opposed to Women Suffrage (NAOWS), founded in 1911 in New York City. In 1917, its members, generally Protestant, middle-class, middle-aged women, established a national headquarters in Washington, D.C. In its newspaper, the *Woman's Patriot*, the NAOWS repeated its belief that women could best effect reform through their influence on male family members. It also tried to discredit woman suffrage by linking it with Socialism.

Unfortunately, the NAWSA leaders did not recognize such female antis as worthy adversaries. In 1915, Catt stated, "The respectable ladies who pose as antis are not dangerous opponents." Because Catt identified "the real enemy" as male, the NASWA did little to bring female antis around to the suffrage position.

Male antisuffrage groups were numerous. They included the National American Constitutional League, state-level Man-Suffrage Associations, and conservative ethnic and religious groups. Opposition to woman suffrage also came from what Catt called the "Vice Trust." These were male employers who feared that voting women would oppose child labor, and male liquor interests who worried that voting women would support a state or national prohibition of alcohol. And in the South, right-wing Democrats—or Dixiecrats—resisted the suffrage measure, even though the Democratic party had long supported woman suffrage "on the same basis as men."

Despite such opposition, the NAWSA soon became the nation's largest voluntary organization. Through it, 2 million women voiced their support of state and federal suffrage legislation. In Washington, the central office of the NAWSA exerted steady pressure on President Wilson to change his conservative views and endorse woman suffrage.

The Woman's Party

The NAWSA was not the only woman suffrage association to fight for the vote. First organized as the Congressional Union in 1913, suffragist Alice Paul's National Woman's party (NWP) had years of experience with suffrage campaigning. Although a Quaker, Paul believed in using high-pressure techniques such as she had observed in England. In 1916, Paul broke with the NAWSA and founded the National Woman's party. Beginning in 1917, the party initiated twenty-four-hour pickets of the White House, with female picketers bearing banners reading "Democracy Should Begin at Home," "How Long Must Women Wait For Liberty!" and "Kaiser Wilson." The resulting riots, arrests, and hunger strikes by those women imprisoned attracted even more publicity and created greater tension for President Wilson. When jail matrons force-fed women on hunger strikes, dramatic headlines splashed across the nation's dailies.

A member of the Woman's party who was arrested during White House demonstrations smuggled her thoughts out of prison on small scraps of paper directed to her husband and to other suffragists. "If this thing is necessary we will naturally go through with it," she wrote early in her prison stay, but she added, "force is so stupid a weapon." In later notes, she described fainting spells and vomiting caused by the tube used to force-feed her. One of the most alarming messages read: "Alice Paul is in the psychopathic ward." She added that Paul had dreaded the forced feeding, an emotion she well understood. "I had a nervous time of it," she continued, "gasping a long time afterward, and my stomach rejecting during the process. The poor soul who fed me got liberally besprinkled during the process. I heard myself making the most hideous sounds."

These hunger strikes and other actions of Woman's party members embarrassed the NAWSA leaders, who saw them as irrational and unproductive. Undaunted, the Woman's party maintained that its militant tactics would force the hands of President Wilson and members of Congress.

Hispanic Women Suffragists

Not all suffragists were middle-class white women. Using New Mexico as an example, it is clear that a number of Hispanas participated in the campaign for woman suffrage. In 1915, Alice Paul sent a representative to New Mexico, where less than 10 percent of New Mexico's suffragists were Hispanas. Paul's organizer worked through the white women's club movement but nonetheless managed to recruit some Hispanas to the cause, among them Aurora Lucero, charged with preparing announcements in Spanish and speaking Spanish at rallies. Lucero was a good choice. Daughter of New Mexico's first secretary of state, she was well educated and aware of women's issues.

Adelina Otero-Warren also proved active and influential in the woman suffrage movement. Because she came from an elite background and was bilingual, Otero-Warren managed to reach out to Hispanas of other classes, convincing many of them that the patriarchal system could change—that women could and should have the right to vote. She also lobbied New

Mexico's senators and representatives. Otero-Warren served as president of New Mexico's chapter of the NWP until 1919, when she became chair of the women's division of the Republican State Committee for Women. In this position, Otero-Warren unsuccessfully lobbied Republicans to adopt woman suffrage on the state level. She remained poised to urge New Mexican legislators and the governor to adopt the federal woman suffrage provision.

African American Women Suffragists

A significant number of black women also supported woman suffrage, sometimes joining and even becoming leaders of white suffrage groups. In New York City in 1917, the largely white New York Woman Suffrage party elected a black suffragist as vice-chair. Generally, however, white woman suffrage leaders avoided the involvement of black women in their efforts, both because of their own prejudice and because they did not want to risk alienating white southern male voters.

White women's hesitancy to involve black women made black people hostile and suspicious. Also in 1917, the *Crisis*, the official newspaper of the National Association for the Advancement of Colored People (NAACP), warned black women that, once enfranchised, white women were sure to vote for antiblack programs and policies. Other black leaders warned that white women voters would introduce a "grandmother" clause to deny most black women the right to vote.

Unfortunately, such sentiments had a basis in fact. In hopes of gaining the support of southern white suffragists and white supremacist Democrats, Catt and other white suffrage leaders gradually distanced themselves from the enfranchisement of black women. By 1919, the NAWSA officially rejected black female members. In the South, white female suffragists stated that the most "capable" women should vote, implying that "untutored" black women should not. They also hoped that southern white men would extend suffrage to white women only in order to offset the vote of black men.

While not all white women opposed giving the vote to black women, the support of black woman suffrage was increasingly unpopular. Even those southern white women who supported black women's right to vote hesitated to state their views publicly, quietly hoping that once white women got the vote they would extend the same privilege to black women. As one woman put it, "One war was enough at a time."

Despite these developments, large numbers of black women refused to desert the suffrage cause. They recognized the potential influence they could wield and the good they might achieve as voters, especially in southern states. The extreme complexity of the situation drove these black women to pursue the vote separately from white women, but much like their white counterparts, black suffragists organized suffrage clubs, participated in rallies and demonstrations, lectured, and wrote articles. According to several observers, black women, especially in the South, wanted the vote even more than white women did. Certainly, such black women's groups as the National Federation of Afro-American Women, the National Association of Colored Women, and the Northeastern Federation of Colored Women's Clubs enthusiastically joined the fight.

Jeannette Rankin and the "Anthony" Amendment

As women suffragists hoped, President Wilson changed his mind regarding their cause. On 9 January 1918, Wilson advised a group of Democrats to vote for the suffrage amendment "as an act of right and justice to the women of the country and of the world." The day after Wilson's announcement a stirring drama occurred in the House of Representatives. The galleries overflowed with women who fastened their eyes on Representative Jeannette Rankin, a suffragist from Montana and the first woman elected to Congress. (Although women could not vote in federal elections, they could vote and run for office in some states, including Montana.) Suffrage leaders had chosen Rankin to introduce the "Anthony" amendment, as the suffrage measure was called, for consideration, which she proceeded to do. Simple in its language, the amendment said "The right of citizens of the United States to vote shall not be denied or abridged by the United States or by any State on account of sex."

To support the amendment, suffrage leaders went to great lengths. One very ill representative was carried in on a stretcher to cast his vote. Another came straight from the deathbed of his suffragist wife. When the tally came in it stood at 274 votes for and 136 against, one vote more than the necessary two-thirds majority. As women of the NAWSA and the Woman's party streamed into the hallways, they sang "Praise God from whom all blessings flow."

The suffrage amendment moved next to the Senate, where it remained for a year and a half. Meanwhile, the NAWSA worked against the reelection of four antisuffrage senators, while the Woman's party again took to the streets in protest. President Wilson personally addressed the Senate on behalf of suffrage. Finally, after several negative votes, on 4 June 1919 the Senate approved woman suffrage by a vote of sixty-three to thirty.

Now the suffrage provision went to the states for ratification. To pass, the measure needed the support of three-fourths (thirty-six) of the states. Eleven ratifications poured in during the first month. Eleven more states approved the amendment during the next five months. The opposition, which proved tough and well organized, needed to hold back only thirteen states. The NAWSA and the Woman's party worked hard to combat the "antis," but it was unclear whether thirty-six of the states would indeed ratify the amendment.

The tension peaked in August 1920. By this time, thirty-five states had ratified woman suffrage. Only the approval of one more state was needed, and only one state was a potential supporter—Tennessee. Accordingly, suffragists poured into Nashville to campaign and lobby. On 13 August, the Tennessee Senate ratified the measure. When the issue went to the House, the vote tied. It now rested in the hands of Representative Harry Burn, at twenty-four years of age the youngest member of the Tennessee House of Representatives. When he cast his decision for suffrage, the amendment carried. Reportedly, he had just received a message from his mother instructing him to "vote for suffrage and don't keep them in doubt. . . . Don't forget to be a good boy and help Mrs. Catt put 'Rat' in Ratification."

The Nineteenth Amendment

On 26 August 1920, the secretary of state proclaimed the ratification of the Nineteenth Amendment to the U.S. Constitution. American women could, at long last, vote. Seventy-two years had passed since the 1848 convention at Seneca Falls, where women had first asked for the franchise. Many suffragists were elated and believed they had gained a way to solve their problems and those of society.

Because they had invested so much emotional energy and hope for the future in the vote, activist women were crushed when they learned it was not the answer after all. Within a few years, it became evident that women did not vote in blocs or react uniformly to women's issues. Like men, individual women voted in terms of such factors as their social class, educational level, race, religious affiliation, and geographical location.

Another unexpected complication developed when the NAWSA, the Woman's party, and other women's groups disagreed on how further reforms for women might be activated, or if they were necessary at all. Most American women seemed to feel that women now had all necessary rights, and that the unending discussion concerning women could finally cease. Women's efforts after 1920 were thus fragmented. Anna Howard Shaw foresaw this development when she stated, "I am sorry for you young women who have to carry on the work for the next ten years, for suffrage was a symbol, and now you have lost your symbol."

Just as Shaw prophesied, the suffrage movement soon broke into factions. Feminists advocated enlarged roles for women. Social feminists dedicated themselves to the reform of society. Pacifists argued that women could, and must, bring peace to the world. Other women were interested in changing the milieu of labor and the professions. "We all went back to a hundred different causes and tasks that we'd been putting off all those years," one former suffragist explained. "We just demobilized."

League of Women Voters

Because some women leaders believed that further progress would result only from women's political education and action, in 1919 the NAWSA president Carrie Chapman Catt announced to the NAWSA convention in St. Louis: "Let us then raise up a league of women voters . . . that shall be nonpartisan and nonsectarian in nature." In 1920, the NAWSA officially became the League of Women Voters.

League members hoped to demonstrate that women could become effective, involved citizens. The League advocated political education for women, social reform, and the elimination of discriminatory laws against women, all within the framework of a nonpartisan and moderate position. Gradually, League programs provided a solid training ground for women. For instance, the Director of the Maryland League in 1920 won election to the Maryland state legislature, and in 1936 achieved appointment as an officer of the U.S. Social Security Administration.

Unfortunately, because League members believed in "the aloof detachment of the scientific method" and in "wooing our legislators in a dignified and league-like manner," they frequently produced more speeches and literature than action. In late 1920, the League increased its influence by creating the Women's Joint Congressional Committee (WJCC). This umbrella organization brought together ten women's groups, including the League of Women Voters, the National Women's Trade Union League, the General Federation of Women's Clubs, the Women's Christian Temperance Union, and the National Consumer League.

The Women's Joint Congressional Committee engaged largely in lobbying. Recognizing that 250,000 children died—many of preventable diseases and neglect—in the United States each year, the WJCC supported the Sheppard-Towner Act of 1921, which established public health centers and prenatal clinics. The following year, the WJCC campaigned for the Cable Act, which granted individual citizenship to married women; this prevented American women from losing their U.S. citizenship when they married foreign nationals, except for Asians. By 1924, the WJCC had expanded to include twenty-one women's groups.

As with the earlier club movement, few black women found membership attractive in any of the predominantly white women's political groups. Instead, black women developed a wide range of organizations and philosophies of their own design. Most chose to join the Colored Women's Political Group and similar clubs. By 1920, "Colored Women's Voters Leagues" existed throughout the South. Some black women were even radicals. In 1922, one black female Socialist exhorted black women to "explain the correct use of the ballot . . . then make a demand and see to it that it is carried out by those whom you have elected into office."

Equal Rights Amendment

A handful of other women believed that suffrage and women's political action were inadequate and that further constitutional gains were needed. Alice Paul and her National Woman's party now maintained that an equal rights amendment to the Constitution was an absolute necessity to protect women from discriminatory laws and practices at the national and state levels. These women proposed a simply stated provision that "men and women shall have equal rights throughout the United States and every place subject to its jurisdiction." The NWP initiated its campaign for a single cause, the Equal Rights Amendment (ERA). In 1923, Paul introduced the ERA to Congress but found both members of Congress and the American public generally disinterested in any further "women's" amendments.

The NWP's commitment to the ERA kept the spirit of feminism alive during the 1920s, but its clear-cut stance made cooperation among women activists difficult. Feminists, such as those in the NWP, supported both the ERA and equality in all areas of life. They also hoped to eradicate protective labor legislation for women because they viewed it as unfair and restrictive of women's work rights. Social feminists believed the ERA too extreme and desired equality primarily in social and economic areas. They also strongly supported protective labor legislation. As a result of their many differences, feminists and social feminists formed two separate, and often warring, factions, which ultimately hurt the effectiveness of both groups.

At the Crossroads

Overall, American feminists seemed pleased with their progress. In 1923, only three years after American women obtained the right to vote, Charlotte Perkins Gilman proclaimed that the "breath of woman's new freedom" blew strongly through the land. She cited women's mental and physical development, advances in education, and success in the professions, politics, and independent lifestyles as evidence of "rapid and serious change." In spite of the "new status of women," Gilman reassured worried Americans that "women are first, last and always mothers." Besides, she added, "in our dread of the 'new woman' we should not lose sight of the fact that we never were satisfied with the old kind."

Just four years later, in 1927, a special issue of *Current History* devoted to the topic, "The New Woman," asked former suffragists to comment on changes they had witnessed. Charlotte Perkins Gilman again emphasized the progress of women in politics, reform, jobs and professions, and the development of autonomy. Carrie Chapman Catt reminded readers that suffrage had been the result of a long and difficult struggle dating back to

1848. She added that women wanted the vote to enhance their reform efforts, an ideal that had only been partially achieved.

Unlike Catt, Americans typically believed that women had achieved all their due rights. In her autobiography, playwright Lillian Hellman recalled: "By the time I grew up the fight for the emancipation of women, their rights under the law, in the office, in bed, was stale stuff. . . . My generation were not conscious that the designs we saw around us had so recently been formed or that we were still part of that formation." At the same time, psychiatrist Sigmund Freud told women that they would continue to be incomplete and ridden by "penis envy" until they had fulfilled themselves through childbearing.

Other writers and commentators argued that consumerism, fashion, beauty, and sex constituted valid female activities. One even warned women, "The return to the home is going to be almost as long and hard a struggle as the struggle for women's rights." In a 1927 issue of *Harper's Magazine*, journalist Dorothy Dunbar Bromley summed up the situation: "Feminism has become a term of opprobrium to the modern young woman" who "freely admits that American women have so far achieved but little in the arts, sciences, and professions as compared with men." According to Bromley, a "Feminist–New Style" had more interest in individual expression than in "women's" issues and preferred to combine career, marriage, and family.

Modern Femininity: White and Black

During the 1920s, an immense—and also antifeminist—interest developed in beauty, youth, and thinness for women. Advertisements depicted young, slim women doing their housework with the vast array of home appliances now available to them. Such advertisements clearly sent the message that women were most feminine at home, pursuing domestic tasks and consuming commercial goods.

This early version of what would later be termed the *feminine mystique* also emphasized that artificial means, especially cosmetics, were crucial to a woman's attractiveness. Moreover, an undergarment known as the brassiere was increasingly important in molding one's figure into an appealing shape. Ida Rosenthal's Maidenform, Inc., first produced the brassiere, the idea for which was reportedly inspired by the flappers' habit of binding their breasts to look boyish.

In 1921, businesspeople in Atlantic City capitalized on new marketing trends by staging the first Miss America pageant. Although the pageant's organizers attempted to emphasize the athletic skills and wholesome aspects of the contestants, the pageant soon took on a coarse side. Contests took place in a festival atmosphere, often amid charges of bribed judges. Although the Miss America contest halted in 1927 (until 1933), the idea had taken hold. Across the nation Miss New Yorks, Miss American Rodeos, and Miss Cherry Blossoms provided a legitimate display of female charms.

Silent films also reinforced such "feminine" behaviors and values. The 1920s became the age of giant studios, such powerful movie moguls as Louis B. Mayer, and the "star" system. The first female movie heroines emerged during the war years. They ranged from the sexy woman to the pure innocent girl. The ultimate vamp was Theda Bara, who popularized the dramatic makeup developed for her by Helena Rubenstein. The girl-next-door was Lillian Gish. A similar contradiction in female images continued during the 1920s. Clara Bow, the "It Girl," personified the kittenish yet sexy flapper. Mary Pickford, "America's Sweetheart," characterized the eternally youthful, innocent, and feminine woman.

Two movie stars who especially provided role models for young women, Gloria Swanson and Joan Crawford, played characters exhibiting women's new sexual freedom. According to a 1929 study concerning the impact of films on American youth, Swanson and Crawford established a standard of behavior and appearance for many female moviegoers. One sixteen-year-old girl commented, "These modern pictures give me a feeling to imitate their ways. I believe that nothing will happen to the carefree girl like Joan Crawford but it is the quiet girl who is always getting into trouble and making trouble."

Entrepreneurs and advertisers quickly jumped on the bandwagon of this newly invented femininity. Elizabeth Arden and Charles Revson (Revlon cosmetics) created new cosmetic products that underwrote business empires. Advertisements counseled women watching their weight to "Reach for a Lucky [Strike cigarette] Instead of a Sweet." At the same time, producers of mass media cranked out novels, magazines, radio shows, and films giving Americans the type of women they seemed to want.

The essence of such ideas of beauty and femininity ephasized whiteness in coloring, complexion, and hair. No place existed for women of color in early beauty pageants. Yet women of color had their own ideas of beauty and style. Among black women, Sarah Breedlove (Madam C. J.) Walker stands out. After she invented, around 1905, a chemical method for hair grooming, she patented the Walker method as well as other products. Soon a millionaire and philanthropist, Walker refuted the accusation that she had designed a product to "straighten" black women's hair. Rather, Walker explained to an Indianapolis reporter, she intended to help "the great masses of my people to take a greater pride in their personal appearance and to give their hair proper attention."

During the 1910s, Madam Walker's business and philanthropic interests continued to grow. By 1916, when Walker moved the main branch of her company to New York's Harlem, it employed 20,000 female and male agents. Madam Walker used her visibility and wealth to support such causes as the Negro Silent Protest Parade of 1917 and the antilynching crusade. After her death in 1919, her daughter A'Lelia became president of the Madam C. J. Walker Manufacturing Company. During the 1920s, A'Lelia continued her mother's tradition of instilling pride in African Americans, especially those in the arts.

Change and Continuity during the 1920s

Marriage and Family

During the 1920s positive changes for women seemed to be the order of the day. New attitudes, new practices, and new achievements dominated women's lives. Although some women appeared content with personal pursuits like playing bridge, home decoration, gardening, and keeping current with fashion trends, many others rejected such domesticity as old fashioned. To them, the attainment of personal autonomy was a worthy goal.

Concepts of marriage and family shifted into a "modern" mode. Consumerism and advertising raised women's expectations of standards of living in marriage to unrealistic levels. Media also encouraged women to act like "flappers," which the *Ladies Home Journal* described as "morbid" women who smoked, wore short skirts, performed obscene dances, favored one-piece bathing suits, and leaned toward Bolshevism.

During the 1920s, companionate marriage, or one based more on partnership than patriarchy, became the ideal. The "new family" bound its members by affection rather than rules. Novelist F. Scott Fitzgerald and his wife Zelda captured the popular imagination as the "ideal" couple. The Fitzgeralds reflected the 1920s flapper mode, acting thoroughly spoiled, selfish, and hedonistic. Although the Fitzgeralds modeled an impractical marriage, thousands of Americans found it charming and admirable. At the same time, lesbian love fell into disrepute. People of the 1920s increasingly viewed lesbian relationships as a threat to the institution of marriage.

On a daily basis, idealized images of heterosexual romance and everlasting happiness proved unworkable. Women who could now vote and hold paid employment were less willing to suffer abuse at the hands of spouses than were their mothers and grandmothers. Little wonder that marriages failed at a rising rate during the 1920s. By the end of the decade slightly more than one in six marriages ended in divorce.

During the 1920s, childrearing developed a different twist as well. Motherhood now required "psychological" knowledge. Advice literature counseled mothers to refrain from controlling their children. "How can tied hands ever learn to be useful?" one expert asked. The new ideal was to raise children as rational and educated adults. This goal gave a different meaning to the discussion of family size. Mothers and fathers wanted fewer children so they could raise those they had to be happy and healthy. As they had throughout human history, women sought ways to limit the number of children they bore.

The Birth-Control Movement

A public health nurse in New York City, Margaret Sanger, had long been concerned about women's desire to control family size. Sanger, credited with coining the term "birth control," had seen too many of her female patients harmed, or worse, by illegal or self-induced abortions. In 1914, she distributed a monthly publication, the *Woman Rebel*, on the streets and through the mail. Aimed at working-class women, the *Rebel* advocated women's right to sexual freedom and control of their own bodies. Although the journal did not describe birth-control techniques, its support of birth control was enough to draw opposition. Because she faced arrest under the Comstock Law, which, as mentioned, prohibited the mailing of birth-control information, Sanger fled to Europe where she studied family-planning clinics.

When Sanger returned to the United States in late 1915, she continued her crusade. Reportedly, she had smuggled into the country a number of diaphragms hidden in her girdle. One year later, Sanger and her sister established the first birth-control clinic, for which they were arrested and sentenced to the workhouse, where Sanger's sister went on a dramatic hunger strike that almost killed her. Although publicity brought the issue of birth control before the public, the episode alienated suffrage leaders and feminists who hoped for a more dignified reform. Nonetheless, Sanger's efforts led to a court decision allowing physicians to dispense a restricted amount of birth-control information.

Sanger enlarged her base of support, turning to middle-class women and medical doctors for psychological and financial backing and lobbying Congress for modifications in the Comstock Law. Using the term "voluntary parenthood" rather than "birth control," lobbyists argued that American citizens should have the right to make decisions regarding family size.

In 1921, the year of the first American Birth Control Conference, Sanger founded the American Birth Control League (ABCL). The ABCL offered birth-control information and dispensed spring-type diaphragms and lactic-acid jelly. It also gave out the names of New York physicians willing to help women with birth control. Although Sanger's efforts drew criticism and threats of riots from people who feared "race suicide" (meaning middle- and upper-class white native-born Americans) and increased promiscuity, she persevered, responding, "We want children to be conceived in love, born of parents' conscious desire and born into the world with healthy and sound bodies and sound minds."

In 1923, Sanger opened the Birth Control Clinical Research Bureau, the first birth-control clinic in the United States staffed by licensed physicians. The bureau trained doctors, who, at the time, received no birth-control instruction in medical schools. Sanger and her network established three hundred other birth-control clinics in the United States, which helped native-born white women.

Although Sanger wanted to reach out to immigrant and rural women, as well as those of color, such factors as illiteracy, religious beliefs, and cultural attitudes stood in the way. First-generation immigrant women believed in large families in which the husband ruled. A study of Polish families in Chicago showed that wife beating was acceptable practice and that the patriarchal family structure remained strong. The concept of "choice" was unknown to most of these women.

For them, change had to wait until their daughters grew up. Second-generation immigrant women who held paid employment outside their homes gradually developed expectations similar to those of native-born white women. The most popular women's journal, *Good Housekeeping,* helped immigrant women do things the "American" way. The movies indoctrinated thousands more into the values and beliefs of American women. One of the most popular film series during the 1920s, *Perils of Pauline,* stunned its women viewers. For twenty episodes, Pauline challenged tradition, including flying an airplane, racing an automobile, and refusing a suitor in favor of a career. American women appeared free to do as they pleased.

Women Actors

It certainly seemed that women were everywhere. On stage, black singer and dancer Josephine Baker delighted audiences. During the 1910s, she traveled with the Dixie Steppers. In 1921, Baker captured a part in Eubie Blake's and Noble Sissle's musical, *Shuffle Along,* which catapulted her to stardom. After captivating American audiences, Baker repeated her triumph in Paris. On one occasion, she appeared at the Folies-Bergère wearing a costume of rhinestone-studded bananas, an outfit that she adopted as her trademark. Baker performed in a traditional black style that incorporated rhythms with roots in the slave quarters and the ghetto. While African American audiences appreciated Baker, white critics viewed her as exotic, even "primitive." Baker not only persevered, but she legitimized African American dance forms. She sang in six different languages and was a fine comedian. Although Baker is thought of as an acclaimed artist today, in her lifetime she never gained widespread acceptance and confronted much racial prejudice in the United States. As a result, she often chose to live and perform abroad. Eventually, in 1937, she became a French citizen. Although Baker toured the United States, she resisted returning on a permanent basis: "They would make me sing mammy songs and I cannot feel mammy songs, so I cannot sing them."

A few years later, an unnamed dancer invented the striptease at Minsky's Burlesque House in New York City. During a 1925 police raid, she broke her shoulder strap and the audience went wild. The woman repeated the performance in subsequent shows. Most of her imitators developed routines based on the gradual removal of long gloves, evening gowns, and undergarments. Perhaps the most inventive act was that of the stripper who wrapped herself in newspapers. She read the headlines to music, while allowing people in the box seats near the stage to tear sheets off and slowly expose her body.

Women Artists

In the art world, women smashed old conventions. They experimented with such techniques as cubism and fauvism, and they established places to exhibit their work. In New York City, these included the Société Anonyme, the first gallery dedicated to modern art, and the Whitney Studio Club, which became the Whitney Museum of Modern Art.

The most controversial female artist of the 1920s was Georgia O'Keefe. Her New York skylines, abstract landscapes, and erotic flowers that filled entire canvases mystified her critics, who often dismissed O'Keefe's work as expressions of extreme female "sensibility" and emotionalism. According to O'Keefe, her work spoke to the pressures of life in the early-twentieth-century United States. Although she painted what she saw in a flower, O'Keefe magnified it so that viewers would "be surprised into taking time to look at it." She vowed that, "I will make even busy New Yorkers take time to see what I see of flowers."

Women Athletes

The 1920s, known as the Golden Age of Sports, saw women athletes make their marks. In 1922, a woman defeated the reigning bowling champion, a man. In 1926, another woman became the first female to swim the English Channel, with a time that improved on the existing male record by two hours. Yet another was the first female to break eighty for eighteen holes of golf.

The era also witnessed the golden years of rodeo. With Wild West shows in decline and western films not yet a genre, thousands of Americans satisfied their interest in the mythology of the American West, cowboys and cowgirls, and cattle and horses by following the rodeo circuit. In the United States, contests of ranching skills were held everywhere from New York City's Madison Square Garden to Los Angeles's Santa Anita Racetrack.

Women rodeo stars, who wowed audiences with their roping, trick riding, and bronco-busting, destroyed images of women as physically weak and mentally timid. Wearing split skirts, bloomers, or trousers tucked into high boots, rodeo women did men's work yet retained their femininity. As one said, "I love dresses and everything that goes with them. I can't tolerate the mannish woman any more than I can stand the womanish man."

The most famous of the cowgirls during the 1920s was Tad Lucas, who earned titles in bronco-riding, trick-riding, and all-around cowgirl. Lucas, who was born in Nebraska but grew up in Texas, learned her trade appearing in local Texas rodeos. In 1922, she became a full-time professional cowgirl. When Lucas toured with 101 Ranch Wild West, one of the most renowned Wild West shows, she developed an interest in trick riding. Two years later, she competed in trick riding in London. Back in the United States, Lucas established a reputation as a frequent winner. Among her many appearances, she scored high in Madison Square Garden, Chicago, Fort Worth, Philadelphia, and Cheyenne. One commentator summed up her career by saying, "She is considered the world's greatest rider."

Women Aviators

Barnstorming and stunt flying enthralled Americans during the 1920s. After all, the airplane was America's new fascination. Women were among the dauntless pilots who swooped and dived over everything from air fields to corn fields.

Unfortunately, such heroics sometimes led to disaster. Bessie Coleman, who in 1921 became the first black woman to earn a pilot's license, crashed and died while practicing for an air show in Orlando, Florida. After Coleman's death, her friends and fans took up her dream of establishing a flying school for black Americans, naming it the Bessie Coleman School.

By the end of the decade, women pilots were commonplace. They vied against each other in formal competition. In 1929, the first national aviation competition, the Women's Air Derby, offered monetary awards as well as the opportunity for women to prove themselves as accomplished aviators. Soon after the derby, a woman pilot at the Curtiss Flying Service on Long Island, New York, asked four women pilots to help her write to the 126 licensed women pilots in the United States to explore the possibility of organizing a female pilots' organization. Ninety-nine women responded. On 2 November 1929, twenty-six women gathered in a Curtiss hangar and established the Ninety-Nines, named for the number of charter members.

The most famous woman pilot during the 1920s was Amelia Earhart, who set her first world record in 1922. Flying her own Kinner Canary, she achieved the highest altitude flown by a woman. Soon, Earhart experimented with long-distance flights. With her short, curly blond hair and slim figure, she looked boyish in her white flying suits. Although Earhart was not an avowed feminist, she served as a model for adventurous and energetic women. Known as "The First Lady of the Air," Earhart wrote, lectured, and became aviation editor of *Cosmopolitan*. In 1929, Earhart was a founding member of the Ninety-Nines and served as the group's president until 1933. In 1937, Earhart was lost in the Pacific Ocean during an attempt to fly around the world.

Female Religious Leaders

A few women even challenged biases against them as ministers. The most successful way for a woman minister to get ahead was by founding her own religious sect. Evangelist Aimee Semple McPherson was not the only female religious leader in the United States at the time, but she certainly gained the most fame. When seventeen years old, Aimee had experienced conversion at a Pentecostal revival. Within the year she married Robert James Semple, the evangelist who had converted her. After her husband died, Aimee and her daughter worked for the New York City Salvation Army. In 1912, Aimee married Harold McPherson and had a son. After a long illness, Aimee returned to preaching; between 1918 and 1923, she worked her way across the country and back eight times.

In 1921, Aimee began building her dream, the Angelus Temple near Los Angeles, California. The temple became the center for her conservative "Church of the Foursquare Gospel." There McPherson preached every evening and three times on Sunday to crowds of five thousand people or more. Her enthralled listeners included women and men, young and old, whites and people of color. By the late 1920s, "Sister Aimee," as she was now called, had toured the United States, the British Isles, and Paris, preaching her message of redemption to thousands of persons anxious to hear what she had to say.

Women Scientists

The barriers restricting women from the sciences crumbled a bit more, allowing some women to distinguish themselves in their chosen fields. Alice Hamilton, the country's leading industrial toxicologist, had begun her career well before World War I. She had combined her interest in reform and medicine by taking in 1897 the position of Professor of Pathology at the Woman's Medical School of Northwestern University and by living at Hull House. Given the industrial reform agenda of Hull House leaders, it was inevitable that Hamilton would have interest in the contamination of factory workers and the pureness of products. Beginning in 1925, she worked with the National Consumers League and in 1925 published *Industrial Poisons in the United States*, which established her reputation worldwide.

Women Writers

During the 1920s, women published more books, essays, and poetry than in any previous era. They contributed novels, articles, and essays, and autobiographies. Some wrote about southern and western women. Others experimented with Realism. Yet others created hundreds of bold women characters who overcame and conquered every barrier they confronted. In other words, it was an inspiring time for women writers.

In 1920, Edith Wharton, who wrote about women in New York society, was the first woman to receive the Pulitzer Prize. In addition to her prize-winning *Age of Innocence*, Wharton wrote several other novels and eighty-five short stories. Known for her attention to detail and sensitive portrayals of female characters, Wharton revealed the intricacies and pitfalls of the New York social scene.

In poetry, Edna St. Vincent Millay dominated the era. Living in New York City's Greenwich Village during the 1920s, Millay's work reflected post–World War I thinking regarding women. Her always-witty female characters were independent and sexually free. They not only promoted reform, notably world peace, but they spoke against authoritarian ideas of the period such as Fascism.

Patron of the arts Mabel Dodge Luhan, who presided over the most illustrious salon in New York City's Greenwich Village, remembered the 1920s as exciting times indeed. Luhan recalled that her parties attracted "Socialists, Trade-Unionists, Suffragists, Poets, Relations, Lawyers, Murderers, Old Friends, Psychoanalysts, I.W.W.'s, Single Taxers, Birth Controlists, Newspapermen, Artists, Modern-Artists, Clubwomen, Woman's-place-is-in-the-home Women, clergymen, and just plain men" who all met in her home to exchange "a variousness in vocabulary called, in euphemistic optimism, Opinions."

Luhan failed to mention women of color, but they contributed to the literary ferment of the 1920s as well. An American Indian woman, Humishu-ma (Chrystal Quintasket), gained renown for her novel, *Co-ge-wea, the Half Blood* (1927). African American as well as Hispanic writers also created female images important to their people, writing of mothers, entertainers, and other women who possessed great beauty and sensuality.

At the other end of the United States, West Coast journalist Delilah Beasley researched and wrote the first history of California's black pioneers. Because no publishers believed Beasley's history would sell, in 1919 she borrowed money to publish *The Negro Trail Blazers of California* herself. Because Beasley had to market the book single-handedly, it achieved only modest sales. In 1923, her column "Activities Among Negroes" appeared in the Oakland, California, *Theme*. One focus of Beasley's columns was African Americans' civic responsibility. The tidbits she gleaned from black newspapers across the country emphasized reform and self-help efforts. Beasley also taught black history in her columns, always careful to give the background to events, telling, for example, how black singers had traveled through Europe in the 1870s to raise money for the first building at Fisk University in Nashville, Tennessee. Overlooked in her own day, Beasley is now seen as a trail blazer in her own right.

The Harlem Renaissance

The migration of southern rural African Americans to northern cities introduced black oral traditions and traditional rhythms to northerners in general and to New Yorkers in particular. During this time white audiences became interested in the work of black artists. The epicenter of this cultural renaissance was New York's Harlem, a vibrant Upper East Side neighborhood that since the early 1910s incubated the renewal of black culture, providing a model for African Americans living in the rest of the country.

With Harlem as their backdrop, black women demonstrated African Americans' literary talents and creative imaginations to the nation. In 1928, Nella Larsen's *Quicksand* gave American literature its first black heroine, a character that revealed the inner turmoil of a woman of a mixed racial background who never fully resolved her identity. The following year, Larsen's *Passing* revealed a similar crisis of identity faced by a light-skinned black woman who did not know which culture she should call her own. Another writer, Jessie Redmon Fauset, explained that she chose black Americans as her subject "partly because of all the other separate groups which constitute the American cosmogony none of them, to me, seems to be naturally endowed with the stuff of which chronicles may be made."

Harlem's black women also included pianists, composers, and orchestra conductors. They sang in the tiny Glory Hole cabaret or the huge, and hugely popular, Cotton Club, which attracted mixed audiences of blacks and whites. Out of these places came some of the most innovative and important musical styles of the era.

At the heart of the Harlem Renaissance were female blues singers. During what we now refer to as the "classic" blues era of the 1920s, such singers as Gertrude Pridgett "Ma" Rainey and Bessie Smith created a unique form of artistic expression, their lyrics reflecting the common anxieties of black women of the day, especially the fear of poverty and abandonment by men. Another dominant theme was migration, South to North and rural to urban, in which men often left women behind. Called the "railroad blues," this genre featured such songs as "Freight Train Blues" and "Chicago Bound Blues."

Among blues aficionados, Ma Rainey, who sang in a throaty, haunting voice, was known as "Mother of the Blues." During the early 1900s, Rainey appeared in tent shows, minstrel shows, and on the black vaudeville circuit. Not until 1923, however, did she achieve national stardom by recording with Paramount Records. Thereafter, Rainey's renditions of such blues standards as "See, See Rider" brought her phenomenal record sales and standing-room-only audiences. Unlike other blues singers of the time, Rainey composed more than one-third of the ninety-two songs she recorded. In late 1928, Paramount stopped recording Rainey because company executives believed that her style had gone out of fashion.

Meanwhile, Bessie Smith established herself as the "empress of the blues" and the "world's greatest blues singer." Smith, who began her career in 1912 touring with the acclaimed Rabbit Foot Minstrels on the black vaudeville circuit, not only worked with Gertrude Rainey but developed a friendship with her that lasted the rest of their lives. In 1913, Smith located in Atlanta. In 1923, she moved again, this time to Philadelphia, where she recorded with Columbia records. The sales of her first two records, which included "Down-hearted Blues" and "Gulf Coast Blues," far outdistanced Columbia's expectations. To many people, Smith's voice sounded rough and gravelly, but to others Smith's voice epitomized the blues. During her prime years, 1923 to 1930, Smith's powerful, husky voice reached millions of ears via radio. Ultimately it was the popularity of radio that undercut her record sales and the onset of the Great Depression that ended her recording career. Along with others, Rainey and Smith pioneered what is now known as the classic blues style, hooking black and white people alike on funky rhythms and doleful lyrics. In so doing they provided a continuity from African American music to the blues and to jazz. These were tremendous accomplishments in a short slice of time.

Lingering Barriers

Within the mantle of change for American women was a strong thread of continuity, for barriers lingered everywhere. Even areas that seemed to have undergone drastic revision were often not, upon closer examination, experiencing significant change.

For example, for many years after the adoption of the Nineteenth Amendment, not all women were actually allowed to vote. In southern jurisdictions, officials found ways to prevent black women from registering to vote. Registrars asked black women (knowing they were illiterate) to read from and interpret state and federal constitutions. In other cases, southern registrars required black women to pay a poll tax (which they could not afford) or kept them waiting at polling places for hours or even days, hoping they would simply go away in frustration.

Furthermore, laws against inter-racial marriage continued to exist in many states. Incredibly, policy and law makers continued to spend a good deal of time defining racial categories. In Virginia in 1924, legislators listed the races as Caucasian, Negro, Mongolian, American Indian, Asiatic Indian, Malay, or any mixture thereof, or any other non-Caucus strains. Also in 1924, Virginia legislators adopted the strictest marital code yet: white people could marry only other whites, or a white person with some American Indian blood.

Even though there were some changes in the U.S. Congress, most women who became senators or representatives were widows, nominated to take the place of their deceased husbands in office. When in 1924 Nellie Tayloe Ross was elected governor of Wyoming, she succeeded her husband, who had died in office. She made it clear that she was "not interested" in feminist issues. Instead, she wanted to retain her "femininity" and demonstrate that gender was unimportant in politics.

In education, women received one-third of graduate degrees but accounted for only 4 percent of full professors. In the professions in general, women maintained practices, especially in the West, but they remained exceptions. The number of female medical doctors increased slightly, but women who wished to become active lawyers still faced numerous difficulties. Finally, quotas determined the number of female students admitted to law and medical schools.

In the work force, women failed to catch up with men in terms of numbers working or wages received. In 1920, 23 percent of American women held jobs; by 1930 that percentage had risen by only one point. Meanwhile 80 percent of employed black women still performed menial labor, including cooking, washing clothes, and field work. White women clerical workers staffed offices but had to accept low wages and the lack of opportunity for advancement, seldom filling executive, managerial, or other high-level positions. Those businesswomen who did succeed did so by designing and marketing products for other women.

In the 1920s, women pilots gained their positions because the airline industry hoped to convince passengers that they would be as safe in the air with women in the cockpit as they would be at home with "mother." By the end of the decade, women were more often hired by airlines as "hostesses," a job which at the time required a nursing degree.

Ongoing Reform

Although some Americans thought of the 1920s as a magical time, it had its dark underside, and the need for reform continued. World War I and its aftermath demonstrated a greater need than ever for improvement in American society. Reforms as called for by the Women's Trade Union

League, the Consumers League, and the YMCA required women's attention.

In the wake of World War I, the United States achieved the position of a world leader. Americans considered peace with new eyes. In hopes of leading the world to peace, two groups organized in 1921: the Women's Peace Union of the Western Hemisphere and the Women's Committee for World Disarmament. In that same year, the PTA lent its support to the cause of peace as well, arguing that schools must educate the next generation of Americans to avoid war. In 1925, Carrie Chapman Catt organized the National Conference on the Cause and Cure of War. Meanwhile, Jane Addams continued to play an active role in the Women's International League for Peace and Freedom.

Educated and skilled women also voiced concerns about their place in postwar America. In 1919, a group of teachers and clerical workers formed the National Federation of Business and Professional Women's Clubs to achieve equal rights for professional women. For the first time, college-educated women formed a national association. In 1921, the Association of Collegiate Alumnae (1882) merged with the Western Association of Collegiate Alumnae (1883) and the Southern Association of College Women (1903) to form the American Association of University Women (AAUW). Like its forerunners, the AAUW awarded scholarships for women and funded women's dormitories. AAUW supported the admission of female students, the hiring of women faculty, and better salaries for female faculty members.

For female reformers, the dominant issue of the 1920s was the prohibition of alcoholic beverages in the United States. Women's long-term fight for temperance culminated in the total banning of alcoholic beverages. With the passage of the Eighteenth Amendment, ratified in 1918, and the Volstead Act, passed in 1919, the United States barred the manufacture, sale, and transportation of liquor and established harsh penalties for those who disobeyed.

But rather than bringing salvation from a long-standing problem, national prohibition drove liquor consumption underground. During the 1920s, illicit alcohol production turned into a corrupt, and highly lucrative, industry. Part of what made the "Roaring Twenties" roar stemmed from the activities of bootleggers, gang wars, and a general disrespect for law and order. Women, who were no longer arrested for merely smoking in public, now smoked and drank openly.

Prostitution thrived as well. In Silverton, Colorado, "boardinghouses" with such colorful names as the "Diamond Bell" and the "Mikado" lined Blair Street. According to one long-time resident, during the 1920s Silverton was "like a little Las Vegas, the gambling houses and bordellos were open 24 hours a day, seven days a week. You could buy bootleg booze in any saloon or whorehouse."

Calls for the repeal of prohibition accelerated by the end of the 1920s. The depression strengthened such arguments. For one thing, farmers needed another market for their wheat and corn. Although Congress considered repealing prohibition, it made no move to do so during the 1920s.

Environmental Conservation

Conservation of the physical environment remained another pressing need that engaged women during the 1920s. Because they had the spare time and financial resources, middle- and upper-class white women were the most likely to be conservation-minded. Women of color were interested in their environments as well, but more pressing "environmental" issues for them were public health programs and regular garbage pick-up.

Largely white women formed clubs to study science, nature, photography, and conservation; others centered around hiking and nature travel. Clubwomen participated in the growing field of nature study, begun in the early twentieth century. During the 1920s, approximately 60 percent of the members of the Nature Study Association were women; 90 percent of nature study teachers were female. The latter introduced into American classrooms scientific activities and techniques such as nature walks, school museums, weather (data-collection) stations, aquariums, and terrariums.

Other women supported the educational and lobbying efforts of such conservation clubs as the Save-the-Redwoods-League, founded in 1918 in San Francisco's Palace Hotel. Some of these club women gave speeches or wrote articles or books, emphasizing the need to preserve the fragile environment. By so doing, women raised peoples' awareness and often caused them to take direct action or at least support environmentalism.

The women's club movement proved instrumental in the conservation campaign. Since the late nineteenth century, club women had viewed conservation of home, family, schools, and the larger environment as a woman's special duty. Virtually every white women's club in the nation appointed a conservation committee or established an environmental goal. During the 1920s, local club agendas included highway beautification, forest and wildflower protection, and clean-up campaigns.

In addition, women's clubs supported the establishment of a National Park Service and such parks as Colorado's Estes Park, California's Sequoia National Park, and Arizona's Grand Canyon National Park. Garden Club of America affiliates all over the nation joined in the campaign to create parks and reserves.

Moreover, individual club women fought for conservation. In 1929, Rosalie Barrow Edge, a New York clubwoman, suffragist, and devoted birdwatcher, founded the Emergency Conservation Committee (ECC). As a one-person organization, Edge wrote letters, testified, lobbied, and spoke in support of such ECC causes as "defending and creating National Parks. Edge explained that because of business commitments, most men found it difficult to "take a strong stand on the side of public interest." Edge summed up many women's feelings about environmentalism when she added, "But women can do it, and they should."

Individual women used their expertise on behalf of the environment. Among them, Florence Merriam Bailey was foremost. During her Smith College days from 1882 to 1886, Bailey protested the slaughtering of birds by companies who provided feathers and whole birds to adorn women's hats. Shortly after the Audubon Society began, she and another student organized a Smith College Audubon Society for the Protection of Birds. "The birds must be protected," the pair decided. "We must persuade the girls not to wear feathers on their hats."

After graduating from Smith, Florence moved to Washington, D.C., although she often worked in the West, notably New Mexico. In 1899 she married biologist Vernon Bailey, who sometimes accompanied Florence on her western jaunts. While he studied mammals, birds, reptiles, and plants, she concentrated on birds, her passion and lifetime conservation project. Florence Bailey wrote articles protesting bird slaughter for the *Audubon Magazine* and newspapers, including the Washington D.C. *Evening Star* and *Watertown (New York) Times*. In 1913, when Congress had before it a plumage act that would stop milliners from using feathers and birds as decorations, Bailey joined the fight.

For years, Bailey collected data on birds. In 1928, her comprehensive *Birds of New Mexico* appeared. For this work, a hallmark in natural history, Bailey became, in 1929, the first woman elected a fellow of the American Ornithologists Union. One expert called her the "greatest woman ornithologist in the United States." In her later years, she continued to promote the Audubon Society and teach bird classes.

Thanks in part to Florence Bailey, a growing awareness of the need to protect birds and their habitats developed among American women. In 1919, the Bird Lovers' Club of the Southwest Museum formed in Los Angeles. This largely female group held weekly bird walks and monthly study meetings. During the 1920s, the Bird Lovers engaged in letter-writing, lobbying, and speech-making campaigns in support of local and statewide issues. In 1925, the group fought the California Fish and Game Commission's decision to stop protecting cormorants and pelicans.

American Indians

After slipping out of mainstream (white) America's consciousness at the close of the nineteenth century, Native Americans gained public attention during the 1920s. The situation of American Indians was dismal and their numbers were hitting a plateau or declining. Some Indians died in the worldwide influenza epidemic. Others were not counted, for census-takers were hasty and careless when dealing with Indians. The question of who was truly Indian caused further confusion. Census-bureau investigators used physical appearance and residence as the basis for classifying people. If a person looked like an Indian or lived with a group of other Indians, he or she was deemed Indian. If a person looked more "white" than "Indian" or lived in a city, he or she was recorded as white.

As a result, the number and residences of Native Americans was unclear. Generally, however, American Indian women lived in one of two places: government reservations or urban ghettoes. In addition, some rural Indian women were scattered and lived isolated from their people. Typically, Indian women worked as domestics and agricultural laborers. Wherever they resided, they experienced poverty. During the 1910s, a rural Pima woman rose daily at 3:00 AM to prepare beans and stacks of tortillas for her husband and sons to eat before scratching out a living with a horse-drawn plow on their small forty-acre farm.

According to many Indian women, white people were to blame for the miserable conditions Native Americans faced. In 1915, one woman faulted white men for destroying Indian farming lands: "the white people plow up the ground, pull up the trees, kill everything." Native American women also condemned the federal government. Misguided policies had forced capitalistic means of production on Indian societies, thereby destroying their social fabric and, with it, women's traditional roles. Women resisted these changes. When the U.S. Agricultural Extension Service established a program to teach New Mexico women canning techniques, Indian women refused to purchase or use jams, jellies, and canned goods, preferring the traditional and more efficient technique of drying foodstuffs.

Unhappy with their peoples' plight, Native American women recognized that unity was important to improving life in Indian communities. Like other groups of American women, they formed social clubs and self-help organizations. Among the Ojibway of Minnesota, women founded the First Daughters of America, which met twice monthly to do beadwork, knit, quilt, and study methods of gardening. The groups also undertook community improvement projects. In some cases drawing on the resources offered them by Catholic and Episcopal churches, Indian women might use the churches as meeting places for family dinners, First Daughters' events, and holiday celebrations.

Similarly Indian women in Alaska stood together. In 1920, Tlingit women formed the Alaska Native Sisterhood, which brought together local women's clubs. Although the Sisterhood supported the programs of the Alaska Native Brotherhood, the Sisterhood soon developed its own agenda. Women's programs included lobbying the Alaska Territorial government and U.S. Congress to preserve Native cultural identity, protect Native fishing grounds, and settle Native land claims.

In addition to groups of women, individual Native women took up reform causes. A Dakota Sioux named Gertrude Simmons Bonnin, also known as Zitkala-Sa or "Redbird," worked with the Society of American Indians, founded in 1911. Bonnin campaigned for U.S. citizenship for Indians, which Congress finally granted in 1924. She also wanted an equitable settlement of Indian land claims and investigations of the federal government's relations with individual tribes. In 1926, Bonnin founded the National Congress of American Indians, which she led for years. Moreover, Bonnin convinced the General Federation of Women's Clubs to join the Indian Rights Association and encourage the documentation of Indian grievances. Through her writings in such journals as *Atlantic Monthly, Harper's Monthly,* and *The American Indian Magazine,* Bonnin brought Native dilemmas before the American public.

During the 1910s and 1920s, white women wishing to help Indians found themselves in the middle of a national argument about Indian reform: should Indians' culture be restored or should government welfare programs take care of Indians? When people asked Native Americans for their opinions they got one of three answers: support Indian nationalism; give Native peoples American citizenship; or leave Indian peoples alone to live according to their respective cultures.

In 1924, writer and Indian reformer Mary Austin pointed out, "[What] the Indian Bureau has utterly failed to reckon with is the rapidly growing appreciation of such Indian culture[s] as remain to us, as a National Asset, having something the same valuation as the big trees of California and the geysers and buffaloes of Yellowstone." As the conservators of society and the environment, women stepped in to preserve Indians and their culture. Austin believed that health programs, education, and fair-minded officials who recognized that "Indians do not belong to them, but to us" would be a "starter" toward a more effective Indian policy.

Female scholars, including anthropologists, archaeologists, and ethnologists, also took steps toward Indian reform. They did fieldwork that retrieved pieces of Native culture. Because these investigators were female, they had a keen interest in family, kin, children, and household practices, all of which had been overlooked by male anthropologists. Women reconstructed an Indian history that revealed human beings, who like others before and after them, had families, relationships, and households.

Other women believed that the customary visual images of the "savage" Indian needed revision. Instead of presenting Indians as warriors, female artists and photographers focused on women, children, and family life. Unfortunately, some women photographers were tempted by financial gain. During the 1910s and 1920s, one female photographer took idealized photographs of Indians in northern California, which she sold in her San Francisco salesroom. Nevertheless, the majority of women artists and photographers introduced a humanized view of American Indians. The works of these artists had wide dissemination. During the 1920s, one painter sold her renditions of Glacier Park's Blackfeet, including children and families, to the Great Northern Railroad for use in nationwide advertisements.

White clubwomen, too, worked to save Native cultures. In 1924, Mary Austin declared that an improved "public consciousness" regarding Indians was due, in great measure, to clubwomen. During the 1920s, the Utah Federation of Women's Clubs set out to help American Indians living on the Goshute Reservation. Utah clubwomen raised the Indians' standard of living and lobbied the Bureau of Indian Affairs in Washington, D.C., for reforms. Women also brought about the arrest and conviction of a corrupt Indian agent and his wife, and the dismissal of an ineffective teacher.

Yet other clubwomen collected and preserved Indian artifacts. In Arizona, philanthropist and clubwoman Maie Bartlett Heard assembled a fine variety of Indian art. Because Heard had worked in the tourist industry, she had seen firsthand the destruction of Native cultures that pandering to the tourist market could cause. Heard tried to offset such damage by purchasing and saving whatever pieces of American Indian material culture she could find. In 1929, her collection became Tucson's Heard Museum.

White women's efforts to help Native peoples produced mixed results. From the white point of view, women writers drew much-needed attention to the Indians' situation. From the Native American outlook, this attention was often intrusive. White female reformers tried to teach Indian women how to act like "ladies," as defined by white culture. White women initiated the Native arts and crafts movement, yet set the standards for Indian women's art. Indian women responded by meeting white women's expectations on the surface, but going their own ways in their daily life. Most kept their misgivings to themselves. Many Indian women associated white women reformers with bitter memories of Indian schools that had taken them from their families.

Hispanas

For many decades, white Americans had largely ignored Spanish-heritage peoples living in the United States. White Americans knew little about the culture, customs, and complaints of Hispanic Americans. By the 1910s and 1920s, however, it was increasingly important for white people to understand the Hispanic point of view.

During World War I and thereafter, continuing turmoil in Mexico combined with the demand for unskilled labor in North America created a powerful motivating force for immigration to the United States. At first, Mexican migrants lived in Arizona, California, New Mexico, and Texas. In the 1920s, they fanned out over the Midwest, the men working as industrial and agricultural laborers, especially for railroads, in steel mills and automobile plants, and in sugar beet fields. Migrant women and children sought wage work in the fields and in canneries. Despite their efforts to support themselves, most Hispanics suffered inadequate nutrition, poor sanitary conditions, and scattering of their extended families.

A number of individual Hispanas tried to remedy the situation. Beginning in 1924, a young civil rights leader from Mexico, María Hernández, spoke and wrote in Texas on behalf of rights for *Tejanos* (Mexican Texans). Hernández advocated cooperation between women and men in fighting against the racial segregation their people faced. She campaigned for improved education in *barrios* (ghettos) and Hispanic activism in politics and the workplace. In 1929, Hernández and her husband organized a male civil rights group, the *Orden Caballeros de America*. Later, she helped develop the *Raza Unida* party in Texas.

On the East and West Coasts, other Spanish-speaking women and their descendants struggled to preserve their native language and culture. To New York City, Puerto Rican men migrated to seek work as cigarmakers, shoemakers, and industrial workers, whereas women migrated to work as domestic servants and cooks. Puerto Ricans formed *colonias* (neighborhoods), especially in Harlem and Brooklyn, where women attempted to conserve the Puerto Rican legacy. They used everything from the celebration of traditional holidays to public storytelling to keep their culture alive and vital in the community.

Asian Women

American Indians and Hispanics were not the only groups facing racial prejudice and discrimination. During the 1910s and 1920s, Americans' long-standing hostility toward Asian immigrants worsened. Whites feared losing their jobs to Chinese workers willing to accept lower wages. In 1920, 40 percent of the Chinese population lived in San Francisco and New York, usually employed in segregated businesses and industry. Because so few

Chinese women obtained permission to immigrate, 80 percent of the Chinese American population was male, who typically took refuge in urban Chinatowns. Although gender still determined Chinese women's roles, customs such as foot-binding and total seclusion disappeared in America.

Unlike Chinese immigrants, the majority of Japanese immigrants worked as migratory laborers in agriculture, canneries, and for railroads. A significant number went to Hawaii, where men performed taxing field work in the expanding sugar-cane industry. On the mainland, Japanese established themselves as small farmers. In cities, *Issei* (first-generation immigrants) clustered in Little Tokyos. Women divided their time between domestic duties and paid employment, often helping out in family businesses or working in domestic service or factories. Women of the upper classes, usually wives of merchants, spent a greater proportion of their time in domestic activities and assisting their husbands. *Nisei* (second-generation) Japanese women adopted such American ideas as better education and professional training for women.

Smaller groups of Asians, including Filipinos, Asian Indians, and Koreans, also migrated to the United States. Because the Philippines had become an American territory after the Spanish-American War (1898), all 5,603 Filipinos residing in the mainland United States in 1920 could claim U.S. citizenship. By that time, 6,400 Asian Indians and 1,677 Koreans lived in the United States as well. Of Korean immigrants, 75 percent were male. Korean women migrated primarily as "picture brides." Among Asian agricultural workers, women ran kitchens and laundries or worked in the fields alongside men. Like others, Asian women spent a great deal of energy maintaining their own language and culture.

African Americans

To most Americans, the phrase "racial issues" meant one thing: white-black relationships. Although the two groups had lived together in North America for three hundred years, by the 1920s they were more divided than ever. Each harbored prejudice against the other and blamed them for many of America's problems.

Working through organizations, black women stepped forward in an attempt to bridge the gap. In 1921, eight Montana clubs met in Butte to organize a statewide federation, the Montana State Federation of Negro Women's Clubs, dedicated to fighting for civil rights. Their program included providing college scholarships for black students and opposing discrimination in athletics and school events.

Three years later, in 1924, clubwoman Nannie Burroughs helped establish the National League of Republican Colored Women in Washington, D.C. Burroughs served as the group's first president. Because Burroughs was a spell-binding orator, she traveled and spoke widely. At political conferences, she was one of two or three black women among hundreds of white women. She learned to see issues from many sides and used her powers as a speaker on behalf of domestic servants, black wage workers, equal justice, and black pride. Rather than wait for "deliverance" at the hands of white people, Burroughs urged black Americans to "arise and go over Jordan" to the promised land on their own.

Better education for black children also demanded the attention of black women reformers. In 1927, an African American woman founded the National Congress of Colored Parents and Teachers. Although Texas contained the most and the best black high schools in the South, other states had to catch up. As a child-advocacy group, the National Congress intended to help school districts, especially in the South, improve their segregated schools.

To offset the effects of racism, thousands of other black women joined community improvement organizations, women's clubs of various types, and churches. The black Baptist church especially provided black women with a social center and training ground. In turn, black female activists helped black churches become powerful self-help institutions.

Wherever they gathered, black women found themselves divided on the question of joining forces with white women. Some opposed the inclusion of white women in black projects. Jamaican-born black-nationalist Amy Jacques Garvey spoke and wrote on behalf of the most successful Pan-African movement ever. As supporter and spouse of Marcus Garvey and his Universal Negro Improvement Association (UNIA), Amy Garvey was a strong voice for cultural unity as a vehicle for racial uplift. When her husband was jailed during the mid-1920s, Amy represented him and the UNIA as a writer, speaker, and advocate. After Marcus's release and deportation from the United States, the Garveys went to Jamaica, where Amy continued as a strong voice for Pan-Africanism.

Other black women believed that interracial cooperation must underwrite change. Cases of black-white cooperation occurred in the Commission on Interracial Cooperation of the Women's Council of the Methodist Episcopal Church, which in 1920 sponsored a major conference on race relations. Also in 1920, a group of black women appealed to the predominantly white YWCA for the development of some black-oriented programs. They called for integration of black women into the administration and black representation on the national board. The first black woman on the staff of the YWCA emphasized, "White women do not properly appreciate the strength of our colored women throughout the country." During the early 1920s, the YWCA responded to these complaints. In 1924, it elected the first black woman to its national board.

The most pressing issue to black women during the 1920s, lynching, frequently led to collaboration between black and white women. The anti-lynching movement dated back to the 1890s, notably to the campaign of Ida Wells-Barnett. In 1922, another black woman reformer, Mary B. Talbert, organized the Anti-Lynching Crusade. She hoped to bring together "a million women," black and white, "to stop lynching" in the United States. The group released studies disclosing that eighty-three women had been lynched since 1892. Members of racist groups like the Ku Klux Klan were responsible for these cowardly and appalling acts of violence. Klan membership, which reached its peak during the 1920s, included white women.

The great majority of white women, however, opposed lynching. In 1922, the National Council of Women, representing 13 million white women, voted to endorse the Anti-Lynching Crusade. By the following year, more than seven hundred women leaders in twenty-five states had joined the crusade, using such tactics as pressuring Congress and state legislatures for antilynching legislation, publicizing the grisly details of specific lynchings, and suing lynchers.

In 1924, the League of Women Voters established a Committee on Negro Problems. Southern white women supported this program, which included a call for an end to lynching. The persistence of the image of the southern lady may have hampered the committee's effectiveness, however. Though crusty with age and heavy with the weight of tradition, old-fashioned notions of the southern female plagued women activists throughout the postwar decade.

Labor Reform

As growing numbers of women entered the job market during the 1920s, labor problems increased. In 1920, one out of every five workers was female. Of women workers, 25.6 percent worked in such business-related jobs as store clerk or receptionist.

Another 8.2 percent worked in domestic service, 12.9 percent in agriculture, and 23.8 percent in manufacturing, especially the automobile industry. According to a 1927 issue of *Motor Magazine*, the automobile industry had "almost over night become a feminine business with a feminine market."

For women of color the statistics were more dismal. Fully 75 percent of all employed women of color labored in three fields: domestic service, laundry work, and agriculture. In cities, the proportion of black women and other women of color in domestic service rose to 85 percent. Restrictive policies barred them from factories and offices. If hired in factories and shops, women of color had to work in separate rooms from white employees and went without amenities like lunchrooms and clean bathrooms.

In 1920, the U.S. government responded to the needs of working women by creating a new division within the Department of Labor. The Women's Bureau collected data, studied women on the job, and lobbied for protective legislation. In a 1920 report, the Women's Bureau observed that World War I had "forced the experiment of woman labor in the craftsmanly occupations." The Bureau also reported the surprise of employers when observing the skills and abilities of women workers. According to one manufacturer, "There is hardly a line of work in which a woman cannot adapt herself."

The Women's Bureau also supported the passage of protective laws for women. In the years of peak activity, 1912 to 1919, fourteen states, mainly in the Midwest and on the West Coast, enacted such legislation. Three new legal codes limited the number of hours women worked, prohibited night work, and excluding women from selling liquor, carrying mail, running elevators, and working in foundries and mines. In addition, women's employers had to provide seats, rest periods, ventilation, and good lighting.

Other women tried a different approach. Such experienced labor reformers as Mary "Mother" Jones and Lucy González Parsons, who had grown disillusioned with Socialism, joined the Communist party, which had organized in the United States in 1919. During the 1920s, these and other women pushed the American Communist party in the direction of championing the rights of working women, white and of color.

Other labor reformers remained convinced that only strikes, protests, and even violence would compel employers to institute needed reforms. Unfortunately, such demonstrations often resulted in tragedy. In a 1919 strike in West Natrona, Pennsylvania, Allegheny Coal and Coke Company deputy sheriffs shot and killed a female Socialist labor organizer. Some thought she had been killed intentionally, for she had alienated many employers by organizing female garment workers and helping black workers, who had been brought north as strikebreakers.

Ten years later, a 1929 strike in Elizabethton, Tennessee, turned violent. When textile workers left their machines to protest low wages, work quotas, and "hard rules," laborers in a nearby plant joined them. On the spot, the striking workers organized a local of the United Textile Workers of the American Federation of Labor (UTW-AFL). The strike spread over the entire area, resulting in chaos and defiance, the strikers ignoring injunctions against picketing. In retaliation, a local business owner kidnapped a union organizer. Meanwhile, women, who constituted 37 percent of rayon workers in Elizabethton, wrapped themselves in American flags. So attired, they walked through the streets, blocked roads with their bodies, and, with fists and picket signs, assaulted members of the National Guard. Although many women ended up in jail and the six-week strike brought workers only minimal gains, they felt empowered. Furthermore, their courageous stand set off a wave of protests against other southern textile factories.

As the stock market took its monumental tumble in 1929, the era of World War I and the 1920s ended. The national scene had changed. Americans' disappointment with the outcome of World War I, rising fear of communism, an experiment with the prohibition of alcohol, and witnessing women's entry into the political arena had reshaped their ideas, values, and society.

Were American laws, policies, and expectations regarding women significantly different? Probably not. Too many of the changes had originated in wartime emergency and could easily be forgotten. Other changes were only anticipated—what suffrage could bring and what women officeholders might achieve. And even though the 1920s seemed radical in many ways, people, let alone society, could not transform overnight.

Anticlimactic as they might in some ways seem, such innovations as woman suffrage, the antilynching movement, and birth-control practices were now firmly in place. Not only were these giant steps forward, but they were building blocks for the future.

Study Guide

Checklist of important names, terms, phrases, and dates in Chapter 7. Think about what or who each was and why she, he, or it was significant.

Woman's Peace Party (WPP)
"meatless," "wheatless," and "butterless" meals
Lugenia Burns Hope
National War Labor Board
Women's Land Army (WLA)
Army Nurse Corps (ANC)
Navy Nurse Corps (NNC)
National American Woman Suffrage Association (NAWSA)
Carrie Chapman Catt
"Winning Plan"
"antis"
Alice Paul
National Woman's Party (NWP)
Adelina Otero-Warren
Jeannette Rankin
"Anthony amendment"
1920
Nineteenth Amendment
League of Women Voters
Women's Joint Congressional Committee (WJCC)
Equal Rights Amendment

companionate marriage
Margaret Sanger
American Birth Control League (ABCL)
Josephine Baker
Georgia O'Keefe
Tad Lucas
Bessie Coleman
Aimee Semple McPherson
Alice Hamilton
Edith Wharton
Edna St. Vincent Millay
Delilah Beasley
Harlem Renaissance
Nella Larsen
Gertrude "Ma" Rainey
Bessie Smith
Florence Merriam Bailey
Gertrude Simmons Bonnin
Mary Austin
María Hernández
colonias
Nannie Burroughs
Amy Jacques Garvey
Anti-Lynching Crusade

Chapter 7 issues to think about and discuss:

- What gender-associated reasons do women have for opposing wars?
- What factors began to break down black/white prejudice during the World War I years and thereafter?
- In what ways did World War I help—and hurt—the employment prospects of white women? Of black women?
- Why did the military begin to accept women during World War I?
- Why did woman suffrage leaders continue their campaign during World War I?
- Why did the "antis" oppose woman suffrage?
- Why did some white suffragists recruit Hispanas but not black women?
- Is violence necessary to achieve reform?
- If women had not organized and fought for suffrage, when might it have finally occurred?
- Why do American women need an Equal Rights Amendment? Why don't they?
- Opponents of birth control feared medical complications and a decline in population, especially the white population. Did those events occur once birth control became available? What changes in American society have taken place as a result of birth control?

- In what ways do you think the Harlem Renaissance was important for black civil rights?
- Why did many white Americans fear peoples of color?
- Why did employed men fear employed women?
- If you were a labor reformer during the 1920s, what techniques and strategies would you choose as the most effective?

Suggestions for Further Reading

Women During World War I, 1914–1918

Breen, William J., "Black Women and the Great War: Mobilization and Reform in the South," *Journal of Southern History* 44 (August 1978): 421–40.

Conner, Valerie J., "'The Mothers of the Race' in World War I: The National War Labor Board and Women in Industry," *Labor History* 21 (Winter 1979–80): 31–54.

Graebner, William., "'Uncle Sam Just Loves the Ladies': Sex Discrimination in the Federal Government, 1917," *Labor History* 21 (Winter 1979–80): 75–85.

Greenwald, Maurine Weiner, *Women, War, and Work: The Impact of World War I on Women Workers in the United States* (Westport, CT: Greenwood Press, 1980).

———, "Working Class Feminism and the Family Wage Ideal: The Seattle Debate on Married Women's Right to Work, 1914–1920," *Journal of American History* 76 (June 1989): 118–50.

Higonnet, Margaret R., Jane Jenson, Sonya Michel, and Margaret C. Weitz, eds., *Behind the Lines: Gender and the Two World Wars* (New Haven, CT: Yale University Press, 1987).

Kennedy, Kathleen, *Disloyal Mothers and Scurrilous Citizens: Women and Subversion during World War I* (Bloomington: University of Indiana Press, 1999).

Malin, Nancy E., "How 'Ya Gonna Keep 'Em Down? Women and World War I," *Prologue* 25 (1994): 113–18.

Martelet, Penny, "The Woman's Land Army, World War I," 136–46, in *Clio Was a Woman: Studies in the History of American Women,* edited by Mabel E. Deutrich and Virginia C. Purdy (Washington, DC: Howard University Press, 1980).

Rouse, Jacqueline A., *Lugenia Burns Hope: Black Southern Reformer* (Athens: University of Georgia Press, 1989).

Steinson, Barbara J., "'The Mother Half of Humanity': American Women in the Peace and Preparedness Movements in World War I," 259–84, in *Women, War, and Revolution* edited by Carol R. Berkin and Clara M. Lovett (New York: Holmes and Meier, Inc., 1980).

Zeiger, Susan, "She Didn't Raise Her Boy to be a Slacker: Motherhood, Conscription, and the Culture of the First World War," *Feminist Studies* 22 (Spring 1996): 7– 39.

Woman Suffrage Triumphant

Alonso, Harriet Hyman, "Jeannette Rankin and the Women's Peace Union," *Montana the Magazine of Western History* 29 (Spring 1989): 34–49.

Alpern, Sara, and Dale Baum., "Female Ballots: The Impact of the Nineteenth Amendment," *Journal of Interdisciplinary History* 16 (Summer 1985): 43–67.

Baker, Jean H., ed., *Votes for Women: The Struggle for Suffrage Revisited* (New York: Oxford University Press, 2002).

Beauchamp, Cari, *Frances Marion and the Powerful Women of Early Hollywood* (New York: Scribner, 1997).

Becker, Susan D., *The Origins of the Equal Rights Amendment: American Feminism Between the Wars* (Westport, CT: Greenwood Press, 1981).

Camhi, Jane Jerome, *Women Against Women: American Anti-Suffragism, 1880–1920* (Brooklyn, NY: Carlson, 1994).

Cott, Nancy F. "Feminist Politics in the 1920s: The National Woman's Party," *Journal of American History* 71 (June 1984): 43–68.

DuBois, Ellen Carol, "The Radicalism of the Woman Suffrage Movement: Notes Toward the Reconstruction of Nineteenth-Century Feminism," *Feminist Studies* 3 (Fall 1975): 63–71.

Easton, Patricia O'Keefe, "Woman Suffrage in South Dakota: The Final Decade, 1911–1920," *South Dakota History* 13 (Fall 1983): 206–26.

Finn, Barbara R., "Anna Howard Shaw and Women's Work," *Frontiers* 4 (Fall 1979): 21–25.

Geidel, Peter, "The National Woman's Party and the Origins of the Equal Rights Amendment, 1920–1923," *Historian* 42 (August 1980): 557–82.

Graham, Sally Hunter, "Woodrow Wilson, Alice Paul, and the Woman Suffrage Movement," *Political Science Quarterly* 98 (Winter 1983–84): 665–80.

Green, Elna C., *Southern Strategies: Southern Women and the Woman Suffrage Question* (Chapel Hill: University of North Carolina Press, 1999).

Jensen, Billie Barnes, "'In the Weird and Wooly West': Anti-Suffrage Women, Gender Issues, and Woman Suffrage in the West," *Journal of the West* 32 (July 1993): 41–51.

Jensen, Joan M., and Lois Scharf, eds., *Decades of Discontent: The Women's Movement, 1920–1940* (Westport, CT: Greenwood Press, 1983).

Landsman, Gail H., "The 'Other' as Political Symbol: Images of Indians in the Woman Suffrage Movement," *Ethnohistory* 39 (Summer 1992): 247–84.

Lathem, Angela J., "Packaging Women: The Concurrent Rise of Beauty Pageants, Public Bathing, and Other Performances of Female 'Nudity,'" *Journal of Popular Culture* 29 (Winter 1995): 149–67.

Lemons, J. Stanley, *The Woman Citizen: Social Feminism in the 1920s* (Charlottesville: University Press of Virginia, 1990).

Lunardini, Christine A., and Thomas J. Knock, "Woodrow Wilson and Woman Suffrage: A New Look," *Political Science Quarterly* 95 (Winter 1980–81): 655–71.

———, *From Equal Suffrage to Equal Rights: Alice Paul and the National Woman's Party, 1910–1928* (New York: New York University Press, 1986).

Perry, Elisabeth Israels, *Belle Moskowitz: Feminine Politics and the Exercise of Power in the Age of Alfred E. Smith* (New York: Oxford University Press, 1987).

———, "Women's Political Choices After Suffrage: The Women's City Club of New York, 1915–1990," *New York History* 71 (October 1990): 417–34.

Rosen, Marjorie, *Popcorn Venus: Women, Movies and the American Dream* (New York: Avon Books, 1973).

Salas, Elizabeth, "Ethnicity, Gender and Issues in the 1922 Campaign by Adelina Otero-Warren for the U.S. House of Representatives," *New Mexico Historical Review* 70 (October 1995): 367–82.

Salyer, Lucy E., *Law Harsh as Tigers: Chinese Immigrants and the Shaping of Modern Immigration Law* (Chapel Hill: University of North Carolina Press, 1995).

Shaw, Stephanie J., "Black Club Women and the Creation of the National Association of Colored Women," *Journal of Women's History* 3 (Fall 1991): 1290–91.

Strom, Sharon Hartman, "Leadership and Tactics in the American Woman Suffrage Movement: A New Perspective from Massachusetts," *Journal of American History* 12 (September 1975): 296–315.

Terborg-Penn, Rosalynn, "Discontented Black Feminists: Prelude and Postscript to the Passage of the Nineteenth Amendment," 262–78, in *Decades of Discontent: The Women's Movement, 1920–1940*, edited by Joan M. Jensen and Lois Scharf (Westport, CT: Greenwood Press, 1983).

———, *African American Women in the Struggle for the Vote, 1850–1920* (Bloomington: Indiana University Press, 1998).

Thomas, Mary Martha, *The New Woman in Alabama: Social Reforms and Suffrage, 1890–1920* (Tuscaloosa: University of Alabama Press, 1992).

———, "The Ideology of the Alabama Woman Suffrage Movement, 1890–1920," 109–28, in *Southern Women: Histories and Identities*, edited by Virginia Bernhard, Betty Brandon, Elizabeth Fox-Genovese, and Theda Perdue (Columbia: University of Missouri Press, 1992).

Turner, Elizabeth Hayes, "'White-Gloved Ladies' and 'New Women' in the Texas Woman Suffrage Movement," 129–56, in *Southern Women: Histories and Identities*, edited by Virginia Bernhard, Betty Brandon, Elizabeth Fox-Genovese, and Theda Perdue (Columbia: University of Missouri Press, 1992).

Vigil, Maurilio E., "The Political Development of New Mexico's Hispanas," *Latino Studies Journal* 7 (Spring 1996): 3–28.

Whaley, Charlotte, *Nina Otero-Warren of Santa Fe* (Albuquerque: University of New Mexico Press, 1994).

Wheeler, Marjorie Spruill, *The New Women of the New South: The Leaders of the Woman Suffrage Movement in the Southern States* (New York: Oxford University Press, 1993).

———, ed., *Votes for Women! The Woman Suffrage Movement in Tennessee, the South, and the Nation* (Knoxville: University of Tennessee Press, 1995).

Wilson, Joan Hoff, "Jeanette Rankin and American Foreign Policy: Her Life Work as a Pacifist," *Montana the Magazine of Western History* 30 (Spring 1980): 38–53.

Young, Louise M., *In the Public Image: The League of Women Voters, 1920–1970* (Westport, CT: Greenwood Press, 1989).

Change and Continuity during the 1920s

Allen, Michael, "The Rise and Decline of the Early Rodeo Cowgirl: The Career of Mabel Strickland, 1916–1941," *Pacific Northwest Quarterly* 83 (October 1992): 122–27.

Barnet, Evelyn Brooks, "Nannie Burroughs and the Education of Black Women," 97–108, in *The Afro-American Woman: Struggles and Images*, edited by Sharon Harley and Rosalyn Terborg-Penn (Port Washington, NY: Kennikat Press, 1978).

Beisel, Nicola, *Imperiled Innocents: Anthony Comstock and Family Reproduction in Victorian America* (Princeton, NJ: Princeton University Press, 1997).

Benson, Susan Porter, *Counter Cultures: Saleswomen, Managers, and Customers in American Department Stores, 1890–1940* (Urbana: University of Illinois Press, 1988).

Blackwell, Joyce, *No Peace without Freedom: Race and the Women's International League for Peace and Freedom, 1915–1975* (Carbondale: Southern Illinois University Press, 2004).

Blee, Kathleen M., *Women of the Klan: Racism and Gender in the 1920s* (Berkeley: University of California Press, 1991).

Blewett, Mary H., *The Last Generation: Work and Life in the Textile Mills of Lowell, Massachusetts, 1910–1960* (Amherst: University of Massachusetts Press, 1990).

Brady, Marilyn Dell, "Kansas Federation of Colored Women's Clubs, 1900–1930," *Kansas History* 9 (Spring 1986): 19–31.

Broker, Ignatia, *Night Flying Woman: An Ojibway Narrative* (St. Paul: Minnesota Historical Society Press, 1983).

Brown, Dorothy M., *Setting a Course: American Women in the 1920s* (Boston: Twayne, 1987).

Carby, Hazel V., "It Jus Be's Dat Way Sometime: The Sexual Politics of Women's Blues," *Radical America* 20 (1986): 9–24.

Chalfen, Richard, *Turning Leaves: The Photograph Collections of Two Japanese American Families* (Albuquerque: University of New Mexico Press, 1991).

Chan, Sucheng, *Entry Denied: Exclusion and the Chinese Community in America, 1882–1943* (Philadelphia: Temple University Press, 1991).

Chesler, Ellen, *Woman of Valor: Margaret Sanger and the Birth Control Movement in America* (New York: Simon & Schuster, 1992).

Coburn, Carol K., "Learning to Serve: Education and Change in the Lives of Rural Domestics in the Twentieth Century," *Journal of Social History* 25 (Fall 1991): 109–22.

———, *Life at Four Corners: Religion, Gender, and Education in a German-Lutheran Community, 1868–1945* (Lawrence, University Press of Kansas, 1992).

Conway, Jill, "Women Reformers and American Culture, 1870–1930," *Journal of Social History* 5 (Winter 1971–72): 164–77.

Corn, Joseph J., "Making Flying 'Thinkable': Women Pilots and the Selling of Aviation, 1827–1940," *American Quarterly* 31 (Fall 1979): 556–71.

Davis, Thadious M., *Nella Larsen, Novelist of the Harlem Renaissance: A Woman's Life Unveiled* (Baton Rouge: Louisiana State University Press, 1993).

Downey, Betsy, "Battered Pioneers: Jules Sandoz and the Physical Abuse of Wives on the American Frontier," *Great Plains Quarterly* 12 (Winter 1992): 31–49.

Ewen, Elizabeth, *Immigrant Women in the Land of Dollars: Life and Culture on the Lower East Side, 1890–1925* (New York: Monthly Review Press, 1985).

Fine, Lisa M., "Between Two Worlds: Business Women in a Chicago Boarding House, 1900–1930," *Journal of Social History* 19 (Spring 1986): 511–20.

———, *The Souls of the Skyscraper: Female Clerical Workers in Chicago, 1870–1930* (Philadelphia: Temple University Press, 1990).

Foner, Philip S., *Women and the American Labor Movement: From World War I to the Present* (New York: The Free Press, 1980).

Gertzog, Irwin N., "The Matrimonial Connection: The Nomination of Congressmen's Widows for the House of Representatives," *Journal of Politics* 42 (August 1980): 820–33.

Gillespie, Michele, and Catherine Clinton, *Taking Off the White Gloves: Southern Women and Women Historians* (Columbia: University of Missouri Press, 1998).

Glazer, Penina M., and Miriam Slater, *Unequal Colleagues: The Entrance of Women into the Professions, 1890–1940* (New Brunswick, NJ: Rutgers University Press, 1987).

Glenn, Evelyn Nakano, "The Dialectics of Wage Work: Japanese-American Women and Domestic Service, 1905–1940," *Feminist Studies* 6 (September 1980): 432–71.

———, "Occupational Ghettoization: Japanese Women and Domestic Service, 1905–1970," *Ethnicity* 8 (December 1981): 352–86.

———, *Unequal Freedom: How Race and Gender Shaped American Citizenship and Labor* (Cambridge, MA: Harvard University Press, 2004).

Golden, Claudia, *Understanding the Gender Gap: An Economic History of American Women* (New York: Oxford University Press, 1990).

Gordon, Linda, *Moral Property of Women: A History of Birth Control Politics in America* (Champaign Urbana: University of Illinois Press, 2002).

Hall, Jacquelyn Dowd, "Disorderly Women: Gender and Labor Militancy in the Appalachian South," *Journal of American History* 73 (September 1986): 354–82.

———, "Private Eyes, Public Women: Images of Class and Sex in the Urban South, Atlanta, Georgia, 1913–1915," *Atlanta History* 36 (Winter 1993): 24–39.

Hamilton, Michael S., "Women, Public Ministry, and American Fundamentalism, 1920–1950," *Religion and American Culture* 3 (Summer 1993): 283–303.

Harrison, Daphne Duval, "Black Women in the Blues Tradition," 58–73, in *The Afro-American Woman: Struggles and Images,* edited by Sharon Harley and Rosalyn Terborg-Penn (Port Washington, NY: Kennikat Press, 1978).

———, *Black Pearls: Blues Queens of the 1920s* (New Brunswick, NJ: Rutgers University Press, 1988).

Higginbotham, Evelyn Brooks, *Righteous Discontent: The Women's Movement in the Black Baptist Church, 1880–1920* (Cambridge, MA: Harvard University Press, 1993).

Hinckley, Ted C., "Glimpses of Societal Change Among Nineteenth-Century Tlingit Women," *Journal of the West* 33 (July 1993): 12–24.

Hine, Darlene Clark, *Black Women in White: Racial Conflict and Cooperation in the Nursing Profession, 1890–1950* (Bloomington: Indiana University Press, 1989).

Horowitz, Daniel, *The Morality of Spending: Attitudes Toward the Consumer Society in America, 1875–1940* (Chicago: Ivan R. Dee, Inc., 1993).

Ichioka, Yuji, "Amerika Nadeshiko: Japanese Immigrant Women in the United States, 1900–1924," *Pacific Historical Review* 49 (May 1980): 339–58.

Jacobs, Margaret D., *Engendered Encounters: Feminism and Pueblo Cultures, 1879–1934* (Lincoln: University of Nebraska Press, 1999).

Jaros, Dean, *Heroes Without Legacy: American Airwomen, 1912–1944* (Niwot: University Press of Colorado, 1993).

Jensen, Joan M., "The Evolution of Margaret Sanger's Family Limitation Pamphlet, 1914–1921," *Signs* 6 (Spring 1981): 548–55.

———, "Canning Comes to New Mexico: Women and the Agricultural Extension Service, 1914–1919," *New Mexico Historical Review* 57 (October 1982): 361–86.

Johnson, David L., and Raymond Wilson, "Gertrude Simmons Bonnin, 1876–1938: 'Americanize the First Americans,'" *American Indian Quarterly* 12 (Winter 1988): 130–43.

Jordan, Teresa, *Cowgirls: Women of the American West* (Lincoln: University of Nebraska Press, 1992).

Koester, Susan H., "'By the Words of the Mouth Let Thee Be Judged': The Alaska Native Sisterhood Speaks," *Journal of the West* 27 (April 1988): 35–44.

Krause, Corinne Azen, "Urbanization Without Breakdown: Italian, Jewish, and Slavic Immigrant Women in Pittsburgh, 1900–1945," *Journal of Urban History* 4 (May 1978): 291–305.

Ladd-Taylor, Molly, *Mother-Work: Women, Child Welfare, and the State, 1890–1930* (Champaign, University of Illinois Press, 1994).

LeCompte, Mary Lou, *Cowgirls of the Rodeo: Pioneer Professional Athletes* (Champaign: University of Illinois Press, 1993).

Levine, Susan, "Workers' Wives: Gender, Class, and Consumerism in the 1920s United States," *Gender and History* 3 (Spring 1991): 45–64.

Lieb, Sandra R., *Mother of the Blues: A Study of Ma Rainey* (Amherst: University of Massachusetts Press, 1984).

Martin, Patricia Precíado, ed., *Images and Conversations: Mexican Americans Recall a Southwestern Past* (Tucson: University of Arizona Press, 1983).

May, Elaine Tyler, *Great Expectations: Marriage and Divorce in Post-Victorian America* (Chicago: University of Chicago Press, 1981).

Meyerowitz, Joanne J., *Women Adrift: Independent Wage Earners in Chicago, 1880–1930* (Chicago: University of Chicago Press, 1988).

Muncy, Robyn, *Creating a Female Dominion in American Reform* (New York: Oxford University Press, 1991).

Nielsen, Kim, *Un-American Womanhood: Antiradicalism, Antifeminism, and the First Red Scare* (Columbus: Ohio State University Press, 2001).

Norwood, Stephen H., *Labor's Flaming Youth: Telephone Operators and Worker Militancy, 1878–1923* (Urbana: University of Illinois Press, 1990).

Pleck, Elizabeth H., "Challenges to Traditional Authority in Immigrant Families," 482–503, in *The American Family in Social-historical Perspective,* edited by Michael Gordon (New York: St. Martin's Press, 1983).

Rakow, Lana F., *Gender on the Line: Women, the Telephone, and Community Life* (Urbana: University of Illinois Press, 1992).

Rodríguez, Clara E., *Puerto Ricans: Born in the U.S.A.* (Boston: Unwin Hyman, 1989).

Rossiter, Margaret W., *Women Scientists in America: Struggles and Strategies to 1940* (Baltimore: Johns Hopkins University Press, 1982).

Rushing, Andrea Benton, "Images of Black Women in Afro-American Poetry," 74–86, in *The Afro-American Woman: Struggles and Images,* edited by Sharon Harley and Rosalyn Terborg-Penn (Port Washington, NY: Kennikat Press, 1978).

Rymph, Catherine E., *Republic Women: Feminism and Conservatism from Suffrage through the Rise of the New Right* (Chapel Hill: University of North Carolina Press, 2005).

Sánchez, George J., "'Go After the Women': Americanization and the Mexican Immigrant Woman, 1915–1929," 284–97, in *Unequal Sisters: A Multicultural Reader in U.S. Women's History,* edited by Vicki L. Ruiz and Ellen Carol DuBois (New York: Routledge, 2d ed., 1994).

Scharff, Virginia, *Taking the Wheel: Women and the Coming of the Motor Age* (New York: Free Press, 1991).

———, "Feminism, Femininity, and Power: Nellie Tayloe Ross and the Woman Politician's Dilemma," *Frontiers* (1995): 87–106.

Scott, Anne Firor, *Making the Invisible Woman Visible* (Urbana: University of Illinois Press, 1984).

Seller, Maxine Schwartz, ed., *Immigrant Women* (Philadelphia: Temple University Press, 1981).

Stephens, Sandra L., "The Women of the Amador Family, 1860–1940," 257–78, in *New Mexico Women: Intercultural Perspectives,* edited by Joan M. Jensen and Darlis A. Miller (Albuquerque: University of New Mexico Press, 1986).

Strom, Sharon Hartman, *Beyond the Typewriter: Gender, Class, and the Origins of Modern American Office Work, 1900–1930* (Champaign: University of Illinois Press, 1992).

Takaki, Ronald, *Strangers from a Different Shore: A History of Asian Americans* (New York: Little, Brown, 1989).

Tamura, Eileen H., "Gender, Schooling and Teaching, and the Nisei in Hawai'i: An Episode in American Immigration History, 1900–1940," *Journal of American Ethnic History* 14 (Summer 1995): 3–26.

Taylor, Ula Yvette, *The Veiled Garvey: The Life and Time of Amy Jacques Garvey* (Chapel Hill: University of North Carolina Press, 2002).

Tentler, Leslie Woodcock, *Wage-Earning Women: Industrial Work and Family Life in the United States, 1900–1930* (New York: Oxford University Press, 1979).

Todd, Ellen Wiley, *The "New Woman" Revised: Painting and Gender Politics on Fourteenth Street* (Berkeley: University of California Press, 1993).

Tucker, Cynthia Grant, *Prophetic Sisterhood: Liberal Women Ministers of the Frontier, 1880–1930* (Boston: Beacon Press, 1990).

Van Rapphorst, Donna L., *Union Maid Not Wanted: Organizing Domestic Workers, 1870–1940* (New York: Praeger, 1988).

Vargas, Zaragosa, "Armies in the Fields and Factories: The Mexican Working Classes in the Midwest in the 1920s," *Mexican Studies/Estudios Mexicanos* 7 (Winter 1991): 47–71.

Ware, Susan, *Still Missing: Amelia Earhart and the Search for Modern Feminism* (New York: W. W. Norton & Co., 1993).

Wolf, Beverly Hungry, *The Ways of My Grandmothers* (New York: William Morrow and Co., Inc., 1980).

Yang, Eun Sik, "Korean Women of America: From Subordination to Partnership, 1903–1930," *Amerasia* 2 (Fall/Winter 1984): 1–28.

Yung, Judy, *Unbound Feet: A Social History of Chinese Women in San Francisco* (Berkeley: University of California Press, 1995).

Chapter Eight

"Making Do and Pitching In": The Great Depression and World War II, 1929 to 1945

Shortly after the stock market collapsed during the fall of 1929, the American economy crumbled. The controversial recovery program called the New Deal soon emerged. Following the Great Depression of the 1930s, the nation was barely getting on its feet again when in 1941 it became involved in the largest and most destructive war in history.

The years between the beginning of the Great Depression in 1929 and the end of World War II in 1945 were indeed trying ones. Most people felt unnerved and uncertain. Did economic forces drive their lives? How much could political action achieve? What was the role of human willpower? Was democracy any longer viable?

Because former certainties regarding these questions now seemed meaningless, people set out to reconstruct their lives and beliefs. In the process, women contributed their skills and energies in the home, workplace, and military. Traditional gender expectations and the forces that underlay them wavered and modified, in some case temporarily, in others permanently.

The Great Depression of the 1930s

The Stock Market Crash of 1929

When the stock market plunged on "Black Tuesday," October 29, 1929, the crash brought the fads and fashions of the 1920s, American prosperity, and even individual lives to an end. One former flapper discovered her father hanging from the end of a rope, one of many suicides committed to escape economic ruin.

The situation rapidly worsened. Between 1930 and 1933, 5,504 banks closed their doors and the national banking system teetered on the brink of collapse. As the collateral effects of the stock-market crash spread across the nation, the economies of the South, Midwest, and West reeled. In towns and cities, factories shut their doors and managers told workers to go home—and stay there. Because unemployed laborers could no longer buy groceries and other goods, grocery and department stores shuttered their doors as well.

Farm families were also hit hard. Before that fateful autumn day, the price of corn stood at 81 cents a bushel. By the end of 1929, the price had jumped to 90 cents. By 1931, the price of corn had dropped to between 10 and 12 cents a bushel. Prices for eggs, hogs, and cattle collapsed as well. According to one Iowa farmer, "The depression had really set in." Because corn was now cheaper than coal, some farm families burned corn for fuel. One farmer paid a hospital bill in eggs. Soon thereafter, the nation's midsection suffered a severe and prolonged drought, creating, in time, the great American "Dustbowl."

During the 1930s and thereafter, families across the nation struggled to keep their farms going. Others dreamed of returning to farms they had already lost. The combination of heavy mortgages, falling crop prices, and the need to borrow money to purchase seed, stock, and equipment put farm families on, and sometimes over, the edge. Farm women stretched their meager resources as far as they would go, then told their families that they would have to do without. Selling what they could, including butter, eggs, and bread, farm women also "helped out" by adding some form of paid employment to their already heavy workloads. In this capacity, they sewed for others, worked in shops in town, and took paid jobs off the farm in such agribusiness enterprises as meat-packing plants. Gradually, these women helped provide the income that kept farms solvent.

In this dire situation, people's attention naturally riveted on jobs and money. They sold whatever they could to raise cash, and when that was gone, they turned to the federal government for assistance. President Herbert Hoover tried to promote economic recovery, but his solutions were too shallow and the causes of the depression too deep. In 1932, American voters, desperate for relief from economic distress, carried Democrat Franklin Delano Roosevelt into the White House. Having lost faith in President Hoover's policies, the apex of a decade of Republican-led "normalcy," they were willing to take a chance on Roosevelt's radical ideas.

After the 1932 election, journalist Anne O'Hare McCormick wrote, "Now the question is: Where are we? What's the government going to do?" She concluded that this might be "our last chance to prove that there is initiative enough left in democracy to make it worth saving." President Roosevelt faced an overwhelming number of seemingly unsolvable problems, many of them involving the nation's women.

Employed Women

In 1930, 22 percent of all American workers were female, including white women and those of color. Pushed now by economic necessity, women took whatever jobs they could find. Because women could often land low-paying "women's" jobs, many of them worked while their fathers, husbands, and sons faced unemployment. During the 1930s, approximately three out of every ten female workers held clerical and sales positions, two were factory operatives, two were in domestic service, one was a professional (usually a teacher or a nurse), and one worked in a service job. By 1940, 25 percent of all employed laborers were women.

For all jobs, women received low wages. During the early 1930s, a woman could earn an average of $525 yearly. Men averaged $1,027. The typical domestic worker earned only $312.60 per year. Because employment of any stripe often stood between them and starvation, female workers tolerated long hours, bad working conditions, and abusive treatment from employers and supervisors. Because a woman held paid employment did not mean that she and her family would survive the depression.

The Hispanic community is illustrative. At this time Hispanics settled in *colonias*, or small, ethnically concentrated villages. During the depression, Hispanas became more important than ever to their communities. In the orange-producing regions of southern California, Hispanas took jobs as pickers and packers. One young woman remarked, "All my friends and cousins, we all worked as packers." These Hispanas enjoyed the companionship of other women while at work and exerted increased economic power at home. In the colonias, Hispanas sometimes built their own homes and often supplied their families with food by raising chickens, ducks, goats, and pigs when not at work. They planted everything from vegetables to medicinal herbs in home gardens. In addition, they sewed clothing and washed it by hand, using old-fashioned wash-boards and wash-tubs, canned cactus, and brewed their own beer. In short, Hispanas were indispensable to their families and communities.

Unemployed Women

The depression proved disastrous for African American women. Because a majority of them held the lowest-paying jobs in the United States, they were hit fast and hard. In 1929, nearly 40 percent of black women and girls were in the work force, nearly two-thirds of which toiled in domestic service and agriculture. Just two years later (1931), more than one-quarter of these black wage-earning women had lost their jobs. As usual, employers fired women of color first, with black women suffering a far higher rate of job loss than did white women. As the depression worsened, more than half of all employed black women lost their jobs; meanwhile, three out of ten white women did so.

Throughout the 1930s, black women had higher rates of unemployment than did white women. To make matters worse, black women could not turn to the old standby of domestic service because the number of these jobs had declined, with unemployed white women snapping up the remaining few. Barred from clerical, sales, and factory jobs because of the color of their skin, many black women found themselves with no employment opportunities at all. Finally, relief and welfare programs were designed to aid males—whom society expected to be the "breadwinners"—all but ignoring black women workers.

Women of color coped by using a strategy of downward mobility—they took whatever jobs they could find. Rural black women often left their homes to migrate to southern, northern, and western cities. The number of urban-bound black women outdistanced the numbers of black men who migrated.

Once in urban areas, black women scrabbled for a few cents to buy food, often becoming small-scale entrepreneurs, peddling such goods as home-baked bread or home-raised vegetables on the streets or door to door. Urban black women also responded to economic hard times by gathering into so-called slave markets on street corners each morning. They offered their labor to the highest bidder on an hourly basis, often for as little as ten cents an hour. In New York City, an observer noted that hundreds of "forlorn and half-starved" girls were lucky to find a few hours' work one or two days each week.

Such poverty-stricken and desperate black women called on the federal government for assistance. They often told tales of racial discrimination in hiring. A Chicago woman wrote directly to President Roosevelt: "We are citizens just as much or more than the majority of this country." She continued, "This is supposed to be a free country regardless of color, creed or race but still we are slaves. . . . Won't you help us?"

President Roosevelt faced a dire situation. By 1933, the year of his inauguration, more than 25 percent of American workers were unemployed. Unemployment not only affected people of color and working-class families, but white workers and middle-class families as well. One college-educated, middle-class white woman described the terrors confronting those whose "normal" lives the depression had interrupted. She and her husband lost their jobs in 1933, shortly before their first child was due. They spent their last twelve dollars on a rat-infested, leaky, and cold apartment.

This couple also turned to the federal government for help. They applied for emergency relief funds, usually available to white workers. After numerous investigations and delays, they received woefully small checks. Their baby was born in a public ward, and the mother returned home weak from inadequate care and nutrition. She and her husband devoted all their time to searching for work, begging for relief, and carrying home bits of coal and other necessities. So they could afford to buy milk for their sickly baby, they ate only one meal a day. "We feel ourselves always on the edge of a precipice," she wrote, "with nothing to save us, sooner or later, from the abyss."

The Right-to-Work Issue

Given such desperate conditions, many Americans opposed the employment of married women on the assumption that they had husbands to support them. Public opinion, as well as the leaders of male-dominated unions like the American Federation of Labor (AFL), believed that all available positions should go to men, arguing that men had to support families and women did not. They also resurrected the old "pin-money" rationale, whereby women supposedly worked for incidental funds rather than to support themselves or their families. Quite the contrary, many married women had to work to support children as well as unemployed husbands.

Another argument against married women working was the upheaval this role reversal might cause in families. If men held marginal employment or none at all while women worked and provided the family's primary support, men would be psychologically devastated. Advocates of this position pointed out that wife- and child-abuse had increased during the depression because of the strain it put on families. They did not, however, suggest a workable way to provide jobs for all married men so that all married women might stay home.

Nevertheless, such old-fashioned, tired thinking resulted in laws barring married female workers from certain jobs, the so-called "right-to-work" laws. Under the Economy Act of 1933, two members of the same family could no longer hold positions in federal governmental service. Although they elicited protests from the League of Women Voters and the National Woman's Party, these laws forced a number of workers to resign, three-fourths of whom were women.

State and local governments also refused to employ married women. In 1931, three out of four school boards banned the hiring of married female teachers. In that year, one New York official termed the employment of married women "reprehensible," calling on the "federal, state and local governments" to remove "these undeserving parasites." Even women's colleges urged their graduates to wait until recovery before seeking paid employment.

Denying Americans the right to work was an action born of panic. It ignored the fact that many women had to work. Indeed, the number of wage-earning married women actually increased during the 1930s. In 1930, 11.7 percent of married women held jobs. By 1940, 15.3 percent did so. Most of these married women held paid jobs because their husbands earned inadequate or no wages. Others worked to supplement their family's income. Even the few who worked because they preferred to do so often cited poverty as the reason, for economic need was the only socially acceptable reason for women to work at the time.

Even with public opinion against them, working women had their advocates. Women's agencies opposed rules against women working. The Women's Bureau pointed out that denying a woman the right to work posed a potential threat to all citizens who also might be refused employment. Similarly, the Business and Professional Women's Club declared in its newspaper, *The Independent Woman*, the importance of fighting for "the freedom to seek self-realization," a freedom "that men and women should guard jealously." For its part, the League of Women Voters opposed anti-nepotism (appointing two or more members of a family to positions in the same workplace) rules in the federal civil service, as well as other legislation that barred married women from jobs.

Despite these efforts, widespread public sympathy never developed for married women workers. Frequently, the *Ladies' Home Journal* declared that women should hold paid employment only when necessary. As one editorial observed, women who "deserved" employment had "no selfish desire for a career . . . simply the pressure of financial need." Obviously, such arguments did little good for the feminist movement. Bans on female workers suggested that they were expendable but male workers were not.

Women in the Professions

Right-to-work laws especially threatened women in the professions, for those who trained for such positions were seen as selfishly career-minded. Because teaching was a profession dominated by women, it came under attack early in the depression. Once other job opportunities tightened, men entered or re-entered teaching. At first, male teachers took the places of married women teachers, whether these women had been working out of need or not. Next, male teachers blocked young single women from teaching jobs. At the beginning of the 1930s, men accounted for 19 percent of all teachers; by the end of the decade, male teachers constituted 24.3 percent of all teachers. During these same years, the number of men enrolled in teacher-training programs rose from 31 to 40 percent of total enrollments.

Similar developments occurred in other professions, so that by 1940, the proportion of women in the professions had fallen from 14.2 percent (in 1930) to 12.3 percent. Women lost ground in medicine, law, science, and university teaching. In nursing, social work, and librarianship, the trend toward feminization came to a sudden halt.

Discouraging women from entering the professions denied American society the skills and contributions of accomplished professionals, and it robbed young women of positive role models. One of the few remaining role models was Reva Beck Bosone, a Mormon, lawyer, and Democrat. In a coal-mining town in central Utah named Helper, Bosone gave legal assistance to Italian and Greek miners and on occasion gave legal advice to convicted prostitutes. In 1932, Bosone won election to the Utah state legislature. During two terms, Bosone sponsored minimum-wage and maximum-hour laws for women and children. She later moved to the judicial bench as Utah's first woman judge.

The decline of women in the professions created a multiplier effect. Once female role models decreased, fewer women aspired to learned positions. In 1930, women constituted 43.7 percent of college enrollments. By 1940, this figure had dropped to 40.2 percent. Instead of pursuing professions and careers, women moved into clerical, sales, and similar jobs lower on the economic and status scale.

The Women's New Deal

Americans looked to the government for help, a response born during the Progressive Era, when the best solutions had seemed to come in the form of local, state, and federal legislation. Heeding the call, President Roosevelt oversaw the development of an innovative and broad recovery program—the New Deal—which generated relief agencies such as the National Industrial Recovery Act (NIRA), the Agricultural Adjustment Act, the Works Progress Administration (WPA), and the Civilian Conservation Corps (CCC). In the hope of priming the fiscal pump to get the economy flowing again, these agencies lent money to state and local governments and businesses.

Many of the programs helped women; together they constituted the "women's" New Deal. In 1933, Congress established the Federal Emergency Relief Administration (FERA), which gave federal funds to states for direct distribution to individual recipients, of whom 12 percent were women. In that same year, Congress approved the Civil Works Administration (CWA) to pursue large-scale construction projects. Before its termination in March 1934, the CWA hired approximately 300,000 women in light jobs and clerical positions. In 1935, the Works Progress Administration (WPA) initiated building projects as well. The WPA hired women in research, health and nutrition, clerical, and library positions and funded the Federal Art Project, which hired artists to paint murals in public buildings. The Music,

Theater, and Writers Projects also employed women. Some 400,000 women benefited from WPA programs alone.

Also in 1933, the NIRA established maximum-hour and minimum-wage guidelines for female and male workers. It addressed a long-standing problem by limiting and regulating industrial piecework done at home, mostly by women and children. When in 1935 the Supreme Court declared this legislation unconstitutional, Congress replaced it with the Fair Labor Standards Act of 1938, which reaffirmed maximum-hour and minimum-wage standards.

The program aimed most directly at women was the Social Security Act of 1935, which included the Aid to Dependent Children (ADC) program. Among other provisions, ADC furnished prenatal care for poor women and pediatric treatment for their infants and children.

New Deal programs especially helped white women, not only in the workplace and the home, but in the arts as well. Realizing that the nation's artists would have to turn to other work or go begging, law and policy makers endowed the Federal Art Project to help support the work of female painters and sculptors. Such works as the WPA-sponsored murals—most often done in post offices and other public buildings—were not only often painted by talented women but typically portrayed strong, courageous women surviving economic reversals, drought, and other hardships.

In the field of photography, the Resettlement Administration and the Farm Security Administration employed photographer Dorothea Lange to document the harsh conditions that rural Americans endured. Through skilled manipulation of lighting and composition, Lange revealed the tragedy of the depression in a southern woman's face. Lange also used her camera to capture the quiet suffering of those reduced to standing in bread lines, the unemployed, and migrant workers in the West. Lange's best-known work, "The Migrant Mother" (1936), laid bare the emotion of a young woman in despair.

Not surprisingly, women of color fared less well under New Deal programs. WPA projects hired women of color, but in far smaller numbers than white women. Although they were eligible for ADC, many women of color felt degraded by what they thought of as "charity." In general, black women felt shut out of government assistance programs.

A notable exception was in the arts. The WPA's Federal Theater Project and Federal Art Project gave black performers and artists an unprecedented opportunity to reach thousands of Americans. In addition, black women taught their skills to children through New Deal–funded community art centers in such places as Harlem, Atlanta, Chicago, and Memphis. In 1939, black sculptor Augusta Savage declared, "If I can inspire one of the youngsters to develop the talent that I know they possess, then my monument will be in their work. No one could ask more than that."

Franklin D. Roosevelt

In addition to fostering New Deal legislation that proved beneficial to women, President Roosevelt helped women challenge gender expectations in three areas. One was public service. As a result of his years in New York state government, Roosevelt trusted women with important policy-making positions. During the New Deal, he appointed women to high-level jobs. These positions included secretary of labor, head of women's and professional projects for the WPA, assistant secretary of the treasury, director of the mint, assistant treasurer of the United States, and civil service commissioner. In the diplomatic field, women received appointments as minister to Denmark and ambassador to Norway. Many of Roosevelt's appointments were "firsts" for women: first woman cabinet member, first woman director of the mint, and first woman ambassador.

A second area was social work. President Roosevelt initiated social welfare programs that demanded trained social workers to administer them. From the Consumers League, the Women's Trade Union League, and other reform organizations came trained women eager to undertake governmental assignments. Women had decades of experience in being the "moral housekeepers" of society. Now FDR offered them the chance to apply their expertise on a national scope.

A third area was enlarging the influence of the First Lady. Roosevelt integrated his wife Eleanor into the political scene. Already a crusader for women's issues, African Americans, and the poor, Eleanor Roosevelt became the social conscience of America. In addition, she provided access to the president for scores of women. As one of Eleanor Roosevelt's colleagues put it, "When I wanted help on some definite point, Mrs. Roosevelt gave me the opportunity to sit by the President at dinner and the matter was settled before we finished our soup."

Eleanor Roosevelt

Eleanor Roosevelt arrived at the position of First Lady by a circuitous route. Born to a wealthy and prestigious New York couple in 1884, Eleanor had lost both her parents by the time she was ten years old. Raised by her maternal grandmother, she lived a lonely life. When she was eighteen years old, Roosevelt initiated her lifelong commitment to social reform by joining Florence Kelley's National Consumers League. As she visited workplaces to conduct inspections for the league, Roosevelt observed firsthand the hardships endured by working women. At the same time, she participated in the Junior League and the Rivington Street Settlement House in New York City.

In 1905, Eleanor Roosevelt married a distant cousin, Franklin Roosevelt. Because Franklin's mother Sara dominated the household, Eleanor's feelings of inadequacy as a wife and mother were reminiscent of those she had felt as an ungainly young girl. When Franklin gained election as Democratic assemblyperson from Dutchess County, New York, in 1910, Eleanor sought fulfillment in contributing to her husband's political career. After Franklin's appointment as assistant secretary of the navy in 1913, Eleanor developed expertise in orchestrating social and political gatherings. Once World War I began, Eleanor Roosevelt resumed with a passion her interest in welfare work and social reform.

After World War I, Eleanor Roosevelt participated in the League of Women Voters and the Women's Trade Union League. When polio struck Franklin in 1921, Eleanor acted as his political representative. At the Democratic National Convention of 1924, she worked for platform planks supporting equal pay, child-labor legislation, and other women's reform issues. By 1928, Eleanor Roosevelt had built a wide reputation as a reformer and politician in her own right.

When Franklin ran for the presidency in 1932, Eleanor coordinated the activities of the Women's Division of the Democratic National Committee. Along with her friend and Democratic colleague, Molly (Mary) Dewson, Eleanor mobilized huge numbers of women activists as potential administration members. Once she became First Lady, Eleanor toured the country observing the condition of workers, visiting relief agencies, and speaking on behalf of human rights. Beginning in 1936, she also wrote a syndicated newspaper column called "My Day." She reached millions of other Americans through radio programs in which she took part or hosted.

Despite the fact that the Roosevelts' marriage suffered in 1918 because of Franklin's involvement with Lucy Mercer, Franklin and Eleanor remained married and worked together as an effective political team. Eleanor Roosevelt poured her emotional energies into close relationships with women. Publicly, Roosevelt devoted her vigor and growing influence to reform causes.

Eleanor Roosevelt was a conservative feminist who did much to advance the cause of women. One example was her initiation of press conferences for women only, which gave a tremendous boost to female journalists. One of these, who covered Eleanor Roosevelt for the Associated Press, commented that "no newspaperwoman could have asked for better luck." Certain reporters became Roosevelt's closest friends, particularly Lorena Hickok, who some scholars believe was Eleanor's long-term companion and lover. The two women listened to each other's problems, traveled together, and cowrote a book.

Eleanor Roosevelt also helped shape the New Deal in ways beneficial to women: she supported the appointment of hundreds of women to official positions; acted as clearing agent of women's project proposals to the WPA;

emphasized the need for numerical guidelines regarding women's employment in New Deal programs; helped organize the White House Conference on the Emergency Needs of Women; pushed for the inclusion of women in the WPA and CCC; and worked for the establishment of minimum-wage and maximum-hour laws for female workers.

Roosevelt also emerged as an advocate for African Americans. She lobbied for civil rights and supported the causes of the National Association for the Advancement of Colored People (NAACP). Roosevelt backed a law that made lynching a federal crime. She argued for the inclusion of black men and women in the WPA and the CCC, and she encouraged the work of black writers, artists, and performers.

Early in the 1930s, the accomplished operatic star Marian Anderson, an African American, benefited from revised ideas. Anderson had sung largely in Europe to escape racist policies, including segregated audiences, in her native United States. In 1935, she returned home, and in 1939 she was the first black person to appear at New York City's Metropolitan Opera. Later that year, Anderson was preparing for a scheduled performance at Constitution Hall in Washington, D.C., when the Daughters of the American Revolution (DAR), who objected to hosting an African American, called off the show. Incensed by this blatant display of prejudice and insensitivity, Eleanor Roosevelt promptly and publicly resigned her membership in the DAR (which no doubt embarrassed the organization) and arranged an outdoor concert for Anderson in front of the Lincoln Memorial. Although Anderson hesitated to appear at the alternate venue, she later admitted: "I had become, whether I liked it or not, a symbol, representing my people. I had to appear." In a groundswell of appreciation and respect, seventy-five thousand people attended the concert, at which, all agreed, Anderson was magnificent.

In 1940, Eleanor Roosevelt gave women credit for "the government's attitude of concern for the welfare of human beings." She added, "There has been a tremendous change in the outlook of government, which can be attributed to the fact that women have the ballot." Roosevelt failed to mention her own numerous contributions.

New Deal Women

A huge number of women assisted Eleanor Roosevelt in her efforts. Largely professional women interested in reform, they hoped to improve women's condition in the family and in the labor force. Whether purposefully or not, they laid the foundation for a resurgence of women's rights and feminism.

One of these was the black woman leader, Mary McLeod Bethune. Between 1935 and 1943, Bethune served as director of the Division of Negro Affairs of the National Youth Administration (NYA), organized in 1935 to provide employment for students and nonstudents. As a member of President Roosevelt's so-called black cabinet—advisers who helped implement black programs in New Deal projects—Bethune exercised great influence. Yet she seldom challenged segregation, apparently hoping to offend no one while extending her vision of racial equality to all. When necessary, however, Bethune proved a strong advocate for the rights of blacks. In 1937, she told the director of the NYA in no uncertain terms, "It is about time that white folks recognize that Negroes are human too, and will not much longer stand to be the dregs of the work force."

Another important black woman was Juanita J. Sadler, who, like Bethune, worked as an administrator in the Division of Negro Affairs during the organization's formative period. Unlike Bethune, Sadler openly questioned the NYA's and President Roosevelt's stand on desegregation, arguing for the total integration of blacks into New Deal programs in particular and American society in general.

Other black women formative in the New Deal strove to improve their own condition as well as that of their communities and their race. In 1935, many became activists, forming the National Council of Negro Women, which elected Bethune as its first president. The Council coordinated the efforts of more than twenty national and ninety-five local groups representing almost 850,000 black women. Black women also continued their crusade to abolish lynching in the South.

Among white women in the New Deal, one standout was Frances Perkins, a social reformer and the first female cabinet member in the nation's history. As secretary of labor, Perkins helped draft New Deal legislation, including the Federal Emergency Relief Act, the Social Security Act, and the National Labor Relations Act. She also helped President Roosevelt make appointments, maintain harmonious relations with union leaders, and bring the United States into the International Labor Organization in 1934. As a woman, Perkins's leadership of the Labor Department helped establish an image of women as competent, trustworthy individuals. Perkins herself once said that "doing" means "digging your nails in and working like a truck horse," an adage her own record bore out.

Another important New Deal woman was social worker Molly Dewson, who had long campaigned for minimum wages for women. When in 1933 Dewson became a top echelon New Deal politician—as director of the women's division of the Democratic party—she urged the equal representation of women in party membership and leadership positions. Partially because of Dewson's efforts, women campaign workers numbered 73,000 in 1936 and swelled to 109,000 by 1940. Dewson also helped secure an unemployment insurance act in New York state in 1935 and minimum-wage laws in Illinois and Ohio. She served on the President's Commission on

Economic Security and had a hand in shaping the Social Security Act of 1935. As a member of the Social Security Board in 1937 and 1938, Dewson helped improve federal-state relations in the administration of the Social Security Act.

A lesser-known female figure of the New Deal was Ellen S. Woodward, the director of women's work under the Federal Emergency Relief Administration. Woodward also contributed programs to the CWA. In 1935, she became the director of Women's and Professional Projects of the WPA. At the time, many political commentators viewed Woodward as President Roosevelt's most important noncabinet female appointment. She reeducated Americans, helping them view women as heads of families, and created programs to train women as mattress makers, bookbinders, seamstresses, and household workers. Unlike most New Deal officials, Woodward emphasized the importance of reaching both white and black women through federal programs.

Unionization

Although many Americans counted on state and federal governments to pull them through the Great Depression, labor unions began to assume a new importance. In previous economic depressions, labor unions had all but disappeared, with workers grabbing what jobs they could and putting the issues of better wages and shorter hours on hold. During the 1930s, however, workers felt isolated and powerless. Their only hope seemed to lie in unity; President Roosevelt and members of the U.S. Congress apparently agreed. In 1933, the National Industrial Recovery Act (NIRA) guaranteed workers the right "to organize and bargain collectively through representatives of their own choosing."

Women had their own reasons for joining unions. The New Deal disappointed many women, especially those who worked for wages. Female immigrants fell outside the New Deal because they were not yet citizens. Due to discrimination based on race, black and other women of color got little help from the government. Many of these women perceived unionization as the solution to some of their problems

A number of women reformers favored unionization as well. The Women's Trade Union League and female members of the Communist party urged women who worked in female-dominated industries like textiles, canneries, clothing, paper products, cigar and candy making, restaurants, and laundries to organize or to join existing unions.

These messages did not go unheard by labor leaders. The passage of the NIRA encouraged male leaders of the thirty-three-year-old but nearly defunct International Ladies' Garment Workers' Union (ILGWU) to launch a membership drive. During the mid-1930s, a revived ILGWU organized several strikes that won workers lower hours and higher wages. The membership of the ILGWU soared. For the first time, the ILGWU recruited black, Hispanic, and Asian women. In the Southwest, union leaders organized Hispanic garment workers, who accounted for approximately one-third of the labor force in the nation's garment industry. By late 1934, membership of the ILGWU reached 200,000. Six years later, the union claimed 800,000 members, most of whom were women.

Female Hispanic wage workers proved especially active in union ventures. Hispanas joined unions and participated in labor protests at a greater rate than did Hispanic men. Although they risked dismissal and deportation, a number of Hispanas even became labor organizers and spokespersons. During the 1930s, Manuela Solis Sager organized garment and agricultural workers in Laredo, Texas. Sager helped establish a statewide Mexican labor movement and, in 1935, assisted the formation of the South Texas Agricultural Workers' Union (STAWU). She joined ranks with San Antonio labor organizers, notably Emma Tenayuca.

Tenayuca's name was well known in the southwestern United States. Her grandfather was a Socialist, her husband a Communist, and she herself an effective speaker who blended these ideologies in her defense of workers' rights. Initially, Emma Tenayuca tried to organize all workers of Spanish heritage into a single union. When that effort failed, she founded the Workers' Alliance to distribute civil rights literature and protest the indiscriminate deportation of Hispanics by the federal government. During a 1937 sit-in at San Antonio's city hall that she organized, Tenayuca was arrested. The following year, the twenty-two-year-old Tenayuca led a walkout that affected 170 pecan-shelling plants and some 6,000 to 8,000 workers. When one union rally ended in a violent attack by white opponents and the police, it spurred Tenayuca's resignation.

During the 1930s, the American Federation of Labor (AFL) concentrated on organizing skilled workers and craftspeople. One effective AFL organizer was Luisa Moreno, a Guatemalan who emigrated to the United States in 1928 with her Mexican husband. Moreno had begun her career in the fertile ground of Puerto Rican colonias in New York's Spanish Harlem. Moreno built on existing reform associations to unify Puerto Rican women garment workers in the city. In 1936, the AFL hired Moreno to work a wider field. Besides unions, Moreno established the first Congress of Spanish Speaking People, an umbrella organization for Mexican American and other Spanish-speaking laborers throughout the United States.

Also during the 1930s, a new labor union appeared. In November 1935, a splinter group of the AFL, calling itself the Committee for Industrial Organization, recruited workers without regard to gender, race, or skills. In 1938, this group took the name Congress of Industrial Organizations (CIO). Instead of organizing by craft, as did the AFL, the CIO organized workers by the industry that employed them. Because women made up 40 percent of the automobile, steel, and textile industries, they swelled CIO ranks.

Women also took part in labor demonstrations. Gone were the days when they hesitated to participate in militant action. Union women, as well as wives, sisters, and daughters, marched and bore signs on the picket lines. The female relatives of union members provided support services. They formed women's auxiliaries or groups called Women's Emergency Brigades, supporting a union or its strikers. During the heat of strikes, these women's groups created diversions to draw police or strikebreakers away from the pickets. When these women thought police were about to gas workers inside the plants, they picked up rocks and sticks and hurled them at factory windows. They also provided food and first aid to picketers and distributed union literature throughout their communities. Such female supporters knew that strikers appreciated their efforts. When one young Minnesota woman took part in her first strike during the mid-1930s, she could hear the union men inside the occupied factory's doors shouting, "Let the women in—we need women."

Women's efforts proved important in the most famous of "sit-down" actions, Flint (Michigan) Auto Workers' Strike of late 1936 and early 1937. Disgruntled by their employers' refusal to negotiate with union representatives over "speed-ups" on the assembly line, male workers sat down at their machines and refused to leave the factories. Although women were excluded from the factories, they assisted by providing food, clothing, and medical supplies for the protestors.

When police threatened to evict the men by force, women formed a Women's Emergency Brigade. Daily, 350 women stood as a picket line between the police and the strikers. One January day, police shot into the milling crowd and hit fourteen people. As the crowd surged forward and threw stones, coal, and milk bottles, the police broke and ran. The event took the name of the Battle of Bulls' (slang for police) Run. In February, the final crisis occurred when women's brigades poured into the area. As they congregated, a woman's voice boomed over the loudspeaker: "We don't want any violence; we don't want any trouble. . . . But we are going to protect our husbands."

Ultimately, the Flint Auto Workers' Strike forced General Motors to recognize unions and negotiate with union representatives. For the United Auto Workers this meant a huge increase in membership. For women, the strike marked their coming of age as labor activists. As one female participant said, "Women who only yesterday . . . felt inferior to the task of organizing, speaking, leading, have, as if overnight, become the spearhead in the battle of unionism."

The aforementioned Pecan-Shellers' Strike of 1938 in San Antonio marked another turning point for women. In this Hispana-dominated industry, women earned an average of $2.73 a week by monotonously shelling pecans. According to one worker, Hispanas sat "crowded elbow to elbow on long wooden benches without backs." The United Cannery, Agricultural, Packing, and Allied Workers of America (UCAPAWA), a CIO-chartered union, had organized these women. In 1938, workers in 170 plants went on strike. Employers and police used tear gas and beatings to halt the strike. Police arrested hundred of picketers. Prison officials shoved as many as thirty-three women into cells meant for six, or forced the protestors to share quarters with prostitutes. When some of the plants closed, women realized the power of unity.

By 1938, an estimated 800,000 women had joined unions—a 300 percent increase since 1918—yet women remained under-represented. The old idea that women belonged in the home continued to carry weight among most male union leaders, who expected women workers to be content with membership in gender-segregated locals. Only a few women rose to the position of organizer or union official. In addition, union-approved contracts often sanctioned unequal pay scales. Nearly fourteen of every fifteen female laborers remained outside the union structure. In other words, union leadership overlooked some 5 million women workers.

Other working women had no opportunity to join a union. No unions existed for rural white women in the South and West, American Indian women, or Asian women. In the South and West, women continued to serve as unpaid domestic artisans and field workers on family farms. In the South, women engaged in sharecropping and other forms of tenant-farming. In the West, they worked as day- and migrant-laborers. In both regions, poverty, farm mortgages, and hard work characterized the lives of working women.

Black women constituted another group neglected by unions. In 1930, 90 percent of black women laborers worked as domestic servants or farm hands. Throughout the 1930s, only 10 percent of black women worked in industry. Factories were segregated and black women were excluded from white workers' plan to join unions. In the cotton mills of Durham, North Carolina, black women not only labored in separate areas, but they earned lower wages and were considered inferior to white women performing similar tasks.

Before long, black women developed cohesion among themselves, and some groups managed to form their own unions. In 1934, a black New

York City woman helped organize household workers into the Domestic Workers' Union. Three years later, the National Negro Congress sponsored a Domestic Workers' Association in New York. Once again, African American women had taken matters into their own capable hands.

Life during the 1930s

The Feminine Ideal

In 1930, a male journalist remarked that American women spent $2 billion a year on cosmetics. In their pursuit to appear "feminine," he said, women annually applied 52,500 tons of cleansing cream, 6,562 tons of bath powder, and 2,375 tons of rouge. The 1930 Sears Roebuck catalog confirmed women's interest in looking feminine. Fashion advertisements emphasized long, flowing skirts, highly defined bustlines, tiny waistlines, and a modernized version of the corset. The catalogue explained, "The new mode calls for a definitely higher indented waistline, long tapering hips and the molded bust. To wear the new frocks, you must wear the smart, new corsetry."

Movie stars and the characters they played reinforced these trends. Jeanne Harlow bleached her hair and became the original blond temptress of the "big screen." Others like Marlene Dietrich, Bette Davis, and Greta Garbo became models of steamy sensuality, replete with "bedroom eyes," painted lips, and camellia-like complexions. Mae West carried the style to a new high. West was not only a sensual woman, but she loved in a "masculine" style, committing herself neither to one man nor to the idea of marriage.

The Evolution of "Dating"

Given these role models, it is not surprising that relationships between women and men continued to change. During the 1930s, the traditional custom of a man "calling" on a woman in her family's home for the purpose of "courting" virtually disappeared. Instead, reinforcing the trend that had emerged during the 1920s, men invited women to accompany them unchaperoned to public places like amusement parks and bowling alleys. The man was expected to pay the cost of such "dates." The rise of the personal automobile further accelerated the development of dating, providing increased mobility *and* unheard-of privacy to unwed couples, becoming, some said, a bedroom on wheels.

Hundreds of books and articles appeared to explain the etiquette of dating. According to new standards, a young woman or man should "date" as many different people as possible; this would demonstrate one's popularity and better his or her chances of finding the "perfect" mate. No one, however, discussed the issue of the changing power relationships between women and men. In the day of the formal "call," women had controlled courting by inviting men to their homes and exposing them to their families' assessment. Now, men invited women to share their company away from home, out of sight of family members, and in situations funded by them.

Women, who felt free to do as they pleased—yet somehow indebted to their male dates—increasingly participated in premarital sexual activity. Although most women expected to marry the men with whom they were involved, many ended up pregnant and unwed instead. During the 1930s, the Florence Crittenton Home for Unwed Mothers established additional branches all over the United States. Now staffed by professional social workers rather than benevolent middle- and upper-class ladies, Crittenton homes offered pregnant women vocational training so they could find employment.

Marriage and Family

Given such changes, educators and social scientists decided that Americans needed formal training in courtship, marriage, and family life. Because educators and counselors believed that parents were unable to cope with their children's dating and premarital sex lives, they hoped to impart the guidance of experts to young people. They expected this training to lead to lasting marriages. Accordingly, during the 1930s, colleges and universities, as well as some high schools, introduced "marriage and family" courses. As enrollments climbed and research in family living flourished, teachers catered to white middle- and upper-class students and researchers limited research pools to white, middle-class subjects. Teachers and researchers thus reinforced gender expectations traditional among the white middle class.

For the majority of Americans, harsh economic realities, rather than "expert" advice, dictated family decisions and lifestyles. For most women, sustaining family life during the Great Depression meant learning how to "make do." The slogan "Use it up, wear it out, make it do or go without" became words to live by. Women put their pride aside, sought welfare for their families, and took whatever jobs they could find to help keep themselves and their families afloat.

During the 1930s, more than half of American families lived on annual incomes of between $500 and $1,500. Under such conditions, conspicuous consumption declined. Because women controlled approximately 80 percent of a family's spending and were the primary keepers of household budgets, they purchased less and made more themselves. They dressed more simply and planned family entertainments that cost little or no money. As the home again became the focal point for American families, quilting reappeared. Quilts made during these hard times document the Depression Era through the scenes they portray. They also demonstrate women's thrift by including pieces of flour and seed bags, or rags and scraps of cloth that women had saved in rag-bags.

It fell to women to stretch the $20 to $25 allotted each week for food and shelter. In northern cities, milk sold for ten cents a quart, butter for twenty-three cents per pound, bread for seven cents a loaf, and ground beef for twelve cents a pound. With careful shopping, a woman could feed a family of six for $5 a week. Even formerly wealthy women soon grasped the nuances of economizing. They too bought day-old bread, relined coats with old blankets, and moved to smaller living quarters.

On such limited budgets, divorce became an expensive luxury for most dissatisfied couples. In "Middletown" (Muncie, Indiana), the divorce rate fell 43 percent between 1929 and 1933. A similar drop occurred on the national level. In some areas of the nation, however, the divorce rate remained level or even rose. The latter was true in Cedar Rapids, Iowa, an industrial city in the center of an agricultural area. Moreover, anecdotal evidence suggests that although overall divorce rates declined, desertion rates increased. Many deserters planned to obtain formal decrees once the economy improved and they could pay the costs of a divorce.

At the same time, the marriage and birth rates fell. People who felt they could not afford to get married or have another child postponed these events. By the mid-1930s, for the first time in the nation's history, the birth rate dropped below replacement level.

Women and Reform

In spite of hard times, female reformers hung on to their causes, among them environmental conservation. Although women had few resources to commit to environmental conservation, they did what they could. A number of them worked in museums, often for little or no pay and few fringe benefits. Museum work allowed women to pursue activities they loved and establish conservation programs. In 1926, avid collector Ellen Quillin had become the first director of the Witte Memorial Museum in San Antonio. With her husband, Quillin explored southwest Texas, especially the Big Bend area. She also pursued an active writing career. In 1928, she published *Texas Wild Flowers* (1928). During the 1930s, Quillin wrote a series of children's books. She also built the first reptile garden in the country, in order to teach people that snakes were important creatures worth preserving.

Many women gardeners participated in environmental activities. As civilizers and conservators of home and society, women applied their gardening skills to community, state, and national parks, public gardens, recreation areas, and forests. When the Garden Club of America organized in 1913, its mission included environmental concerns. Under the first presidency of Margaret McKenny of Olympia, Washington, the Garden Club encouraged the observance of Arbor Day and tree-planting projects. After McKenny returned to Olympia, she served on the state tourism commission and lectured on Washington's natural resources. McKenny chaired the Conservation Committee of Washington Garden Clubs and was president of the Audubon Society. In 1939, two of McKenny's well-known books appeared: *Birds in the Garden and How to Attract Them* and *A Book of Wild Flowers.* During the 1930s, Garden Club groups spoke, wrote, and lobbied for the establishment of national parks and monuments, such as Joshua Tree National Monument, which was instituted in 1936 in the Mojave Desert of southern California.

Other reformers discovered that their causes had fallen out of the public's sympathy. Few people of the 1930s worried about conditions affecting female prisoners. For one thing, funds for prison reform were seldom available. For another, women had been going to prison with great regularity. During the suffrage era, women had been arrested largely for picketing and rioting. During the prohibition years, a large number of women had gone to jail for bootlegging and prostitution. Few people had sympathy for women committing these crimes.

And the idea of female criminals seldom shocked people. When the murderous Bonnie Parker grabbed headlines along with her partner, Clyde Barrow, people were more disturbed by her actions than by her gender. In 1932, Parker and Barrow set off on a spree of crime and violence. After taking a New Mexico sheriff hostage and leaving him in Texas, the couple raided a National Guard Armory in Fort Worth, taking machine guns, automatic rifles, and shotguns. They moved across the South and Midwest, using their new weaponry with thoughtless malice. Because Parker and Barrow robbed grocery stores and small businesses, their biggest take was only $1,500, but in the process Bonnie and Clyde shot and killed fifteen people, including several police officers. Their rampage came to an abrupt end in May of 1934, when a posse gunned them down in a roadside ambush near Gibland, Texas.

Female prison reformers could muster little concern for a criminal like Bonnie Parker. At the same time, female prisoners in unhealthy situations went largely ignored. During the 1930s, prison philosophy had reverted from reform and rehabilitation to simple custodianship.

As the depression dragged on, female reformers shifted their attention from social ills to the economic situation and from national programs to helping individuals. They and the organizations they headed set new goals or reordered existing priorities. One of the most pressing claims on women's energies was to provide the necessities of life to those in need. As early as November of 1930, the Young Women's Christian Association (YWCA) transformed itself into a welfare agency, providing poor women food, shelter, clothing, and medical care. It also offered job-skills classes and an employment service. The YWCA assisted single women, who were denied government relief, and helped thousands of homeless women who lived in city streets or went on the road as hoboes, known then as "sisters of the road."

Despite this trend, women refused to abandon the antilynching campaign. Lynching was one "social evil" that remained a high priority. Although hard hit by the depression, black women dedicated whatever resources they could to ending lynching. White southern women joined the effort as well. In 1930, Texas reformer Jessie Daniel Ames founded the Association of Southern Women for the Prevention of Lynching (ASWPL). Ames, widowed in 1902 at the age of thirty-one and with three small children to support, had learned early about poverty and discrimination. As an ardent suffragist, Ames had objected to the general exclusion of black women from the national suffrage movement. All along, Ames had called on both sides to break down the racist stereotypes separating black and white women in their reform efforts.

In founding ASWPL, Ames hoped to unite black and white women. Appalled that American society rationalized the lynching of black people as necessary to protect white womanhood, Ames wanted to mobilize southern white women to end lynching. Under Ames's leadership, ASWPL issued a public statement: "Women dare no longer allow themselves to be the cloak behind which those bent upon personal revenge and savagery commit acts of violence and lawlessness."

The Concept of Comparative Cultures

White women's awareness of racial prejudice had expanded since the 1910s and 1920s; because social scientists had popularized the concept of comparative cultures, educated white women had begun to realize that their way was not the only way. White women's ability to empathize with African American, Native, and even foreign cultures was fostered by the work of two female anthropologists. Ruth Fulton Benedict gained distinction as the country's leading female professional anthropologist. In 1930, Benedict went to Columbia University as an assistant professor. Four years later, she published her renowned *Patterns of Culture*, which analyzed Zuni, Dobu, and Kwakiutl cultures. In the southwestern United States, Benedict studied Serrano, Zuni, Pima, Apache, and Blackfeet Indians. In 1940, in *Race, Science, and Politics* she discredited Nazism and other racist philosophies by demonstrating that differences between groups of people were cultural rather than biological.

Another anthropologist, Margaret Mead, the first American woman to earn a Ph.D. in anthropology, became world-famous. In 1928, Mead published her acclaimed *Coming of Age in Samoa*. In 1935, her equally celebrated *Sex and Temperament* appeared. Like Benedict's pioneering work, Mead's studies indicated that culture shaped individual personality. According to her findings, individual behavior resulted more from cultural patterning than genetic determinants. When not in Samoa and New Guinea conducting research in the field, Mead served as Curator of Ethnology at the American Museum of Natural History in New York City. Mead not only legitimized the study of anthropology, she popularized the concept of comparative cultures.

During the late 1930s, scores of female scientists were at work across the country. Partly in response to the work of Benedict and Mead, these women initiated projects studying Native peoples. The Nevada botanist Edith Van Allen Murphey undertook government fieldwork on Indian reservations. Wearing knee-high boots, breeches, a long-sleeved shirt, and a floppy brimmed hat, she set out to explore Nevada armed only with a long-handled, double-bladed hoe. Murphey studied Indian food and medicine.

At the same time, women archaeologists excavated Hopi and other Native American sites. These investigators unearthed artifacts that were put on display in such institutions as the Museum of New Mexico and Museum of American Archaeology in Santa Fe. In reports, articles, books, and speeches, these women did their best to retrieve and preserve Native cultures so that other Americans might better understand and come to appreciate them.

Farther west, in Hawaii, Martha Warren Beckwith, who received a doctorate from Columbia University in 1918, studied Hawaii's native peoples. Her landmark work, *Hawaiian Mythology*, appeared in 1940. Working from her base in the Bernice Pauahi Bishop Museum in Honolulu, Beckwith promoted respect for the native traditions of Hawaii.

Granted, these individual scientists were all educated white women. Nonetheless, each of them made inestimable contributions to the preservation of Native life and aroused a keen interest and sympathy for Native Americans among the American public.

Preserving Native American Culture

Scholarly studies helped motivate other women to use their skills to preserve Indian culture. During the 1930s, Ann Nolan Clark picked up where New Mexican writer Mary Austin (see Chapter Six) left off. While working as a teacher and administrator for the Bureau of Indian Affairs, Clark wrote many articles on the dilemma of the Navajo Indians: caught between cultures, their own and that of white people. Clark had taught in a large Indian boarding school, where she "saw something awful happening to Indian children." In her view, forcing Native children to assimilate into "American" culture destroyed ancient and irretrievable cultural patterns. To help remedy the situation, Clark wrote children's books especially for Indian girls and boys. She was also an active clubwoman in Santa Fe, New Mexico, and a popular speaker who supported the preservation of Native cultures wherever she went.

Many women gained their interest in the West's Native peoples as tourists. They returned home from the West determined to learn about and preserve whatever they could of Native life. In some ways, tourism also revised cultural practices. White travelers were astonished when curious, blanket-covered Native Americans peered into the windows of their Ford or Buick touring cars. Indians, who quickly saw the potential profit in amusing tourists, donned garish beaded outfits and performed "war" and "rain" dances for paying audiences.

Women Speak Out

For women of "other" cultures, the time was right to speak out. During the 1930s, black author Zora Neale Hurston turned from the short story to the novel. In 1934, she published her first novel, *Jonah's Gourd Vine*. Hurston's 1937 masterpiece, *Their Eyes Were Watching God*, subtly considered the critical influence of race and gender. Hurston's genius lay in exploring and authenticating African American culture.

During the 1930s, other women writers revealed different cultures to the mainstream American reading public. In many cases, federal employment projects had encouraged and funded their work. A number of Hispanas, for example, wrote books dealing with their history, folklore, and customs through the Federal Writers Project. In 1936, Nina Otero Warren's *Old Spain in Our Southwest* tied Mexican culture to its Spanish roots.

Women also demonstrated the richness of nonwhite cultures through music. The 1930s witnessed growing interest in ethnomusicology: the collection, writing down, and arrangement of folk music. Women musicians and composers participated in this movement, traveling through the Appalachian Mountains, the South, and the Southwest searching out the music of "hillbillies," cowboys, African Americans, Creoles, Hispanics, American Indians, and other groups. On radio, such groups as *"El Despertador y Los Chicos"* performed on KFOX in Los Angeles. Columbia Records joined the trend by hiring Hispanas to record folk songs and other music

Women spoke out not only regarding race relations, but also about homosexuality, in particular lesbianism. In 1932, Gertrude Stein published *The Autobiography of Alice B. Toklas*, a fictional work based on Stein's real-life companion and lover. Stein's work had never before attracted large audiences, perhaps because of her unconventional style—for instance, she favored repetition, as in her famous sentence "A rose is a rose is a rose." In bringing her sexuality before the public in the autobiography of Toklas, Stein enjoyed huge sales.

Stein was not alone. Through lectures, radio broadcasts, columns, and books, the sharp-tongued journalist Dorothy Thompson commented on the American scene. A supporter of women's issues and an early and outspoken critic of Nazism, Thompson focused on the plight of European Jews. She conducted an interview with Hitler in 1931 and five years later, initiated her "On the Record" column for the *New York Herald Tribune*. In 1936, she began to write for the *Ladies' Home Journal*. Although she had been married twice and had one child, Thompson declared herself a lesbian and spoke on her own and other lesbians' behalf.

Meanwhile, in 1934 the playwright Lillian Hellman brought lesbianism before the theater-going public in her first play, the Broadway hit *The Children's Hour*. Through the chilling story of two teachers accused of lesbianism, Hellman produced a sensitive and probing treatment of the issues surrounding homosexuality in American society. Hellman, a political activist and antifascist during the 1930s, also wrote several film scripts, but Hollywood eventually blacklisted her for political activism. Although many thought of Hellman as America's greatest female playwright, others were unprepared for her searching honesty.

In the fine arts, another woman supported lesbians. Romaine Brooks first achieved notice for her paintings of lesbians during the 1920s. During the 1930s, Brooks experimented with drawings composed of a single, unbroken line. Because of a forty-year lesbian relationship, Brooks was more comfortable living in France and Italy, where people were more tolerant of homosexuals. Nevertheless, because her work caught the eye of American critics and buyers alike, Brooks spent the mid-1930s in Chicago and New York, showing and selling her works.

Biases Continue

Despite the willingness of many women to speak out, gender discrimination was alive and well in America, as was racial discrimination. In 1939 a San Diego, California, court spent six weeks debating whether a widow had any "Negro blood." If it determined the widow was "white," her marriage, which had taken place in Arizona, was legal and she could inherit her dead husband's estate. If she was part "Negro," the marriage was invalid and she would get nothing. Ultimately, the court ruled that the woman had one-eighth "Negro blood." The case indicates how strongly—and for how long—white Americans clung to racial categories.

Farther north, in Hollywood, racial categories not only existed but determined casting decisions. During the 1930s, Asian actors found themselves limited to stereotyped film roles. Anna May Wong, who entered the film industry against the wishes of her traditional parents, discovered that Hollywood producers reserved major roles in Class A films for white actors.

White women played Asian as well as Mexican characters. The only parts Wong landed were Asian female villains in such films as *Limehouse Blues* (1934). In fact, *Time* magazine once called Wong the "foremost Oriental villainess." Despite this limitation, Wong tried to show a different side of Asian women. In *Daughter of Shanghai* (1937), she played a role sympathetic to Asian women.

At the same time, directors and producers cast black women in the stereotypical roles of maid, vamp, tragic mulatto, or—the best known of all—the "Mammy," an artless yet affectionate mother figure. Louise Beavers projected the lovable, wholesome "Aunt Jemima" image in a number of films, including *Imitation of Life* (1934). She later became TV's Beulah the maid. Another black performer, Hattie McDaniel, won an Academy Award for her version of the simple-minded and loyal, yet tough, black servant in *Gone with the Wind* (1939). Although these women portrayed the Mammy image so despised by black women, those who wished to appear in Hollywood films had little choice.

Black female singers faced similar problems. Despite their brilliance in innovation and styling, most never broke into the musical "mainstream." Most visible among them was Ethel Waters, the blues singer who, during the 1930s, rolled blues over into jazz. As the first important jazz singer, Waters experimented, as when she added "scat," or the singing of melodic syllables, to numbers such as "Dinah," and "Heat Wave." In 1939, in *Mamba's Daughter*, Waters became the first black woman to appear on Broadway in a dramatic role.

Another jazz singer who rocketed to celebrity during the 1930s was Billie Holiday, hailed as the "greatest jazz singer of the era." Although Holiday suffered physical abuse as a child and was arrested for prostitution as a teenager, her talent and determination triumphed. As the first singer to use a microphone to convey vocal subtleties, Holiday recorded such hits as "Me, Myself and I" and "Sailboat in the Moonlight." Holiday appeared with Teddy Wilson and his women's jazz orchestra. In spite of her fame, Holiday, a light-skinned African American, suffered discrimination: when she appeared with Count Basie's all-black band, she had to tint her skin to look darker; when appearing with Artie Shaw's all-white band, she had to eat and lodge separate from white band members.

Even white women musicians confronted prejudice, but it was gender based. The case of conductor Antonia Brico is instructive. After being rejected time and time again by major, male-dominated orchestras, Brico formed an all-women's orchestra in New York City. Brico's orchestra attracted a significant proportion of the city's symphony goers to its excellent performances.

Popular Culture

In popular culture, white women reigned supreme. Everything from movies to cartoons made it appear that white heterosexual women had achieved many gains. Hollywood films featured successful women as corporate executives, reporters, attorneys, detectives, and even spies. Sounding a new note, these films presented female characters of wit, intelligence, and sophistication. Dressed in suits with padded shoulders, these women depicted strong-minded, aggressive, and forceful leaders who ran empires and amassed fortunes. In virtually every case, however, the end of the story witnessed these successful women learning that marriage and family were all that really mattered. In film after film, such stars as Joan Bennett, Rosalind Russell, Ginger Rogers, Claudette Colbert, Joan Crawford, and Katharine Hepburn gave up thriving careers for the man of their dreams. Such films usually stopped short of revealing just how these superwomen reconciled their ambitions with the demands of traditional marriage and family.

In such popular press magazines as the *Saturday Evening Post*, women were contradictory creatures. On the one hand, idealized white women were clever, achieving, and assertive, exhibiting feminist overtones. On the other hand, women were vain and silly or happily married despite the fact that they had sacrificed a career in order to help a husband advance in his vocation.

Conflicting views of women also appeared in newspapers and on the radio. In newly popular comic strips, women took various guises. In 1930, Chic Young's Blondie began to manipulate the inept Dagwood. In 1940, female cartoonist Dale Messick (who was actually a woman, Dalia Messick) created "girl reporter" Brenda Starr. The new radio soap operas, including "Our Gal Sunday," "Backstage Wife," and "Romance of Helen Trent," also vacillated between portraying women as beings who could make their way in the world and those who found their fulfillment solely through the adoration of men.

In sports, however, women were fearless and victorious. The real-life white female athlete predominated, the most famous being Mildred "Babe" Didrikson Zaharias. In the 1932 Los Angeles Olympics, Zaharias not only won gold medals in the javelin and hurdles, but she captured the silver medal in the high-jump. Zaharias also excelled in women's basketball and softball. She not only demonstrated women's athletic potential, but provided a model for other talented female athletes. Zaharias also went on to be a professional golfer, popularizing women's golf.

Changing ideas regarding women athletes affected average women as well. The most popular sports of the era were basketball, swimming, bowling, tennis, golf, and ice skating. Women's softball and basketball teams, sponsored by industrial organizations and businesses, flourished. Even though white women's choice of sports had not changed much, the same could not be said for their choice of sports attire. Lighter and shorter tennis dresses and satin basketball shorts accentuated women's athletic skills as well as their athletic bodies.

Losses and Gains

Between 1929 and 1941, American women lost ground in some areas and gained it in others. On the negative side, the harsh economics of the Great Depression caused a reemphasis on women's domestic roles as wives and mothers. In turn, these ideas led to the erosion of earlier gains in employment and the professions. On the positive side, the New Deal offered helpful programs that brought women into prominent government positions. The public's desire to escape the stress of difficult times through media such as films, music, and comic strips also created a receptive atmosphere for women in literature, the arts, and popular culture. Feminism may not have been highly visible during the 1930s, but it had not disappeared—and was more influential than historians once thought.

World War II, 1941–1945

Pearl Harbor

The United States was pulling out of the depression when a new challenge exploded on the scene. On 7 December 1941 the Japanese bombed the U.S. Pacific Fleet as it lay in Pearl Harbor, Hawaii, catapulting the United States into World War II. Although the war would bring prosperity to the United States during the 1940s, the nation's sudden entry into the conflict brought problems, the most pressing of which was how to mobilize effectively manpower for the front and womanpower for the homefront. Under the capable leadership of President Roosevelt, now in an unprecedented third consecutive term as the chief executive, the government turned its attention to winning the war.

The course of United States history had made it obvious that Americans regarded women as a flexible labor supply to be pulled out of, and pushed back into, the home as needed. But in 1941 an especially difficult situation existed. Throughout the course of the Great Depression, women had been lectured on their responsibilities as wives and mothers. They had been advised to avoid paid employment unless it was an absolute necessity. Now, the U.S. government wanted and needed these same women, as well as their daughters, to take wage-paying employment.

With their backs to the wall, government agencies such as the War Manpower Commission (WMC) and the Office of War Information (OWI) undertook the difficult assignment of reshaping the image of women from homemakers to potential workers. Fortunately, they could draw on the experience gained in mobilizing women during World War I. In April 1942, Congress created the WMC to oversee labor placement, training, and utilization. Desperate for more workers, the WMC launched a massive public-message campaign to attract women into the work force. Especially in areas experiencing labor shortages, the WMC used high-visibility propaganda including films, posters, billboards, and radio broadcasts to recruit women workers.

Rosie the Riveter

Initially, the War Advertising Council, an offshoot of the WMC, and the OWI produced ads emphasizing the high wages women could earn. Next came the character of "Rosie the Riveter." Much like the famous recruiting poster featuring the Uncle Sam character ("Uncle Sam Wants You!"), Rosie the Riveter posters (some with Rosie declaring, "We Can Do It!") soon covered walls and sides of buildings and barns. Rosie also appeared in newspaper, magazine, and other advertisements. Dressed in overalls, her hair covered by a bandanna, Rosie called out to housewives across the nation to join the homefront army of the employed.

Rosie fired the public's imagination. Films like *Swing Shift Maisie* hit the big screen. Magazines ran articles proclaiming, "I Take Part in the War Effort." Advertisements declared, "There's a new woman today doing a man's job so that he may fight and finish this war sooner." Songs titled "Rosie the Riveter" and "We're the Janes Who Make the Planes" became instant hits.

Because the OWI believed that effective propaganda included "highly emotional, patriotic appeals," its campaign developed a "feminine" dimension. Advertisements compared acetylene torches to vacuum cleaners, arguing that women could handle any kind of machinery. The agency encouraged the design of special fashions to guarantee "vain" women that they would look glamorous while on the assembly line. It distributed war recruitment literature and posters that stressed a woman's patriotic duty to her country: "The More Women Work—The Sooner We'll Win." It also played on a woman's sense of loss and her duty to her man: "Longing Won't Bring Him Back Sooner—Get A War job!"

The wartime propaganda directed at women had two major effects: it created an image of women as dynamic citizens, and it persuaded millions of women to go to work. Between 1940 and 1945, the number of women working outside the home increased by slightly more than 50 percent. In 1940, there were 11,970,000 women workers; by 1945, this figure had reached 18,610,000. In other words, the percentage of American women working for wages, three-fourths of whom were married, rose from 17.6 to 37 in this period.

Women with small children also took wartime jobs. To assist working mothers, the Lanham Act of 1942 established Child Care Centers in forty-one states. The government intended these centers only as an emergency wartime measure rather than a sign of women's acceptance into the labor force. After the war, the centers were to be closed or converted to other uses.

During the war women replaced male workers in ordnance plants, shipyards, aircraft factories, and steel mills. They also seized newly opened opportunities as musicians, scientists, doctors, attorneys, university professors, governmental officials, athletes, and teachers. The federal government hired a huge number of women.

Women received high wages for their labor, as well as regulated hours and decent working conditions. Additionally, the Lanham Act provided such support services as canteens (social centers). Moreover, the Women's Bureau, the War Production Board, and the War Manpower Commission endorsed the principle of equal pay for equal work. In 1942, the one agency that had influence over equal pay—the National War Labor Board (NWLB)—ordered equal wages for women who performed "work of the same quality and quantity" as male laborers. Unfortunately, the equal-pay policy was difficult to enforce so in practice, women drew lower wages than men. Nonetheless, the NWLB had established the principle.

Women also gained ground in unions. Although many male workers still resisted working with women, some union leaders accepted the idea of women wage workers. From its inception in 1935, the CIO had admitted all workers. The AFL had long included the ILGWU as an affiliate. Now the AFL opened membership to women in craft-oriented affiliates. By the end of the war, between 3 and 3.5 million women (including women of color) belonged to unions, an increase of more than 12 percent since 1940. Yet the struggle for women's access to unions had not ended. They faced prejudice of male members and restricted memberships, while very few women rose to positions of leadership within the large labor organizations.

Women made wartime gains outside the factory, too. This period saw the end of age requirements for teachers. Nor could school boards any longer refuse to hire married women teachers. In addition, approximately half of black domestic servants switched to jobs with higher pay and more status. And factory employment opened to women of color as well as disabled women.

Black Women

World War II gave black women a long-awaited break. As jobs formerly closed to them opened, they inched up the economic ladder. Approximately 600,000 black women entered the labor force between 1941 and 1945.

Many of those already employed bettered their positions. Aided by the Fair Employment Practices Committee (created in 1941), the National Council of Negro Women, and the NAACP, the number of black factory operatives more than doubled. Between 1940 and 1944, the percentage of black women workers rose from 6.8 to 18. By 1945, the number of black clerical, sales, and professional workers also increased. Perhaps most telling was the percentage of black women in domestic service, which fell from 59.9 to 44.6.

These developments encouraged African American women to migrate from the rural South to the urban North and West. Once relocated these women often found jobs, but they also lived in crowded and segregated neighborhoods, which tended not to have public transportation or child-care. In California, more than 50,000 African American women migrated to Los Angeles, where black families already had a terrible time finding housing. In Texas, one woman explained that she "finally decided to break up housekeeping and go to the city. I decided I wanted to make more money." Racial prejudice followed black women west. Although most found jobs, they were often in domestic service rather than defense industries.

Even when they broke into industry, urban black women earned lower wages than did white women. Black women remained segregated, often engaged in heavy, dirty, and hazardous work with inadequate wages. In defense factories in Detroit and St. Louis, black women worked in segregated plants and workshops. Even in the federal civil service, black women not only labored in separate offices but were denied opportunities for advancement.

Black women turned to the labor unions. In 1941, Sabina Martínez, an African American who organized workers for the Amalgamated Clothing Workers of America, encouraged black women workers to have confidence in "the principles of organized labor." She urged black women to join the union appropriate to their field of employment. Other black union women worked to organize female workers in the southern tobacco industry, domestic laborers, and black factory operatives.

Women in the Military

Another large group of women joined the armed services. Women served in the military as nurses, accepting dangerous assignments caring for injured soldiers on landing ships. In 1941, the Navy counted 787 nurses, 95 of which saw duty overseas, primarily in base hospitals or on hospital ships. More than 60 of these Navy nurses served in the Caribbean or the Pacific theater. Some female navy nurses lived through the Japanese attack on Pearl Harbor, during and after which they ministered to hundreds of wounded men—and assigned the dead to a temporary morgue in the basement of the Pearl Harbor Naval Hospital. Other nurses spent the war years stationed on naval bases, ships, and in prisoner-of-war camps. By mid-1945, the navy counted 5,431 nurses in its service. Too often overlooked, these courageous military nurses made it possible for numerous American troops to survive the horrors of the greatest and most devastating war in world history.

After Pearl Harbor, women participated in military corps for the first time. The U.S. Army organized the Women's Army Auxiliary Corps (WAAC) in May 1942. Although WAAC had only partial military status and offered no benefits, women thronged to it. Top military officials judged army women as superior in performance of duty, but rank-and-file men resented female intrusion into a male world. Some of these men spread rumors regarding the women's sexual behavior that demoralized WAAC leaders and members.

Initially, the WAAC included only white women; but in response to pressure from the black press, civil rights groups, and black women's organizations, the War Department agreed that WAAC should accept black women. Nonetheless, a quota was established: no more than 10 percent of total WAAC female officer candidates could be African American. A 1942 press release reported, "Forty negro women, successful in a nationwide competition for enrollment in the Officer Candidate School of the Women's Army Auxiliary Corps, are scheduled to report today." These women, virtually all college graduates, were among 440 women who comprised the first class of WAAC officer candidates.

Members of the WAAC confronted many difficulties, the worst of which, not surprisingly, were sexism and racism. These women also endured widespread predictions of the corps's failure, stories of WAACs in sexual liaisons with military men, and rumors of lesbianism within the corps. In truth, these women proved themselves effective and efficient military personnel who handled a variety of duties. It was not long before army commanders were asking for more WAACs, primarily to fill such traditional female jobs as typing and filing.

In July 1943, the WAAC became the Women's Army Corps (WAC), the formation of which was a definite step up for women. The WAC offered female recruits the same rank, title, and pay as male reservists. It provided better salaries and better chances for advancement than did peacetime employment. The WAC built an even finer reputation than had the WAAC. According to a WAC publication, its women were proud to "do every job—little or big—with a thrilling competence that awakens respect in the eyes of even the ablest G.I. Wherever they serve, Wacs are doing a gallant, soldier's job." The WAC further distinguished itself by commissioning the first African American woman officer, who led the first all-black female unit to serve overseas. At the same time, however, the WAC required black officers to live separately and lead racially segregated WAC companies.

By mid-1942, the U.S. Navy joined the trend toward recruiting women. In July, it created the Women Accepted for Volunteer Emergency Service (WAVES), which offered pay and benefits comparable to that tendered male reservists. Before long, women accounted for approximately 2 percent of the navy's active duty roster. Reportedly, none of these women served overseas. Instead, they performed clerical and administrative jobs in the United States. One-third of the women trained pilots, packed parachutes, and operated weather stations. The WAVES excluded black women until 1944, when President Roosevelt ordered the navy to admit them. This directive came so late in the war that less than one hundred black WAVES saw duty.

The U.S. Marine Corps was the last branch of the military to establish a women's corps. Known as women marines, or as marine reserves, these women took pride in performing State-side duty so that more men would be available for combat duty. Women marines provided one-third to one-half of post troops, mechanics, and aviation personnel. At Cherry Point, North Carolina, all of the flight instructors were female, women marines packed parachutes, and women largely ran the control tower.

The U.S. Army Air Force did not recruit women, but it did hire them in special positions. Photojournalist Margaret Bourke-White worked as an official photographer for the air force. In 1942, she was the first woman to don a war correspondent's uniform. Bourke-White had worked hard during the 1930s to achieve this honor. In 1936, she joined the staff of *Life*, where she helped develop the photographic essay as a genre. Bourke-White's photographs not only captured an event, but commented on it. She chose to explore with her photographic techniques the topics of industry and war. She journeyed across the United States photographing such scenes as the Fort Peck Dam in Montana for *Life, Fortune,* and other major magazines. During the war years, Bourke-White documented with her camera such atrocities as the concentration camps at Buchenwald. Her professionalism and courage led her into places previously "off-limits" to women. Through her lens, she saw Patton enter Germany and American troops arrive in North Africa.

In 1942, the Army Air Force (AAF) created the Women's Auxiliary Ferry Squadron (WAFS), followed by the Women's Flying Training Detachment (WFTD). In 1943, the two organizations merged into the Women Airforces Service Pilots (WASP). These female pilots were Civil Service employees on assignment with the Army Air Force. They received military training as pilots but held no military rank. By ferrying aircraft from one site to another, female pilots released male aviators for combat assignments.

These women pilots undertook such other tasks as towing gunnery targets, jamming radar, and testing new aircraft. In 1943, one of them flew the first U.S. jet fighter plane. By the end of the war, 1,074 women had completed the Army Air Force's training program. They had ferried 12,650 aircraft and logged more than 300,000 flight miles.

All told, during World War II, 350,000 women served in the U.S. armed forces. For the first time, women engaged in almost every military activity. Most achieved regular status in women's military units. Combined with the authoritative and tailored uniforms they wore, women's military records created a new public image of women.

The women's armed forces also achieved a measure of racial integration. During the conflict, black women created many of their own opportunities and raised awareness of the restrictions on them by filing complaints with the Fair Employment Practices Committee or enlisting the aid of civil rights groups. Early in 1945, the efforts of black activists and civil rights proponents led to the end of segregated assignments.

In addition, a number of other women of color distinguished themselves in the service. Chinese and Japanese women served, as did an entire WAC unit of Puerto Rican women. Approximately eight hundred Native American women enlisted in the WACs. Officials integrated American Indian women into black and white units. In addition, Indian women reported less prejudicial treatment than did black women. A number of Lakota women said that their experience at Indian boarding schools had accustomed them to group living, curfews, and orders. These women felt they adjusted better to military life than did women who had lived with their families until time of enlistment. Indian women's war service changed their public image from "passive servants" to capable and achieving Native women.

Sex in the Military

Women serving in the military raised a number of fears in peoples' minds. Would men in the military exploit these women sexually? Would women lose every shred of femininity? Were these women lesbians?

The director of the Women's Army Corps, Colonel Oveta Culp Hobby, replied to these questions with a resounding no. She maintained that women could serve in the military without sex playing an unhealthy role in their lives. Although the WAAC was a female-dominated corps in the midst of men, Hobby believed that women could remain chaste and feminine. By no means did women's armed service brand them as prostitutes or lesbians. Hobby asked a number of religious leaders to make public statements assuring Americans that the army provided a secure and decent life for the nation's young women. She added that WACs were of good moral character and had come from good families. The army, Hobby said, continued to serve as parents to its female recruits.

Besides Colonel Hobby, other army officials reassured the American public that female recruits would come to no harm at the hands of their fellow servicepeople. In addition, press releases maintained, "Soldiering hasn't transformed these WACs into Amazons." Rather, army women had "retained their femininity," as well as their heterosexuality.

Regarding sexual activity, Hobby refused to admit that service women would consider such a thing. She ignored the placement of condom vending machines near women's restrooms. Instead, Hobby distributed "social hygiene" pamphlets to WAC officers and stressed the need for "morality" among female recruits. As always, Hobby's major concern was in maintaining a "clean" public image that would allow her to induct more women into the army.

In retrospect, Colonel Hobby's policies derived from the long-standing double sexual standard in the United States. Most Americans expected male GIs to engage in sexual activity, but few thought female GIs should do so. Hobby was mortified when in 1943 a rumor campaign accused army officials of giving contraceptives to female personnel. When the army stationed African American women at posts where only African American men served, many critics assumed that the army intended service women to raise the "morale" of service men, sex included. Actually, the stationing of black women and men at the same base resulted from the army's segregation policy.

In addition to rumors, the army had to deal with the issue of military women and men dating. The only existing rule stated that officers could not "fraternize" with enlisted people. This translated to mean that male officers could not date enlisted women. In certain posts, local rules existed as well. Women had to stay within the compound. A heterosexual couple could not have a "date" without others present. Women should bring their male friends to communal day rooms and recreation areas where informal supervision existed. Women could not dance together or wear their hair in masculine styles. Unsurprisingly, service women, whether heterosexual or lesbian, objected to these limits on their personal lives.

Army policy makers tried to respond to complaints in a fair manner. Yet the army had to assure parents and communities that young women would not be corrupted while in the service. The result was an uneasy understanding between WACs and army officials. Each tried to respect the other's territory. Nonetheless, the issue of sexuality in the army was not settled in any definitive way. Nor was the term "female soldier" defined. Instead, World War II left the questions surrounding sex in the military to later generations to solve.

War Correspondents

Thanks in large part to Eleanor Roosevelt's "women-only" press conferences, women journalists were numerous by the early 1940s. When war broke out, many male reporters, anxious to get to the fighting front to cover the "real" stories, left the United States. Female reporters filled the positions they had vacated. Eager to get a foot in the door of journalism, women performed every necessary task, including setting type and running presses. By 1943, women accounted for about 50 percent of the staffs of small newspapers—and they were grateful to be there. As one woman put it, "It was easier for a newcomer to get a reporting job once the U.S. entered the war and the men went off."

At first, the State Department refused to issue passports to women reporters and the War Department withheld from women formal accreditation as war correspondents. Yet newspaper women knew that the biggest stories would come from the front, and many were determined to get there.

Once they made it to the front, female journalists confronted difficulties they had not anticipated. One rule restricted them from going any closer to the fighting line than members of women's corps. Some officers treated female reporters with hostility and male reporters scrambled to get the best assignments. Women usually reacted to these impediments with grace, and they refused special treatment and avoided controversy in the press camps. At the site of a story, however, they acted like any other reporter. As one observer explained, "When ever you find hundreds of thousands of sane people trying to get out of a place and a little bunch of madmen struggling to get in," you know the latter group are journalists. Women did "get in" and they produced quality reporting. They made the most of their opportunities and landed where they wanted to be—covering the "big" stories.

Women's Land Army

With the memory of the World War I Women's Land Army vivid, in 1943 the federal government established a Women's Land Army (WLA) to help the nation's farmers cope with the labor shortage they faced. Although the first Women's Land Army was a private organization, its reincarnation was a government agency. It offered female workers fair pay along with clean, adequate housing.

The WLA operated all over the United States. On the East Coast, women cultivated vegetables and picked fruit. They also tended poultry and dairy cows. Working as seasonal labor, WLA members ranged from upstate New York to New Jersey. On the West Coast, women picked citrus fruit. On the Great Plains, women pitched hay and herded cattle. The greatest number of WLA members, however, worked in Texas. There, approximately

75,000 women provided the seasonal labor that helped farmers make it through planting, cultivation, and harvest seasons.

In the Midwest, where grain farmers depended on large machinery rather than individual workers, WLA women did incidental field tasks and helped farmer's wives with their chores. At first, midwesterners were hesitant to accept WLA workers on their farms. One Iowa farm woman believed that "city women and girls" could not be away from "bathrooms and nail polish" long enough to learn farm work, but she thought they might be of some help in the kitchen. Urban women proved these notions wrong; from fields to kitchens, WLA workers provided useful service everywhere they went.

Besides white women, the WLA recruited Chinese women. Farmers, in the belief that most Chinese women had worked in agriculture in China, even paid Chinese women a high wage. When the depression forced a number of Chinese businesses to close, many Chinese women found themselves unemployed. The WLA offered them employment opportunities, mostly on the East and West coasts.

Over the course of the war, some 3.5 million women took part in WLA programs. Initially, many farmers accepted WLA workers because no male laborers were available. Each year, however, more farmers praised the women of the land army and awaited their return. In 1945, the last year of the war, WLA leaders recruited a record number of women. One measure of the WLA's success was that farm output and incomes rose during the war. Another came from appreciative farmers. One admitted that he had accepted female workers because he "was in an awful jam." He added that, "Now I will say they were eminently successful, and helped me get the job done."

Women's Other Contributions

Women served their nation in other ways as well. As in earlier wars, female entrepreneurs offered their services to the war effort. During the American Revolution, Philadelphia's foremost printer, Mary Katherine Goddard, had supplied for distribution copies of the Declaration of Independence. During World War II, the contributions of female entrepreneurs included modern technology. Notably, Olive Ann Beech turned her small commercial airline company into a major defense contractor. During the war, Beech supplied 90 percent of the planes used to train American bombardiers and navigators.

In another industry, Tillie Lewis helped refine the canning of food. Canned food played an essential role in feeding troops at the front. Lewis also brought the Italian tomato industry to California and developed the first artificially sweetened canned fruit. By the end of the war, Lewis had become the first woman director of the multibillion-dollar Ogden Corporation.

A different case was that of Lillian Evelyn Gilbreth, who contributed scientific management techniques to wartime industry. The holder of a Ph.D. in industrial psychology from Brown University, Gilbreth married and bore twelve children. When widowed, Gilbreth not only raised her family on her own but continued to work. To do this successfully, Gilbreth developed efficiency techniques for the home, techniques that were later applied to industry and used with effectiveness in World War II plants.

Besides assisting the war effort, a number of women looked ahead to the postwar world. They wanted to be involved in the nation's peace plans. In 1943, a group of women formed the Women's Action Committee for Victory and Lasting Peace. Other women chose to work through such existing associations as the National Council of Negro Women. In 1944, women's demands for seats at peace conferences prompted a White House conference called "How Women May Share in Post-War Policy Making." This meeting led to the nomination of several female delegates to international peace conferences. Individual states, notably Texas, held state-level "White House" conferences to give other women a chance to get involved in peace deliberations. Women's interest and enthusiasm for peace planning demonstrated that they were willing to do more than speak and march for the pacifist ideals they cherished.

Women at Home

Nearly two-thirds of the adult female population did not hold employment outside their homes or serve in the military. Instead, they worked on behalf of the war through their communities. For instance, women in Chinese neighborhoods formed chapters of the New Life Movement to organize women for war-relief efforts. These and millions of other women gave their time and energy to the Red Cross and the Office of Civil Defense. They provided entertainment for military men and women at USO canteens. They sold war bonds, raised victory gardens, canned their own foods, and collected tin cans and newspapers for recycling—all the while stretching their families' food and gasoline rationing stamps as far as they would go.

Moreover, so-called war brides provided a support system for the many men in the armed forces. Between 1940 and 1943, one million more marriages occurred than prewar rates would have predicted. Some 8 percent of all brides, or four to five million women, married servicemen. As "war brides," these women traveled all over the country to live on or near the bases at which their husbands were stationed. In addition, they joined the Red Cross, volunteered as motor pool drivers, and worked in hospitals and United Service Organizations (USOs). In 1944, one journalist described war brides as "wandering members of a huge unorganized club" but neglected to comment on their invaluable contributions to the war effort.

The "Nature" of Women

The activities of American women during the war years raised questions regarding the "inherent" nature of women. Were women really "natural" mothers who were happiest and most fulfilled when surrounded by children?

Certainly, childbearing statistics disputed this long-held belief, for the average number of children had dropped to two to three per mother. Many women shopped for the latest in birth-control technology and advice. In 1942, the American Birth Control League renamed itself the Planned Parenthood Federation of America, its officers believing that "planned parenthood" had more public appeal than did "birth control." The transformed organization no longer targeted working-class women but hoped to serve all classes. In addition to using birth control, American women increasingly rejected the attentions of midwives in favor of "physician-managed" childbirth in their homes or in hospitals.

During the war years, psychologist Helene Deutsch revised the traditional Freudian image of women to match contemporary realities. As a disciple of Freud, Deutsch accepted his hypothesis that women became hysterical because of sexual repression. In her classic two-volume *Psychology of Women* (1944), Deutsch anticipated feminist psychoanalysis by some thirty years. She argued that women's dependency grew out of their learned reliance on their mothers. Women had repressed rage, Deutsch explained, which put them in danger of developing neuroses. Deutsch stopped short of her feminist promise, however, for she continued to describe women as basically passive, even masochistic. Although Deutsch contributed to the ferment of thought regarding women and their innate nature, she reinforced some traditional ideas.

By the time that the war came to a welcome end in 1945, American women had experienced many modifications in their images, roles, and lifestyles. The war years had dramatically broken women's usual life cycle of childhood, schooling, employment, marriage, motherhood, and widowhood. Instead, it offered women the chance to experience paid employment, military service, travel, and patriotic activities firsthand. That the war proved a critical life stage for many American women was revealed in an army nurse's postwar assessment of herself: "More mature, more realistic, more open-minded."

Survival of Regionalism during the Depression and World War II

The South, 1930–1945

Although the war had helped homogenize the United States, the South retained a regional personality. For one thing, the South still reeled from its loss in the Civil War and the ending of black slavery. For another, Reconstruction left such deep scars in the southern psyche that they lingered well past their time. Even the rise of southern industrialization failed to pull the region out of its economic doldrums. Rather than disappearing, racial prejudice remained very much in place. Given these conditions, many white southerners retreated into the fantasy known as the "Magnolia Myth," choosing to remember the Old South, pre–Civil War days, as an epoch marked by grace, charm, and dignified living. Needless to say, few black southerners remembered the Old South quite so fondly.

During the depression era, the South suffered poverty and want. Although this changed some aspects of southern women's lives, others remained much the same as they had always been, especially among working-class women. During the depression, the government identified the South as "the nation's economic problem Number 1." Farm tenancy, sharecropping, soil erosion, illiteracy, and the highest birthrate in the country plagued the region. Sociologist Margaret Jarman Hagood studied black and white farm-tenant women in North Carolina, Georgia, and Alabama during the late 1930s and published her results in *Mothers of the South* (1939). She remarked on women's powerlessness, poverty, and the debilitating demands placed on them by raising too many children.

During the war years, poor southern women took paid employment outside their homes when it was available, but white and black southern women continued to work at different tasks for unequal pay. In North Carolina's tobacco industry, black women earned the lowest wages of all workers. Employers engaged black women only for certain types of jobs. Much like the days of slavery, supervisors created an auction setting when hiring black women. They lined the women up against walls and chose the sturdy-looking ones. One woman remembered that she had to demonstrate her strength and agility by holding "up one leg at a time" and bending "each backwards and forwards."

Once hired, women toiled in incredible discomfort due to substandard working conditions. Because black and white women worked separately, each group organized its own local unions. Black and white workers established racial and gender unity among their groups, rather than among women workers as a whole. Much as they did in slave times, black women viewed their home as the only place where they commanded respect and wielded influence. Raising children and participating in church activities gave them an additional sense of dignity and strength.

The West, 1930–1945

The West also retained its regional distinctiveness. Americans liked to think of the West as a place brimming with opportunity for all. Los Angelenos especially believed that their city was one of opportunity and optimism. Yet, like southerners, westerners faced many lingering problems, including widespread racism.

In the West, Native Americans had important issues. Although they lived largely secluded on reservations, American Indian women did receive attention from New Deal reformers. The Indian Reorganization Act of 1934, designed by John Collier, Commissioner of Indian Affairs between 1933 and 1945, encouraged a revitalization of Native culture. Under Collier's administration, the Bureau of Indian Affairs (BIA) offered reservation Indians improved education and medical services. Collier also believed in religious freedom for Indians as well as the need for an American Indian artistic and cultural revival. While the Indian New Deal was widely criticized, woefully underfunded, and poorly enforced, it broke sharply with the belief that Indians should strive to become pseudo-whites.

The Indian New Deal also included a number of programs and activities designed to aid women. Under it, Native women could apply for direct relief or social service jobs. Some worked as supervisors and laborers in CCC Indian Work Camps, as file clerks for the WPA, or as clerks and seamstresses for the CWA. They were eligible for extension services that provided training in cooking, sewing, canning, handcrafts, and childcare.

The Indian New Deal was a conscious attempt to encourage Native women's renewed participation in Indian affairs. Of the 135 Native constitutions drawn up under the Reorganization Act, not one denied women the right to vote or to hold office. In 1936, one Assiniboine woman and one Gros Ventres woman were elected to the Fort Belknap tribal council. Other women, customarily limited to the domestic realm, moved into leadership positions among Colorado River tribes, Oneida, and Blackfeet. Collier proudly noted that Indian women "are increasingly interested in tribal affairs, and are being given every opportunity to vote and hold office."

During World War II, Collier broke further with tradition in redesigning educational programs for young Native women. In 1942, he explained, "In the earlier days, white teachers refused to recognize Plains Indians customs which assigned work with the farms, gardens or small livestock to the women. . . . We are recognizing that in many Indian homes there will be no garden, no chickens, and no goats if the woman doesn't provide them—we are training girls to do these things well." The BIA also offered Native women courses in secretarial work and nursing, so that they might support themselves off reservations.

In 1944, Collier urged women to serve as delegates in the first National Congress of American Indians. Most were pleased with the suggestion. Although American Indian women had long built power bases by running farms, leasing out their land, and making craft items for sale, they wanted a direct voice in matters affecting them. In addition, having observed everything from women's clubs to labor unions, Indian women had seen the power of unity and protest.

Native women also worked on their own. One Dakota Sioux, Ella Deloria, assisted anthropologist Ruth Benedict in studying and recording Sioux culture. Deloria performed a great deal of fieldwork, especially interviewing elders on her home reservation, the Yankton Indian Reservation in South Dakota. In 1932, Deloria published *Dakota Texts*, which included the myths and tales she had collected. In 1944, Deloria's *Speaking of Indians* offered a description of Dakota culture and life. Perhaps Deloria's greatest achievement was to show for the first time Dakota culture through women's eyes.

In Southeast Alaska, another energetic woman, a Tlingit Indian named Elizabeth Peratrovich, served as president of the Alaska Native Sisterhood during the war years. Peratrovich opposed the discriminatory treatment of Native peoples in movie theaters, restaurants, and other Juneau businesses. As Peratrovich spoke, lobbied, and petitioned, she attacked the prevalence of "un-American" prejudice at home, even as Tlingit men were risking their lives in service to the United States. She was largely responsible for Alaska's Anti-Discrimination Bill of 1945. In addition, Peratrovich traveled at her own expense to locate markets for Indian- and Eskimo-produced items.

Hispanas received far less attention from the government and reformers. About 20 percent or less of relief funds went to Hispanics. During the depression, President Roosevelt's short-lived Good Neighbor Policy of 1933–34 encouraged friendly relations in the Western Hemisphere and inspired an interest in Spanish-style art, architecture, and culture. The CCC and WPA hired Hispanas, but segregated them in menial jobs. This segregation contributed to Hispanas' problems; in 1930, 15 percent were wage workers who earned inadequate pay as field hands, domestics, and unskilled factory workers. In 1931, a sociologist who studied Hispanas noted that those who worked often turned over their wages to husbands, for the "supremacy of the male is seldom disputed." More recent evidence refutes this observation, indicating instead that many Hispanas were far from subservient.

Perhaps the groups that fared worst of all during World War II were Asians and Asian Americans in the American West. Especially in California, racist attitudes kept Japanese American women out of office and sales jobs. Restricted primarily to domestic service, these women used their minimal wages as a lever to achieve small gains in American society. Moreover, engaging in wage work may have given them more influence in the traditional Japanese family structure as well.

During World War II, a groundswell of fear against Japan, the United States' arch enemy in the war, led to the implementation of a racist federal policy that deprived 120,000 Japanese Americans of their freedom, their property, and their pride. Although thousands of Japanese American men and women served with the U.S. armed forces, their families, under an executive order that cited "national security" concerns, spent the war years incarcerated in detention camps scattered throughout the American West. There, the prisoners, whose only crime was their heritage, lived in flimsy, crowded, and noisy barracks, small rooms that afforded no privacy and were furnished only with wooden tables and steel army cots.

Despite the stark conditions and humiliation, Japanese American women took advantage of the situation. They strengthened their roles as conservators of the family and Japanese culture. Moreover, the detained women held camp jobs, thereby shattering certain Japanese traditions restricting women's work. Still, the detention experience was hardly one women enjoyed. As one explained, "It is the effect on the spirit." Another, who was sixteen years old at the time, admitted, "I relive and re-experience the terror, the frustration, and total helplessness of those times."

Often mistaken for Japanese, other people of Asian heritage suffered discrimination during the war years. Only the Chinese commanded any respect. Because China joined the United States as an ally in World War II, people of Chinese heritage were "acceptable" to mainstream Americans. In 1942, the California League of Women Voters initiated an educational campaign to revise immigration laws. Chinese women were even hired to work in defense plants.

Between 1930 and 1945, the flapper of the 1920s gave way to the strong woman of the depression and New Deal years. In turn, she prepared the way for Rosie the Riveter, a heroine who was easier to create than to discredit at war's end. In 1945, women stood on the edge of the nest ready to fly, bolstered by a new consciousness of themselves as people of ability and strength.

Nonetheless, much of what women saw before them was disheartening. Changes implemented during times of national crisis were easily reversible. Americans who longed for the "good old days," a U.S. society that they idealized as simple and family oriented, urged a return to prewar ideals. This retrenchment in thought had a direct impact on American women. Two steps forward would again be accompanied by one step backward in the agonizingly slow dance known as "progress."

Study Guide

Checklist of important names, terms, phrases, and dates in Chapter 8.
Think about what or who each was and why she, he, or it was significant.

Great Depression
Right-to-Work Issue
Women's New Deal
Dorothea Lange
Eleanor Roosevelt
Marian Anderson
Mary McLeod Bethune
Juanita J. Sadler
Frances Perkins
Molly Dewson
Ellen S. Woodward
International Ladies' Garment Workers' Union (ILGWU)
Manuela Solis Sager
Emma Tenayuca
Luisa Moreno
Congress of Industrial Organizations (CIO)
Women's Emergency Brigades
Pecan-Sheller's Strike of 1938
"dating"
Florence Crittenton Home for Unwed Mothers
Ellen Quillin
Margaret McKenny
Bonnie Parker
Jessie Daniel Ames
Association of Southern Women for the Prevention of Lynching (ASWPL)
"comparative cultures"
Ruth Fulton Benedict

Margaret Mead
Zora Neale Hurston
Gertrude Stein
Dorothy Thompson
Lillian Hellman
Romaine Brooks
Anna May Wong
Ethel Waters
Billie Holliday
Antonia Brico
"Blondie"
Mildred "Babe" Didrikson Zaharias
"Rosie the Riveter"
Sabina Martínez
Women's Army Auxiliary Corps (WAAC)
Women's Army Corps (WAC)
Women Accepted for Volunteer Emergency Service (WAVES)
Margaret Bourke-White
Women Airforce Service Pilots (WASP)
Oveta Culp Hobby
Woman's Land Army (WLA)
Olive Ann Beech
Tillie Lewis
Lillian Evelyn Gilbreth
New Life Movement
Helene Deutsch
"Magnolia Myth"
Ella Deloria
Elizabeth Peratrovich
Japanese detention camps

Chapter 8 issues to think about and discuss:

- Would the Great Depression have been more difficult to survive in a city or on a farm? In the Northeast, South, or West?
- Were right-to-work laws immoral? Why weren't they based on race instead of gender?
- What factors caused Eleanor Roosevelt to be so sympathetic and understanding? Did her husband's infidelity give Eleanor Roosevelt more leverage personally and politically?
- Did strikes and other union activities help or hurt efforts to end the Great Depression?
- Is it possible to teach people how to be a "good" spouse or parent?
- How has the concept of comparative cultures shaped U.S. law and policy?
- Is lesbianism a culture?
- If you had been in Oveta Culp Hobby's position during World War II, what policies would you have put in place regarding service women's sexual activities?

- What is the "nature" of women?
- During the 1930s, did the South and the West have more racial issues to confront than did the Northeast?

Suggestions for Further Reading

The Great Depression of the 1930s

Beasley, Maurine, "Eleanor Roosevelt's Vision of Journalism: A Communication Medium for Women," *Presidential Studies Quarterly* 16 (Winter 1986): 66–75.

————, *Eleanor Roosevelt and the Media: A Public Quest for Self-Fulfillment* (Urbana: University of Illinois Press, 1987).

Berger, Jason, *A New Deal for the World: Eleanor Roosevelt and American Foreign Policy, 1920–1962* (New York: Columbia University Press, 1982).

Bergman, Andrew, *We're in the Money: Depression America and Its Films* (Chicago: Ivan R. Dee, Inc., 1993).

Black, Allida M., *Casting Her Own Shadow: Eleanor Roosevelt and the Shaping of Postwar Liberalism* (New York: Columbia University Press, 1996).

Blackwelder, Julia Kirk, "Women in the Work Force: Atlanta, New Orleans, and San Antonio, 1930 to 1940," *Journal of Urban History* 4 (May 1978): 331–53.

————, *Women of the Depression: Caste and Culture in San Antonio, 1929–1939* (College Station: Texas A&M University Press, 1984).

Chacón, Ramón D, "The 1933 San Joaquín Valley Cotton Strikes: Strike-breaking Activities in California Agriculture," 33–70, in *Work, Family, Sex Roles, Language,* edited by Mario Barrera, Alberto Camarillo, and Francisco Hernández (Berkeley, CA: Tonatiuh-Quinto Sol Press, 1980).

Chaudhuri, Nupur, "'We All Seem Like Brothers and Sisters': The African-American Community in Manhattan, Kansas, 1865–1940," *Kansas History* 14 (Winter 1992–92): 270–88.

Christian, Barbara, *Black Women Novelists: The Development of a Tradition, 1892–1976* (Westport, CT: Greenwood Press, 1980).

Clark-Lewis, Elizabeth, *Living In, Living Out: African American Domestics in Washington, D.C., 1910–1940* (Washington, DC: Smithsonian Institution Press, 1994).

Cobble, Dorothy Sue, *Dishing It Out: Waitresses and Their Unions in the Twentieth Century* (Urbana: University of Illinois Press, 1991).

Cook, Blanche Wiesen, *Eleanor Roosevelt, 1884–1933* (New York: Viking Press, 1992).

Fink, Deborah, *Cutting into the Meatpacking Line: Workers and Change in the Rural Midwest* (Chapel Hill: University of North Carolina Press, 1998).

Green, George N, "ILGWU in Texas, 1930–1970," *Journal of Mexican-American History* 1 (Spring 1971): 144–69.

Hanson, Joyce A., *Mary McLeod Bethune and Black Women's Political Activism* (Columbia: University of Missouri Press, 2003).

Kennedy, Susan Estabrook, *If All We Did Was to Weep at Home: A History of White Working Class Women* (Bloomington: Indiana University Press, 1979).

Kessler-Harris, Alice, *Out to Work: A History of Wage-Earning Women in the United States* (New York: Oxford University Press, 1982).

Korrol, Virginia E. Sánchez, *From Colonia to Community: The History of Puerto Ricans in New York City, 1917–1948* (Westport, CT: Greenwood Press, 1983).

Lash, Joseph P., *Eleanor: The Years Alone* (New York: W. W. Norton & Company, Inc., 1972).

Melosh, Barbara, *Engendering Culture: Manhood and Womanhood in New Deal Public Art and Theater* (Summit, PA: Smithsonian Institution Press, 1991).

Neth, Mary, *Preserving the Family Farm: Women, Community, and the Foundations of Agribusiness in the Midwest, 1900–1940* (Baltimore: Johns Hopkins Press, 1995).

Orleck, Annelise, "'We Are That Mythical Thing Called the Public': Militant Housewives during the Great Depression," *Feminist Studies* 19 (Spring 1993): 147–72.

Patterson, James I, "Mary Dewson and the American Minimum Wage Movement," *Labor History* 5 (Spring 1964): 134–52.

Patterson, Victoria D., "Indian Life in the City: A Glimpse of the Urban Experience of Pomo Women in the 1930s," *California History* 71 (Fall 1992): 402–31.

Ross, B, Joyce, "Mary McLeod Bethune and the National Youth Administration: A Case Study of Power Relationships in the Black Cabinet of Franklin D, Roosevelt," *Journal of Negro History* 60 (January 1975): 1–28.

Scharf, Lois, To Work and to Wed: Female Employment, Feminism, and the Great Depression (Westport, CT: Greenwood Press, 1980).

———, *Eleanor Roosevelt: The First Lady of American Liberalism* (Boston: G. K. Hall, 1987).

Sklar, Kathryn Kish, *Florence Kelley and the Nation's Work* (New Haven, CT: Yale University Press, 1995).

Swain, Martha H, "'The Forgotten Woman': Ellen S. Woodward and Women's Relief in the New Deal," *Prologue* 15 (Winter 1983): 200–13.

Wandersee, Winifred D., *Women's Work and Family Values, 1920–1940* (Cambridge, MA: Harvard University Press, 1981).

Ware, Susan, *Beyond Suffrage: Women and the New Deal* (Cambridge, MA: Harvard University Press, 1981).

———, *Holding Their Own: American Women in the 1930s* (Boston: Twayne Publishers, 1982).

———, *Partner and I: Molly Dewson, Feminism, and New Deal Politics* (New Haven, CT: Yale University Press, 1987).

Westin, Jeanne, *Making Do: How Women Survived the Depression* (Chicago: Follett Publishing Company, 1976).

Wortman, Roy, "Gender Issues in the National Farmers Union in the 1930s," *Midwest Review* 15 (1993): 71–83.

Youngs, J. William T., *Eleanor Roosevelt: A Personal and Public Life* (Boston: Little, Brown and Co., 1985).

Life during the 1930s

Ammer, Christine, *Unsung: A History of Women in American Music* (Milwaukee, WI: Hal Leonard Corporation, 2001).

Anderson, Karen, *Changing Woman: A History of Racial Ethnic Women in America* (New York: Oxford University Press, 1996).

Babbitt, Kathleen R., "The Productive Farm Woman and the Extension Home Economist in New York State, 1920–1940," *Agricultural History* 67 (Spring 1993): 83–101.

Bailey, Beth L, "Scientific Truth … and Love: The Marriage Education Movement in the United States," *Journal of Social History* 20 (Summer 1987): 711–32.

———, and David Farber, *The First Strange Place: The Alchemy of Race and Sex in World War II Hawaii* (New York: Free Press, 1992).

Bogle, Donald, *Brown Sugar: Eighty Years of America's Black Superstars* (New York: Harmond, 1980).

Boris, Eileen, "Regulating Industrial Homework: The Triumph of "Sacred Motherhood,"" *Journal of American History* 71 (March 1985): 745–63.

Calderón, Roberto R., and Emilio Zamora, "Manuela Solis Sager and Emma Tenayuca: A Tribute," 30–41, in *Chicana Voices: Intersections of Class, Race, and Gender*, edited by Teresa Córdova et al. (Albuquerque: University of New Mexico Press, 1990).

Campbell, D'Ann, "Was the West Different? Values and Attitudes of Young Women in 1943," *Pacific Historical Review* 47 (August 1978): 453–63,

Cayleff, Susan E., *Babe: The Life and Legend of Babe Didrikson Zaharias* (Urbana: University of Illinois Press, 1995).

Harris, Ann Sutherland, and Linda Nochlin, *Women Artists, 1550–1950* (New York: Alfred A, Knopf, 1979).

Kent, Kathryn, *Making Girls into Women: American Women's Writing and the Rise of Lesbian Identity* (Durham, NC: Duke University Press, 2003).

Kunzel, Regina G., "The Professionalization of Benevolence: Evangelicals and Social Workers in the Florence Crittenton Homes, 1915 to 1945," *Journal of Social History* 22 (Fall 1988): 21–43,

———, *Fallen Women, Problem Girls: Unmarried Mothers and the Professionalization of Social Work, 1890–1945* (New Haven, CT: Yale University Press, 1993).

Leong, Karen J., *The China Mystique: Pearl S. Buck, Anna May Wong, Mayling Soong Chiang, and the Transformation of American Orientalism* (Berkeley: University of California Press, 2005).

Lewandowski, Michael J., "Democracy in the Workplace: Working Women in Midwestern Unions, 1943–1945," *Prologue* 25 (Summer 1993): 157–69.

Madsen, Carol Cornwall, "'Sisters at the Bar': Utah Women in Law," *Utah Historical Quarterly* 61 (Summer 1993): 208–32.

Matsumoto, Valerie, "Desperately Seeking 'Deirdre': Gender Roles, Multicultural Relations, and Nisei Women Writers of the 1930s," *Frontiers* 12 (1991): 19–32.

Morton, Marian J, "Seduced and Abandoned in an American City: Cleveland and Its Fallen Women, 1869–1936," *Journal of Urban History* 11 (August 1985): 443–69.

Ogden, Annegret S., *The Great American Housewife: From Helpmate to Wage Earner, 1776–1986* (Westport, CT: Greenwood Press, 1986).

Reverby, Susan M., *Ordered to Care: The Dilemma of American Nursing, 1850–1945* (New York: Cambridge University Press, 1987).

Rosenfeld, Rachel Ann, *Farm Women: Work, Farm, and Family in the United States* (Chapel Hill: University of North Carolina Press, 1985).

Schwieder, Dorothy, and Deborah Fink, "Plains Women: Rural Life in the 1930s," *Great Plains Quarterly* 8 (Spring 1988): 79–88.

Sochen, June, "Mildred Pierce and Women in Film," *American Quarterly* 30 (Spring 1978): 3–20.

———, *Mae West: She Who Laughs, Lasts* (Wheeling, IL: Harlan Davidson, Inc., 1992).

Todd, Ellen Wiley, *The 'New Woman' Revised: Painting and Gender Politics on Fourteenth Street* (Berkeley: University of California Press, 1993).

Whaley, Charlotte, *Nina Otero-Warren of Santa Fe* (Albuquerque: University of New Mexico Press, 1994).

World War II, 1941–1945

Anderson, Karen Tucker, *Wartime Women: Sex Roles, Family Relations, and the Status of Women during World War II* (Westport, CT: Greenwood Press, 1981).

————, "Last Hired, First Fired: Black Women during World War II," *Journal of American History* 69 (June 1982): 82–97.

Campbell, D'Ann, *Women at War with America: Private Lives in a Patriotic Era* (Cambridge, MA: Harvard University Press, 1984).

————, "Servicewomen of World War II," *Armed Forces and Society* 16 (Winter 1990): 251–70.

————, "Women in Combat: The World War II Experience in the United States, Great Britain, Germany, and the Soviet Union," Journal of Military History 57 (April 1993): 301–23.

Carpenter, Stephanie Ann, "Regular Farm Girl: The Woman's Land Army in World War II," *Agricultural History* 71 (Spring 1997): 163–85.

Clive, Alan, "Women Workers in World War II: Michigan as a Test Case," *Labor History* 20 (Winter 1979): 44–72.

Fletcher, Jean W., Joyce S. McMahon, and Aline O. Quester, "Tradition, Technology, and the Changing Roles of Women in the Navy," *Minerva* 11 (Fall/Winter 1993): 57–85.

Gallaher, Jean, *The World Wars Through the Female Gaze* (Edwardsville: University of Southern Illinois Press, 1999).

Gluck, Sherna Berger, *Rosie the Riveter Revisited: Women, the War, and Social Change* (Boston: Twayne, 1987).

Goossen, Rachel Waltner, *Women Against the Good War: Conscientious Objection and Gender on the American Homefront, 1941–1947* (Chapel Hill: University of North Carolina Press, 1999).

Gouvela, Grace Mary, "'We Also Serve': American Indian Women's Role in World War II," *Michigan Historical Review* 20 (Fall 1994): 153–84.

Gutierrez, Gail M., "The Sting of Discrimination: Women Airforce Service Pilots (WASP)," *Journal of the West* 35 (January 1996): 15–23.

Hartmann, Susan M., *The Home Front and Beyond: American Women in the 1940s* (Boston: Twayne Publishers, 1982).

Heacock, Nan, *Battle Stations! The Homefront in World War II* (Ames: Iowa State University Press, 1992).

Hirshfield, Deborah Scott, "Women Shipyard Workers in the Second World War: A Note," *International History Review* 11 (May 1989): 278–85.

Honey, Maureen, "Images of Women in The Saturday Evening Post, 1931–1936," *Journal of Popular Culture* 10 (Fall 1976): 352–58.

————, *Creating Rosie the Riveter: Class, Gender, and Propaganda during World War II* (Amherst: University of Massachusetts Press, 1984).

————, *Bitter Fruit: African American Women in World War II* (Columbia: University of Missouri Press, 1999).

Jaros, Dean, *Heroes without Legacy: American Airwomen, 1912–1944* (Niwot: University Press of Colorado, 1993).

Jeansonne, Glen, *Women of the Far Right: The Mothers' Movement and World War II* (Chicago: University of Chicago Press, 1996).

Litoff, Judy Barrett, and David C. Smith, eds., *Since You Went Away: World War II Letters from American Women on the Home Front* (New York: Oxford University Press, 1991).

————, *What Kind of World Do We Want? American Women Plan for Peace* (Wilmington, DE: Scholarly Resources, 2000).

Matsumoto, Valerie, "Japanese American Women During World War II," *Frontiers* 8 (1984): 6–14.

Merryan, Molly, *Clipped Wings: The Rise and Fall of the Women Airforce Service Pilots (WASPS) of World War II* (New York City: New York University Press, 2001).

Meyer, Leisa D, "Creating G.I. Jane: The Regulation of Sexuality and Sexual Behavior in the Women's Army Corps during World War II," *Feminist Studies* 18 (Fall 1992): 581–601.

Milkman, Ruth, *Gender at Work: The Dynamics of Job Segregation by Sex during World War II* (Urbana: University of Illinois Press, 1987).

Moore, Brenda L., *Serving Our Country: Japanese American Women in the Military during World War II* (New Brunswick, NJ: Rutgers University Press, 2003).

Newman, Debra L., "The Propaganda and the Truth: Black Women and World War II," *Minerva: Quarterly Report on Women and the Military* 4 (Winter 1986): 72–92.

Peterson, Susan C., and Amy K. Rieger, "'They Needed Nurses at Home': The Cadet Nurse Corps in South Dakota and North Dakota," *South Dakota History* 23 (Summer 1993): 122–32.

Rupp, Leila J., *Mobilizing Women for War: German and American Propaganda, 1939–1945* (Princeton, NJ: Princeton University Press, 1978).

Sheldon, Sayre P., *Her War Story: Twentieth-Century Women Write about War* (Edwardsville: University of Southern Illinois Press, 1999).

Shukert, Elfrieda B., and Barbara S. Scibetta, *War Brides of World War Two* (New York: Penguin, 1989).

Spickard, Paul R., "Work and Hope: African American Women in Southern California during World War II," *Journal of the West* 33 (July 1993): 70–79.

Tomblin, Barbara Brooks, *G.I. Nightengales: The Army Nurse Corps in World War II* (Lexington: University Press of Kentucky, 2003).

Wagner, Lilya, *Women War Correspondents of World War II* (Westport, CT: Greenwood Press, 1989).

Survival of Regionalism during the Depression and World War II

Antell, Judith Anne, *American Indian Women Activists* (Berkeley: University of California Press, 1990).

Armitage, Susan, and Elizabeth Jameson, eds., *Writing the Range: Race, Class, and Culture in the Women's West* (Norman: University of Oklahoma Press, 1997).

Bernstein, Alison, "A Mixed Record: The Political Enfranchisement of American Indian Women during the Indian New Deal," *Journal of the West* 23 (July 1984): 13–20.

Butler, Anne M., *Gendered Justice in the American West* (Urbana: University of Illinois Press, 1997).

Coburn, Carol K., *Life at Four Corners: Religion, Gender, and Education in a German-Lutheran Community, 1868–1945* (Lawrence: University Press of Kansas, 1992).

Daniel, Cletus E., *Bitter Harvest: A History of California Farmworkers, 1870–1914* (Ithaca, NY: Cornell University Press, 1981).

Durón, Clementina, "Mexican Women and Labor Conflict in Los Angeles: The ILGWU Dressmakers' Strike of 1933," *Aztlan* 15 (Spring 1984): 365–75.

Fink, Deborah, *Agrarian Women: Wives and Mothers in Rural Nebraska, 1880–1940* (Chapel Hill: University of North Carolina Press, 1992).

García, Richard A., *The Rise of the Mexican American Middle Class: San Antonio, 1923–1941* (College Station: Texas A&M University Press, 1991).

Glenn, Evelyn Nakano, "The Dialectics of Wage Work: Japanese-American Women and Domestic Service, 1905–1940," *Feminist Studies* 6 (Fall 1980): 432–71.

Gonzalez, Gilbert G, "Women, Work, and Community in the Mexican Colonias of the Southern California Citrus Belt," *California History* 74 (Spring 1995): 58–67.

Gonzalez, Rosalinda M., "Chicanas and Mexican Immigrant Families 1920–1940: Women's Subordination and Family Exploitation," 59–84, in *Decades of Discontent: The Women's Movement, 1920–1940*, edited by Joan M. Jensen and Lois Scharf (Westport, CT: Greenwood Press, 1983).

Harvey, Lola, *Derevinia's Daughters: Saga of an Alaskan Village* (Manhattan, KS: Sunflower University Press, 1991).

Janiewski, Dolores, "Flawed Victories: The Experiences of Black and White Women Workers in Durham during the 1930s," 85–109, in *Decades of Discontent: The Women's Movement, 1920–1940*, edited by Joan M. Jensen and Lois Scharf (Westport, CT: Greenwood Press, 1983).

———, *Sisterhood Denied: Race, Gender, and Class in a New South Community* (Philadelphia: Temple University Press, 1985).

Jellison, Katherine, "Women and Technology on the Great Plains, 1910–40," *Great Plains Quarterly* 8 (Summer 1988): 145–57.

———, *Entitled to Power: Farm Women and Technology, 1913–1963* (Chapel Hill: University of North Carolina Press, 1993).

Jones, Beverly W., "Race, Sex, and Class: Black Female Tobacco Workers in Durham, North Carolina, 1920–1940, and the Development of Female Consciousness," *Feminist Studies* 10 (Fall 1984): 441–52.

Jones, Jacqueline, *Labor of Love, Labor of Sorrow: Black Women, Work, and the Family from Slavery to the Present* (New York: Basic Books, 1985).

Laslett, John H. M., "Gender, Class, or Ethno-Cultural Struggle? The Problematic Relationship Between Rose Pesotta and the Los Angeles ILGWU," *California History* 72 (Spring 1993): 20–39.

Lothrop, Gloria Ricci, "Westering Women & the Ladies of Los Angeles: Sisters Under the Skin?" *Californians* 12 (1995): 12–23.

Nelson-Cisneros, Victor B., "UCAPAWA and Chicanos in California: The Farmworker Period, 1937–40," *Aztlan* 7 (Fall 1976): 453–77.

———, "UCAPAWA Organizing Activities in Texas, 1935–50," *Aztlan* 9 (Spring/Summer/Fall (1978): 71–84.

Osburn, Katherine B., *Southern Ute Women: Autonomy and Assimilation on the Reservation, 1887–1934* (Albuquerque: University of New Mexico Press, 1998).

Scadron, Arlene, ed., *On Their Own: Widows and Widowhood in the American Southwest, 1848–1939* (Urbana: University of Illinois Press, 1988).

Schackel, Sandra, *Social Housekeepers: Women Shaping Public Policy in New Mexico, 1920–1940* (Albuquerque: University of New Mexico Press, 1992).

Taylor, Quintard, *In Search of the Racial Frontier: African Americans in the American West, 1528–1990* (New York: W. W. Norton, 1998).

Taylor, Sandra C., "Leaving the Concentration Camps: Japanese Americans and Resettlement in the Intermountain West," *Pacific Historical Review* 60 (May 1991): 169–94.

Tsuchida, Nobuya, ed., *Asian and Pacific American Experiences: Women's Perspectives* (Minneapolis: Asian/American Learning Resource Center, University of Minnesota, 1982).

Walker, Melissa, *All We Knew Was to Farm: Rural Women in the Upcountry South, 1919–1941* (Columbia: University of Missouri Press, 2003).

Images and Realities

Top: Zambrano family and others at baby's funeral in early 1900s, UT Institute of Texan Cultures at San Antonio, No. 81-0154.
Bottom: Tejanas and Anglos (French) among this class, El Carmen, Texas, c. 1896. UT Institute of Texan Cultures at San Antonio, No. 078-0561.

Top: Sawmill crew near Pekin, North Dakota, c. 1897. Author's collection.
Bottom: Unidentified couple in front of dug-out cabin on the Dragseth Ranch,
Evelyn Cameron, photographer. Montana Historical Society, Helena, Mon-
tana, #MHS vintage Cameron.

Top: Gathering cotton, c. 1900. Library of Congress, #LC-USZ62-75650.
Bottom: Polly Bemis of Warrens, Idaho. Idaho State Historical Society, Accession #71-185.29.

Top: Trimming currency, Bureau of Engraving and Printing, Washington, D.C., 1907. Library of Congress.

Bottom: A physical education class in the Armory, University of North Dakota, Grand Forks, 1904. State Historical Society of North Dakota, Bismarck, #E-398.

Top: Na-tu-ende, Apache, ca. 1883. Photo by Ben Wittick, courtesy Museum of New Mexico, Neg. #15910.
Bottom: A teacher with her Flathead Indian pupils in Montana, 1910. Montana Historical Society, Helena, Montana, Neg.#954-659.

*Top: Doctors Tai
Heong Kong (Li) and
Kai Fai Li. Bishop
Museum, Honolulu,
I.D. #CP86221.
Bottom: Washing
clothes in a stream
near Ft. Pierre, 1911.
Photo courtesy of the
South Dakota State
Historical Society—
State Archives.*

Top: *Hispana in New Mexico, c. 1915. Courtesy Museum of New Mexico, Neg. #31501.*
Bottom: *Two elderly women at a convention of former slaves, 1916. Library of Congress, #LC-USZ62-35649.*

Top: Working in the dry goods store, Lakota, North Dakota. State Historical Society of North Dakota, A-2831.
Bottom: Nancy Hendrickson, planting corn, Morton County, North Dakota, c. 1918. State Historical Society of North Dakota, 24-45.

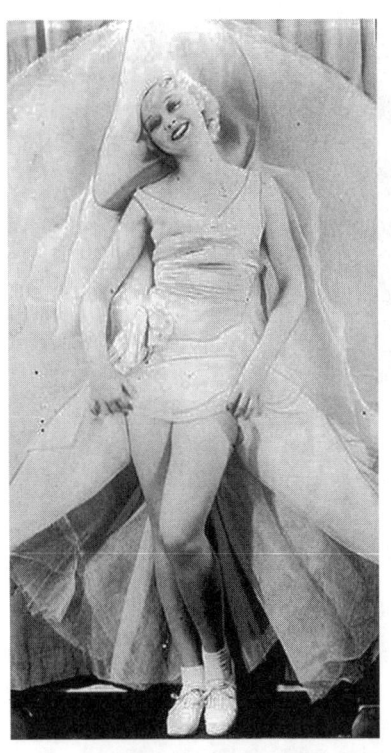

Top: Showgirl with floppy hat and short stockings, c. 1920. Denver Public Library, Western History Collection, Harry M. Rhoads, #codhawp 00186995.
Bottom: Flappers, c. 1920. Western History Collection, Harry M. Rhoads, Denver Public Library, Rh 1936.

Top: Creating beauty in the barrio, El Paso, Texas, 1949. Russell Lee
Photograph Collection, The Center for American History, The University of
Texas at Austin, Neg. #VN1920-34.
Bottom: Creole women in Plaquemines Parish, Louisiana, 1939. Louisiana
State Library.

Top: Migrant family on the road, 1939. Dorothea Lange photo. Library of Congress, #LC-USZ-34-T01-020993. Bottom: Cigar factory strike, August 1933. San Antonio Light Collection, UT Institute of Texan Cultures at San Antonio, No. 1476-A SAL.

Top: Women's Air Force service pilots at Scott Field, Illinois, 1943.
UT Institute of Texan Cultures at San Antonio, No. 085-0482.
Bottom: Riveters in the Long Beach plant of Douglas Aircraft Co., 1942.
National Archives.

Top: Dressmaking class at Manzanar, a Japanese American relocation center, 1943. Library of Congress, #LC-DIG-ppprs-00126.
Bottom: African American war workers at the shipyards. Library of Congress, #LC-USW3-028675-C.

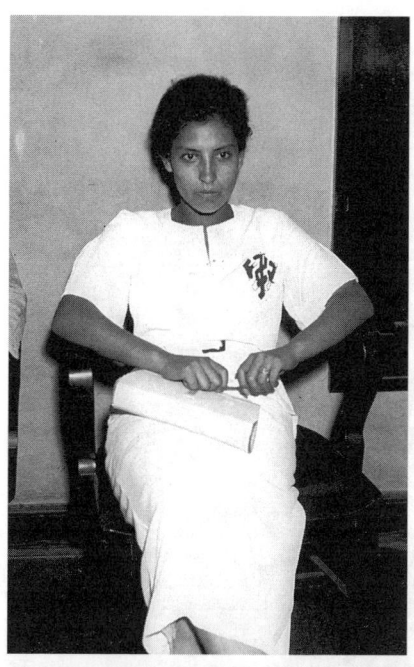

Top: Emma Tenayuca, union organizer, at age 19. San Antonio Light Collection, UT Institute of Texan Cultures at San Antonio, No. 1006-B SAL. Bottom: Eleanor Roosevelt greeting Mary McLeod Bethune at a women's dormitory for black war workers, May 1943. Library of Congress, #LC-USW3-028297-C.

Top: Elizabeth Eckford attempts to enter her desegre- gated high school in Little Rock, Arkansas, 1957. AP/Wide World. Bottom: Dolores Huerta signaling to strikebreakers in fields near Delano, California, September 24, 1965. The Harvey Richards Film Collection, Estuary Press.

Top: Betty Friedan (third from left) leading a small march to present 894 resolutions to the U.N. International Women's Year conference, Mexico City, 1975. Photo courtesy of Jacqui Ceballos.
Bottom: Barbara Jordan giving a speech. Library of Congress, #LC-U9-32937-32A/33.

Top Elizabeth Ochoa, STS-110 mission specialist, #JSC2003-E-08185. Courtesy of NASA.
Bottom: Young professional golfer Michelle Wei of Hawaii lines up a putt at the U.S. Women's Open in Colorado, 2005. AP Photo/Chris Carlson.

Chapter Nine

The Feminine Mystique and Beyond, 1945 to 1965

$\mathcal{I}$n 1945, Americans expressed a desire to "get back to normal," by which they meant a return to a happy, industrious lifestyle in an idyllic country. Although such a time had never existed in the nation's history, a war-weary generation clung to their illusions. In 1946, such events as the opening of the new United Nations Organization and the United Nations Atomic Energy Commission created optimism in the United States. The postwar years included, however, testing of atomic bombs, as well as the news that the Union of Soviet Socialist Republics (USSR) had taken over the governments of a string of Eastern European nations, drawing an "Iron Curtain" between itself and Western nations. In an era in which Americans feared communism almost to the point of irrationality—some built bomb shelters in their backyards—it seemed reassuring to think of wives and mothers safely back in traditional roles.

Postwar America had definite plans for the nation's women. Many people believed that women would return from wartime employment to their homes, where they could contentedly keep house and bear children. Now that women had helped the nation meet the monumental challenge of World War II, newspaper articles, political speeches, sermons, and casual conversations indicated that "true" women should, and would, limit their activities to their homes, and leave the endeavors of the "outside" world to men.

This "feminine mystique," as the feminist writer Betty Friedan would soon label such principles, was more or less an updated version of the nineteenth-century cult of domesticity; such ideas placed women in a domestic setting and largely applied to white, middle- and upper-class women. As in the nineteenth century, these beliefs met with resistance from numerous women. By the early 1960s, a significant number of them—along with other types of women—created the contemporary feminist movement. The supposed "nature" of woman was no longer a given. Rather, it provided grist for an open and controversial discussion.

Back-to-the-Home Movement
of the Late 1940s and the 1950s

Demobilization

In 1945, the Women's Bureau reported that a significant number of female workers hoped to keep their jobs after the war. Probably motivated more by high pay than feminist ideals, fully 80 percent of employed women wanted to keep working. Of these, 57 percent were single, 34 percent married, and 15 percent widowed or divorced. In that same year, however, a study of women workers in Michigan defense plants revealed that a majority of them had no desire to continue their wartime lifestyles. Rather than viewing the war as an opportunity for emancipation, they, like most men, perceived it as a temporary call to duty. These women intended to return to their domestic duties at war's end.

As far as U.S. government agencies were concerned, women needed to leave their jobs so that returning veterans could find work. Soon after the war, government propaganda reversed 180 degrees, with postwar depictions showing Rosie the Riveter throwing down her welding torch and returning to the suburbs. The media cooperated in this effort by encouraging women to marry and bear children, to recreate the warm home life that the national emergency had interrupted. Above all else, women were to act sweet, supportive, and motherly toward the returning veterans.

Accordingly, layoffs of women workers came quickly and day-care centers closed abruptly. In early 1946, a *New York Times* reporter commented, "The courtship of women workers has ended." True to the historical pattern, employers fired women of color, then white women. After losing their wartime jobs, women sought other employment—in department stores, offices, or service industries. Rather than returning to domestic or agricultural labor, many black women took clerical, retail, and other similar positions. One million other women withdrew from the labor pool entirely; half of them listed themselves as unemployed, meaning that they wanted to work and were seeking employment.

Even women in the military were expected to retreat to their homes. Military officials expected WASP pilots to find husbands and establish homes in which to live happily ever after, without the aid of well-deserved military benefits. Unlike their male counterparts, former WASP pilots did not receive educational allowances, life insurance policies, or government-backed farm or home loans. One WASP, who lost an arm in a propeller accident, received only 10 percent of the traditional (male) disability compensation. In short, these women had served their nation well, only to be told to go home.

Sex and Marriage

Initially it appeared that women, especially those of the white middle and upper classes, accepted with joy the postwar return to domestic life. Being at home full-time with one's children seemed to be an American dream come true.

Women had many reasons for wanting to return home. Because World War II had lasted far longer than World War I, it caused longer delays in marriage for single women and in childbirth for married women. Many such women were anxious to move forward with their lives. Others were tired of the demands of simultaneously running a home and holding paid employment. Still others swallowed postwar propaganda, declaring it was their patriotic duty to bear children to replace Americans killed in the war. As domestic consumers, dictums added, women would fuel the postwar economy. As mothers, they would instill principles of democracy into their children, securing the nation's faith in itself in the face of the spread of communism overseas.

But once redomesticated, women found their roles less than clearly defined. It seemed that American society had one foot planted in the postwar world and the other in the prewar one, as a period of contradiction marked the late 1940s and 1950s. For instance, American society encouraged women to act open and sensual, yet societal norms imposed taboos on women's sexual behavior. Although sex appeared everywhere in postwar advertisements and media, the old rules regarding personal conduct remained in place.

One example of this contradictory thinking was the emergence of *Playboy* magazine. Although this publication featured photographs of unclothed women in sexual poses, it appeared on the shelves of newsstands and stores nationwide. At the same time, *Playboy* faced government censorship and gained only grudging public acceptance. Hardly a publication that one would leave on the coffee table for guests to see, *Playboy* was more likely to be found under an adolescent boy's bed or hidden in his father's garage.

Another example of inconsistent attitudes toward human sexuality was the new degree of respectability that vaudeville striptease artists attained. Gypsy Rose Lee (Rose Lee Hovick) fascinated, yet repulsed, the American public. She turned her vaudeville stardom into a career as a writer and film actor. Lee's 1944 film, *Belle of the Yukon,* and her 1957 book, *Gypsy, A Memoir,* focused not only on sex but on women as sex objects. She would later be celebrated in the Broadway musical, *Gypsy.*

During the late 1940s and early 1950s, sex invaded the traditional Hollywood Western, but not without a moral message. In 1946, sex provided the motif for *Duel in the Sun,* referred to popularly as "Lust in the Dust." In this film, Gregory Peck as Lewt seduces Jennifer Jones as Pearl, who eventually pays with her life for her unbridled sensuality. Openly sexual women suffer similar fates in *The Gunfighter* (1950) and *The Maverick Queen* (1956).

Women of color faced a more complicated situation. When Hispanas landed a part in a Western, their skin tone dictated which character they would portray, with light-skinned women cast as virgins and dark-skinned women as whores. The virgins were carried off by the likes of John Wayne and Gary Cooper, but the whores were shot to death. Although sex furnished the postwar film industry with a new theme, the message remained prewar: women had the responsibility to act morally and hold amoral men to "proper" social standards.

The mixed messages the media delivered were not lost on American women. Before marriage, nice girls could experiment with sex, especially "petting." They did not, however, "go all the way." If they did, they refused to admit it to their friends and certainly not to their mothers. Many women justified their actions by planning to marry the men with whom they were sexually involved. Of course, such plans often fell through, leaving women to blame men for having seduced them or to rationalize their behavior to themselves.

The fear of an unwanted pregnancy further restricted sexual behavior. Although Planned Parenthood offered diaphragms and most drugstore pharmacies sold condoms, neither form of contraception was easily available to single women. When used, these devices were not totally reliable. In addition to contracting a sexually transmitted disease, a woman engaging in sex could become pregnant. The choices open to an unwed pregnant woman included illegal abortion, having the child "out of wedlock" as it was called, or forcing the child's father into marriage.

After marriage, however, women were allowed—even expected—to be sensual but only in a "wifely" way. Rather than acting like a "loose" woman, a wife was to be sexy for her husband. In other words, she was to project a chaste image to the outside world, the perfect wife and mother during the day; at night, however, this same person was to become a passionate and compliant lover.

Naturally, this climate of opinion confused women. It also scared them. Being single and sinful was bad enough. Being pregnant was worse. Given the situation, women felt they were better off married. During the late 1940s, the average age of women at time of first marriage was twenty years. By 1951, one out of every three women married by the age of nineteen. By 1958, more women married between the ages of fifteen and nineteen than in any other age category.

The Baby Boom

Once married, women's sexuality was supposed to lead to childbirth. To be truly fulfilled, a wife had to become a mother. Such thinking fit the age. Most returning male veterans from World War II and the Korean War (1950–53), as well as their wives, wanted children. Postwar prosperity made the financial support of four or more children possible for millions of couples. Americans' hopes for the nation's growth further encouraged childbearing.

In 1946, a dramatic rise in the birth rate began. Known as the "Baby Boom," this trend marked the late 1940s and the 1950s, when most women bore children in their late teens and early twenties; the average woman bore her last child by the age of twenty-six. Birth rates differed between women in different regions of the country. Generally, women of color and immigrant women bore more children than did native-born white women, and the former continued giving birth through a later age than did native-born whites. Rural women had more children and bore their last ones later in life than did urban women.

These differential birth rates resulted from diverse cultural attitudes and religious beliefs. Some women appreciated large families more than others. Some felt that using birth control was immoral; whereas some who might have used birth control had no access to the necessary knowledge or devices, or could not afford it. While Planned Parenthood helped as many women as possible, its offices were located in urban areas and mostly served white, middle-to upper-class women. Nor did the organization encourage single women to take advantage of its services.

The experience of childbirth changed as well. Many women who carried their pregnancies to term brought new ideas and input to the birthing process. Because women now considered "natural" childbirth the healthiest form of delivery (for themselves as well as their newborns), increasing numbers of pregnant women decided to employ the labor technique known as "Lamaze," after the name of the French doctor who developed it. Through instruction in special exercises and breathing patterns, the Lamaze method encouraged women to have their babies with little or no anesthesia. It also urged expectant fathers to participate in prebirth training classes and to attend the birth. Because most American hospitals did not allow fathers in delivery rooms, men usually had to remain in waiting rooms during the birth of their children. Some innovative hospitals connected sound systems between delivery and waiting rooms so that concerned fathers might listen in. After birth, an organization dedicated to promoting the health benefits of breast-feeding for mothers and babies, the La Leche League, advised mothers to nurse rather than bottle-feed their newborns. Members of the La

Leche League provided information and, if necessary, counsel to mothers experiencing difficulties in consistently breast-feeding their children.

In 1953, the Baby Boom peaked with a record 4.3 million births. The decline in the birth rate was gradual and often went unnoticed. Three years later, *Look* magazine rejoiced that the American woman "marries younger than ever, bears more babies and looks and acts far more feminine than the emancipated girl of the 1920s and even '30s." The magazine also applauded women's ability to raise "bumper crops of children."

Homebound in Suburbia

The Baby Boom underwrote a population exodus, especially of middle- and upper-class white Americans, to a new form of residential area, the suburb. City life changed dramatically as residents left urban areas to relocate in outlying communities, which spread in concentric rings around cities and towns. No longer was the city a place in which the affluent both worked and raised a family. Those left behind, the poor and people of color, re-mained full-time urban dwellers. Every weekday at 8 AM, massive numbers of people, typically white males, poured into the city by automobile, bus, and train to report to offices and other workplaces. Meanwhile, white women and children remained "safe at home" in the suburbs, either keeping house or attending school.

On weekends, urban residents and suburbanites led different lives. Ur-ban dwellers used front stoops and streets as places of recreation. Children played basketball in neglected lots or stickball in the street, dodging the passing car when necessary. Such neighborhoods fostered the creation of "gangs" of young adults. Meanwhile, in suburbia, backyards and well-equipped parks provided kids ample recreational areas. Because most subur-ban families had one or two cars, children were shuttled to entertainments and activities in Young Women's and Young Men's Christian Associations, schools and churches, and movie theaters. Problems like youth gangs, alco-hol, and drugs had not yet reached the "burbs."

Because of its relative isolation, suburban living required a commitment on the part of women to home, family, and child-care. A building boom created 1 million new homes a year, each needing decoration, furnishing, and upkeep. In addition, women had to orchestrate family unity. Modern architectural styles reinforced what *McCall's* magazine in 1954 termed "to-getherness." Suburban homes substituted open arches for kitchen walls, a dining "area" for a formal dining room, and a family room for what used to be the parlor. During mealtimes, families increasingly huddled around tele-vision sets, their TV dinners on individual TV tables. In summertime, they adjourned to decks and patios behind their houses. As they barbecued steaks on charcoal grills, they might look across open yards to see their neighbors doing the same thing.

In this system, women ran families. Driving the "second car" that most suburban families found necessary, mothers chauffeured their children from one activity to another. Mothers drove themselves to meetings and to a new phenomenon, the suburban grocery store. There, among long, well-stocked aisles, they selected items from an unprecedented variety of foodstuffs and products, all hauled to the suburbs in huge refrigerated trucks.

Because "housewives" soon became the primary consumers in suburban families—in which women made 75 percent of all purchases—Madison Avenue focused its energies on convincing this new market that domestic consumption offered fulfillment and satisfaction. As one advertising expert pointed out, "The buying of things can provide a sense of identity, purpose, creativity, and self-realization" for women. Ironically, at the same time, advertisements often depicted women as silly or flighty. One of the most successful marketing promotions of the 1950s was Maidenform's "I dreamed I went shopping in my Maidenform bra" campaign. Although a woman founded the company and her daughter took it over, they apparently saw no problem with sponsoring an ad campaign that featured a woman in a grocery store or other venue wearing a Maidenform bra but no blouse.

In some ways, suburban women's lives sounded ideal. In truth, however, a new set of tasks replaced the old one in these women's lives. Although technology had freed them from heavy labor, they now had to select, purchase, and operate a vast array of new "labor-saving" gadgets, including variable-speed, multitask blenders and washing machines and dryers with a plethora of settings. It also fell on women to choose and bring home all the food, clothing, and other household products their family members consumed. Much like pioneer women, suburban women supplied their families with everything they needed. The difference was that suburban women did not spend their time producing domestic goods; instead, they spent their time "shopping" for them and transporting them home in cars. By the end of the 1950s, women's household workload had not declined. On the contrary, it had increased from fifty-two to fifty-four hours per week.

If these women had doubts about their lifestyles, they could turn to a variety of psychological "experts" for advice and reassurance. Such professionals reinforced the importance of modern-day domesticity at every turn. For example, in 1946, psychoanalyst Helene Deutsch insisted that a feminine woman "leaves the initiative to the man, and out of her own needs, renounces originality and experiences her own self through identification." The following year sociologist Marynia Farnham and historian Ferdinand Lundberg published *Modern Woman: The Lost Sex*, which blamed such contemporary problems as world war and economic depression on women having left their homes and families to pursue employment or other endeavors. Clearly antifeminist in tone, this book argued that the "independent woman" was an oxymoron, that no "true" woman could be independent. They further posited that a woman's interest in feminism revealed mental instability. According to these social scientists, only a woman suffering from a psychological disorder would question the rightness and inevitability of male dominance.

During the 1950s, a number of other authors elaborated on the themes of domesticity. In 1952, a book titled *Natural Superiority of Women* emphasized the importance of "mother love" to human development and progress. Its author believed that women's ability to bear and raise children invested them with natural superiority over men. Meanwhile, Dr. Benjamin Spock, whose *Baby and Child Care* reached 1 million readers each year between 1945 and 1960—and continues to sell well in a considerably revised form— reinforced the image of the ideal mother. This woman neither worked outside the home nor left her child for extended periods. Indeed, should a mother feel the need to seek paid employment, Spock advised her to obtain psychological counseling and examine the costs involved in working, notably the deprivation and potential delinquency of her "abandoned" children.

Popular magazines like *Ladies' Home Journal* carried the experts' messages to additional readers. In 1956, a special issue of *Life* chose a thirty-two-year-old mother of four as the ideal American woman, describing her as a wife, hostess, volunteer, and "home manager." Above all, the editors applauded her as a "conscientious mother" who spent "lots of time with her children, helping with their homework and listening to their stories or problems."

Hollywood films also portrayed women as simple and innocent homebodies. Debbie Reynolds and Doris Day were cute and sweet, the ideal "girls-next-door." Even Marilyn Monroe and Elizabeth Taylor combined their sexuality with dependence on men. They were the vamps of the 1920s reborn in modern America, and both of them left a string of broken marriages in their wake. Taylor explained that when she fell in love with a man, she felt compelled to marry him. Much to her disadvantage, she had adopted the dictums of the late 1940s and 1950s.

The new medium of television added images of its own to the mix. Families who appeared on the "small screen" were white and well ordered. From their posts in the kitchen, mothers ran homes efficiently. The ideal number of children was two, a girl and a boy. Of course, this type of family had never been the norm in American society. According to television, however, this unit represented the model that all American families should emulate. Only by watching closely might a viewer note a contradiction. In such television shows as *I Love Lucy*, *Father Knows Best*, and *Leave It to Beaver* supposedly scatterbrained women manipulated their mates and children into doing what they wanted them to do.

Women's fashions also reflected the new "domesticity." Rather than choosing practical clothes, women bought outfits that projected a "feminine" image. In 1947, Christian Dior's "New Look" replaced the mannish, utilitarian styles of the war years. Dior's creations incorporated long, full skirts, defined bustlines, and tiny waists. During the 1950s, the "baby doll" style introduced cinch-belted waists, padded brassieres, and full skirts over crinoline petticoats. Shoes featured pointed toes and heels so high and spindly that they had to be made of steel to avoid breakage. Much like in the "corset" era of the nineteenth century, in postwar America, women were to be alluring and attractive rather than mobile and useful.

Women and Activism

Unsurprisingly, women's organizations declined in strength. During the postwar years, the League of Women Voters and the Consumers League lost members at an alarming rate. In 1947, the Women's Trade Union League disbanded. Nonetheless, the Woman's party, the National Federation of Business and Professional Women's Clubs, and the National Federation of Women's Clubs survived and continued crusading for an Equal Rights Amendment to the Constitution. In 1950 and again in 1953, the Senate adopted equal rights resolutions, yet these groups were unable to push the bills any farther along the legislative route. Americans generally believed that women had all the rights and protection they could possibly want.

In harmony with the back-to-the-home message, women directed their efforts toward local activities. Women spent untold hours engaged in projects related to Parent-Teacher Associations (PTAs), the Young Women's Christian Association (YWCA), churches, and schools. "Women's rights" was a phrase seldom heard anywhere in the land. Nor were politics regarded as worthwhile female pursuits. By the early 1950s, women held less than 5 percent of political offices, from the federal through the local level. In 1952, the Democratic party abolished its Women's Division; leaders explained that they intended to "integrate" women into the party's overall structure. Later that year, the Republican party introduced a similar integration program.

It was evident that women were not expected to question prevailing ideas. Seemingly, the vitality and change generated by female reformers was no longer necessary to the the well being of the nation. Nevertheless, women's activism did not disappear entirely. Women participated in local groups and kept reform traditions and interests alive. These associations involved women in public service and trained them in managerial and leadership skills. At the same time, school and campus organizations opposing the "new" social ills of the postwar years—racial segregation, the proliferation of nuclear weapons, and gross materialism—drew young women into civic re-form at an earlier age and in greater numbers than ever before.

Trouble in Suburbia

The thousands of guidebooks, homemaking articles, and other forms of prodomestic propaganda that appeared during the postwar years indicated that women did not fit easily into prescribed domestic roles. Had domesticity been compelling, women would have no need of books and articles giving them advice on how to achieve happiness.

In truth, many women felt themselves stranded in the suburbs. Not only were they largely cut off from family and kin networks in the "old" neighborhood (in the city), but suburban women lived far from access to public transportation and lacked the time to drive downtown and make it back home before their children returned from school or their husbands returned from work. After their initial fascination with car-pooling and frantic rounds of volunteer and social activities, women found such enterprises less than riveting. Worse yet, women spent their days in domestic achievement only to discover that standards rose with the introduction of each new appliance or soap powder. According to one widespread advertisement, a conscientious woman's laundry had to look "whiter than white" and "brighter than bright." One cake-mix manufacturer removed the eggs from their premade products and added several extra steps to the directions so that women could provide their families with "somethin' lovin' from the oven."

Women also discovered that even though society urged them to perform housework, it demeaned the results of such toil. Regardless of how their kitchen floors shined, their lack of a paycheck put housewives on the bottom rung of an industrial culture that judged people by their earning power. Women began to respond to the question "What do you do?" with the answer, "I'm *just* a housewife."

During the mid-1950s, some college-educated wives and mothers publicly admitted that they felt ill at ease in their domestic roles. As one Barnard College graduate put it: "We stagger through our first years of child-rearing wondering what our values are in struggling to find some compromise between our intellectual ambition and the reality of everyday living."

Some women responded to their disillusionment by seeking paid employment, but because their household incomes were more than adequate, they had trouble justifying their actions. Often they would claim they had gone to work to purchase a better car or to fund a child's college education. In other words, women served as supplementary wage earners. Also, the very consumerism that urged women to stay at home now became the motivation, and the rationale, for them to seek paying jobs. Yet other suburban women acted out their unhappiness by abusing alcohol or prescription medications or by rejecting their spouses. As a result, the rates of alcoholism and divorce rose alarmingly. The national consumption of prescription tranquilizers jumped from virtually none in 1955 to 1.15 million pounds in 1959.

While most Americans, including suburban women, refused to notice these blatant signs of trouble, a few dissenting voices rose to warn people that all was not well in suburbia. One of these was French commentator Simone de Beauvoir who in 1949 published *The Second Sex*. When the book appeared in the United States in 1952, it gained a limited audience, but those who read it began to see the back-to-the-home movement and postwar domesticity as gender prejudice. De Beauvoir questioned why men's experience was deemed normal whereas women had to explain and rationalize their lives. De Beauvoir also revealed the richness of womanhood by exploring the female experiences of motherhood, daughterhood, and lesbianism.

The following year, 1953, sex researcher Alfred C. Kinsey attacked prevailing notions of womanhood in *Sexual Behavior and the Human Female*. After interviewing scores of volunteers, Kinsey and his team prepared a report that shocked the nation. According to Kinsey, women were highly sexual beings. Breaking with conventional wisdom, Kinsey characterized American women as not only sexually active but troubled over their sex lives. With great guilt, women engaged in premarital and extramarital sex. Mired in shame, women explored sexual activities ranging from masturbation and oral sex to lesbian relationships. Kinsey further startled Americans by maintaining that, despite long-held beliefs to the contrary, the possibility of a vaginal orgasm was doubtful. To be fulfilled sexually, women needed more understanding and physical stimulation from their partners.

In the same year the Kinsey report appeared, sociologist Mirra Komarovsky argued in *Women in the Modern World: Their Education and Dilemmas* (1953) that women's supposed lack of accomplishments resulted from their cultural conditioning. Women were not, she said, inferior to men. In interviews with college-educated women, Komarovsky discovered that wives and mothers often felt overwhelmed by the demands of child rearing. They were disenchanted with volunteer activities and envious of their husbands' careers. Komarovsky lacked a solution, however, and perpetuated the view of women as primary caretakers of home and children, with men playing secondary domestic roles as fathers and wage earners.

Many Americans sensed that all was not well with the ideal American woman, yet it did not seem a good time to explore the issue. In addition to other events, war got in the way of reform for women. In June of 1950, President Harry S Truman ordered the U.S. Air Force and Navy to support

South Korean troops against North Korean aggression. Because the Soviet Union backed communist North Korea, U.S. troops were dispatched to a far-off land, of which few Americans had heard, to stop the "Red Menace." With communists as well as the "arms race" clouding America's bright horizon, the problems of suburban women paled by comparison.

Repression of Dissent

Why did women not speak up? Complain? Rebel? Perhaps because it was unwise to criticize anything during the late 1940s and the 1950s. Most white Americans wanted to believe that postwar peace and prosperity had ended the nation's problems, that a female utopia had been achieved. At the same time, the "Cold War" and the Chinese Revolution spread an umbrella of fear of nuclear holocaust across the nation that inhibited people and fostered paranoia toward anything out of the "norm."

As a result of the rabid "Red-baiting" of Senator Joseph McCarthy and his House Un-American Activities Committee (HUAC), Americans developed a phobia regarding communist infiltration in the United States. Always loosely defined, a communist might be anyone, including a feminist or a lesbian. Acting on such fears, the U.S. armed services dismissed lesbians or those rumored as lesbians, and urban police raided lesbian bars.

One Cleveland, Ohio, woman recalled that as a girl she returned from school every afternoon to watch the McCarthy trials on television and to absorb clear messages. Her parents, too, preached a doctrine of repression: be quiet, stay out of trouble, marry well, and establish a happy family. Little wonder that she avoided questioning her teachers, or later her college professors. She refrained from dissent at all costs, only daring to speak out when the postwar mania had finally dissipated.

Another case was that of Helen Gahagan Douglas, a Democrat from California's fourteenth district, who in 1944 gained a seat in Congress. In spite of the mood of fear, Douglas opposed legislation that threatened to undermine Americans' civil liberties. Gaining re-election to the House in 1946 and 1948, she ran for the Senate in 1950. During her senatorial campaign, accusations of being a communist, other smear tactics, and opposition of big business combined to defeat Douglas, who then retired from politics.

During this same time, the film actor Ida Lupino suffered for displaying a feminist attitude. After she tired of playing women in crisis in modern melodramas, Lupino formed in 1949 an independent production company called The Filmmakers, writing, acting in, directing, and producing such films as *Hard, Fast, and Beautiful* (1951), *The Bigamist* (1953), and *The Hitchhiker* (1953). In all these works, Lupino analyzed women as consumers. She also examined women's divisive allegiances to marriage, family, and career. Given the fact that Americans were just beginning to consider such ideas regarding women, it is little wonder that Lupino's characters alienated mainstream critics. Lupino scored high only with feminist and European reviewers.

Beyond Suburbia: The Late 1940s and the 1950s

Employed Women

The postwar notion that the "typical" American woman was a simple, cheerful, and financially secure suburban housewife ignored reality in numerous ways, the primary one being that the majority of American women lived outside domestic ideologies. Even before the problems of suburban white women emerged, most other women had already experienced change and considered its implications for the future.

For one thing, many women who did not have to hold paid employment preferred to do so anyway. Thanks to the postwar economy, jobs were plentiful, and consumerism gave women a reason to earn additional income. Suburban women held jobs ranging from receptionists and clerks to factory operatives. Ironically, although women earned lower wages than men, it was often women's income that allowed families to make a move to the suburbs in the first place.

Second, other women, especially those in urban areas, worked because economic necessity demanded they do so. Thousands of women who lived in poor neighborhoods supported, or helped support, themselves or their families. Still others who were divorced, separated, or deserted worked to survive without the aid of male partners.

Despite the back-to-the-home mentality, the number of employed women grew during the late 1940s and the 1950s. As the base of the national economy began to shift from industry to service, the number of jobs in "women's work" areas like education, social services, clerical, secretarial, and health care increased. This proved a boon for women who had to work and a temptation for those considering paid work. As a suburban woman watched her last child leave for school, she recognized that she had to face each day alone in the house for many years unless she sought outside employment.

Even when their husbands earned good salaries, growing numbers of women sought paid employment, but this group tended to move in and out of the labor force. Bored at home and rationalizing that they needed money for some reason, they took a job. Underutilized, underpaid, and bored at work, they returned home. Soon they repeated the cycle, making it appear that women workers had short attention spans and high attrition rates. In 1956, *Look* magazine described these women, who constituted one-third of the nation's labor force, as people who "work casually . . . as a way of filling a hope chest or buying a new home freezer," adding that these women conceded the top rungs of the job ladder to men.

During the mid- to late-1950s, women escalated their claim that middle-class families had to have two incomes in order to enjoy postwar standards of living. Money was not women's only concern, however. A *Fortune* magazine poll reported that a startling 25 percent of American women would have preferred to have been born male. They expressed a desire to perform wage labor or pursue a career. Instead of regretting leaving their homes, they exulted in the prospect of joining the world of employment.

In 1957, *Life* addressed what it termed the "American Woman's Dilemma." Women faced two options: a husband, home, and family; or a combination of family and paid work. The magazine's writers puzzled over how this could have happened in a society that urged women to remain at home and discouraged their independence and autonomy.

Certainly, women did not gain much financially or in career advancement during these years. Because of the rationale that they worked to "help their families," women sought gender-defined jobs, including clerks, secretaries, or department store salespeople, which offered low pay and little hope of promotion. Women generally failed to gain access to the professional, technical, and managerial fields. Under these circumstances, union hostility against women revived. Once again, union men feared that by accepting low wages, women would depress the earning power of all workers.

Despite these difficulties, during the 1950s the number of women employees grew at a rate four times that of men. In 1950, women accounted for 29 percent of the total work force. By 1959, this figure had jumped to nearly 35 percent. In that year, 40 percent of all women over the age of sixteen held a job, and 30 percent of all married women worked outside the home.

Other trends in women's employment emerged. Increasing numbers of women worked full time. More women continued to work after marriage. And more mothers returned to work after their children entered school—the number of working mothers rose by 400 percent. By the late 1950s, women no longer spent most of their lives doing housework and caring for children. In spite of the back-to-the-home movement, a lifetime devoted to home and family was an exception rather than a rule for American women.

Throughout these developments, the Women's Bureau represented the interests of working women. The Bureau fielded complaints of discrimination in the workplace, demands for equal-pay legislation, calls for the establishment of day-care facilities for the children of working mothers, and protective legislation. In 1955, the Women's Bureau also tackled the problem of reconciling the back-to-the-home movement with the rising numbers of women in the labor force. In that year, at the White House Conference on Effective Uses of Woman Power, Bureau officials aired the legitimate grievances of working women.

One Bureau speaker urged acceptance of women in all occupations. She emphasized that women were "achievement-oriented" individuals who had the right to work. Other speakers advocated an increase in the utilization of the nation's "woman power." Although the conference report declared, "The structure and the substance of the lives of most women are fundamentally determined by their functions as wives, mothers, and homemakers," its very convening marked a subtle shift in governmental policy.

Changes for women had minuses and pluses. On the downside, women workers tended to accept conditions that would hurt later generations of female laborers. Foremost, their acceptance of low wages caused the median income of all female workers to drop. In 1955, women earned 63.9 percent of that earned by men. In 1960, they received only 60 percent of the average wages paid to men. On the positive side, women workers effected meaningful change. By entering the labor force and remaining in it, women challenged traditional notions of just where women's place lay. Americans began to view women as a permanent part of the labor force rather than a temporary or emergency resource.

Rural and Native American Women

Other women who lived outside the back-to-the-home philosophy were those on farms and in rural areas. On backcountry farms, women lived as had their mothers, without such modern conveniences as electricity and indoor plumbing. Many suffered poor health, unemployment, and poverty.

Among these were American Indian women, many of whom lived on reservations scattered throughout the West. After plateauing in the 1920s, the number of American Indian women began to rise in 1950, the rate of increase well outdistancing projected figures. In addition, many women found honor among their tribes as grandmothers and elders. In these roles, Indian women influenced the education and training of young people.

Unfortunately, the nation's postwar prosperity never reached the reservation. Indian women's standard of living remained lamentable. Daily, most suffered scarcity and despair. If they had not already done so, they were under constant pressure to accept Christianity and the exclusive use of the English language. They further endured such policies as involuntary sterilization performed by reservation medical staff. Some even lost their children through forced adoptions by "concerned" white families. It appeared that, in white eyes, Native American women did little right.

The 1950s proved especially disruptive for Native American women. In 1953, the Termination Act cut off a number of tribes from federal assistance. Three years later, the Relocation Act decreased government services to those tribes still under its jurisdiction and encouraged Indians to relocate to urban areas. One Nez Perce woman commented that the government's relocation program "created large urban populations without any sort of support system for that population."

Frequently, urban Indian women faced discrimination, unemployment, and segregated housing. They saw alcoholism and petty crime rates rise among themselves their relatives, friends, and neighbors. Yet the Nez Perce woman explained that she would "continue on anyway." She added that, "I don't feel that discrimination is as rampant as it might have been before." She was anxious to cooperate with other Americans for the survival of the United States as a democratic and powerful nation.

To facilitate such Indian-white cooperation, many Indian women took on the role of cultural broker, telling the Indian's side of the story. In her 1964 autobiography, Polingaysi Qoyawayma, a Hopi woman, revealed the conditions she had faced in her life. On one occasion, reservation officials had forced Hopi girls and women to walk naked through a livestock dipping vat to avert a suspected epidemic. Qoyawayma did not oppose assimilation, but neither did she wish to lose her native culture. Between 1924 and 1954, she taught Hopi children, giving them the government-prescribed instruction in English as well as slipping in Hopi and Navaho language whenever possible.

Other Indian women bridged cultures through art. Potter Maria Montoya Martinez of the San Ildefonso pueblo in New Mexico developed a technique that created distinctive and highly sought-after pottery. After hand-turning clay on a disk made from a gourd, Martinez polished the surface of the pottery with a river stone and painted it with designs based on ancient Indian motifs. She then fired her pots in a kiln alongside cow manure, the burning carbon resulting in a unique silvery black glaze. Martinez's work proved popular and lucrative, helping revive the pueblo economy. Her award-winning pots also fanned interest in Southwestern and Indian art in general. She traveled extensively, teaching other Native women her method and exhibiting her pottery to people who knew little about pueblo cultures.

Even more than Martinez, Osage Indian Maria Tallchief from Oklahoma took her talent on the road to demonstrate to audiences around the world what Indian women could achieve. Tallchief became the first Native American prima ballerina in the United States. Between 1947 and 1960, she performed with the New York City Ballet. Later, she directed the Chicago City Ballet.

Working through different media, these women performed outreach work for Native Americans. On the one hand, these and other women called attention not only to the problems facing Indians, but also to talents that went largely unappreciated and underutilized by the nation. On the other hand, Indian women were unable to break down traditional stereotypes of them as ageless, wise, and at one with nature. In white eyes, such women continued to appear as cookie-cutter versions of Indian women, rather than individuals with different experiences and cultural backgrounds.

Hispanas

Except for some of the middle and upper classes, Hispanas also lived largely outside the suburban myth. During the late 1940s and the 1950s, the majority of Hispanas worked for wages. In California, they labored in the cannery industry under appalling conditions. Working seasonally for low wages, often based on how many "pieces" they processed, they endured gradual speedups on the production line without commensurate pay increases.

Like other groups of women, Hispanas sought innovative solutions. Mothers, daughters, sisters, cousins, and aunts took jobs in the same cannery, persuading employers to hire yet one more family member. Although some saw employment as an avenue to independence, most used it to strengthen family ties. In addition, workers established networks within canneries. Hispanas worked women's departments that were often race-segregated as well. This gave them an opportunity to develop a sense of unity. Because they spoke Spanish and their supervisors spoke English, these women could communicate freely.

Employers soon learned to fear Hispana workers because of what one termed their propensity toward "labor militancy." Hispanas, who composed 75 percent of the work force in California canneries, resented their lack of promotion to supervisory positions. Hispanas, who had a tradition of labor activism, soon made up one-half of the membership of the United Cannery, Agricultural, Packing, and Allied Workers of America (UCAPAWA). Hispanas also served as organizers and strikers. They fought for equal wages, maternity leave, and improved working conditions. In so doing, they not only gained self-esteem, but they had the opportunity to meet and work with women of other racial and ethnic groups.

Hispanas also improved their lot by applying pressure on working men. In a 1950 strike in the New Mexico mines, male workers opposed Empire Zinc Company's wage cuts and unsafe conditions. Women asked that improved housing be included in the demands, but male strikers ranked this a low priority. After the company obtained an injunction forbidding miners from picketing, women took the men's places on the picket line. Even when the company trucked in loads of nonunion workers to break the strike, the women refused to budge. While men ran households, fed children, and cooked meals, women marched with babies in their arms. As police arrested them, the defiant women sang and shouted, which they continued to do as wardens packed them into jail cells. These women demonstrated their importance to labor movements, for their actions convinced men that when women said they needed better housing, they meant it. Perhaps most important, these women had recognized their own power.

In New York City a slightly different pattern developed. There, Puerto Rican women also worked in segregated conditions. They earned woefully inadequate wages as cigar makers, seamstresses, and factory operatives. They too maintained strong family ties and preserved their native culture. More than 90 percent of them continued to speak Spanish at home. Unlike the situation in the Southwest, a number of Puerto Rican women were craftworkers, supervisors, and sales people. Of all groups of workers, however, Puerto Ricans fell disproportionately below the poverty line.

These conditions existed, at least in part, because skilled and craft unions barred Puerto Rican workers, especially women. Union leaders overlooked or ignored Puerto Ricans' strong tradition of labor activism, simply leaving Puerto Ricans to fend for themselves. Lack of union representation was particularly hard on women. Because of death, desertion, separation, and divorce, Puerto Rican women had the highest proportion of female-headed households. These women had to bring home a living wage to support themselves and their children.

Puerto Ricans responded to the dire situation by caring for their own. Fortunately, their culture had a long history of self-help organizations; numerous Puerto Ricans adapted the association model from their homeland to New York City. In 1934, for example, Sister Carmelita established the Casita Maria, an agency that provided social services during the depression, World War II, and the postwar years. Other aid and social organizations such as the Puerto Rico Civic Club sponsored dances and held holiday celebrations. They also supplied meeting places for single people looking for friends and potential spouses.

Disregarding the national fear of anything deemed "socialist" or "communistic," Puerto Rican women spoke up. Sometimes they spoke collectively, sometimes as individuals. Julia de Burgos, who in 1940 left Puerto Rico for New York City, wrote essays and stories, encouraged by the Circle of Ibero-American Writers and Poets (CEPI). Between 1943 and 1945, Burgos worked for *Pueblos Hispanicos*. To this Spanish-language publication, she contributed editorials, news stories, and interviews. Throughout her career, Burgos called for social reform for Puerto Ricans. She especially urged improvement in the living conditions of working-class Puerto Ricans.

Gradually, Burgos became a feminist and poet who used verse to critique the societal restrictions placed on women's lives.

During the late 1940s, Puerto Ricans also formed labor groups. The Puerto Rican postal workers' union, the *Associación de Empleados Civiles de Correo*, implemented work, civic, and social programs. The *Associación* not only grew, but welcomed Puerto Rican women as members. When the group incorporated in 1951, its goals were clear: "To promote friendship and encourage social and intellectual intercourse among veterans born in Puerto Rico employed in the service of the United States of America." The group was large and articulate. Its members had passed civil service exams, including proficiency in two languages. Many of them were college graduates. They drew on their talents to sponsor fund-raising events in support of labor issues, cultural events, and recreational activities.

African American Women

Nor did the back-to-the-home fantasy have much meaning for African American women. For one thing, discriminatory housing policies excluded black women from suburban life. Black women, even those of the middle- and upper-classes, lived in segregated neighborhoods. Some black communities were middle class and included professionals such as doctors and dentists. Most were ghettoes, however, where black women faced poverty, disease, and the possibility of sexual assault as a matter of daily life. In her 1944 novel, *Strange Fruit,* Lillian Smith attacked such racial segregation. Smith, a Southern white woman, told the story of a tragic love affair between a black woman and white man in a small Georgia town. In 1949, Smith's *Killers of the Dream* revealed the determination of the white population of Georgia to preserve segregation and white supremacy.

African American women also spoke out. Like Hispanas, they had a history of activism and were unafraid of the witch-hunt of supposed communists. The work of several contemporary black authors of fiction captured the plight of black women. Ann Petry wrote many short stories and several novels, including *The Street* (1946) and *Country Place* (1947). Petry's talent lay in demonstrating how much the lives of black women differed from those of white women. In *The Street*, which sold 1.5 million copies and received a Houghton Mifflin Literary Fellowship Award in 1946, Petry detailed the decline of Harlem's hard-working, earnest, and honest Lutie Johnson. In *Country Place*, Petry, whose father was a druggist, explored tensions affecting black professionals and their families. Throughout her writings, Petry emphasized the achievements and humanity of black women in America.

Other black women proved assertive in the demand for civil rights. In the great reform tradition established by their mothers and grandmothers,

African American women did not shy away from asking for what their people needed. Charlotta Spears Bass, editor of the *California Eagle*, the largest black newspaper in the state, attacked racial stereotypes in editorials, essays, and speeches. She lambasted the Ku Klux Klan, restrictive housing covenants, and discriminatory hiring practices. During the 1940s, Bass entered local politics. In 1948, she helped found the Progressive party. When running for the vice presidency in 1952, Bass used the slogan: "Win or lose, we win by raising the issue." As a dynamic woman who fought for the civil rights of thousands of African Americans who had migrated to California during both world wars, she helped formulate the themes of what would be the Black Power movement.

Some signs of change did appear during this period. In 1948, the same year the Progressive party organized in California, the state's supreme court allowed a black man and a white woman to marry. Then the court went one step further. It declared California's antimiscegenation law unconstitutional. The four judges who ruled against the law cited the arbitrary nature of racial classifications. They added that prohibiting certain Americans from marrying certain other Americans ran counter to the nation's principles of equality. In this landmark case, the California court had called into question racist laws that had been in place since Reconstruction or earlier. In this sense, the California decision was revolutionary. It would not prove enough, however, to divert the battle over civil rights then emerging in the United States.

Another legal advance came in 1954, with the case of *Brown* v. *Board of Education of Topeka*, in which the United States Supreme Court declared unconstitutional "racial discrimination in public education." When news of the decision reached the public, many white southerners rioted, demanding school closures to thwart integration. Fed-up with the longevity of racial prejudice in the United States, African Americans rose up against their antagonists. Black men and women, including Rosa Parks, Septima Clark, and Bernice Robinson helped generate a black freedom movement.

These women and many other civil rights leaders learned their skills and gained their voices through church membership. They drew on a solid background of black religious values and beliefs. The Baptist and Methodist churches provided activists encouragement, information, money, and places in which to hold meetings. The Roman Catholic Church supported black civil rights as well. Church leaders and individual Catholics had a long-standing interest in organizing interracial efforts to combat social and economic ills. As early as 1933, Dorothy Day had begun the Catholic Worker Movement, a program that established interracial hospitality houses in which black female volunteers worked alongside whites.

During the 1930s, 1940s, and 1950s, black women also helped staff Catholic settlement-type houses from New Orleans to Harlem. Catholic

Interracial Councils, begun during the 1930s, included black women too. After Vatican II changed the Church, and the black civil rights movement changed the United States, black Catholic women assumed leadership roles in both. Again and again, women pointed out that racial prejudice and discrimination were immoral. For all Christians, they maintained, such attitudes defied the commandment to love one's neighbor as one's self.

Another influence on the black civil rights movement was the Highlander Folk School in Grundy County, Tennessee. Begun in 1932 to help industrial and rural workers in Appalachia, Highlander soon became a regional training center for labor organizers and social reformers. In 1944, when Highlander shifted its focus to desegregating the public schools, it attracted black activists. In 1953, Highlander added to its curriculum summer workshops for white and black leaders and educators.

In 1955, Rosa Parks participated in one of Highlander's summer programs. She later recalled, "That was the first time I lived in an atmosphere of complete equality with the members of the other race." After her Highlander summer, Parks returned home, where she was to initiate the legendary Montgomery, Alabama, bus boycott. On that fateful day, Parks refused to give up her seat to a white person and move to the "back of the bus," where "colored" people were required to sit. When black women rallied around Parks, a massive bus boycott resulted. Women, who constituted 56 percent of the black population in Montgomery and regularly used buses to reach their jobs in domestic service, staged a thirteen-month boycott. In observance of the boycott, some women had to walk as many as twelve miles each day. "I'm walking for my children and grand-children," one elderly woman said.

The following year, 1956, Septima Clark lost her teaching job in Columbia, South Carolina, after the state legislature declared that city employees could not belong to civil rights organizations. Because Clark refused to withdraw from the NAACP, she was dismissed. Now Clark became the full-time director of Highlander's workshop program, personally distributing workbooks that included voter registration and other application forms. The books gave information on voting requirements, political parties, taxes, and other civil matters. Through Highlander, Clark directed a citizenship program, and she traveled throughout the South, teaching African Americans how to write and how to vote as informed citizens.

Meanwhile, Bernice Robinson served as the first teacher in the citizenship program that Septima Clark directed. Robinson proved to be an innovative and popular teacher on South Carolina's Sea Island, where she conducted her citizenship-training classes. Before long, she became a civil rights activist in her own right, and her citizenship-training methods spread across the South. Robinson had developed the model for what later became the southern voter education program.

Asian Women

Because of their diversity and increasing numbers, Asian and Asian American women lived on both sides of the back-to-the-home movement. For these women, the late 1940s and the 1950s proved a turning point.

In 1945, Congress passed the War Brides Act, allowing Asian American men and other U.S. citizens to send for war brides, wives, and families they had left behind in Asia. The ensuing migration included thousands of Chinese, Japanese, Filipino, and Korean women. Once in the United States, these women faced numerous difficulties, including learning English and finding jobs. Worst of all was prejudice from white Americans, as well as from other Asians who resented the newcomers.

Also in 1945, the War Relocation Authority (WRA) established a program to release Japanese Americans from such detention camps as Tule Lake in California and Heart Mountain in Wyoming. The following year, the WRA closed all the camps. Despite the government's relocation efforts, detainees returned home to find that their property had been taken over or sold by white "neighbors" and that their assets and investment slates had been wiped clean. Much more devastating was the emotional trauma they now carried. One woman recalled that it took nearly thirty years for her to outgrow "the shame and the guilt and the sense of unworthiness" she felt from the internment experience.

Additional legislation aimed at redressing the injustices done to Japanese Americans by the war-camp program. In 1948, President Harry S Truman signed the Evacuation Claims Act to help former detainees recover some of their losses. Despite Truman's efforts, Japanese Americans recouped only ten cents on each dollar lost. In 1952, the McCarran-Walter Act abolished racial qualifications for citizenship. In 1953 and 1957, Refugee Relief Acts allowed refugees of the Chinese civil war and the Korean conflict to immigrate to America.

The percentage of women among these immigrant groups increased markedly. The male to female ratio among Chinese living in the United States finally stabilized. In 1940, there were 2.9 Chinese men to every 1 woman. In 1950, this had dropped to 1.8 men per woman. In 1960, there were 1.3 Chinese men for each woman. In that year, nearly 40 percent of the 217,000 people of Chinese ancestry living in the United States were women.

Many of these women had been left behind in China by husbands who migrated to the United States. Most never expected to reunite their split families, but they now had the opportunity to do so. In entering the United States, they had to undergo detention and investigation, to which the American Civil Liberties Union and Chinese American groups protested, arguing that the wives of U.S. citizens deserved better treatment. By the late

1950s, the U.S. Immigration Service resolved women's rights of entry at the point of departure in China, making women's entry into the United States relatively easy.

Chinese and other female immigrants settled in Asian communities in New York, Boston, Los Angeles, and San Francisco, in which they found a familiar culture, possibly family members, and support networks. As Asian communities became balanced in gender they grew family oriented. At the same time, Chinatowns and Little Tokyos experienced overcrowding, lack of social services, and job segregation. Asian women labored as seamstresses and tailors, cannery workers, domestic servants, and farm laborers. Others worked in laundries, restaurants, and small businesses. Even those who were able to enter clerical work or technical and professional fields earned less than equally qualified white workers.

The story of Song Zem Ping is representative. At the age of thirteen she had married a Chinese man who later migrated to the United States. After the war, she could migrate only by posing as a war bride, which required her to leave her son behind. When she arrived in the United States, she spoke no English, but she took a job as a seamstress. Although she bore four more children, Song Zem Ping continued to work: "I can still recall the times when I had one foot on the pedal and another one on an improvised rocker, rocking one son to sleep while the other was tied to my back. Many times I would accidentally sew my finger instead of the fabric because one child screamed or because I was falling asleep on the job."

To make their acculturation easier, Asian women had to learn to speak English. Churches and women's groups responded by offering English and vocational classes. Teachers showed Asian women how to wear Western styles of dress and how to cook American food. First-tier immigrants then taught newer arrivals and helped those in need by founding such groups as the Chinese Benevolent Association.

During the 1950s, tensions surrounding the Cold War largely halted Asian migration. Americans' fear of communism led to violent attacks on such groups as the Chinese American Youth Club and the Chinese Workers' Mutual Aid Association. Although some Asians and Asian Americans waited quietly for this hostility to dissolve, others protested this persecution. For instance, Chinese Benevolent Associations launched educational campaigns to convince the American public that, in the words of one of its female leaders, Chinese were "democratic, freedom-loving people" rather than communists.

Many women of Asian heritage were, of course, American-born. They led a different kind of split lives, following Asian customs at home and Western ways in public. Jade Snow Wong's autobiography *Fifth Chinese Daughter* (1945) revealed the tension in these women's lives. She told her parents, "You must give me the freedom to find some answers for myself." Because even the most conservative families recognized the value of education for daughters, more Asian American women attended college than ever before. Among Chinese American women, a larger proportion graduated from college than among white women. In addition, many young Asian women joined the labor force despite continuing discrimination against them.

A few even surmounted the blockades of prejudice to become everything from stage stars to political leaders. In 1946, Ruth Ann Koesun, the first woman of Asian heritage to become a prima ballerina, joined the American Ballet Theatre, where she soloed for the next twenty-three years. Yet other women played an active role in public life, such as holding elected seats on local school boards.

Most Asian women's social lives continued to center on their own communities. In California's Chinatowns, for example, women formed such organizations as the Oakland Waku Auxiliary. This group sponsored women's sporting events, including basketball, volleyball, and softball. Beginning in 1958, Chinatown boosters sponsored Miss Chinatown contests. A number of individual families held debutante balls so their daughters could properly enter Chinese American society. In their desire to assimilate to their adopted culture, these women and their families copied white society. It was a way to achieve a feeling of belonging in an often inhospitable country.

Other Asian American women, especially those of the middle and upper classes, moved to white urban neighborhoods or out to the suburbs. Thus relocated, these women missed the support they had known in their ethnic enclaves. Furthermore, they resented the marginal positions they held in their newly adopted communities. One Chinese woman who grew up in a white section of Brooklyn, New York, during the 1950s remembered: "I felt very lonely when I grew up. We were simply not like the other people in the neighborhood." Another Chinese woman living in Mississippi concurred: "We were made fun of all the time. . . . We had to meet certain expectations that our parents wanted of us and at the same time, deal with those who could not totally understand us."

In a sense, these women had sacrificed their ethnic identity, yet they were not allowed to assimilate fully into the broader American culture. Even though unmarried women had to accept mates of their parents' choosing, they had to honor parents' wishes that they marry Asian men. By now, most antimiscegenation laws had been repealed, and approximately one-fourth of Asian American men married outside their racial-ethnic group. Although the men intermarried frequently, Asian American women were not expected to do so.

Competent Women of the 1960s

The year 1960 marked the beginning of a unique decade in American history. In February, a sit-in movement erupted after four black college students took seats at a "whites-only" Woolworth lunch counter in Greensboro, North Carolina. When they refused to vacate the seats, a riot nearly occurred. That fall, the boyish and charismatic John F. Kennedy defeated Richard M. Nixon for the presidency of the United States. For a time after Kennedy's inauguration in 1961, young Americans believed that all things were possible.

For women, opportunities abounded. The nation's switch to a service industry created more jobs for women. Improved technology allowed women to handle more and heavier jobs. And women were determined to enter or reenter the labor force despite social expectations to the contrary.

Rather than encouraging women to stay home, a variety of commentators discussed ways in which women could combine homemaking and work. The director of the Women's Bureau remarked, "Today's homemaking chores are no great challenge" to women. She added that women's "sense of frustration is likely to heighten after children go to school and there is even less need for her in the home."

Researchers and sociologists, too, argued that women should work. After all, they said, employed women exercised a greater role in family decision making and fostered greater self-reliance in their children. Research showed that working mothers were less protective of and more confident in their children than were nonworking women. In 1965, one prominent sociologist asserted, "Employment emancipates women from domination by their husbands, and secondarily, raises their daughters from inferiority to their brothers." In his view, "the male-dominated, female-serviced family is being replaced by a new symmetry."

Obviously, attitudes toward women were undergoing change. By 1960, Americans no longer harbored fears regarding the disruption of homes and families during World War II. At the same time, the discontentment of women—especially white, educated, middle-class women—gained recognition. Various media commented on women's dual role as wife/mother and worker. The continuing education movement turned its attention to training women.

President's Commission on the Status of Women, 1961

During John F. Kennedy's 1960 presidential campaign, approximately 6 million women worked on his behalf. Young women saw him as a messiah.

One alienated her anti-Catholic father, who called the Roman Catholic Kennedy "the Pope's candidate," by voting for JFK.

Once Kennedy achieved the presidency, he was unable to appoint a female cabinet member as he had promised, so he tried to make up for this breach of faith in another way. In 1961—several years before a revitalized feminist movement flared up in America—President Kennedy created the President's Commission on the Status of Women. At the urging of Democratic party women and the Women's Bureau, he appointed Eleanor Roosevelt as the Commission's chairperson.

Two years later, the Commission presented a sixty-page report on its deliberations. This included the Commission's endorsement of improved access to education for all women, and aid and child-care services for working mothers. The report also supported equal employment opportunities, a wider role for women in government, and equality of rights under the law (preferably under the existing Fifth and Fourteenth Amendments rather than under the proposed ERA). The report also asked for continuing governmental action on behalf of women, a recommendation that led President Kennedy to establish the Interdepartmental Committee on the Status of Women and the Citizens' Advisory Council on the Status of Women.

While the Commission's findings were somewhat conservative, they had widespread influence. The Commission's deliberations helped initiate a national debate on women's issues. In time, every state established a commission on the status of women. Furthermore, the federal government had committed itself to a comprehensive policy of reform for women. Kennedy hoped to do more for women than simply appointing a few to office, as the Truman and Eisenhower administrations had done.

The Equal Pay Act of 1963, recommended by the Commission on the Status of Women, further demonstrated the resolve of the Kennedy administration. This act attacked a long-term problem, one traceable to the early years of the industrial revolution in the United States. The Equal Pay Act, the first major federal legislation concerning women's employment since the Progressive Era, required that employers pay equal wages to women and men who performed jobs requiring equal skill and effort.

The long-awaited Equal Pay Act proved less effective than women had hoped, however. The U.S. Labor Department attempted to enforce its provisions by making routine workplace inspections and taking specific complaints, but the act's wording was unclear as to what constituted "equal skill." In addition, the law did not apply at all to women who performed specialized "women's work" at lesser pay.

Women and Civil Rights

The cause of working women was not the only one on the reform docket. During the early 1960s, the civil rights movement became a stirring crusade. To some observers, the movement seemed inevitable. Demographers had often remarked on the growing numbers of African Americans, Hispanics, and Asian Americans among the U.S. population. During World War II, with jobs plentiful and well-paying, members of these groups saw firsthand how white people lived and realized the full weight of the restrictions on their lives. Consequently, women and men of color objected to unequal limits on their political, civic, and social rights.

The civil rights movement burst out on two fronts simultaneously: among Hispanics and among African Americans. Of course, Hispanics had long been activists in the areas of employment and social ills. In multipurpose organizations they had worked for political, economic, social, and cultural improvements. For years they had watched their people suffer exclusion from white-dominated labor unions. Furthermore, discriminatory poll taxes, literacy tests for voting, voter residency requirements, and gerrymandering kept Hispanics from the polls and reduced their political influence.

The emerging Hispanic civil rights movement received little exposure in the national media. Because its leaders were Puerto Ricans in New York City and Hispanics in the Southwest, white Americans dismissed this protest. This was shortsighted. During the post–World War II years Hispanics in New York and the Southwest grew more politically oriented. In Texas, the League of United Latin American Citizens (founded in 1929) encouraged the formation of other activist groups. During the 1950s, the League worked to desegregate movie theaters, restaurants, and other public facilities.

Because of the lack of media attention, Hispanas had to speak for themselves. During the 1960s, a Hispanic Renaissance encouraged artists, musicians, and writers. The work of female writers almost shouted with pride. These female authors celebrated their combined Indian and Spanish ancestry and explored contemporary problems like urban living.

Other women raised their voices for civil rights. Dolores Huerta exercised particular influence. In 1960, Huerta participated in the Viva Kennedy campaign. She assisted the newly formed Community Service Organization (CSO) in registering Hispanic voters. She also went to Sacramento to lobby the California legislature for CSO programs. Her demands included the right to register voters door to door, to offer drivers' license examinations in Spanish, and to provide disability insurance for California's migrant farm workers. In 1962, Huerta helped Cesar Chavez organize the National Farm Workers Association (NFWA), for which she recruited women as members. She also helped with policy-making and public relations—to her, these areas were "the creative part of the organization." She not only joined picket lines herself, but she recruited other female marchers. In fields and towns, Huerta delivered fiery speeches, usually in Spanish but sometimes in English. And she never stopped lobbying the California legislature. Her energy and activity mark the beginning of Hispanas' critical role in the farm labor union movement. Certainly, Huerta established a new style for other Hispanas to imitate.

Meanwhile, a Chicano student movement emerged, which included groups such as La Raza Unida Party, the Crusade for Justice (which involved middle- and upper-class college and university students), United Mexican American Students, and the Mexican American Youth Organization. Typically, these young people's groups protested housing and health care discrimination, police brutality, substandard education, and unemployment. Although women initially filled traditional "helper" roles in these organizations, they soon demanded their own place in them and in the movement in general.

At the same time, African Americans took similar steps. Because waves of migration of southern blacks to northern and western cities had created communities, black Americans lived together and shared common grievances. Among them were women writers who revealed the African American cause to a larger public.

As the first black female playwright to see her work produced on Broadway, Lorraine Hansberry opened many eyes. During its first Broadway run in 1958–59, *A Raisin in the Sun* related to audiences of many races the story of a proud black family struggling against whites attempting to keep them out of the neighborhood. The play not only won the New York Drama Critics' Circle Award as best play of the season but contributed to a rising awareness of the problems black Americans faced. Hansberry, who supported civil rights, said over and over that black people lived "in a hostile circumstance in the United States." In her view, African Americans had "a great deal to be angry about."

In 1960, poet Gwendolyn Brooks, the winner of a Pulitzer Prize in 1950, echoed such sentiments. Living and writing in her home area on the South Side of Chicago, Brooks depicted brave, hopeful women who endured the difficulties of being black in postwar America. In one of her best-known works, an anthology of poems called *The Bean Eaters* (1960), her portrayal of the African American community was a powerful, sometimes bitter, one. A sought-after speaker, Brooks toured, reading her work in diverse places, ranging from bookstores to prisons. By the mid-1960s, she addressed such issues as black pride and black power.

The time was ripe for a black civil rights movement. Northern blacks had numerous complaints, but southern blacks had even more. The civil rights movement came out of the South for several reasons. Although the plantation economy was dead, vestiges of plantation society remained. African Americans in the South still had to defer to white people and remain on their side of the Jim Crow line. By the 1960s, black southerners were fed-up with shuffling for white folks.

The arrest in 1960 of the four black students who "sat-in" at the segregated Woolworth's lunch counter in Greensboro, North Carolina, inspired similar actions all over the South. African Americans also organized Freedom Rides, during which black protestors rode interstate transportation that ordinarily denied them passage. Thousands of Americans exchanged apathy for concern. Young African Americans rose up and gained inspiration and support from the 1960s white youth who believed in John F. Kennedy and his promise to change the nation. Like Kennedy, the nation's young people wanted to participate in civic affairs. They listened to, and repeated among themselves, his famous summons: "Ask not what your country can do for you. Ask what you can do for your country."

Kennedy's appeal diminished somewhat, however, in 1961, when the president dispatched to Vietnam four hundred Special Forces soldiers and one hundred military advisers. He then authorized clandestine warfare against North Vietnam. In response, American women and men, especially the young, protested. Hundred of marchers carried placards opposing the nation's involvement in the affairs of the Southeast Asian Country. At the same time, other people picketed for civil rights legislation, meaning concrete governmental assurance of equal opportunities regardless of race, gender, or ethnicity.

Throughout these events, the nation's women lacked a feminist consciousness. Black women believed they had to deal with racial problems before addressing gender issues. During the early 1960s, black women found themselves burdened with a range of social problems, including marital instability. As a result, the number of female-headed households increased. In addition, the black illegitimacy rate soared. In 1940, it had stood at 17 percent. By 1960, it reached 29 percent. During the 1960s, 58 percent of black women, many of them heads of household, held paid employment outside their homes.

To help themselves and their families, black women remained active in churches, which trained and positioned them as activists at a crucial moment in history. Fannie Lou Hamer, for example, went from singing gospel hymns to organizing voter registration drives in 1962. Hamer worked for the Mississippi Freedom Democratic Party (MFDP), even giving a televised speech to the 1964 Democratic National Convention in Atlantic City, New Jersey. Although she unsuccessfully opposed a white male candidate for a congressional seat in 1964, for the rest of her life, Hamer remained active in the fight for civil rights.

Other black women participated in civil rights associations, social service organizations, and the last Highlander summer workshop in 1961. Although the Tennessee state court revoked Highlander's charter in that year, the school had done its job. It had produced people who went on to lead sit-ins, Freedom Rides, and other protests throughout the South during the 1960s.

In spite of women's involvement in the Southern Christian Leadership Conference (SCLC) and the Student Nonviolent Coordinating Committee (SNCC), they remained subordinate to male leaders in these organizations. SNCC leader Stokely Carmichael went so far as to say, "The only position for women in our movement is prone." Sadly, he and others had overlooked the very real achievements of the women who surrounded them. For instance, SNCC board of directors' member Septima Clark not only assisted southern blacks in challenging the denial of voting rights, but she had helped organize the SNCC in the first place!

Carmichael and other male activists also failed to recognize that women had learned a great deal through the civil rights movement. Women had acquired a language that described oppression and advocated revolt. They had grasped the strategy and techniques of organization. And they had begun to see themselves as objects of discrimination. Because of their independence, black women experienced frustration when civil rights leaders offered them a heightened sense of self-worth on the one hand and forced them into traditional sex roles on the other. Too many of black women's male colleagues expected them to make coffee, serve doughnuts, and provide other domestic services. Black men ignored the gender prejudice they perpetuated even as they decried race-based forms of discrimination.

Naturally, activist women had no interest in being men's servants; women wanted to join in writing pamphlets, making speeches, and marching in protest. Cynthia Washington, an engineering student who joined SNCC in 1963, rose to leadership positions and became director of a freedom project in Mississippi. She had observed firsthand the limitations placed on women workers in many parts of the civil rights movement. She was annoyed that white women, who crossed color lines to fight for civil rights, were treated by men as lesser beings. Washington listened to, and encouraged, these women to take up the mantle of civil rights for women of all races.

In 1964, the first written analysis of sexism in the civil rights movement appeared. In it, white activist Casey Hayden charged the SNCC with rampant paternalism: "Assumptions of male superiority are as widespread and deep rooted and every bit as crippling to the woman as the assumptions of white supremacy are to the Negro." Other protests followed. Right in front of male civil rights leaders' eyes, disgruntled women became feminists.

During the "freedom summers" of 1964 and 1965, 650 northern white women went south to work for civil rights. They confronted a movement that defined oppression and equality in terms of race and class rather than gender. Working within the Congress on Racial Equality (CORE), the SCLC, and the SNCC, women demanded that their interests and abilities, rather than their gender, determine their job assignments. Nevertheless, they were seldom asked to participate in policy decisions and they were often the recipients of unwelcome sexual advances.

In 1965, white freedom fighters Casey Hayden and Mary King left the civil rights movement, but not before addressing a memorandum to black women workers that expressed the following hope: "Perhaps we can start to talk with each other more openly than in the past and create a community of support for each other so we can deal with ourselves and others with integrity and can therefore keep working."

Perhaps Hayden and King left too soon, for 1965 proved a turning point. In that year, the U.S. Congress approved the Voting Rights Act, ensuring black men's and women's right to vote. This action encouraged the black power movement and feminism, especially black feminism.

The Feminine Mystique

Even though it may appear that the black civil rights movement developed before feminism, it is more likely that the former was simply more visible. Certainly, the civil rights movement helped raise all women's awareness, politicized women, and legitimized women's actions and claims. Yet, feminism emerged in its own right during the early 1960s.

In 1961, writer Tillie Olsen set the tone. Her first novella, *Tell Me a Riddle,* demonstrated that women carried limits in their lives into their writing and other forms of expression. Born in 1913, Olsen explained that she did not write sooner because, "In the twenty years I bore and reared my children, usually had to work on a paid job as well, the simplest circumstances for creation did not exist." In "I Stand Here Ironing," Olsen presented a touching narrative of her feelings as a writer. In 1961, Olsen won the O. Henry Award for literature.

Two years later, a young Jewish woman coalesced the emerging feminist movement with the release of a seminal book, *The Feminine Mystique.* Its author, Betty Friedan, had graduated from Smith College and received a fellowship to the University of California at Berkeley to study psychology. But, like many other women of her era, she withdrew from the program and married. For years, she alternated work with marriage and childbearing. When her second pregnancy led to her dismissal at work, Friedan retreated into a suburban home on New York's Long Island. Rather than finding contentment in suburbia, she experienced a vague but pressing lack of fulfillment. Curious if her peers could relate, during the late 1950s, she sent a questionnaire out to other Smith College graduates. Her findings revealed a similar unrest among other women like her, a feeling that Friedan labeled "the problem that has no name."

In *The Feminine Mystique*, Friedan reported on her findings and described "the problem that has no name" as "a strange stirring, a sense of dissatisfaction, a yearning that women suffered in the middle of the twentieth century in the United States." She added that a vague discontent gnawed at wives and mothers who supposedly lived "happy" and "fulfilled" lives. Furthermore, they felt guilty and ill at ease about having these feelings. "What kind of a woman was she if she did not feel this mysterious fulfillment waxing the kitchen floor?" Friedan asked. "She was so ashamed to admit her dissatisfaction that she never knew how many other women shared it." Friedan concluded that women needed to add other pursuits to "occupation housewife" and the "comfortable concentration camp" of the home.

Friedan also attacked the ideas of psychiatrist Sigmund Freud, objecting to his theory of "penis envy," which held that women felt dissatisfied because they were physically lesser than men. Friedan disliked Freud's tendency to stereotype women according to gender expectations, pointing out that he used men to establish norms, then posited that women wanted to act and feel like the norm. There was, Friedan argued, so much more to women than how they related to men. She issued a call to action.

Thousands of women heeded Friedan's call. One of the most effective and visible of these was New York attorney Bella Abzug. Abzug, who had championed defendants during the sinister McCarthy anticommunist trials of the 1950s, now gave legal advice to civil rights workers. In 1964, Abzug assisted the passage of civil rights legislation. The following year she helped pass the Voting Rights Act. Throughout the 1960s, Abzug lobbied for the Women's Strike for Peace and supported nuclear disarmament. Colorful and outspoken, Abzug often called men to task for their deeds and urged women onward in their fight for equality.

White southern women emerged as feminists as well. Across the region college-age women joined picket lines and helped black and white women register to vote, occasionally landing in jail for their efforts. Older women, often professionals, lobbied state legislatures and spoke publicly about the discrimination that limited their lives. At this time in North Carolina, a state law required a married woman to present a signed release from her husband to sell her own property. In most other southern states, women could not secure credit or home loans. As late as 1968, a female legislator in Mississippi obtained for women the right to sit on juries. One southern woman objected to being assigned "the legal status of a child." Another opposed what she called "protective custody." She added that women "do not need any special protection . . . or law that treats us differently from other citizens."

Everywhere in the nation, white women and those of color raised their voices, protesting gender prejudice. In scouring history to find female idols, feminists rediscovered Emma Goldman. Hailing Goldman as "Red Emma" for the communist sympathies she refused to disavow to avoid her deportation in 1919, feminists took her as a symbol. Young or old, white or black, feminists put Emma Goldman's likeness on everything from tee-shirts to buttons and coffee cups. Like Goldman, the emerging feminists defied authority and demanded reform.

Affirmative Action

One early result of contemporary feminism was affirmative action programs, mandating the hiring of women and people of color. In 1964, the U.S. Congress passed Title VII of the Civil Rights Act. This legislation prohibited racial discrimination on many fronts, as well as discrimination by employers on the basis of race or gender. Employment agencies and labor unions also fell within Title VII guidelines. To enforce these provisions, the act created an Equal Employment Opportunity Commission (EEOC).

The Office of Federal Contract Compliance (OFCC) enforced these regulations through fifteen different departments and compliance agencies that conducted periodic reviews. Nonetheless, the OFCC had a small staff and limited funding, and its ability to enforce Title VII provisions fell short. The agency showed its weakness by reprimanding few employers. Furthermore, it received widespread criticism when it exercised what many Americans viewed as preferential treatment on behalf of people of color and women.

Senator Everett Dirksen of Illinois remarked that Title VII was Congress's attempt to "remake the social pattern of this country," yet the EEOC had more power in theory than in practice. Women activists urged the EEOC to take seriously the ban on gender discrimination, yet affirmative action remained problematic because of the difficulty of enforcing its principles.

Backlash and Antifeminism

Opponents of feminist goals argued that if the American family were to survive, women must remain domestic and maternal. Although the nation's high divorce rate had temporarily plateaued, antifeminists pointed to divorce as a warning sign of the demise of the "American family," that is, the traditional patriarchal family. Indeed, this traditional family was disappearing, to be replaced by different and, according to feminists, more democratic forms.

Generally, antifeminists attracted a cohort composed of political and religious fundamentalists. Women like Phyllis Schlafly and Mirabelle Morgan built careers around campaigns to send women back to the home. Ironically, they utilized trademark feminist techniques, including public-speaking tours, petitions, and lobbying campaigns, to advance what they called "profamily" messages. They especially pointed to the growth of "displaced homemakers," that is, women without saleable job skills who were divorced yet unable to support themselves. The existence of these women, antifeminists claimed, was proof that American women must resume their maternal "destiny," meaning a domestic and subordinate role within the family.

Women's Lives: The Early 1960s

Consumerism

During the early 1960s, consumerism reached a new peak. Based on a seemingly insatiable desire for innovative fashions, novelty items, and new technology, consumerism spurred the U.S. economy. Manufacturers tried to anticipate women's patterns, creating household products that women did not yet know they wanted. In cooperation with corporate America, Madison Avenue advertising agencies launched campaigns encouraging women to buy such things as electric shoe polishers and can openers.

A contradiction became apparent. Women as consumers played a critical role in the U.S. economy, yet advertising routinely used patronizing and sexist themes to attract them. Advertising firms viewed women as easily manipulated and gullible purchasers who would, and often did, buy anything. Nonetheless, many women were well aware of their power as consumers and, like colonial women two hundred years earlier, boycotted certain goods to punish companies for social as well as political reasons. One woman who grew up during the 1960s remembered that her mother avoided fad-fashions and refused to buy polyester pantsuits. When feminist leaders pointed out examples of sexist advertising or exposed a manufacturer as a polluter of the environment, additional women turned against the American marketplace.

Sex

During the early 1960s, the so-called sexual revolution was well underway. As diaphragms and birth-control pills became available, recreational sex became less problematic. As the number of "crisis" pregnancies declined, Americans talked a great deal about the "new morality" and "free love."

In the ensuing quest for "better" sex, experts rejected the vagina as a source of orgasm for women. Instead, they identified the clitoris as the orgasmic center. Even writers of anatomy textbooks took note and changed their emphasis. More revolutionary yet, sex researchers recommended masturbation as a substitute for or a supplement to sex. They also claimed that women could experience sexual pleasure with men or women. The tenets that nineteenth-century Americans had idealized, notably the avoidance of masturbation and homosexuality, were turned upside down.

Lesbianism emerged as a public issue. As early as 1955, eight San Francisco women had founded the first lesbian organization, the Daughters of Bilitis (DOB). Named after the erotic poem "Songs of Bilitis," DOB sounded like a traditional woman's club, yet offered a code name to attract lesbians. By 1960, DOB membership included 110 women. DOB chapters existed in such urban centers as Los Angeles, Chicago, and New York City. The association issued a bimonthly newsletter called the *Ladder*, emphasizing lesbian rights. DOB used public education to achieve civil rights and an improved image for lesbians. The organization also provided speakers for radio and television, high schools and colleges, and clubs.

Many Americans could not easily accept lesbianism, or, for that matter, anything contrary to traditional beliefs regarding gender. In the United States, people were expected to behave in harmony with their gender. In cases of children born with amorphous genitalia, Western culture assigned them one gender or the other for their upbringing. Other cultures made very different choices. In some, infanticide settled the problem. In others, such as India, where a caste system was in place, special rank and rules of behavior accrued to hermaphroditic children. Some Native American peoples revered those who were different physically, practiced cross-gender dressing, or established homosexual relationships. But because Western, Christian culture opposed such practices, American society expected all children to assume one gender or the other, and thereafter to adhere to the "rules."

While many Americans hoped the issue would just go away, lesbians grew more militant. During the early 1960s, new, more-assertive and proactively feminist lesbian groups appeared. Opposing what some called "compulsory heterosexuality," some lesbians formed communities and established support networks. These groups demonstrated that lesbianism involved more than sexual rights: it involved civil rights as well. In other words, lesbians demanded public discussion of a long-hidden issue. In turn, the debate provided an important antecedent for the later gay rights movement.

Courtship, Marriage, and Divorce

During the 1960s, formal dating lessened; single people pursued activities in groups. Sex became "casual" and many couples "lived together" out of wedlock. Yet, at the same time, marriage rates rose. In spite of their social activism, young people seemed committed to the institution of marriage.

In 1964, birth rates began to decline, marking the end of the so-called Baby Boom. Americans wanted fewer children for a number of reasons. In the atmosphere of the tense cold war between the United States and the USSR, some refused to produce offspring whom they feared might suffer through nuclear war. Others felt they could not afford the rising cost of raising and educating a child. Yet others wanted to combine child-raising with nondomestic pursuits.

In 1965, a landmark case established Americans' right to practice birth control. In *Griswold* v. *Connecticut* the Supreme Court considered the situation of Planned Parenthood officials who had been arrested and fined for defying Connecticut laws that banned birth-control devices and prohibited the distribution of birth-control information. In its ruling, the Court declared Connecticut's birth-control law unconstitutional; it also established citizens' right of privacy in matters of marital intimacy. Justice William O. Douglas set an important precedent when he ruled for the protected nature of the "intimate relation of husband and wife."

Meanwhile, Americans resumed their tendency to divorce. After remaining fairly constant between 1955 and 1963, the rate of divorce continued its ascent. The incidence of divorce remained higher in urban areas than in rural ones. Regionally, the West had the highest divorce rate; the South rose to second place; and the Northeast dropped to third. African Americans suffered the highest rate of divorce of all racial groups, but divorce among Roman Catholic Hispanics was on the rise. Divorce increased among women employed outside the home as well as mothers with children still at home. In short, divorce affected virtually every American either directly or indirectly through a friend, relative, or colleague.

Supporters of divorce pointed out that the divorce rate was not as threatening as it appeared. They noted that divorce statistics appeared high because modern-day statisticians could provide more-detailed data. In addition, the number of divorces was inflated by people who obtained multiple divorces as well as by those who sought a divorce rather than simply deserting their spouses, as had their forebears. Finally, the fact that people were living longer led couples to divorce rather than wait for the death of a spouse.

Still, women clearly demanded more from marriage than had their mothers and grandmothers. Because so many women worked, either part-time or full-time, they were less economically dependent on husbands. In 1963, one observer maintained that the high divorce rate was an inevitable result of "the emancipation of women—economic, legal, sexual, and intellectual."

Popular Culture

A number of fads characterized the early 1960s. The relaxed "hippie" culture spread over the nation, along with marijuana smoking, hitchhiking,

communal living, and the music of the counterculture. In the matter of attire, both young women and men favored blue jeans, work shirts, combat
boots, and beads. When young men began to look like women by wearing
sandals and long hair, conservative Americans complained. Undaunted,
youths replied that Jesus had favored sandals and long hair too.

In this era of protest and transition, films and other forms of popular
culture sent mixed messages to women. For the most part, popular women's
magazines continued to underwrite the feminine mystique by depicting
white suburban housewives as living ideal lifestyles. One of the few dissenting voices was that of Helen Gurley Brown, editor of *Cosmopolitan*. In
1962, Brown's *Sex and the Single Girl* had been a smash hit. Beginning in
1965, Brown led "Cosmo," as she liked to call it, to a new frankness.
Through Cosmo, Brown supported the sexual revolution as well as women's
participation in the workplace. Cosmo held wide appeal for young women,
single and married, and the magazine's sales and advertising income soared.

Generally, images of women in magazine and newspaper cartoons remained mixed. Female stereotypes included the wild spender, the emotional
wreck, and the shameless gossip. There was also the reckless driver and the
well-meaning dimwit, a woman unable to grasp politics or current events.
Cranky mothers-in-law and sexy, air-headed secretaries were also favorite
targets. In one cartoon, a boss remarked to his secretary as she left the office
on a Friday afternoon: "Nice going, Miss Hamblin. You certainly put in a
full day's work this week!" At the same time, however, Blondie continued to
boss Dagwood around, and Superwoman and Wonder Woman fought their
way through "masculine" adventures.

In Hollywood films, a similar contradiction existed. Although Marilyn
Monroe entered a mental hospital in 1961 and the following year committed suicide, her sex-kitten image lived on. American men viewed Monroe as
a dream lover. Author Norman Mailer described her as "The sweet angel of
sex . . . so gorgeous, forgiving, humorous, compliant and tender that even
the most mediocre musician could relax his lack of art in the dissolving
magic of her violin."

Meanwhile, other Hollywood women avoided creating the Monroe
myth. Katharine Hepburn was one of the most admired and independent
movie stars ever. During the 1960s, Hepburn earned Best Actress Academy
Awards for *Guess Who's Coming to Dinner* (1967) and *The Lion in Winter*
(1968). On screen, Hepburn played strong women who were ornery and
smart. Off screen, she provided a model for American women who disliked
the limitations of traditional female roles.

Hollywood also vacillated on film portrayals of women of color. These
characters were usually sexy and strong. Not unlike Monroe, Nancy Kwan
played a clever but submissive prostitute in *The World of Suzie Wong* (1960).

In other media, Asian women came across as diabolical. In the "Terry and the Pirates" and the "Steve Canyon" series, comic books presented the evil Dragon Lady.

In other cases, women of color rose above their roles to appear assertive and smart. For her role in *Carmen Jones* (1954), Dorothy Dandridge became the first black woman to earn an Academy Award nomination as Best Actress. As Bess in *Porgy and Bess* (1959), she won the Golden Globe Award for best actress in a musical. Although Dandridge tried to develop independence and autonomy in her professional and personal life, she found her acting parts and private activities limited by gender as well as race prejudice. In one of her last films, *Malaga* (1962), Dandridge once again played a love scene with a white man who was not allowed to kiss her (for fear of offending theater audiences). Such racist attitudes had cost Dandridge big parts. For example, when she was sought out for the major role of black temptress Cleopatra, the director's choice was overruled by the studio heads in favor of a white woman, Elizabeth Taylor. In 1965, Dandridge died from an overdose of antidepressants.

The contradictions also appeared in popular music. On the one hand, such singers as Barbra Streisand followed the Broadway musical theater tradition. Although Streisand made the transition from popular recording artist to film actor and director, she appeared feminine and sensual on the big screen, even in the gutsy roles she played, as Fanny Brice in *Funny Girl*, and in *Yentl*. In Los Angeles, the Hollywood Palladium featured such talented and "womanly" singers as Celia Cruz and Nita Cruz. Meanwhile, Aretha Frank-lin and Diana Ross developed the more mellow music of "soul." On the other hand, rock star Janis Joplin gained fame for her hard-driving, flamboyant performances as well as her self-destructive lifestyle. Finally, singer Joan Baez played a significant role in the rediscovery of folk music that characterized the early 1960s. She utilized this music in a political way, to protest various forms of oppression and violence. Active in civil rights and the protest against U.S. involvement in Vietnam, Baez built her reputation on such songs as "Where Are You Now, My Son?" and "Carry It On."

Sports were the one area in which women clearly excelled. From playing paddle tennis on the streets of Harlem, Althea Gibson progressed to being the first black player in the American Lawn Tennis Association championships. In 1957 and 1958, Gibson won at Wimbledon and Forest Hills, respectively, and was named Woman Athlete of the Year in both years. In 1960, Gibson won the world professional tennis championship, opening a previously white-dominated sport to women of color.

Women athletes also pushed for reform. Such groups as the Unified Golf Association worked for further racial integration in women's sports.

The Olympic Games proved especially receptive to integration, with athletes of many racial and ethnic backgrounds not only competing on the same U.S. teams but taking home gold and silver medals.

Professional Women

During the early 1960s, American women increasingly obtained higher education. As they applied for medical and law schools, they challenged quotas on female students. They also earned a growing number of Ph.D.s, especially in the humanities. In 1960, the number of professional women had increased by 41 percent over the 1940 number. Yet women fell short of gaining full professorships and administrative posts. Because most Americans still viewed professions suitable for women as extensions of domestic duties, women remained clustered in teaching and nursing; such professional segregation underwrote lower pay and fewer opportunities for promotion to top-level positions.

Women were expected to leave their jobs when they married. One young college graduate seeking employment in 1960 recalled that the school superintendent who interviewed her first checked with her student-teaching supervisor regarding her marriage plans. Reassured that she was not engaged, he hired her. She left the position within two years anyway—to attend graduate school where she earned an M.A. and a Ph.D.

This portrayal of the conflicting forces on women's lives in no way suggests that women achieved little or nothing during the postwar years. Despite the back-to-the-home movement and the contradictory messages of the early 1960s, women excelled in many fields. Maria Goeppert Mayer, for example, became the first woman to receive the Nobel Prize for theoretical physics. In 1963, Mayer's work in nuclear physics not only gained her the Nobel Prize, it helped the United States enter the nuclear age.

Another leading figure was Hannah Arendt, a German Jew who migrated to the United States in 1940 and became a significant postwar intellectual. Between 1949 and 1952, Arendt served as the research director for the Jewish Cultural Reconstruction and later its executive secretary. Arendt helped reassemble Jewish writings dispersed by the Nazis. Later, she entered academia and became the first woman appointed as full professor at Princeton University. By the late 1950s and early 1960s, Arendt achieved renown for her writings, including *On Revolution* (1958), *The Human Condition* (1958), and *On Violence* (1962), in which she argued that revolution and war constituted the primary forces of the era.

Unfortunately, women like Mayer and Arendt were exceptions. Had women been welcome in graduate and professional schools, and had they received more support and mentoring, the list undoubtedly would have been much longer.

Women in the Military

Women found limited opportunities in the U.S. armed forces. In 1948, President Harry S Truman signed the Women's Armed Forces Integration Act, which made women's corps permanent parts of the armed forces. Yet women soon discovered that the 1948 legislation also constrained them, with restrictions on their terms of service, ranks, and benefits. Moreover, quotas limited the number of women accepted, and women were prohibited from serving in combat. In spite of these restrictions, there were 22,000 women in the armed services when the Korean War began in 1950.

When President Kennedy ordered American forces into Vietnam in 1961, it was clear that the conflict would demand huge numbers of troops. Although personnel shortages existed, the armed forces did not actively recruit women. During the Vietnam years, some 11,000 women were stationed in Vietnam and thousands more located in neighboring countries. Eight percent of these women worked in administration, communications, and personnel positions; the other 92 percent were nurses, eight of whom died as a result of combat.

After the Vietnam War ended, male veterans received military benefits and saw a magnificent memorial erected in their honor in Washington, D.C. Vietnam nurses spent years lobbying and writing letters before a smaller memorial was erected to salute them. Apparently, women's wartime accomplishments were still viewed as emergency, and temporary, assistance.

Reform-Minded Women

During the early 1960s, such issues as civil rights, anti–Vietnam War protests, and feminism grabbed the spotlight. In spite of the decade's emphasis on causes ranging from black and Hispanic civil rights to feminism, women's interest in other social and cultural reforms revived, with a number of women rediscovering the cause of children's rights. Exploitative child labor and child neglect had long interested women reformers, but during the 1960s women seemed most concerned with stopping the physical abuse of children. The medical profession had defined a "battered" child syndrome, yet the media generally skirted the issue. Although female reformers spoke out on child abuse, most Americans regarded it as an unmentionable phenomenon.

In 1965, Project Head Start brought to national attention another kind of child abuse—the lack of services and education suffered by poor children. Head Start began as a summer program as part of President Lyndon B. Johnson's "War on Poverty." Using federal funds, Project Head Start offered health, social, and psychological services for children and their families. It also established an enriched preschool experience to impoverished children. Numerous women, black and white, participated in Head Start activities.

Yet others used the public deification of "mother" to demand change. Women Strike for Peace (WSP) opposed nuclear weapons. In 1961, WSP called for a one-day peace demonstration to protest radioactive fallout from the testing of nuclear weapons in the Soviet Union. More than fifty thousand women participated in the strike, and the demonstration led to the organization of local peace groups in sixty towns and cities. Fully 61 percent of the members of these groups were full-time homemakers. The following year, the House Un-American Activities Committee accused WSP members of being communists. In reply, the founder of WSP stated that the group was concerned with mother love and protecting children rather than influencing politics: "I would like to say that unless everybody in the whole world joins us in the fight, then God help us."

Immigration and Resettlement

Clearly, American women had developed an awareness of many and varied problems, including the existence and pain of discriminatory actions and attitudes. Although many fought prejudice on public and political levels, racial and ethnic hostility remained entrenched in their daily lives. Such major cities as Cleveland, Chicago, Denver, Los Angeles, New York, and Seattle continued to foster segregated streets and sections where only poor, Native American, Hispanic, African American, or Asian American people lived. In Cleveland, one downtown street was considered "black," a parallel street "white."

In 1965, the Naturalization Act formalized divisions between groups by establishing a yearly maximum of 20,000 immigrants from any one nation. Its provisions gave preference to split families, resettlement of refugees, and skilled workers and professionals. Even though the quota system contained in this legislation limited the growth of some racial and ethnic groups in the United States, it led to a more diversified immigration. Under its provisions, more types of Asians, including Chinese, Koreans, Filipinos, and Asian Indians, and more female immigrants entered the country. Indeed, more than half of the "new" immigrants were women. A significant number of these women came from urban backgrounds where they had worked as teachers, nurses, doctors, dentists, and attorneys. In the United States, they faced language problems and discriminatory licensing examinations that kept them from resuming their professions. Of course, exclusion—both formal and informal—further complicated the ordeal of resettlement.

Saving the American Environment

Women also put time and energy into environmental conservation. Although one might expect overwhelming issues like war, civil rights, and feminism to push concern for the environment to the background, it was not the case. Instead, during 1960s the American public was increasingly aware of environmental issues. This occurred, in large part, because the protest movements of the 1960s had taught, or forced, Americans to think about a range of problems and to question sources of power, including the government and big business.

Perhaps best known of all female environmentalists was Rachel Carson, an aquatic biologist with the U.S. Fish and Wildlife Service until 1952 and later an environmentalist writer. Carson wrote *The Sea Wind* (1941) and *The Sea Around Us* (1951) before gaining national attention with *The Silent Spring* (1962). The latter book helped unify the emerging environmental movement much as Friedan's *The Feminine Mystique* had ignited the feminist movement. In her seminal work, Carson drew international attention to the destructive effects of pesticides on the environment, warning Americans that if preventive measures were not undertaken a "silent spring" would one day fall over a lifeless land.

Meanwhile, thousands of other women took on conservation causes. In Texas, birdwatcher and bird protectionist Connie Hagar went on fieldtrips and compiled "nature calendars." Hagar's work included twenty-five volumes of notes, photographs, and other documents. In California, female naturalists joined with female nature lovers to fight to protect the state's endangered redwood forests from lumber companies and land developers.

In addition, from one end of the country to the other, clubwomen initiated environmental programs and projects. In Arizona, the attorney and active clubwoman Nellie Bush rose to the presidency of the General Federation of Women's Clubs. During the sixteen years that Bush spent in the Arizona house of representatives, she demonstrated her abiding interest in preserving the environment for outdoor enthusiasts like herself. In Minnesota, another clubwoman made her farm available to youth campers, designed a course of environmental education for public schools, and helped expand the University of Minnesota's arboretum.

Along with these women's clubs, another prominent women's organization entered the environmental fight, the League of Women Voters. Besides its interest in politics, the League was dedicated to improving American society in general. One Minnesota woman urged League officials to move environmentalism "to a more active place on the current agenda." In 1964, the League's national convention voted on behalf of "long-range planning for conservation and development of water resources."

Perhaps the most colorful political activist of the period was the Nevada lobbyist Velma B. Johnston. By championing the cause of saving Nevada's wild mustangs, Johnston earned the nickname "Wild Horse Annie." She began her crusade during the early 1950s by informing state legislators that these magnificent creatures were not only sold for pet food, but hunted from airplanes for "sport." When Johnston's bill to protect mustangs passed in Nevada in 1955, she turned her attention to the U.S. Congress. There, Johnston told legislators that as a symbol of American freedom, the mustang had a "right to survival."

Similarly, the Federation of Western Outdoor Clubs tried to save other aspects of the "wild" West. In California during the mid-1940s, members of Western Outdoor Clubs had urged Congress to establish a Jackson Hole National Monument in the Grand Tetons (Wyoming). In the 1950s and 1960s, the Federation opposed the opening of national park land to cattle grazing by private ranchers—a battle they lost—and supported U.S. Forest Service plans to preserve virgin timberlands. Female members also prodded the U.S. Forest Service to protect the West's remaining "wilderness" areas before they all disappeared.

During the post–World War II years, numerous forces challenged the back-to-the-home movement. Just as the dream of no problems and prosperity proved illusory, so did the belief in a sweet, docile, model American woman evaporate. Instead, Americans found it necessary to cope with the modern world—and with the modern woman. By the early 1960s, increasing numbers of women argued that they had a right to participate in the public realm. In so doing, they literally created the contemporary feminist movement.

Rather than focusing on improved education, the vote, or other specific rights as they had in the past, for the first time American women called into question the basic nature of American gender expectations, constructs, and beliefs. The national debate that resulted pushed America's women into a new position. Although the traditional model of the invented American woman held some ground, it was fast losing its footing.

Study Guide

Checklist of important names, terms, phrases, and dates in Chapter 9.
Think about what or who each was and why she, he, or it was significant.

back-to-the-home movement
Baby Boom
suburbia
Dr. Benjamin Spock
Alfred C. Kinsey
Margaret Mead
Maria Montoya Martinez
Maria Tallchief
cultural broker
Ann Petry
Charlotta Spears Bass
Brown v. *Board of Education of Topeka*
Highlander Folk School
Rosa Parks
Septima Clark
Bernice Robinson
War Brides Act
Chinese Benevolent Association
Jade Snow Wong
President's Commission on the Status of
    Women

Equal Pay Act of 1963
Dolores Huerta
Fannie Lou Hamer
Casey Hayden
Tillie Olsen
Betty Friedan
The Feminine Mystique
Bella Abzug
affirmative action
Title VII of the Civil Rights Act
"sexual revolution"
Griswold v. *Connecticut*
Helen Gurley Brown
Marilyn Monroe
Katharine Hepburn
Nancy Kwan
Dorothy Dandridge
Joan Baez
Althea Gibson
Project Head Start

Chapter 9 issues to think about and discuss:

- For what reasons did white women accept the back-to-the-home message?
- Compare sexual knowledge and practices of the Victorian era with those of the 1950s.
- After World War II, were American Indians better off living on reservations or in cities?
- How were the situations of American Indian women and Hispanas similar and different during the 1950s?
- How were the situations of African American and Asian American women similar and different during the 1950s?
- What characteristics of the 1960s allowed people to speak up and reform movements to develop?
- In what ways did the black civil rights and feminist movements hurt and help each other?
- What about feminism annoyed antifeminists? Were antifeminists' fears sound?
- What has the sexual revolution of the 1960s done for your generation? Has it had a positive or a negative effect?
- Why does the divorce rate continue to move generally upward?
- Was environmental conservation as significant a reform as civil rights and feminism?

Suggestions for Further Reading

Back-to-the-Home Movement of the Late 1940s and the 1950s

Breines, Wini, *Young, White, and Miserable: Growing Up Female in the Fifties* (Boston, Beacon Press, 1992).

Chato, Genevieve, and Christine Conte, "The Legal Rights of American Indian Women," 229–46, in *Western Women: Their Land, Their Lives,* edited by Lillian Schlissel, Vicki L, Ruiz, and Janice Monk (Albuquerque: University of New Mexico Press, 1988).

Coleman, Barbara J., "Maidenform(ed): Images of American Women in the 1950s," *Genders* 21 (1995): 3–29.

Foote, Cheryl J., "Changing Images of Women in the Western Film," *Journal of the West* 22 (October 1983): 64–71.

Matthews, Glenna, *"Just a Housewife," The Rise and Fall of Domesticity in America* (New York, Oxford University Press, 1987).

Morantz, Regina Markell, "The Scientist as Sex Crusader, Alfred C. Kinsey and American Culture," 145–66, in *Procreation or Pleasure? Sexual Attitudes in American History,* edited by Thomas L. Altherr (Malabar, FL: Robert E. Kreiger Publishing Company, 1983).

Movshovitz, Howard, "The Still Point, Women in the Westerns of John Ford," *Frontiers* 7 (1984): 68–72.

Scobie, Ingrid Winther, *Center Stage, Helen Gahagan Douglas: A Life* (New York, Oxford University Press, 1992).

Solinger, Rickie, *Wake Up Little Susie: Single Pregnancy and Race before Roe v. Wade* (New York, Routledge, 1992).

Weigand, Kate, "The Red Menace, the Feminine Mystique, and the Ohio Un-American Activities Commission, Gender and Anti-Communism in Ohio, 1951–1954," *Journal of Women's History* 3 (Winter 1992): 70–94.

Weiss, Nancy Pottishman, "Mother, the Invention of Necessity, Dr. Benjamin Spock's Baby and Child Care," *American Quarterly* 24 (Winter 1977): 519–46.

Beyond Suburbia during the Late 1940s and 1950s

Ackerman, Lillian A., "Marital Instability and Juvenile Delinquency Among the Nez Perces," *American Anthropologist* 73 (June 1971): 595–603.

Asian American Studies Center and Chinese Historical Society of Southern California, eds., *Linking Our Lives: Chinese American Women of Los Angeles* (Los Angeles: Chinese Historical Society of Southern California, 1984).

Dunne, Sara, "Women as Children in American Comedy, Baby Snooks' Daughters," *Journal of American Culture* 16 (Summer 1993): 31–35.

Gabin, Nancy, "Women Workers and the UAW in the Post–World War II Period, 1945–1954," *Labor History* 21 (Winter 1979–80): 5–30.

Gill, Gerald R., "WIN OR LOSE—WE WIN', The 1952 Vice-Presidential Campaign of Charlotta A, Bass," 109–88, in *The Afro-American Woman, Struggles and Images,* edited by Sharon Harley and Rosalyn M. Terborg-Penn (Port Washington, NY: Kennikat Press, 1978).

Goldin, Claudia, *Understanding the Gender Gap: An Economic History of American Women* (New York: Oxford University Press, 1990).

Hine, Darlene Clark, "Rape and the Inner Lives of Southern Black Women, Thoughts on the Culture of Dissemblance," 177–90, in *Southern Women,* edited by Bernhard, et al. (Columbia, University of Missouri Press, 1992).

Jacobs, Sue-Ellen, "Being a Grandmother in the Tewa World," *American Indian Culture and Research Journal* 19 (1995): 67–84.

Jamieson, Kathleen, "Multiple Jeopardy, The Evolution of a Native Women's Movement," *Canadian Ethnic Studies* 13 (1981): 130–43.

Kessler-Harris, Alice, *In Pursuit of Equity: Women, Men, and the Quest for Economic Citizenship in 20th-Century America* (New York: Oxford University Press, 2001).

Lamphere, Louise, Patricia Zavella, Felipe Gonzalez, with Peter Evans, *Sunbelt Working Mothers: Reconciling Family and Factory* (Ithaca, NY: Cornell University Press, 1993).

Lemke-Santangelo, Gretchen, *Abiding Courage: African American Migrant Women and the East Bay Community* (Chapel Hill: University of North Carolina Press, 1996).

Loveland, Anne, Lillian Smith, *A Southerner Confronting the South: A Biography* (Baton Rouge: Louisiana State University Press, 1986).

Miller, Sally M., "California Immigrants: Case Studies in Continuity and Change in Societal and Familial Roles," *Journal of the West* 33 (July 1993): 25–34.

Ruiz, Vicki L., *Cannery Women, Cannery Lives: Mexican Women, Unionization, and the California Food Processing Industry, 1930–1950* (Albuquerque: University of New Mexico Press, 1987).

Segura, Denise, "Chicana and Mexican Immigrant Women at Work," *Gender and Society* 3 (March 1989): 37–52.

Shoemaker, Nancy, *American Indian Population Recovery in the Twentieth Century* (Albuquerque: University of New Mexico Press, 1999).

Streitmatter, Rodger, *Raising Her Voice, African-American Women Journalists Who Changed History* (Lexington: University Press of Kentucky, 1994).

Williams, Teresa K., "Marriage between Japanese Women and U.S. Servicemen Since World War II," *Amerasia Journal* 17 (1991): 135–54.

Zavella, Patricia, "The Impact of 'Sun Belt Industrialization' on Chicanas," 291–304, in *The Women's West,* edited by Susan Armitage and Elizabeth Jameson (Norman: University of Oklahoma Press, 1987).

Emerging Feminism, The Early 1960s

Bem, Sandra Lipsitz, *The Lenses of Gender: Transforming the Debate on Sexual Inequality* (New Haven, CT: Yale University Press, 1993).

Caraway, Nancie, *Segregated Sisterhood: Racism and the Politics of American Feminism* (Knoxville: University of Tennessee Press, 1991).

Chafe, William H., *The American Woman: Her Changing Social, Economic, and Political Roles, 1920–1970* (New York, Oxford University Press, 1972).

Collier-Thomas, Bettye, *Sisters in the Struggle: African-American Women in the Civil Rights and Black Power Movements* (New York: New York University Press, 2001).

Cott, Nancy F., *The Grounding of Modern Feminism* (New Haven, CT: Yale University Press, 1987).

Crawford, Vicki L., Jacqueline Anne Rouse, and Barbara Woods, eds., *Women in the Civil Rights Movement: Trailblazers and Torchbearers, 1941–1965* (Bloomington: Indiana University Press, 1993).

Deslippe, Dennis A., *Rights, Not Roses: Unions and the Rise of Working-Class Feminism, 1945–80* (Champaign-Urbana: University of Illinois Press, 2000).

Diner, Hasia R, and Beryl L. Benderly, *Her Works Praise Her: A History of Jewish Women in America from Colonial Times to the Present* (Oshkosh, WI: Basic Books, 2003).

Epstein, Cynthia Fuchs, "Positive Effects of the Multiple Negative: Explaining the Success of Black Professional Women," *American Journal of Sociology* 78 (January 1973): 912–35.

———, *Deceptive Distinctions: Sex, Gender, and the Social Order* (New Haven, CT: Yale University Press, 1988).

Evans, Sara, "Women's Consciousness and the Southern Black Movement," *Southern Exposure* 4 (Winter 1977): 10–14.

———, *Personal Politics, The Roots of Women's Liberation in the Civil Rights Movement and the New Left* (New York: Alfred A. Knopf, 1979).

Farnham, Christie Anne, ed., *Women of the American South: A Multicultural Reader* (New York: New York University Press, 1997).

Faulkner, Mara, *Protest and Possibility in the Writing of Tillie Olsen* (Charlottesville: University Press of Virginia, 1993).

Fleming, Cynthia Griggs, "Black Women Activists and the Student Nonviolent Coordinating Committee, The Case of Ruby Doris Smith Robinson," *Journal of Women's History* 4 (Winter 1993): 64–82.

Frankel, Oz, "Whatever Happened to 'Red Emma'? Emma Goldman, from Alien Rebel to American Icon," *Journal of American History* 83 (December 1996): 903–42.

Gabaccia, Donna, *From the Other Side: Women, Gender, and Immigrant Life in the U.S., 1820–1990* (Bloomington, Indiana University Press, 1994).

García, Richard A., "Dolores Huerta, Woman Organizer, Symbol," *California History* 72 (Spring 1993): 56–71.

Garza, Hedda, *Latinas: Hispanic Women in the United States* (Albuquerque, University of New Mexico Press, 2001).

Giddings, Paula J., *When and Where I Enter: The Impact of Black Women on Race and Sex in America* (New York: HarperCollins Publishers, 1996).

Harrison, Cynthia E., *On Account of Sex: The Politics of Women's Issues, 1945–1968* (Berkeley: University of California Press, 1988).

Hartmann, Susan M., *From Margin to Mainstream: American Women and Politics Since 1960* (New York: Alfred Knopf, 1989).

Hoff, Joan, "The Unfinished Revolution: Changing Legal Status of U.S. Women," *Signs* 13 (Autumn 1987): 7–36.

———, *Unequal Before the Law: A Legal History of U.S. Women* (New York: New York University Press, 1991).

Jellison, Katherine, *Entitled to Power: Farm Women and Technology, 1913–1963* (Chapel Hill: University of North Carolina Press, 1993).

Kennedy, Elizabeth Lapovsky, and Madeline D. Davis, *Boots of Leather, Slippers of Gold: The History of a Lesbian Community* (New York: Routledge, 1993).

Kohl, Herbert R., *She Would Not Be Moved: How We Tell the Story of Rosa Parks and the Montgomery Bus Boycott* (New York: The New Press, 2005).

Lee, Chana Kai, *For Freedom's Sake: The Life of Fannie Lou Hamer* (Champaign: University of Illinois Press, 1999).

Mills, Kay, *This Little Light of Mine: The Life of Fannie Lou Hamer* (New York: Dutton, 1993).

Newman, Louise Michele, *White Women's Rights: The Racial Origins of Feminism in the United States* (New York: Oxford University Press, 2001).

Olsen, Lynne, *Freedom's Daughters: The Unsung Heroines of the Civil Rights Movement from 1830 to 1970* (New York; Simon & Schuster, 2002).

Robinson, Jo Ann, *The Montgomery Bus Boycott and the Women Who Started It* (Knoxville: University of Tennessee Press, 1987).

Robnett, Belinda, *How Long? How Long? African-American Women in the Struggle for Civil Rights* (New York: Oxford University Press, 2000).

Romo, Ricardo, "Southern California and the Origins of Latino Civil-Rights Activism," *Western Legal History* 3 (Summer/Fall 1990): 379–406.

Ross, Rosetta E., *Witnessing and Testifying: Black Women, Religion, and Civil Rights* (Minneapolis, MN: Augsberg Fortress, Publishers, 2003).

Roth, Benita, *Separate Roads to Feminism: Black, Chicana, and White Feminist Movements in America's Second Wave* (New York: Cambridge University Press, 2005).

Rothschild, Mary Aickin, "White Women Volunteers in the Freedom Summers: Their Life and Work in a Movement for Social Change," *Feminist Studies* 5 (Fall 1979): 466–95.

Rupp, Leila J, "The Survival of American Feminism: The Women's Movement in the Postwar Period," 33–65, in *Reshaping America: Society and Institutions, 1945–1960,* edited by Robert H. Bremer and Gary W. Reichard (Columbus: Ohio State University Press, 1982).

Rupp, Leila J., and Verta Taylor, *Survival in the Doldrums: The American Women's Rights Movement, 1945 to the 1960s* (New York: Oxford University Press, 1987).

Sawyer, Mary R, "Black Religion and Social Change: Women in Leadership Roles," *Journal of Religious Thought* 47 (Winter/Spring 1990–91): 16–29.

Segura, Denise, and Beatriz Pesquera, "Beyond Indifference and Apathy: The Chicana Movement and Chicana Feminist Discourse," *Aztlan* 19 (Fall 1988–1990): 69–92.

Szasz, Margaret Connell, ed., *Between Indian and White Worlds: The Cultural Broker* (Norman: University of Oklahoma Press, 1994).

Taylor, Sandra C., "Leaving the Concentration Camps: Japanese Americans and Resettlement in the Intermountain West," *Pacific Historical Review* 60 (May 1991): 169–94.

Weigand, Kate, *Red Feminism: American Communism and the Making of Women's Liberation* (Baltimore: Johns Hopkins University Press, 2002).

Women's Lives, The Early 1960s

Berry, Mary Frances, *The Politics of Parenthood: Child Care, Women's Rights and the Myth of the Good Mother* (New York: Penguin USA, 1994).

Breuer, William B., *War and American Women: Heroism, Deeds, and Controversy* (Westport, CT: Greenwood, 1997).

Davis, Madeline D., and Elizabeth Lapovsky Kennedy, "Oral History and the Study of Sexuality in the Lesbian Community, Buffalo, New York, 1940–1960," 450–62, in *Unequal Sisters: A Multicultural Reader in U.S. Women's History,* edited by Vicki L, Ruiz and Ellen Carol DuBois (New York: Routledge, 2d ed., 1994).

Davis, Ronald L., *The Glamour Factory: Inside Hollywood's Big Studio System* (Dallas: Southern Methodist University Press, 1993).

D'Emilio, John, and Estelle B. Freedman, *Intimate Matters: A History of Sexuality in America* (New York: Harper & Row: 1988).

Douglas, Deborah G., *American Women and Flight Since 1940* (Lexington: University Press of Kentucky, 2003).

Eisenmann, Linda, *Higher Education for Women in Postwar America, 1945–1965* (Baltimore: Johns Hopkins University Press, 2006).

Kim, Bok-Lim C., "Asian Wives of U,S, Servicemen, Women in Shadows," *Amerasia Journal* 4 (March 1977): 91–115.

Lim, Shirley Jennifer, *A Feeling of Belonging: Asian American Women's Popular Culture, 1930–1960* (New York: New York University Press, 2005).

May, Elaine Tyler, *Homeward Bound: American Families in the Cold War Era* (New York: Basic Books, 1988).

Meyerowitz, Joanne, "Beyond the Feminine Mystique: A Reassessment of Postwar Mass Culture, 1946–1958," *Journal of American History* 79 (March 1993): 1455–82.

Murphy, Lucy Eldersveld, and Wendy Hamand Venet, eds., *Midwestern Women, Work, Community, and Leadership at the Crossroads* (Bloomington: Indiana University Press, 1997).

Rosenberg, Rosalind, *Divided Lives: American Women in the Twentieth Century* (New York: Hill and Wang, 1992).

Rossiter, Margaret W., *Women Scientists in America: Before Affirmative Action, 1940–1972* (Baltimore: Johns Hopkins University Press, 1995).

Swerdlow, Amy, "Ladies' Day at the Capitol: Women Strike for Peace Versus HUAC," 479–96, in *Unequal Sisters: A Multicultural Reader in U.S. Women's History,* edited by Vicki Ruiz and Ellen Carol Dubois (New York: Routledge, 2d ed., 1994).

———, *Women Strike for Peace: Traditional Motherhood and Radical Politics in the 1960s* (Chicago: University of Chicago Press, 1993).

Zhao, Ziaojian, *Remaking Chinese America: Immigration, Family and Community, 1940–1965* (New Brunswick, NJ: Rutgers University Press, 2002).

Chapter Ten

Modern American Women,
1965 to the Present

$\mathcal{I}$n 1965, President Lyndon Baines Johnson of Texas encouraged Americans to believe in the creation of a "Great Society." In his state of the union address, Johnson proposed enforcing civil rights provisions, accelerating the war on poverty, and improving American education. At the same time, "Lady Bird" (Claudia Alta Taylor) Johnson initiated a highway beautification program. Widely criticized for her efforts, the First Lady was later recognized as a catalyst to the ecology movement of the late 1960s and early 1970s.

Even though the Johnsons achieved much, the escalation of U.S. involvement in the Vietnam War caused a public outcry, including protests, pickets, and riots. Also during 1965, black urban dwellers rioted in such places as the Watts neighborhood of South Central Los Angeles. The following year, the African American leader Martin Luther King, Jr., was assassinated. In 1969, National Guard troops shot to death four students involved in an antiwar demonstration at Kent State University in Ohio. During the presidential term of Richard Milhous Nixon, the Watergate scandal gave Americans even more cause to despair. Even the long-sought pullout of all American troops from Vietnam during 1971, 1972, and 1975 did little to raise the self-confidence of the nation.

Meanwhile, the emerging feminist movement launched a controversy regarding American women. Americans' response was far from unanimous. Some people grasped at the past, hoping that traditional American values would provide ballast in an increasingly stormy sea. Others sailed ahead in anticipation that rough water would give way to arrival at a better port than the one departed. In the midst of this sea change, reform laws and policies were adopted. Yet, as always, difficult situations remained unresolved. When the United States entered the twenty-first century, deep questions and issues related to gender still demanded solutions.

National Organization for Women, 1966

The latter half of the 1960s was an exciting time; words like *ferment* and *change* characterized the era. Yet this was also a dangerous time in which violence and reform often went hand in hand. Nonetheless, leaders of the feminist movement seized their opportunities as they came.

In 1966, a small group of feminists formally organized the modern feminist movement during the Third National Conference of State Commissions on the Status of Women. Tired of ponderous discussion concerning women's issues that often lacked results, twenty-eight women met in Betty Friedan's hotel room in Washington, D.C. There, they contributed ideas and $5 apiece to the founding of the National Organization for Women (NOW). By the time NOW held its first organizational meeting, the number of interested people had grown to three hundred women and men. Unsurprisingly, they elected Friedan as the first president of NOW.

This first meeting also issued a statement of purpose. NOW members attacked "the traditional assumption that a woman had to choose between marriage and motherhood on the one hand and participation in industry or the professions on the other." They felt it was possible to have marriage, motherhood, and paid activity outside the home. NOW leaders had specific actions in mind to achieve this goal. They criticized gender expectations that cast women as passive, emotional, and nurturing. Instead, NOW maintained that so-called female traits were a matter of learning rather than of genetics. If American society stopped teaching its boys to be "manly" and its girls to be "feminine," the two genders could meet in the middle. If such media as children's books, cartoons, and advertising stopped telling boys to grow up "strong" and girls to grow up "weak," both sexes could grow up to share in home, family, and paid work.

NOW members made a second resolution, vowing to bring women into "full participation in the mainstream of American society NOW." They would settle for no less than "truly equal partnership with men." This was a lofty aim, and NOW members had no way of predicting the complications that would occur. Contrary to the rhetoric of their detractors, not all feminists wanted to become pseudo-men. One accomplished feminist, who had achieved renown and independence, complained that she had "become the man I once thought I would marry." In other words, she bought her own house and car, invested in the stock market, and paid for glamorous vacations. She and other women felt they were "being co-opted" into a system created and dominated by men. In their view, there must be a better system than one in which women acted like men. Surely, everyone did not have to follow the dictates of a nine-to-five world.

In the mid-1960s, however, NOW assumed that equality with men provided the best possible goal. Previous reforms, notably the right to vote, had not brought women liberation. Although such "first wave" leaders as Carrie Chapman Catt and Alice Paul had worked hard to obtain suffrage, women's lives remained restricted. To achieve equality, NOW advocated a list of reforms. Effective birth control and legal abortions to terminate unwanted pregnancies would give women control over their bodies and family size. Paid maternity leaves would allow women to take off work during childbirth without fear of losing their jobs. Tax deductions to help cover childcare expenses and daycare centers would further encourage mothers to work, so that the nation could utilize its full human potential, male and female. Job-training programs would teach women who wished to work outside the home employable skills.

In 1967, NOW added to its long and ambitious list the passage of an Equal Rights Amendment (ERA). NOW pressed its case through literature, speeches, public protests, lobbying, and litigation. NOW encouraged the formation of "rap" groups to discuss issues relating to women and consciousness-raising (c-r) sessions that would allow women to see all sides of such issues as legalized abortion and government-assisted daycare. Women thronged to these groups, where they discovered that other women shared their anxieties. One said she had never enjoyed being a medical secretary, but there had not been room in medical school for her—a female who would presumably leave her medical practice behind when she married and had children.

NOW did not stand alone in its crusade for equality. Other newly organized women's groups joined in its reform efforts. One of these was the Women's Equity Action League (WEAL), founded in 1968. WEAL concentrated on women's economic issues. The group sponsored education projects, supported litigation, and lobbied Congress. Other groups formed to benefit particular types of women. The Professional Women's Caucus (PWC) organized in 1970 to deal with issues related to women in the professions. The National Women's Political Caucus (NWPC) formed in 1971 to address political concerns. The organization urged individual women to vote as well as run for office, serve as convention delegates, act as lobbyists, and take part in election campaigns.

Feminist Publications

By the early 1970s, women's voices were heard everywhere. It seemed that an invisible dam had burst, letting women's concerns rush through, gaining momentum as they went. In 1970 alone, four dynamic and controversial books urging feminist reforms appeared.

One of these was Kate Millett's *Sexual Politics*, in which she argued that the ills of American society occurred because it was based on patriarchy. Why, she asked, should men rule when women were at least as smart? Perhaps women would bring special perspectives and insights to problems. Millet asked for immediate revision of American patriarchy.

Similarly, in the *The Dialectic of Sex: The Case for Feminist Revolution*, Shulamith Firestone envisioned a nation in which gender and social class played no role. Rather than stereotyping people as poor or rich, male or female, and judging their potential accordingly, Firestone called for a system that would give each individual her or his own best chance to succeed.

Robin Morgan's *Sisterhood Is Powerful* told women something they were already learning: isolation from each other was a great disadvantage. Remaining divided meant that all women would remain powerless. If all the disparate groups of women joined together, they would possess an unstoppable influence.

Finally, Germaine Greer's *The Female Eunuch* presented yet another side of the feminist argument. Greer, a native of Melbourne, Australia, earned a Ph.D. in Renaissance literature from Cambridge University in 1968. She exercised tremendous influence on the American feminist movement, arguing that because "female sexuality had been masked and deformed" by sexist attitudes and practices, women had to "take possession" of their own bodies. Like Morgan, Greer urged women to seize "their power."

Newly founded magazines reinforced and enlarged upon these themes. The foremost feminist publication of the popular press was *Ms.* magazine, founded in 1971. The first national publication created and controlled by women for women, *Ms.* was the brainchild of Gloria Steinem and the Women's Action Alliance. In the pages of *Ms.*, Steinem hoped to raise the consciousness of female readers concerning women's problems and possible solutions. *Ms.* aimed its points at all women, from professionals to traditional homemakers. The magazine continued discussions of career and lifestyle choices for women. It also ran articles on women's history and published the work of women writers and poets. In many ways, *Ms.* echoed Sarah Josepha Hale's *Godey's Lady's Book* of the nineteenth century. The former, however, was the first explicitly feminist magazine in American history.

From such writings women learned about ideas new to them. For example, although the concept of androgyny, meaning that people should be innately free to express both "female" and "male" traits, had a long history, it was not widely considered in the United States. Androgyny had originated with the Greek comic playwrights, notably Aristophanes. He maintained that the god Zeus originally had created human beings with two faces, one female and one male. Unfortunately, these dual-sided and well-balanced beings were so successful that they challenged Zeus's power. Zeus cut them in two, creating women and men who would forever have to seek their other halves through heterosexual love and sexual relationships. In 1929, writer Virginia Woolf was probably the first to introduce and support the concept of androgyny in the modern United States. In *A Room of One's Own*, Woolf wrote that androgynist beings would achieve fuller and happier lives than "split" ones. During the 1960s, many feminists advocated androgyny. Let women and men, they said, be weak and strong, each at the appropriate time. Let women earn income and make financial decisions. Let women dare to be strong and men dare to cry. Let men become involved in infant care and raising children.

Not all feminists supported the idea of an androgynous world. In 1978, the feminist and lesbian writer Adrienne Rich maintained in *The Dream of a Common Language* that women could stand strong, gentle, and persistent on their own. Like the woman mentioned above who did not like becoming the man she once thought she would marry, Rich believed that women were better off without adopting supposedly male qualities like competitiveness and violence. It was these kinds of debates that the feminist literature carried to American women.

Advertising and the Media

Feminists also took a close look at American advertising and media. Although some people argued that equal pay or legalized abortion was more important, feminist leaders pointed out that the media planted harmful images in the minds of everyone from young children to senior adults. People who watched television for hours each day absorbed ideas both explicit and subliminal.

One of these images was that of the "happy housewife." Feminists took issue with fantasy women who found fulfillment in waxing floors and cleaning toilet bowls. Noting that these models discouraged women from thinking for themselves and speaking out, they urged more women to become writers, editors, publishers, producers, and directors. If more women participated in the creation of media, they posited, it might become more woman-friendly.

A multiplier effect soon occurred. As the numbers of women writers, speakers, producers, and directors grew, these women established the Women's Institute for Freedom of the Press in Washington, D.C. This group fought for changes in the American mass media system. The Institute insisted that all people should have equal access to the means of communication in the United States so that they could represent themselves fairly and fully.

Feminists also recognized that media could act in positive ways. Television especially carried news of achieving women who served as role models for female viewers. One such woman was Coretta Scott King. In 1953 she had married Martin Luther King, Jr., and in 1971 earned a Ph.D. in music. Coretta Scott King, who frequently gave concerts to benefit the Southern Christian Leadership Conference (SCLC), was voted by U.S. college students as 1968 Woman of the Year and Most Admired Woman. King later contributed her energy and expertise to both the SCLC and the foundation of the Martin Luther King, Jr., Memorial Center in Atlanta. When King died in 2006, there was talk of transferring the administration of the King Center to the National Park Service.

Popular media also provided women with a means of expression. Jane Fonda, an outspoken opponent of U.S. involvement in the war in Vietnam during the 1960s and early 1970s, organized a film company known as the Indo-China Peace Campaign (IPC). In 1978, Fonda and her company produced *Coming Home*, which criticized the war in Southeast Asia and what it had done to American service people and their families. In 1979, she released *The China Syndrome*, which dealt with the possibility of a meltdown at a U.S. nuclear power plant. In her 1980 film, *Nine to Five*, Fonda satirized sexist practices in the office and low pay among clerical workers.

Abortion and Gynecology

On another level, feminists confronted a long-standing issue: women's control of their bodies. Since time began, women had tried to limit pregnancies. In the United States, the birth-control movement of the 1910s and 1920s had made that right available, at least to some women.

Modern women wanted more from their doctors than birth-control information, however. For the first time, women posed searching questions to their obstetricians and gynecologists. Rather than focusing on such "women's ailments" as sexual dysfunction, hormones, menopause, and aging, women asked doctors to pay more attention to the whole woman. They were tired of doctors who, much like physicians of the Victorian era, callously ascribed medical conditions specific to women as "female problems."

Women also requested that their doctors refer to them as something other than "girls." They wanted more of a partnership with their doctors, rather than male condescension toward "weak females." One obstetrician said he was "stunned" when he first received such a request. "I've always thought of patients as 'my girls,'" he added. At first he refused to make changes in the patriarchal way he treated patients, but when his caseload declined he thought more seriously about the matter.

This doctor and others had to face women's determination to understand their own health care. Women intended to learn whatever they could and go to their doctors with informed minds. In response to this need, in 1971, the Boston Women's Health Collective, Inc., published the revolutionary *Our Bodies, Ourselves*. This medical handbook attempted to educate women about female health. Its topics included abortion, birth control, menopause, pregnancy, rape, and venereal disease. It questioned the effectiveness of customary medical treatment of women and urged the establishment of female clinics. *Our Bodies, Ourselves* became a national best-seller that went through many editions. It helped create the climate of opinion that supported the appearance of many women's health clinics and rape crisis centers throughout the United States.

As part of this movement to take charge of their bodies, a growing number of women demanded the right to abortion. In 1965, all fifty states banned abortion. Law allowed therapeutic abortions only in life-threatening situations. Feminists argued that abortion should be allowed in cases of rape, incest, and known fetal deformity. Although a number of states liberalized their laws, many did not. Even the most lenient laws required a woman seeking an abortion to provide parental or spousal consent. As in the past, whatever the law in each state, wealthy women were able to circumvent it by traveling to other countries where abortion was a safe, legal procedure. Unfortunately, many women with no such option attempted illegal and self-induced abortions that often resulted in injury or death.

Feminists sought for all women the right to abortion on demand. They insisted that individual women, not the medical community or government, should make decisions regarding childbearing. During the 1970s, most state governments hesitated or refused to offer abortion on demand. In response, feminists created test cases of various antiabortion legislation throughout the United States. As a result of such efforts, the U.S. Supreme Court handed down a historic decision in 1973. In *Roe* v. *Wade*, a young female attorney from Texas argued for the legal right to have an abortion. In the historic decision, the Supreme Court justices overturned state laws that prohibited abortion during the first trimester (twelve weeks) of pregnancy. For the first time in the nation's history, American women could have abortions legally. Furthermore, according to *Roe* v. *Wade*, in life-threatening cases women could have abortions between twelve weeks and viability (the time at which a fetus can survive outside the womb). Subsequent rulings struck down laws requiring parental or spousal consent except in cases involving minors.

Unsurprisingly, in the wake of *Roe* v. *Wade* an antiabortion movement, driven by Americans who believed that abortion violated their values and religious beliefs, developed. To serve these people, antiabortion groups formed. The National Conference of Catholic Bishops created the National Right to Life Committee. By 1980, the Catholic organization had 11 million members. These and other antiabortion advocates protested that abortion constituted murder of unborn children. They opposed the argument that a fetus was not a human being until twelve weeks of age. Rather, they maintained that a fetus was a human being from the moment of conception. Because the commandments ordered Christians not to kill, the Church felt it had a duty to uphold God's word. "There is no choice," one young priest explained, "in matters of human life and God's injunction not to end it."

Women's Studies

Meanwhile, the academic world made changes of its own. When feminists asked, "Where is women's history?" or "Where is women's literature?", college and university professors had few answers. One woman professor said she had "accepted the way things had always been done." Although female, she had not thought to challenge the academic establishment. During the 1960s and 1970s, however, she and thousands of others called for educational reforms that would put women's studies into college and university curriculums.

Accordingly, professors, especially women, developed and offered courses focusing on women. These included women's history, literature, psychology, and sociology. Although some curriculum committees predicted that there would be little student demand for such courses, students, mostly women, enrolled in great numbers. These students found it an exciting revelation that women played important roles in the past and present. By 1972, American colleges and universities offered more than 600 woman-oriented courses. Two years later, this figure had jumped to 2,000. By 1982, some 30,000 courses existed.

The establishment and popularity of these courses led to other educational innovations. The founding of the journals *Women's Studies* and *Signs* recognized the significance of women's issues. They published the latest scholarship on women in all fields. In the meantime, women's courses evolved into women's studies programs. These were interdisciplinary programs analyzing women's experiences from a feminist perspective. In 1974, 39 such programs existed. By 1984, this number had risen to 444. A few schools even offered degrees in women's studies. In 1969, San Diego State University established the first bachelor's degree program in women's studies.

Another breakthrough was the formation of professional women's studies associations. In 1979, the National Women's Studies Association (NWSA) organized. Individual disciplines formed their own women's groups. For instance, to work for reform in the practice and teaching of history, women historians founded the Coordinating Committee for Women in the Historical Profession and Women Historians of the Midwest. In response, scholars retrieved and reestablished the history of women. They also developed a new body of methodology and theory regarding the writing of women's history.

Additional impetus for reform came from scholars in literature and linguistics. They questioned the dominant white male canon in literature. Why, they asked, did students read only books written by white men? Scholars restored women's writings to the canon. They also opposed patriarchal usages in the English language. Why were all people referred to as "men" and "mankind"? Terms like "people" and "humankind" seemed fairer and more inclusive. As a result, feminist literary criticism utilized gender as a basic category of literary analysis. Literary scholars also experimented with deconstruction, the theory of textual analysis that questions whether language truly represents reality. More specifically, scholars attempted to deconstruct language to remove its gender bias. Then they reconstructed it in a bias-free way so that women's topics could be studied free of patriarchal words and "woman-as-other" prejudices.

Math anxiety among women constituted yet another concern. Although some outstanding women mathematicians had existed in the United States, most women still viewed mathematics as a male preserve. In 1971, the Association for Women in Mathematics (AWM) organized to promote equal treatment of women in mathematics training and careers. The AWM established a speakers' bureau, distributed information, and initiated programs intended to eradicate math anxiety among young women.

International Women's Year Conference, 1977

The year 1977 proved significant for the feminist movement. Leaders organized an International Women's Year Conference, held in Houston, Texas. Congressperson Bella Abzug served as primary organizer of the conference, as well as the presiding officer of the meeting.

At the conference, two thousand delegates and twenty thousand observers gathered to devise a plan for the liberation of womankind. The delegates represented Native Americans, Hispanas, whites, African Americans, Asian Americans; in other words, all American women. The wants of rich and poor, young and old, worker and full-time housewife, heterosexual and homosexual were also considered. Betty Friedan, who had once called lesbians the "lavender menace," now defended their right to their sexual preference and civil rights.

The conference created a National Plan of Action, which its leaders presented to President Jimmy Carter on 22 March 1978. The document was wide ranging. Its twenty-six planks addressed such topics as child abuse, childcare, disabled women, education, employment, an Equal Rights

Amendment (ERA) to the U.S. Constitution, health, homemakers, insurance, older women, rape, reproductive rights, rural women, poverty, and women of color. Although few of the suggestions received implementation, the conference and its report defined the problems women faced. The report also generated spirited public discussion.

Antifeminism

The forward motion of feminist reform did not go unopposed. The ERA proved explosive. In 1972, attorney Phyllis Schlafly of Illinois organized a group called STOP ERA. Schlafly declared, "[The] ERA offers absolutely no benefit to women, no new right, no new opportunity that we do not have now." At least partly due to Schlafly's efforts, the ERA fell three states short of achieving ratification before an extended deadline ran out in 1982.

Abortion continued to generate controversy. Although the 1973 Supreme Court decision in *Roe* v. *Wade* supported women's right to choose abortion, it was not widely popular. Opponents became interested in the abortion philosophy of potential federal and Supreme Court justices. As a consequence of sentiment against abortion, as well as the addition of some conservative judges, courts began to backpedal. In 1980, *Harris* v. *McRae* upheld the Hyde Amendment, which limited federal Medicaid funds for abortion to cases involving rape, incest, and life-threatening situations. The following year, a U.S. congressional committee considered a Human Life Amendment, stating that human life begins at conception. Had this amendment been ratified, it would have struck down women's right to choose abortion, but the committee never forwarded the provision to the full Congress for a vote.

Other setbacks to feminist reform came from several U.S. presidents. One curb to the feminist momentum of the 1970s was President Richard M. Nixon's 1972 veto of the Comprehensive Child Development bill. This act would have provided nationwide daycare centers for employed mothers. Nixon believed that daycare was a "communal approach to child-rearing" that had "family-weakening implications." A similar presidential roadblock appeared with the inauguration of President Ronald Reagan in 1981 and again in 1985. The Reagan administration refused to enforce affirmative action laws. It also cut such social welfare programs as Aid to Dependent Children. President Reagan consistently tried to block women's continuing right to choose abortion. He opposed the ERA and its "comparable worth" provision in determining women's wages.

Native American Women

Like the women's rights movement of the nineteenth century and the suffrage movement of the early twentieth century, mid-twentieth century feminism largely appealed to white, middle- and upper-class women. Due to the outcry of women of color, however, feminist leaders gradually expanded their goals to include all types of women.

One of these was Native American women. Still largely confined to reservations or urban ghettoes, Native American women faced prejudice in housing, education, and employment. Because federal Indian policies were derived from the white standard of nuclear families, they ignored the extended kinship systems maintained by numerous Native Americans. In other words, an Indian mother should not seek wage-paying work even though grandmothers and other kin were available to care for her children.

During the 1960s, the reemergence of the movement for Indian self-determination brought a few gains to Native Americans in general. These included more control by Indians of their schools and lands. In 1974, a Wisconsin Menominee woman explained that her people preferred to manage their land holdings themselves rather than putting them in the hands of private developers. In addition, some public recognition occurred of the degrading stereotyping of American Indians in the media. Many Americans realized that the "hostile savage" was a Hollywood invention to act as foil for white male heroes. At the same time, cigar-store Indians disappeared from public streets.

By the late 1970s and early 1980s, the American Indian Movement (AIM) brought attention to the desperate conditions on such reservations as Rose Bud and Pine Ridge in South Dakota. Social problems, notably rampant alcoholism and unemployment among American Indians, were widely discussed. Gradually, Bureau of Indian Affairs schools gave preference to Native American teachers and began to diversify their curriculums. This resulted in more Indian women attending colleges and professional schools.

In 1978, the U.S. Supreme Court and Congress gave Indian women a boost. In *Santa Clara Pueblo* v. *Martínez*, the court ruled that men and women must receive identical tribal rights. The American Indian Religious Freedom Act and the Indian Child Welfare Act reinforced this principle. Even though Indian women had far more influence within their families and communities than most observers thought, these women wanted formal political rights. By the early 1980s, between one-fourth and one-third as many Oglala women as men ran for tribal office. In 1981, for the first time one of the six Oglala candidates for tribal president was female.

Still, Indian women felt overlooked. Drawing on a long-standing tradition of helping themselves, Indian women organized. In 1978, they formed Women of All Red Nations (WARN). This group fought enforced sterilization, which white officials had long imposed on Indian women as a means of controlling Indian population growth. Indian women also opposed

forced adoptions by white families, a government policy intended to integrate Indian children into white society. WARN campaigned against political imprisonment of Indian activists, further loss of Indian lands at the
hands of the federal government and unregulated land developers, and the
destruction of Native cultures. WARN's demands resulted in the 1984 establishment of the Navajo Office for Women, which offered to women
counseling, childcare, family planning advice, and job placement. The following year, the Indigenous Women's Network met in Yelm, Washington,
where it supported WARN's programs. It demonstrated the ability of Indian
women to build networks among themselves and led to additional Indian
studies courses and programs in colleges and universities.

Native American women also continued to act as cultural mediators.
Such writers as Paula Gunn Allen, Leslie Marmon Silko, and Louise Erdrich
carried Indian culture and Indian concerns to a larger public. Although Indian "literature" had long depended on oral tradition, especially songs and
stories that contained the history and traditions of various peoples, these
Native American writers used the written word. In addition, they empowered their female characters, establishing a model for contemporary women
readers. In 1977, Silko won both the prestigious National Book Award and
the MacArthur Award for her novel, *Ceremony*. Erdrich received several
awards for *Love Medicine* (1984) and *The Beet Queen* (1986). Paula Gunn
Allen gained wide recognition both for her poetry and her novel, *The
Woman Who Owned the Shadows* (1983).

Hispanas

Hispanas raised concerns particular to them, ranging from feminist goals to
issues arising from the traditional patriarchy of Hispanic culture. In the
American Southwest, Hispanas had their own culture—and their own
problems. Hispana feminism grew, at least in part, out of a long tradition of
labor protest. The American public first learned of Hispanic militancy in
1966, when grape-pickers struck in Delano, California. The event received
widespread media coverage as did the disgruntled workers (men and
women) who marched 230 miles to Sacramento, their ranks swelling as they
went. On college campuses, students and faculty members added to their
list of protest causes the plight of the mistreated migrant workers.

The following year, Jessie Lopez de la Cruz became the first female organizer for the United Farm Workers of America (UFW). Beginning in
1962, she had worked as a volunteer organizer. In this capacity, de la Cruz
had supported such reforms as a workers' credit union and a consumer cooperative. When she assumed her UFW position in 1967, de la Cruz utilized feminist terms to argue for more female members: "Women can no

longer be taken for granted . . . it's way past the time when our husbands could say, 'You stay home!'" She also became a spokesperson for Hispanas and a member of the California Commission on the Status of Women.

In 1969, the EEOC reported that the majority of Hispana factory workers labored in the agricultural, food, textile, and apparel industries. Thousands of other Hispanas toiled as domestic help in such cities as El Paso and Los Angeles. Most Hispanas were underpaid and lacked maternity leave. The latter meant that upon their return from childbirth, Hispanas had to accept beginning pay and start back on the bottom rung of the seniority ladder. Between 1972 and 1974, Tejanas demonstrated their willingness to organize and demonstrate publicly. In the Farah Manufacturing Company Strike in El Paso, women garment workers brought their children to the picket lines. One Farah worker explained, "Because we were women, we were staying behind. Now we just bring our children to our meetings, and we bring them to picket lines."

In the meantime, numerous Hispanas experienced growing disenchantment with *el movimiento*, the Chicano rights movement that called for an end to discrimination against Hispanics but ignored women's lowly place in Hispanic families and societies. Indeed, Hispanic men disparaged Hispana activists as "women's libbers." Men warned these women that white people wanted Hispanas to adopt feminism to defeat el movimiento. Despite these tactics, Hispana feminists were convinced that they had to obtain their liberation rather than waiting for men to do it for them.

In other southwestern urban areas such as Los Angeles and Houston, Hispanas raised Hispanic and feminist issues. In 1971, more than six hundred women participated in the First National Chicana Conference on Women in Houston, where they demanded representation by Spanish-heritage peoples on school boards, town councils, and police forces, as well as access to forms of federal assistance such as food stamps and bilingual education in schools.

On college and university campuses, Hispanic students questioned women's traditional place. By the 1970s, students formed groups like *Las Chicanas* and *Hijas de Cuauhtemoc*. Among other things, these young people demanded the development of Hispanic studies programs, increased hiring of Hispanic faculty members, and scholarships earmarked for Hispanics. Hispanas especially wanted women included in such reforms.

In the Northeast, Hispana protests took a different direction. There, Puerto Ricans and Cuban Americans were relatively recent arrivals who had brought their own cultural and historical backgrounds with them. Their people had unique needs and concerns. Generally, Hispana feminists in New York City remained separate from white feminists. These Hispanas argued that they could not gain freedom until all Hispanics did so. Rather than originating with labor protests as in the Southwest, community organizations led the northeastern Hispanas' rebellion. The two groups of women shared similar goals, however. Both wanted to destroy the triple oppression of racism, sexism, and poverty.

As more recent arrivals to the United States, New York Hispanas were also less bound by Hispanic American tradition and history. One New York woman urged her friends and coworkers to speak up informing them that times had changed: "It's not like when I was a little kid and my grandmother used to say, 'You have to especially respect the Anglos.' We can stand up! We can talk back!" She added that the time had come for Hispanic American women to reject their customary deference to men.

By the early 1970s, statistics showed that although Hispanas nationwide remained family oriented, they delayed childbirth and limited family size. They also divorced at a higher rate than had their mothers and grandmothers. More revolutionary yet, numerous Hispanas explored such issues as assimilation in American culture, lesbianism, and the limits of family loyalty. Like other groups of women, Hispana writers worked to create their own literary genre.

Hispana poets and writers revealed such complaints as loneliness in urban settings. In 1983, poet Elena Avila wrote these poignant lines in "Coming Home": "Mama! Mama! I've been so cold without you/The big city does not hold me like you do Mama." Other authors laid their problems at the feet of macho men. Some blamed the short-sightedness of those Hispanas who overlooked or ignored feminist issues. Yet others denounced traditional Hispanic literature and art, which deified women as maternal figures, strong yet accepting of the limits placed on them. Even epic *corridos* (story-telling ballads) incorporated few women or disguised female characters to play men's parts. Where were the *soldaderas* (soldiers), modern Hispana writers asked, who had fought alongside men in the Mexican Revolution of 1910, or other famous women of strength and cunning?

Gradually, Hispanas reaped some benefits from their efforts. On the East and West Coasts, Hispanas gained places in Women's Studies and Chicano Studies programs. On the stage, Hispana actors broke away from the typecasting that Rita Moreno and others had experienced in the Broadway play and film *West Side Story*. In sports, Rosemary Casals excelled in tennis. In popular music, Vicki Carr and Linda Ronstadt rose to national fame and critical acclaim. Ronstadt won a Grammy Award in 1988 for her Spanish-language recording *Canciones di mi padre*. Clearly, Hispanas had not let the feminist movement pass them by.

African American Women

African American women developed their own strain of feminism. Unlike white women, a great many black women worked as paid laborers, a status that had long afforded them a degree of equality within the black family structure. Even as the national feminist movement emerged, black women already possessed some of the autonomy that white feminists demanded. Therefore, such issues as domesticity, the feminine mystique, and inequality in the family were less pressing to African American women than their white counterparts.

In addition, African American women tended to see racism as a more pronounced cause of their subordination than sexism. Consequently, they often viewed the feminist movement with distrust, even disdain. The failure of many white feminists to reach out to black women and understand their problems worsened the situation. In 1970, one black female reformer explained, "The black woman is not undergoing the same kind of oppression that white women have gone through in the home." She added that because black women were independent, the "struggle of black women and white women" was not the same. Also in 1970, a woman reporter for the *Washington Post* emphasized that although "the women's liberation movement touches some sensitive nerves among black women . . . they are not always the nerves the movement seems to touch among so many whites." To her, "The first priority of virtually all black people is the elimination of racial prejudice in America." She added that when African Americans were free then perhaps black women would turn to "the elimination of oppression because of sex."

Given the differences in black and white women's needs, why did a black feminist movement develop? The answer, at least in part, is because a number of black women concluded that they too could gain from some of the reforms that the white feminist movement advocated. Such rights as abortion, childcare centers, equal pay, equal access to employment, and the destruction of degrading stereotypes would help all women. They argued that black and white women shared "a common burden because of traditional discriminations based upon sex." Others agreed that both types of women suffered from everything from stereotypes to job discrimination and labor exploitation.

In addition, as a growing number of black women ventured out of their segregated communities they encountered blatant sexism. African American women who pursued a college education, entered a white-collar job or profession, or participated in politics faced gender and racial bias. In politics, far fewer black women than men held political office. In 1974, 337 black women obtained office, as opposed to 2,293 black men.

As a consequence, in 1973 a group called Black Women Organized for Action (BWOA) formed in San Francisco. Later that year, the first conference of the National Black Feminist Organization (NBFO) met in New York. Although these organizations recognized the distance between black and white women on feminist issues, they emphasized the importance of working together for mutual goals, including day care, abortion, equal pay, and maternity leaves. Conference speakers remarked that some of these goals were of even greater importance to black women due to their higher rate of poverty.

In 1977, a black feminist group in Boston, the Combahee River Collective, took the widest view yet. Members of the Collective explained that they battled "interlocking" systems of oppression: racial, sexual, heterosexual, and class. During the late 1970s and early 1980s, the Collective recruited and organized female workers, picketed hospitals for health care for impoverished black women, and founded rape-crisis and childcare centers.

Asian American Women

Much like Hispanas, Asian American women struggled to establish their diverse identities. These women were not simply "Asians," they also were Asian Indians, Burmese, Cambodian, mainland Chinese, Filipino, Hong Kong Chinese, Japanese, Korean, Laotian, Malaysian, Singaporean, Taiwanese, and Vietnamese. They, too, wanted such reforms as affirmative action for both women and people of color, and they increasingly asserted themselves in civil rights matters. In 1975, a group of Chinese American women in Boston boycotted public schools and demanded racial/ethnic/feminist reforms.

Women of Asian heritage had particular issues as well. Within their communities, women fought such traditions as having to perform all the housework even though they were employed outside the home. Another Asian custom kept women from speaking in public forums and leading groups. Yet another urged them to refrain from seeking higher education and political involvement. Fed up with these restrictions, Asian women demanded their right to do these things and more. They wanted to work and enter the professions, and they wanted to join American society on their own terms, that is, as Asian American women rather than imitation whites.

Asian American women established wage parity and employment opportunities as a major priority. In 1980, U.S census data indicated that 1.9 million Asian American women lived in the United States. Of these, 71 percent had a high school education, 20 percent held a college degree, and 57 percent were in the labor force. Two-fifths of those employed worked in clerical, sales, and technical jobs; one-fourth held managerial and professional positions; and one-fifth performed such unskilled and semiskilled tasks as factory work and domestic service. They earned a median annual income of $6,685. Although this was higher than the median income earned by all female workers, it was lower than that earned by Asian men.

To achieve their ends, Asian American women joined white-dominated reform groups, in which they provided leadership and supported assimilation programs. Asian American women worked primarily, however, through educational, ethnic, religious, and political organizations in their communities. These women came together at conferences. In 1980, the first National Asian Pacific American Women's Conference on Educational Equity met in Washington, D.C.

Individual women wielded influence as well. Television reporter Connie Chung and writer Maxine Hong Kingston carried a different aspect of Asian American women to the American public. The efforts of Asian television producers helped eliminate destructive stereotypes. Others scaled political barriers. In California, one Asian American woman sat on the Municipal Court bench in San Francisco; another served as mayor of Monterey Park, and another served as secretary of state.

Lesbians

More than race and ethnicity defined types of women. Another factor was sexual orientation. Although nineteenth- and early twentieth-century lesbians had hesitated to declare their sexual preference, by the mid-1960s lesbians were more willing than ever to speak out. The reform climate encouraged lesbians to state their complaints and goals. Lesbians opposed heterosexist practices and attitudes, which assumed that all women were heterosexual. In its extreme form, heterosexism vilified lesbians by defining lesbianism as perverted behavior.

Many lesbians believed that feminist leaders manifested heterosexism. Seldom were lesbians included in feminist gatherings or lesbian reforms stated in feminist plans. Rather than being marginalized in this way, lesbians argued that women must have the freedom to form bonds with other women.

Lesbians also viewed their lifestyle as an act of resistance against the dominant heterosexual culture. They challenged homophobia (the fear of homosexuality), which led to laws restricting lesbians. Because lesbian couples could not marry, they forfeited such spousal rights as company-sponsored health insurance and social security benefits. Nor could lesbians adopt children. Homophobic policies also caused lesbians to lose jobs, denied them equal access to housing, and excluded them from attending social events as a couple. Numerous lesbians charged that homophobic attitudes were outcroppings of outdated patriarchal and political ideologies. If women were to be freed, then all women had to share in that liberation.

One especially articulate lesbian spokesperson was Rita Mae Brown. As a student at New York University, in 1967 Brown helped found the first Student Homophile League. When NOW leaders rejected Brown because of her outspoken lesbian sentiment, she turned her energies to supporting a group called Radicalesbians. During the late 1960s and 1970s, Brown advocated lesbian separatism. In 1970, Radicalesbians published an influential statement of lesbian-feminist philosophies and beliefs titled "The Woman-Identified Woman." This defined a lesbian as "the rage of all women condensed to the point of explosion."

Brown helped form the first lesbian separatist group, the Furies, a collective in Washington, D.C. In 1972 and 1973, the Furies published a newspaper supporting lesbian separatism. Meanwhile, Brown wrote full time. In 1973, her semiautobiographical novel, *Rubyfruit Jungle*, was the first published narrative to show lesbian lifestyles in positive terms. With it, Brown introduced a new subgenre, the lesbian-comic novel. Brown continued to use her writing, especially *Plain Brown Rapper* (1977) and *Southern Discomfort* (1982), to bring the topic of lesbianism further into the open.

Poet Adrienne Rich also contributed to the discussion of lesbian issues. In 1980, Rich argued for lesbianism as a category of literary analysis. She stated that the societal attitude she called "compulsory heterosexuality" kept many women from expressing their true sexuality. She added that such thinking also limited research regarding women. Perhaps Rich's most important contribution was demonstrating the heterosexist assumptions of most scholarship.

As in the case of other types of women, lesbians made some gains. For the first time, the American public not only faced the existence of lesbianism, but discussed it openly. Also, in 1973, the American Psychiatric Association stated that homosexuality did not constitute deviant behavior. Lesbians were simply women who made different choices than other women.

Hearing-impaired and Disabled Women

Of all types of women, hearing-impaired and disabled women received the least notice. Although women with one or more disabilities had long worked to improve their situations, they gained little recognition for their achievements. As early as 1880, a hearing-impaired Catholic sister persuaded the archbishop to found a school for deaf children in Pennsylvania. In 1928, a Hill City, South Dakota, woman became the first hearing-impaired pilot in the United States. In 1953, swimmer Gertrude Ederle became the first hearing-impaired person to win a place in the Helms Foundation Hall of Fame, honoring physically challenged people.

The civil rights movement and the second wave of feminism helped empower such women. Hearing-impaired women and women who faced physical and mental challenges had special needs. They demanded the recognition of American Sign Language as a valid language in its own right. In 1972, a San Francisco television station offered a daily news program with signers for the hearing impaired. Other women asked for better access to schools, businesses, and public buildings. Yet others fought discrimination in employment. Such activists provided role models for other disabled women and made people think about people with disabilities in new ways.

Consequently, Americans increasingly accepted and supported disabled individuals. During the 1970s, the National Theatre of the Deaf and the Gallaudet College Dancers entertained enthusiastic audiences. In 1980, actor Phyllis French won the Tony Award for her leading role in the Broadway play *Children of a Lesser God*, later released as a film in 1986 starring the deaf actor Marlee Matlin.

Women in Religion

Religiously oriented women showed strength and assertiveness as well. One of the most outspoken of these was Mary Daly, a radical feminist and theologian. In 1968, she published her first controversial book, *The Church and the Second Sex*, in which Daly attacked church policies that banned women from full participation. This polemic almost cost Daly her tenure at Boston College, a Catholic school where she had taught since 1966. After her *God the Father* appeared in 1978, Daly worked on a trilogy presenting a radical feminist argument for women's need to liberate themselves from patriarchy: *Gyn/Ecology* (1978), *Pure Lust* (1984), and *Outer Course* (1987). Daly offered women a new way to think about churches and religious beliefs.

Other women were quick to organize on their own behalf. In 1970, an ecumenical Center for Women and Religion formed in Berkeley, California. Ten theological institutions associated with the Graduate Theological Union sponsored the Center, which attracted an international membership committed to ending sexism and promoting justice through religion and religious values. The Center offered theological curriculums based on feminist ideas. It also sponsored conferences, forums, and publications. Another example was Womanchurch, an ecumenical gathering of women who held their own services. In time, Womanchurch established chapters throughout the United States.

In more traditional churches as well, women struggled for increased participation, especially as ministers and priests. One well-publicized case of reform occurred in the Episcopalian Church, which in 1976 began ordaining female priests. This movement caused so much intra-Church controversy that it cost the Church many members.

The American Jewish community responded more cautiously to the feminist impetus. Nonetheless, after 1971, when groups of Jewish women synthesized American feminism and American Judaism, significant changes occurred, including greater female participation in communal prayer. Women also gained limited acceptance of innovative liturgy and life-cycle rituals, and they held positions of communal authority and status. These shifts encouraged Jewish women to criticize certain Jewish religious texts. They also proposed changes in Jewish pedagogy, with some women pursuing the rabbinate, heretofore reserved for men.

Socialist and Communist Women

Socialist feminists took yet another approach to the problems facing American women. They advocated radical feminism, meaning that they wished to eliminate male dominance from American society. Rather than gaining equality with men, they hoped to institute a leaderless participatory democracy. They used consciousness-raising techniques to educate women and enhance awareness of feminist issues. They also engaged in radical demonstrations and protests that frequently alienated middle-of-the road feminists.

The best known of these women was Angela Davis. Born in Birmingham, Alabama, she graduated from Brandeis University in Massachusetts, where she had studied Marxist philosophy. After graduation, Davis entered the civil rights movement, a member of the SNCC and the Black Panthers. In June 1968, she joined the Communist party. Beginning in the fall of 1969, she taught at the University of California at Los Angeles. After attaining office, conservative governor Ronald Reagan helped pass a state law prohibiting California universities from hiring known Communists; Davis was soon fired. After being rehired, she was fired again, this time for making "inflammatory" remarks supporting three black prisoners accused of killing a white guard.

Reportedly, Davis had purchased a gun for one of the prisoners. After fleeing from California, Davis wound up on the FBI's list of the "ten most wanted fugitives." In 1970, she was arrested, after which she endured a twenty-month trial. Two years later, courts declared Davis innocent of all charges. In 1974, she published *Angela Davis: An Autobiography* to help people understand "why so many of us have no alternative but to offer our lives—our bodies, our knowledge, our will—to the cause of our oppressed people." After that, Davis resumed her aborted academic career, teaching philosophy and women's studies at San Francisco State University. In 1981, she published a scholarly study titled *Women, Race, and Class,* which contained little evidence of her old fire.

Rural Women

Generally, rural women experienced less change than other groups of women. In the rural South, black and white women continued to labor in homes and fields. A study of tobacco farms indicated that sisters, wives, and daughters contributed their unpaid labor to their families. According to one researcher, this family system of survival functioned "under the leadership of the male head" and "blended patriarchal forms with the market economy."

Because of growing economic pressures on family farms during the 1970s and 1980s, farm women also "helped out" by working for pay off the farm. A study of Kentucky farm women in 1980 revealed that 38 percent of them worked off the farm. Other women ran farms while men of the family held outside jobs. Another researcher noted that farm women "not only . . . have to fill in for their part-time farming husbands on the land, but they themselves are increasingly entering the non-farm labor force."

The lives of women migrant farm workers were especially difficult. Largely Hispanas, these women suffered harsh and unsanitary working conditions (often with no restroom facilities whatsoever), low wages, wretched housing, patriarchal family structures, and lack of opportunities to improve their situations. One Hispana recalled the anguish that she felt when, in 1966, her migrant worker father shunned her because she had decided to pursue the education that would free her from the migrant life and an arranged marriage. Other Hispanas, including some women Religious (Catholic sisters), protested the terrible conditions and lack of opportunities suffered by workers living in colonias outside such cities as El Paso.

By the 1980s, rural women developed their own brand of feminism. Although 1978 census figures had indicated that 5 percent of all farmers were female, in 1981 a Department of Agriculture survey showed that 55 percent of all farm women considered themselves the main operators. These results suggest that growing numbers of women demanded recognition as farmers. More specifically, they challenged such discriminatory practices as banks refusing to loan female farmers money. They also criticized male farmers who excluded women from information-sharing sessions. Finally, they demanded that tractor manufacturers consider women's need for smaller-scale equipment.

Assessing Gains and Losses, 1965–1985

The Second Wave

Between 1965 and 1985, the second wave of feminism hoped to finish the work the suffragists of the early 1900s had started. Between 1965 and 1985, traditional gender expectations became more of a myth than a prescription for American women. In addition, improvements for American women seemed to follow one another with incredible speed. How many of these changes can be attributed to the feminist movement is unclear. In all probability, the feminist movement was a cause and an effect of the changing social climate. Certainly, the feminist movement forced Americans to recognize the existence of gender discrimination and grapple with implementing the necessary changes.

Among women, awareness of feminist issues rose quickly. Although a 1962 Gallup poll revealed that less than one out of every three women felt discriminated against, eight years later 50 percent of all women reported that they had experienced discrimination. In 1974, two out of three said they had suffered discrimination. In 1979, another study showed that between 1962 and 1977 the beliefs of women of all classes and ages had shifted toward egalitarianism. Even though they might not describe themselves as feminists, the majority of American women supported feminist demands for daycare, abortion, and equal job and professional opportunities.

Yet another study indicated that during the 1970s many American men revised their attitudes toward women. Some of these men translated attitudes into action. In 1978, officials in Indianapolis, Indiana, appointed two women to police patrol duty. During the late 1970s and early 1980s, the police forces of other American municipalities hired women. Gradually, the term "policeman" turned into "police officer."

Federal Initiatives

The federal government played a key role in feminist reform. Political leaders adjusted existing policies and laws and enacted new ones. In 1967, President Lyndon B. Johnson issued an executive order prohibiting gender discrimination by federal contractors. The growing number of female judges appointed and elected to national, state, and local court benches also spurred change.

Congress proved active as well. In 1972, Congress added Title IX to the Education Amendments Act, forbidding discrimination against students and employees in federally assisted educational programs. Also in 1972, Congress finally approved the Equal Rights Amendment (ERA), which stated, "Equality of Rights shall not be denied or abridged by the United States or by any state on account of sex." After Congress sent the ERA to the states for ratification, the civil rights sentiment of the time made ratification appear likely within the seven-year deadline. Some law schools even introduced special courses to train future lawyers in Equal Rights law.

By 1973, however, only thirty states had ratified the ERA; the approval of eight more states was needed, and opposition to the ERA was well organized and widespread. Congress extended the ERA ratification deadline to 30 June 1982, but a nation experiencing economic instability and a rebirth of political conservatism failed to ratify the amendment.

In 1975, Congress mandated that U.S. military academies accept women. The following year the United States Military Academy at West

Point, New York, and the Annapolis Naval Academy admitted their first female cadets; the first coed classes graduated in 1980. In the meantime, the Supreme Court had to step in and directly order the gender integration of the Citadel in Charleston, South Carolina. If women were to have access to military schools, then they would have access to all of them.

At the same time, federal offices and agencies made an effort to employ more women. The National Aeronautics and Space Administration (NASA) utilized female personnel. Although NASA was formed in 1958, it did not accept women until the mid-1970s. In 1978, NASA hired its first woman astronaut, Sally K. Ride of Encino, California. In 1983, Ride was the mission specialist on a six-day flight of the space shuttle *Challenger*. Ride was later inducted into the National Women's Hall of Fame.

During the 1970s and 1980s, Congress adopted additional initiatives for women. One was the Women's Equity Act, which supported job training programs for women. Congress also supported Women's History Month. This event began in 1977 when Sonoma County, California, schools denoted March as Women's History Month in the hopes of raising interest in women's history and integrating it into school curriculums. In 1980, the National Women's History Project organized in Santa Rosa, California, to supply information on International Women's Day and Women's History Month. In 1981, Congress adopted a national Women's History Week proclamation, later enlarging it to a Women's History Month, now celebrated every March in the United States.

Women in Paid Employment

How did feminist programs affect the day-to-day lives of average American women? Employed women were a large group who needed reform. By 1980, more than half of all married women worked outside the home, and approximately three out of five women with children held jobs. By 1985, more than three out of five women held employment. No longer a temporary or marginal labor force, women workers received long-sought and much-needed benefits, including maternity leaves (some of them paid leaves), daycare, and job-training programs.

Working women demonstrated a growing willingness to participate in labor organizations. Cesar Chavez and Dolores Huerta's National Farm Workers Association (NFWA) had captured the nation's attention with its grape boycott. During the protest, the NFWA became the United Farm Workers (UFW). In 1974, as the UFW's first elected vice president, Huerta said that women and men welcomed her efforts, explaining that all UFW members appreciated "anybody who will come in and help them." By 1977, UFW represented some 30,000 workers. Women served in administrative positions and on the picket lines, becoming a mainstay of the UFW and its nonviolent approach to labor reform.

Besides Hispanas, other women supported unions. Between 1956 and 1976, women workers, many of whom were teachers and public employees, accounted for nearly half of the growth in overall union membership. In 1974, 3,500 union women launched a new organization, the Coalition of Labor Union Women (CLUW). This group hoped to increase affirmative action on the job, encourage female workers to participate in politics, and bring additional women into unions. Department of Labor statistics for 1976 to 1978 indicated that women trade union members increased by 455,000. For the first time, women constituted nearly 28 percent of all union membership.

And for the first time, male union leaders realized that they had to consider the needs of women in the work force; the growing number of women members could affect not only unions' successes but their very survival. In 1980, the new president of the AFL-CIO announced his intention to bring women into top leadership positions. During the 1980s, labor unions recruited nonunion women workers. Most addressed women's issues and activities in their newsletters and other publications. They also included women's issues in lobbying efforts.

The place of black women in the labor force also changed, as black women moved into positions once dominated by white women. In 1965, only 24 percent of employed black women were white-collar workers; by 1981, this percentage had rocketed to 46. As black women abandoned domestic service in significant numbers, recent immigrants from Puerto Rico, Mexico, and other areas of Latin America replaced them. In 1965, 30 percent of all working black women toiled in domestic service; in 1977, this figure had dropped to 9 percent.

In addition, black women joined labor unions. In 1970, a black garment worker, Lillian Rice, complained that unions were of little use to black workers because they discriminated against people of color. This situation improved during the late 1970s and early 1980s, during which time Rice became associate director of District Council 37 for the organization in New York. She later became Labor Commissioner for the State of New York.

Not all of working women's problems reached resolution. The majority of employed women remained stuck in clerical, sales, and office jobs that paid low wages. In 1985, women earned between fifty-five to fifty-seven cents for every dollar men earned. And women's work offered little opportunity for advancement.

Equal pay also remained problematic. Because the Equal Pay Act of 1963 amended the Fair Labor Standards Act of 1938, the U.S. Labor Department was responsible for its enforcement. Department officials conducted routine checks of workplaces for violations and investigated complaints with only limited success, largely due to imprecision in the wording of the act itself. During the 1970s, women brought comparable-worth suits, later called sex-equity suits. In these court cases, women demanded equal pay for work of like value. By 1985, such complainants had obtained favorable judgments in six states. Nonetheless, the concept of comparable worth continued to face resistance from the New Right and other conservative factions.

Education and the Professions

Female reformers had always considered education a high priority. They understood that it provided the step up that so many women needed. Between 1965 and 1985, the U.S. educational system underwent serious modifications. Special programs to eradicate women's "fear of success" and "math anxiety" offset the negative effects of gender stereotyping in female students. Women's athletic programs expanded and, in some respects, became more equitable with men's athletics. The number of female college students also rose noticeably. By 1985, affirmative action programs increased the number of women hired and enrolled.

With more women seeking higher education, the number of women in the professions increased. In 1962, women constituted 3.6 percent of law students. Ten years later, in 1972, women accounted for 12 percent of law students. Between 1971 and 1981, the percentage of female lawyers and judges jumped from 4 to 14. By 1984, women constituted one-third of law school graduates. In medicine, women filled a variety of roles, including that of nurse, nurse midwife, nurse practitioner, physician, and surgeon. Between 1962 and 1972, the percentage of female medical students rose from 9 to 22. Women also attended all types of graduate schools in growing numbers. After 1970, the number of women obtaining doctorates grew more than 1 percent each year. By 1985, women earned nearly 30 percent of all Ph.D.s granted.

At the same time, women challenged old notions of librarianship as a woman's profession. Female members of the American Library Association publicized discriminatory practices against women, especially in matters of pay equity and opportunities for career advancement. Also, women of color fought for expanded access to library training programs and jobs.

On another front, women sought careers in the U.S. Park Service and Forest Service. Although forestry had remained male-dominated since it professionalized around the turn of the twentieth century, a few women gained employment as naturalists, park rangers, foresters, and fire lookouts. By the early 1980s, women decided they had to take action. In Oregon, affirmative action programs had aided a number of women in obtaining Forest Service jobs in two of the state's national forests. When resistance from male workers continued, women used informal pressure and formal grievance procedures to hold onto their jobs and improve the situation for other women seeking careers in forestry.

Overall, women of color participated in educational gains at a lower rate than did white women. Nonetheless, teaching, nursing, and the social sciences attracted women of color, and they entered law and medicine in growing numbers. While the number of black professional women remained small compared to that of white women, black women had benefited from affirmative action and economic opportunity programs.

Women in the Media

Women who wanted to play a larger role in the media borrowed tactics from feminist leaders. They complained loudly and publicly. And they applied legal pressure, using such policies as affirmative action.

As a result, women became notable in media jobs ranging from reporter to disc jockey. African American women especially made a breakthrough. A black female worked as a war correspondent during the Vietnam years. Another became the first black woman columnist for the *Washington Post*. And a black radio broadcaster became known as the "First Lady of Chicago Radio."

Television producers, who depended on advertising and could not afford to alienate female consumers, responded to women's complaints. Some pushed white women into visible positions as news-show reporters and anchors. Barbara Walters became an outstanding and highly paid television journalist. The number of women of color in such positions grew more slowly, but Connie Chung gained a reputation as a respected journalist and offered the viewing public a new perception of Asian women. Meanwhile, African American talk show star and producer Oprah Winfrey won several Emmy awards for the *Oprah Winfrey Show*, now the longest-running daytime talk show in the United States and a vastly influential broadcast. By 2006, Winfrey's net worth would be estimated at $1.4 billion.

On television and in film, gender stereotypes came under attack. Gradually, the number of women's roles and themes increased. In 1985, the television program *Cagney and Lacy*, which featured two female detectives, received high ratings. At the same time, black women played leading roles in such high-profile television series as *The Cosby Show, Head of the Class, 21 Jump Street,* and *I'll Fly Away.* On the Big Screen, the film *Norma Rae* presented a gutsy labor organizer in southern cotton mills, while *Yentl* questioned the prescribed roles of Jewish American women. *Country* demonstrated the courage of women in times of economic crisis, and *Sounder* and *The Color Purple* revealed the strength of black women characters and the talent of those black women who portrayed them. At long last, no longer were black women seen as "Mammies."

Women in Sports

The world of sports had long been receptive to women athletes. During the twentieth century, women had abandoned "genteel" sports in favor of "men's" sports. The Olympic Games were demonstrative. In Olympic competition, female track-and-field stars lowered women's record times and female skaters brought an impressive number of medals back to the United States.

Other sports experienced marked change as well. In basketball, the Women's Professional Basketball League formed in 1978. In golf, a woman won purses whose amounts approached those won by the top male golfers. In horse racing, female jockeys not only rode against male jockeys but frequently beat them. In 1973, Janet Guthrie became the first woman to qualify for and compete at the "Brickyard" in the Indianapolis 500.

In this era, Billie Jean King established women's tennis as a major American sport. After becoming in 1961 the youngest player to win at Wimbledon, King took twenty more titles in the next twelve years. In 1972, *Sports Illustrated* named her Sportswoman of the Year. In 1973, she helped found the Women's Tennis Association, which acted as a players' union. Also in 1973, King startled Americans by defeating male challenger Bobby Riggs. Although King increasingly spoke out on abortion and lesbianism, she continued to reap titles and enjoy a wide fan base. In 1980, King was inducted into the Women's Sports Hall of Fame. Since then, other outstanding U.S. women tennis players have included Chris Evert Lloyd, foreign-born Martina Navrátilova, Lindsay Davenport, and the remarkable Venus and Serena Williams, African American sisters from Lynwood, California.

Women in the Arts

The arts also benefited from feminist reform. In painting, women produced works ranging in style from folk art to surrealism. At the same time, a resurgence of interest in quilting occurred, leading to the formation of quilting clubs and conferences.

Of special note was the work of Judy Chicago. Chicago, a West Coast minimalist sculptor, had in the 1960s founded or helped found the first feminist art programs of Womanhouse, the Woman's Building, and the Feminist Studio Workshop. In 1973, Chicago started the installation of her major work, *The Dinner Party*. This massive project involved four hundred artists who drew on traditional women's crafts, including china painting, embroidery, and weaving. They created thirty-nine place settings, each celebrating an outstanding woman. For example, the "setting" in honor of early feminist Mary Wollstonecraft featured embroidered scenes from Wollstonecraft's life in stumpwork, a type of stuffed and raised needlework done in England during Wollstonecraft's lifetime in the eighteenth century.

When *The Dinner Party* premiered in 1979 at the San Francisco Museum of Modern Art, it attracted 100,000 viewers. Later, it toured the United States. Because of its outspoken feminist and lesbian themes, the piece seldom visited major museums. In 1980, Chicago started *The Birth Project*, which expressed the experience of childbirth among diverse generations and cultures of women.

In music, women also demonstrated creativity and productivity. In 1966, the New York Philharmonic hired its first woman performer, and by 1983 a woman was artistic director of the New York City Opera Company. Among the best-known opera singers was Leontyne Price. A black woman from Laurel, Mississippi, Price first sang in a church choir and later studied at the Julliard School of Music in New York. In 1966, Price celebrated the Metropolitan Opera's move to Lincoln Hall by performing Samuel Barber's *Anthony and Cleopatra*, which Barber had written expressly for her.

In popular music, female stars soon rivaled men for numbers of gold and platinum records. Women musicians also opened new doors. Black jazz singers developed "scatting," a form of singing that uses improvised sounds instead of words. Meanwhile, an artist known as Madonna challenged gender stereotypes and media norms through her live rock concerts and music videos. Beginning in 1982, Madonna grabbed public attention with such hits as "Everybody," "Borderline," and "Into the Groove." Perhaps most important, her 1984 hit, "Like a Virgin," attacked long-standing conventions regarding American women.

Women writers of the time also proved prolific and imaginative. Maya Angelou, who had served as northern coordinator for the Reverend Dr. Martin Luther King's Southern Christian Leadership Conference, wrote poems, essays, and a series of autobiographical works. Perhaps Angelou's most famous work was *I Know Why the Caged Bird Sings* (1970), which described her childhood in the rural community of Stamps, Arkansas, including her rape at eight years of age. At sixteen, Angelou moved to California, where the San Francisco Streetcar Company hired her as its first black woman fare collector. Later, black feminist writer Alice Walker explored relationships among women and within families in *The Color Purple* (1982). In 1983, Walker received the Pulitzer Prize for this poignant exploration of the lives of black women in the rural South.

To this rich outpouring, Maxine Hong Kingston added her autobiographical *The Woman Warrior* (1975), which probed a Chinese American girl's struggle to overcome Chinese traditionalism and American prejudice against Asians. In 1976, Kingston won the National Book Critics Circle Award for nonfiction.

Nicholasa Mohr, an artist, novelist, and essayist, was the first Puerto Rican woman living in the mainland United States to write in English about her ethnic origins. Born of island migrants in New York City, Mohr recalled that she and her family had felt like "strangers in their own country." In *El Bronx Remembered* (1973), *Neuva York* (1977), and *Felita* (1979), Mohr documented the situation of a rural people transported to an industrial society and their segregation into bleak neighborhoods and low-skill jobs. She also revealed the problems caused by an abundance of female-headed welfare households. Yet Mohr's work captured the joyous side of Puerto Rican life as well. In it lives the pervasiveness of family unity, neighborhood solidarity, and vibrant religious celebrations and feast days.

White women further enriched this feminist literature. Some novelists used fiction to build the case against male chauvinism. Others dealt with women's struggle to understand modern society and find a place in it. For instance, Sylvia Plath described limitations on women in *The Bell Jar* (1971). Feminists celebrated Plath as a spokesperson for their cause. To some, she became a cult figure.

Women in Politics

Political change had long fascinated those who believed that only by entering the realm of politics would women stand on an equal basis with men. From Elizabeth Cady Stanton and Susan B. Anthony to Carrie Chapman Catt and Alice Paul, female reformers viewed political participation as the ultimate answer to women's problems. Yet even though women had won the right to vote in 1920, political influence still escaped them.

Starting in 1965, women finally became more visible in politics. Between 1969 and 1981, the number of female state legislators grew from 301 to 908. Between 1975 and 1981, the number of female elected officials increased from 5,765 to 14,225.

Democrats established an especially strong record. The era of President Johnson and "Lady Bird" proved good years for women. Johnson appointed more women to office than any president before or since, with the exception of President William J. Clinton. Black women also benefited. During the late 1960s, three times as many black women as men registered to vote. In 1968, Democrat Shirley Chisholm became the first black woman elected to the U.S. House of Representatives. Chisholm served until 1982 as representative of the Twelfth District of Brooklyn, New York.

In 1972, Representative Barbara Jordan, an African American Democrat from Houston, came into public view when she delivered the nominating speech at the Democratic National Convention. Later, Jordan earned the respect of the nation with her articulate address as a member of the House Judiciary Committee that recommended the impeachment of President Richard M. Nixon. Jordan, who described Nixon's resignation as a "cleansing experience" for American politics, worked for civil rights, the environment, and the underprivileged. Among other key legislation she sponsored during her three terms, Jordan helped extend Social Security coverage to full-time homemakers.

Although the Republican party had a more checkered record regarding women, the Republicans achieved a significant feat in 1978 when Nancy L. Kassebaum of Kansas became the first woman elected to the U.S. Senate who was not the widow of a member of Congress. In 1981, President Ronald Reagan appointed the first woman justice, Sandra Day O'Connnor, to the U.S. Supreme Court. Two years later, Reagan named women as secretary of transportation and secretary of health and human services. He appointed few women, however, to lower judicial and administrative positions.

Meanwhile, as women's votes began to form a bloc, the so-called gender gap appeared. In 1982, 5 percent less women than men voted for conservative candidates. In later elections, female voters showed less support than men did for President Reagan's policies. Female voters disliked Reagan's opposition to the ERA and his military and economic decisions. Women gave more support than did men to such issues as abortion, childcare, and the ERA. By the mid-1980s, women composed approximately 53 percent of the voting population and registered to vote in greater numbers than did men.

The year 1984 proved crucial for women in politics, as New York congressperson Geraldine Ferraro became the Democratic party's candidate for the vice presidency of the United States. Ferraro, an attorney admitted to the New York bar in 1961, left her private practice in 1974 to serve as assistant district attorney for Queens County, New York. In that capacity, she handled cases of child abuse, domestic violence, and rape. In 1978, Ferraro gained a seat in the U.S. House of Representatives. She ran successfully for two additional terms. In the House, Ferraro voted with liberal Democrats on most issues. Despite her membership in the Roman Catholic Church, Ferraro voted for legal access to abortion. Although she and her running mate, Walter Mondale, failed to unseat President Ronald Reagan and Vice President George Bush in 1984, the fact that Ferraro campaigned with intelligence and style throughout the rigors of her bid for national office established her as a memorable role model for women in politics.

In subsequent years, other women assaulted barriers ranging from the local to the federal level. The U.S. Congress provides and excellent example of women's slow yet steady progress. Since 1917, when Jeannette Rankin of

Missoula, Missouri, became the first women in Congress by gaining election to the U.S. House of Representatives, more than 170 women were elected to the House. Among them were Margaret Chase Smith, Clare Booth Luce, Bella Abzug, and Barbara Jordan.

Women and Family

The family was one of the most dramatic arenas of change for women. During the 1950s, 70 percent of American families were composed of a father who worked and a mother who stayed at home to care for the children. By 1980, only 15 percent of families were so constituted. With the assistance of birth-control pills and other forms of contraception, the average family size fell to 1.6 children. At the same time, 23 percent of adults chose to live in single-person households. Of all new marriages, roughly 50 percent ended in divorce.

One result of the rising divorce rate was a debate concerning child custody. In the country's early years, courts had assigned the custody of children to fathers, as judges had considered children the property of the father. But by the mid-twentieth-century, it was far more common for judges to award mothers custody because they believed that children needed mother love. During the late twentieth century, divorced fathers challenged this thinking and sued for custody of their children. Some parents requested "joint custody," meaning that children would live part-time with their mother and part-time with their father. Many judges agreed that children could benefit from knowing both parents.

Another consequence of the high divorce rate was an expanding definition of family. A family might be two employed adults or spouses who lived in separate households. It also might be a single-parent household or a "reconstituted" family made up of two remarried adults and their children from previous marriages. A family might define a "skip-generation" household, one including a grandparent and grandchild but not the child's parent, or a group of unmarried people representing several generations living together. A family could even be an unmarried person living alone. *Dual-career marriage, single-parent family, commuter marriage, supermom,* and *latchkey child* all became common terms.

Besides these modifications, a 1967 Supreme Court decision made it possible for people of any race or ethnic background to marry whomever they pleased. In *Loving* v. *Virginia*, the justices declared Virginia's antimiscegenation law unconstitutional. The decision emphasized "the principle of equality at the heart of the Fourteenth Amendment." In so doing, the court legitimatized the interracial marriage of Richard and Mildred Loving, who by then were the parents of three children.

Americans continued to experiment with gender roles and to reshape gender expectations. A 1980 Gallup poll revealed support for women's reproductive freedom and their right to hold political office. In 1983, another survey indicated that the majority of respondents believed that wives and husbands should share household chores, childcare, and financial and other decision-making. Many women discovered, however, that declaring something as "right" did not affect practice. In general, women remained in charge of households and men acted as "helpers."

Americans also seemed more than willing to expand their sexual lives. Open discussion occurred of vaginal versus clitoral orgasms. At the same time, a profusion of marriage manuals and other self-help literature offered explicit sexual advice to women, men, and couples. Alex Comfort's *The Joy of Sex* (1972) became a long-term best-seller. It described techniques of oral sex—still against the law in many states—advocated masturbation, and endorsed homosexuality. Nothing was too personal to discuss in public, nothing too deviant to try in private.

Feminization of Poverty

On the deficit side of the ledger, an unfortunate development was the "feminization" of poverty. The rise in the number of female-headed households combined with segregation of women into low-paying jobs created a group of American women who lived near or under the poverty level.

In part, women's growing poverty resulted from "no-fault" divorce. Initially implemented in California in 1970 when then-governor Ronald Reagan signed it into law, no-fault divorce gave women who opposed their husbands' wish to divorce them little legal recourse. Because most states no longer required "grounds" to divorce a spouse, a woman's ability to charge her adulterous husband with fault and thereby obtain a favorable settlement to support herself and her children was diluted. Against their wills, wives who had never worked and lacked job skills moved into the category of "displaced homemakers." In 1973, Congress responded with the Comprehensive Employment and Training Act (CETA). This program gave grants to local agencies that would train displaced homemakers and help them find jobs.

The growth of female poverty also resulted from an unprecedented rise in female-headed households. These occurred because of separation, desertion, mutually agreed upon divorce, widowhood, and pregnancy outside marriage. In 1890, women headed only fourteen of every one hundred households; by 1970, this number had risen to twenty-one. In 1980, women headed twenty-six out of every hundred households. Although federal and state governments expanded welfare programs to help these women, the majority of Americans living in poverty continued to be female.

The rise of female poverty especially affected African American women. By 1980, 55 percent of black children were born outside marriage. Also in 1980, 85 percent of black teenage mothers were unmarried and 47 percent of black families had female heads. Lacking skills and discriminated against in employment, most of these women turned for assistance to welfare or to such organizations as the National Council of Negro Women.

Other women of color also headed households. One Puerto Rican woman in Harlem was a good example. A mother of four separated from her husband and living on relief, she waged a daily battle with rats, junkies, and the indifference of landlords. She also had to deal with the incompetence of exhausted and overloaded welfare caseworkers. And stories like this were not uncommon.

Eating Disorders

Another problem that resulted from the growing pressures on women were eating disorders. These included anorexia nervosa, bulimia, and obesity. Although these ailments were not new to the United States, their incidence rose rapidly during the late 1960s, the 1970s, and early 1980s. Paradoxically, women had more societal options available than ever before yet appeared more stressed than ever.

Anorexia and bulimia were widespread. These diseases typically afflicted the daughters of educated and successful parents. Anorexia is a psycho-sociological disease of self-imposed starvation. Bulimia is marked by a binge-purge cycle, in which a person eats huge amounts of food and then purges it through vomiting or the overuse of laxatives. A female medical researcher in Houston, identified three causal factors for such eating disorders. For one, she blamed the increasing emphasis on thinness in the United States. Second, women faced new and heightened pressures to achieve in their personal as well as professional lives. Finally, societal acceptance to experiment with sex at an early age placed additional stress on young women to appear as "attractive" as possible to others.

By the mid-1980s, 80 percent of ten-year-old girls had been on a diet or were currently dieting. To many commentators, that statistic alone called into question prevailing social and cultural values for women.

Since 1985

A Turning Point?

The nation stood at a crossroads in 1985. When Geraldine Ferraro accepted the Democratic National Convention's vice-presidential nomination in 1984 she said, "By choosing a woman to run for our nation's second highest office, you send a powerful signal to all Americans. There are no doors we cannot unlock."

Many who helped initiate the modern feminist movement felt less confident that they would see solutions to the problems most women faced in their lifetimes. Although some Americans voted to elevate a woman to a leadership position, others resented the demands of feminists and reformers. In 1985, one male public figure commented: "So cry not for the Ferraro candidacy. Nobody lost by it. The women were in the kitchen when the thing started, and they're in the kitchen where they belong at the end of it."

The year 1985 was contradictory in other ways as well. On the one hand, it marked the eruption of violence against abortion clinics, as some women and men demanded a return to past policies. On the other hand, a national poll showed that women and men wanted to destroy the traditional double standard that made women responsible for such slips as an unwanted pregnancy. Apparently, Americans were mixed in their sentiment toward feminist reforms.

Agents of Change

There is no doubt that modern feminism created significant revisions in American attitudes and policies. The second wave of feminism, which began in the 1960s, exerted more influence than had the first wave because of four distinguishing characteristics.

First, the second wave of feminism included women of all social classes, races, and ethnicities. Rather than drawing upon middle- and upper-class white women, modern feminism paid attention to women of color, lesbians, and older women. It also sought support from women's organizations, including the Girl Scouts of America, the League of Women Voters, and the Young Women's Christian Association. As a result, modern feminism had a wider base than any previous campaign.

Second, modern feminist leaders refused to focus on one or two solutions. Instead, they questioned all assumptions regarding women and their prescribed roles. For the first time in American history, women held everything up to examination and disputed its fairness. Feminists challenged the inevitability and "rightness" of patriarchy. Although earlier feminist movements had accepted and built on the societal beliefs that women were moral, virtuous, and social housekeepers, modern feminists rejected that strategy.

Third, the second wave analyzed the effect of culture on the development of gender roles and behavior. How, they asked, do societal rules make children act "female" or "male"? They pointed to scientific evidence that showed that up to the point of birth, human development is largely genetic, with chromosomes and hormones determining gender characteristics. At birth, however, culture becomes formative. During its first three years, a child learns well how she or he is expected to behave. In feminists' eyes, traditional societal rules harnessed girls into crippling lifelong roles.

Fourth, American women wielded new kinds of power, which feminists were quick to use. Women outnumbered men in the United States. Female college students outnumbered males. Employed women were freer than ever before of economic dependence on men. As primary consumers, women greatly influenced the economy. Women even purchased approximately 75 percent of such men's products as underwear. They also selected more liberating lines of personal products and clothing for themselves, including jeans, comfortable shoes, and healthier kinds of makeup. Moreover, because women typically outlived men, as widows they often ended up controlling the fortunes that men had earned.

Despite the influence of contemporary feminism, it would be inaccurate to give it full credit for all changes. Certainly, the questioning of rules and authority received a major boost from the civil rights movement and Anti–Vietnam War protests. In addition, U.S. prosperity, and, ironically, the lack thereof, created more jobs for women. Even when the economy contracted, women continued working in order to keep up high "standards" of living. The dual-income couple became common.

Meanwhile, improved technology made it possible for women to perform numerous jobs, including those that had once demanded physical prowess. Women could also control the spacing of childbirth through technology and ease childcare by employing such products as disposable diapers.

A complex of other factors influenced change. Because the United States democratized education and professional training, advanced jobs and professions opened to women. And because modern women lived longer than had their mothers, they had more years of "empty-nest" time in which to pursue graduate degrees or other credentials and careers.

As always, change generated opposition. Some people feared that chaos might result when old rules changed or disappeared. In addition, people with deep religious convictions believed that certain concepts were innate, natural, and God-given. The Roman Catholic Church, for example, still maintained that abortion constituted murder. Viewing itself as countercultural, the Church resisted a society in which individuals, as opposed to God, chose to bring a pregnancy to term or abort it.

Looking back on American history, it is clear that reform always brought opposition. Resistance served a purpose. Naysayers caused people to consider and discuss reforms. Furthermore, they stopped reformers for rushing headlong into further change before society had absorbed the effects of those already achieved.

Accordingly, during the 1980s and 1990s, opposition to abortion led to a reexamination of the base issues. The antiabortion, or Right-to-Life, movement led in 1989 to the case of *Webster* v. *Reproductive Health Services*, in which the U.S. Supreme Court ruled that individual states had the right to limit women's access to legal abortion. Meanwhile, feminist writers debated the cause and effects of "backlash," which was probably more a reflection of a conservative upswelling than a recoil against the women's movement.

Change Triumphant

Despite such opposition, a majority of Americans stood behind change for women. In 1988, the U.S. Congress approved the Civil Rights Restoration Act. This required institutions accepting federal assistance to comply with antidiscrimination laws. When President Ronald Reagan vetoed the bill, Congress overrode it.

By the early 2000s, a record number of women participated in the 107th Congress. Sixty-one held positions as representativess; thirteen as senator. According to the 2006 figures, the 109th Congress topped this record: 67 women were in the House and 14 in the Senate. Among the senators were Barbara Boxer, Hilary Rodham Clinton, Elizabeth Dole, and Dianne Feinstein. In addition, 20 of these congresspeople were women of color. As a result of their activism, many women's voices were heard in the halls of Congress.

Federal offices and agencies also made an effort to recruit and employ more women. For example, after Sally Ride became the first American woman to reach outer space in 1983 as a crew member of the space shuttle *Challenger*, NASA sent thirty-four other women, all but one of whom was an official astronaut, into space as members of shuttle crews. Tragically, four of them, including Christa McAuliffe, a teacher who volunteered to go on a mission to further American children's interest in science, died in shuttle explosions.

The women of NASA included women of color, notably Dr. Mae C. Jemison, a practicing medical doctor in Los Angeles, who boarded the shuttle *Endeavor* in 1992 to become the first African American woman in space, and a Hispana, Ellen Ochoa, Ph.D. (*Discovery*, 1993, 1999; *Atlantis*, 1994, 2002).

The government's attitude toward historical sites altered as well. Although presidents, generals, forts, and battlefields once dominated the subject matter and names of the nation's statues and historic sites, the National Park Service began to dedicate "women's" sites. These include the Women's Rights National Historical Park in Seneca Falls, New York, which interprets the first women's rights convention of 1848 to visitors. Also located there is the National Women's Hall of Fame, first organized in 1968 to honor outstanding American women.

Others include the Maggie I. Walker National Historical Site in Richmond, Virginia, which preserves the home and neighborhood of a leader in Richmond's black community, who was also the first woman bank president in the United States. There is also the Eleanor Roosevelt National Historic Site in Hyde Park, New York; the Clara Barton National Historic Site in Glen Echo, Maryland; the Whitman Mission National Historic Site near Walla Walla, Washington (the 1836 mission of Narcissa and Marcus Whitman); and the Lowell National Historical Park in Lowell, Massachusetts.

Women also gained greater recognition in the realm of fine arts. In 1987, the National Museum of Women in the Arts in Washington, D.C., opened its doors. It comprised permanent collections ranging from Renaissance work to contemporary art, a library, and a research center.

Contemporary literature demonstrated far more change than continuity. Recent black women writers have investigated the African American past, especially the role of slavery in it. During the 1970s, writer Toni Morrison attracted attention with *Sula* (1975) and *Song of Soloman* (1978). In 1988, Morrison won the Pulitzer Prize for her exquisite novel *Beloved*, which assesses the legacy of slavery. In 1993, Morrison became the first black American to win the Nobel Prize in literature. The Swedish Academy described her work as "unusually finely wrought and cohesive, yet at the same time rich in variation." In response to the prize announcement, Morrison explained that her work attempted to remedy "huge silences in literature, things that had never been articulated, printed or imagined, and they were the silences about black girls, black women." In 1997, Morrison was invited to read a poem of her own creation at the presidential inauguration of William J. Clinton.

In the realm of religion, reform also continued. In 1989, the Episcopal Church ordained its first woman bishop. Although the national body did not keep records of women priests, by the late 1990s officials estimated that at least 15 to 20 percent of priests in the Church were women. Nonetheless, according to eleven female priests who met in Philadelphia in 1999 to celebrate the twenty-fifth anniversary of their ordinations, the Episcopal Church had not done enough for its women. The group agreed that the Church had two conflicting factions: one that worked for peace and justice, the other that resisted change.

These women, as well as other critics, raised a large number of questions. Why did church leaders continue to use such gender-specific terms as "Lord," "Master," and "Son" when such titles reinforced the maleness of religion? Reformers, female and male, suggested such changes as calling God the "Eternal Spirit" or "Father-Mother," and Jesus the "Child." Women also tried to answer the conservative challenge, "If Jesus wanted female priests, he would have made female apostles." They pointed out that Paul praised a woman named Junia as a prominent apostle, and that women had participated in the early Christian movement following Jesus' death. According to biblical scholars, the New Testament contains other concrete examples of women's involvement.

By the early twenty-first century, these and other related issues remained in question. In addition, women had achieved mixed success entering the pulpit. Such denominations as Baptists, Episcopalians, Lutherans, Methodists, Presbyterians, United Church of Christ, and Unitarians accepted women in seminaries and ministerial positions. Most women ministers found it necessary to form female clergy groups for encouragement and support, or to initiate Internet chat rooms to reach out to other women ministers. At the same time, Southern Baptists and Roman Catholic leaders continued to prohibit female ministers and priests.

Coping with Change

After 1985 American society entered a transitional phase. Feminist organizations, governmental agencies, researchers and scholars, social workers, sociologists, and private individuals suggested strategies for dealing with change in American society. Workshops and other public programs to assist people in adjusting to the new society proliferated. A huge body of self-help literature appeared, with many titles enjoying best-seller status.

Reformers compiled a long list of objectives, which included:

- enhanced affirmative action programs
- strategies for passage of the ERA
- litigation equalizing wages of female and male workers
- job-training programs for women
- paid maternity leaves
- crisis intervention programs
- nonsexist education
- equal political representation for all
- a general overhaul of outdated notions of femininity and masculinity

In this process, the federal government was active and insistent. In 1988, Congress addressed the problems of divorce with the Family Support Act. This meant that employers would withhold child-support payments from the paychecks of "deadbeat dads," men who reneged on their court-ordered stipends to dependent children. When the provision went into effect on 1 January 1994, some states had already complied; others struggled to do so. In addition, after the televised hearings for the confirmation of Judge Clarence Thomas to the Supreme Court, in which African American attorney Anita Hill stepped forward as a character witness and described

Thomas's alleged sexual harassment of her in the workplace, the government intensified its attack on such treatment of women.

Local officials participated in further change. They recognized the seriousness of rape, or sexual assault. By the 1980s, most cities and towns had strengthened their rape laws and hired female police officers. In addition, many cities and towns offered rape counseling and established rape-crisis centers. For the first time, courts defined marital rape, meaning forced sexual intercourse between marriage partners. Research indicated that spousal rape could cause a victim more trauma than rape between strangers, for the raped spouse had not only trusted her attacker but was usually subject to multiple offenses. By 1989, thirty-eight states had marital rape laws on the books. By 1993, all fifty states declared marital rape a crime.

Individuals also contributed new ideas. Once shrouded in myth and the subject of jokes, menopausal women gained dignity, at least partly through Gail Sheehy's *The Silent Passage: Menopause* (1991). Sheehy pointed out that while menopause usually occurs between the ages of 45 and 50, women's life expectancy was 75 and rising. In other words, menopause in no way signaled the death of the modern woman, who had some twenty-five years after menopause in which to enjoy life, work, and sex.

This is not meant to suggest that after 1985 all such problems neared solution. On the contrary, cases of spousal abuse and family violence became public with regularity. At one time, police officers had considered a wife and children the property of the husband. A man could beat his wife or children if he so pleased, as it was "nobody else's business." During the 1980s and 1990s, police departments held workshops to train officers in "family intervention" techniques. Teachers and social workers were asked to watch for signs of abuse. Many communities established "safe houses," anonymous locations where battered wives and children could reside until their situations were resolved.

In addition, single motherhood among women aged 18 to 44 years rose. In 1982, 15 percent of mothers were unwed. In 1992, 24 percent of mothers were unwed. In that period, the rate of single motherhood rose from 17.2 to 32.5 percent among women with four years of high school. The rate increased from 5.5 to 11.3 percent among women with one or more years of college. The rate went from 10 to 17 percent among white women, from 16 to 27 percent among Hispanas, and from 49 to 67 percent among African American women. The trend accelerated so that between 1979 and 1996, babies born of unmarried mothers jumped from 500,000 to 10 million. By 2005, statisticians estimated that one in three children was born to an unmarried mother.

During the early 1990s, federal and state governments expanded welfare programs. In 1990, two-thirds of female-headed families received some form of welfare. Put another way, more than 80 percent of welfare recipients were female. By the late 1990s, public resistance to the tax burden created by welfare caused the federal government to institute a reform program; no longer would welfare beneficiaries receive help indefinitely. Indeed, unless those able-bodied could provide proof that they sought employment, they risked losing government aid. Single mothers especially declined in their welfare participation. These included young mothers 18 to 29 years of age, mothers with children under 7 years of age, high-school dropouts, African American and Hispanic mothers, and unmarried mothers. The other side of the picture is that single mothers also proved effective in finding employment: high-school dropout mothers achieved 40 percent of work force entry; 18-to-19 year-old mothers found employment at the rate of 71 percent, and black mothers took jobs at an 83 percent increase. The outcome of this reform is as yet unclear, but appears unworkable without job-skills training programs and government-sponsored daycare centers.

During the 1990s and 2000s, some new patterns emerged among single-parent families. Their numbers grew steadily so that by 2005 single parents accounted for 27 percent of families with children under eighteen, but more male-headed households joined the mix. By 2005, about three in ten children lived in a single-parent home, increasingly headed by men. One source estimated that between approximately 1995 and 2005, the number of single-father homes grew by 60 percent. Another claimed that in 2005, 2 million fathers acted as the primary care givers of children under eighteen, a 62 percent increase since 1990.

Single mothers, however, continued to outnumber single fathers nine-to-one. Another way of looking at the situation is that fathers made up anywhere from 13 to 20 percent of single parents. Between 1970 and 2000, the number of single mothers rocketed from 3 to 10 million. At the same time, racially mixed married and unmarried couples increased to approximately 4.5 million in 2005. In 2000, almost 2.8 million children under eighteen identified themselves as racially mixed. Census officials estimate than another 6 to 10 million children have lesbian, gay, or bisexual parents. Clearly, the definition of the "American family" was undergoing cataclysmic change.

Besides poverty, another critical problem facing society was the spread of AIDS, or Acquired Immune Deficiency Syndrome, a fatal disease contracted by transmission of bodily fluids through sexual relations or infected needles. By the spring of 1987, 2,207 women had been identified as AIDS victims. Two years later, this figure had jumped to 7,821. Indeed, heterosexual women became the fastest-growing AIDS population in the United States. More women contracted AIDS through sexual contact than through the use of infected needles. Although the federal government was slow to recognize the threat AIDS poses to women and their children, in the

1990s, President Clinton established AIDS care and research as a national priority.

During the early 2000s, President George W. Bush also committed funds to fighting AIDS. By 2005, the federal government committed nearly $20 million to care, research, assistance, and prevention of AIDS, as well as fighting the problem internationally. Yet the number of AIDS victims grew. Some observers even termed AIDS an epidemic in America. Although accurate statistics are difficult to compile, in 2002 one social service agency maintained that during that year, 32,000 Americans between 13 and 24 had contracted AIDS. Citing a figure of 43,171 new infections in 2003, another organization claimed that nearly 40,000 Americans became infected each year.

Observers noted several clear patterns. AIDS existed in all fifty states and the District of Columbia. It was most prevalent in urban areas such as New York City on the east coast of the nation and Los Angeles on the west coast. Heterosexual transmission had increased, notably among low-income and low-education groups. Women—especially those of color—were increasingly vulnerable; the number of affected women rose from 8 percent in 1985 to 27 percent in 2003.

At the same time, Alzheimer's disease neared epidemic proportions. With people living longer, the occurrence of some form of dementia, of which Alzheimer's is one, became common. Because women constituted the majority of the aged, Alzheimer's disease especially affected women. American health care had grown so costly, as had retirement and assisted-living centers, only a small number of women living with Alzheimer's received proper treatment. As a result, numerous daughters became health-care givers to their aged mothers. Women who, on the one hand, cared for parents and, on the other, had children living at home, became known as the "sandwich generation." Most of these women also held paid employment, which made their commitments overwhelming. To help, community-based workshops and other programs gave female care-givers and their families a small break.

Continuing Fears regarding Environmental Damage

Some feminists devised a philosophy known as ecofeminism. During the 1980s and 1990s, this group maintained that modern science and technology damaged the environment. Only if modern practices were combined with female principles could the Earth and its peoples survive.

Contemporary ecofeminists blamed patriarchy and its values for dominating not just women, but the physical world as well. For them, the environmental crisis was equally a crisis of white male ideology. In 1983, one ecofeminist poet stated that although "men smile like they know everything," thanks to them, the Earth is "wounded and bleeds." Shortly thereafter, practitioners of "radical ecology" argued that no group had the right to exploit nature at the expense of others. During the mid-1990s, other ecofeminists argued that the approach to environmental conservation had to be egalitarian, free of the hierarchies of command, power, and status to which most men were accustomed.

Other women concerned about the environment took more traditional routes. Many were nature writers. From Annie Dillard to Sue Hubbel, female nature writers brought landscapes and wildlife before their readers. A number of these writers focused on the American West. In essays and books, authors described the natural beauty of—and the human damage done to—western marshes, trees, deserts, mountains, prairies, and plains. The naturalist and writer Ann Zwinger celebrated from a woman's point of view the Rocky Mountains and their Aspens, Utah and its Green River, and the Southwest's four great deserts—the Chihuahuan, Sonoran, Mojave, and Nevada's Great Basin. In addition, Zwinger appealed for an informed use of western landscapes and wildlife.

Meanwhile, the number of women writers of color grew. Often, they shared with white women perceptions of nature, but certain themes distinguished some of them. One of these was a sense of place. White women often viewed nature from their farms, ranches, and cabins; women of color more often viewed nature from reservations, hogans and shacks, or urban ghettos. Too, white women were concerned about the preservation of wildlife pastures, the damage done by nearby missile bases, and the erosion of hills and mountains, whereas women of color emphasized the survival of their immediate environments.

For example, in 1990, a member of the Anishinabe tribe in northern Minnesota called for reciprocity with the environment. She explained that when her people gathered wild rice or hunted they always tried to give something back to the environment: "We're an integral part of the ecosystem in our areas . . . reciprocity is an essential part of our value system, which is very contrary to the industrial value system and the industrial society in the United States." Other Native women implemented or inspired experiments with organic food cooperatives, reforestation, and healing methods that employ natural medicines.

Opening the Military

Even though women had always participated in American wars, from the homefront to the front lines, they had seldom done so with recognition, pay, and benefits equal to that given men. Many people still believed that women were too weak and demure to serve in the military in other than "helping" capacities. Traditionally, men had protected women. Some Americans thought the situation should stay that way.

Other Americans did not like to think of their daughters, wives, or mothers serving in combat. A woman with an arm blown off was too terrible even to imagine. Worse yet, what if a woman was taken as a prisoner of war and subjected to torture, including rape? Even if those things did not happen, would not young women be sexual prey for military men? How would the military deal with sexual activity and pregnancy among its troops?

With such questions in mind, Americans still had difficulty accepting women in the military. Changing historic military policy would take time. In addition, reform would have to depend on the feats of individual women who could prove a point for all women. One of the first women to do so was Christine Baker. In 1989, at the age of twenty-one, Baker became the first woman to head the Corps of Cadets at West Point, the U.S. Army Military Academy's highest cadet honor. Selected on the basis of her academic achievement, athletic ability, and military expertise, Baker led West Point's brigade of 4,400 cadets, composed of about 10 percent women.

New technology has also made women's participation at the front more feasible. From the ultralight M-16 automatic rifle to long-range missiles that could be launched with the touch of a button, new weaponry could be handled by women. In addition, space limitations on battleships, submarines, and in warplanes, favored women, who are typically shorter and thinner than men. Also, women had the agility, reflexes, and endurance necessary to undertake most military assignments. In many areas of the armed forces, physical requirements as brute strength were no longer important, for such labor-saving devices as hydraulic lifts moved heavy cargo. Accordingly, designers of military technology took into account the presence of women and added separate bathroom facilities and sleeping quarters on new ships.

In 1990, when President George Bush called for American troops to fight in the Gulf War, women formed part of the battlefield troop movement. In Operations Desert Shield and Desert Storm, female Navy personnel accounted for 7 percent of all Navy forces stationed in the Persian Gulf. Military reports of the operation praised the performance and courage of these 3,700 women.

In 1991, Congresswoman Patricia Schroeder accomplished another coup for military women. On May 8, she successfully attached a rider to a Defense Department bill underwriting the assignment of women to combat aircraft. One female pilot who got the chance to serve in the Gulf War was Rhonda Cornum. Cornum was a soldier, surgeon, helicopter pilot, and one of two female prisoners-of-war. Although she suffered two broken arms, Cornum explained that she survived imprisonment by refusing to give up "control" of her mind to her Iraqi jailers. When she returned home, Cornum said she believed that "America is ready for army women." In her service, she had seen women serve as doctors and nurses, as mechanics and drivers, as intelligence officers and communications experts. She had even spotted women in foxholes as she steered her aircraft overhead. In her opinion, no military action had ever suffered because of the presence of women. On the contrary, she believed that women had served with integrity and courage.

Overall, in the Gulf War the U.S. armed forces lost far more men than women. Of the combat dead, 148 were men and 11 were women. Of course, this data reflects the fact that seldom were women allowed to participate in direct combat. At the same time, military officials showed a commitment to resolve the problems of military women, including the need for some women to leave small children behind, sexual relations and pregnancy among troops, and the possibility of rape by the enemy.

During the early 1990s, the U.S. Army and Air Force recruited and utilized women. Although the Army had a high proportion of combat units, ranging from infantry to artillery, it opened opportunities for enlisted women as well as female officers. By the early 1990s, approximately one in every nine Army officers was female. At the same time, female officers in the Air Force increased, although not as dramatically as in the Army.

Another step forward for women came in 1993 on Veterans Day, on which women who had served in Vietnam were recognized. The U.S. government dedicated a Vietnam Women's Memorial in Washington, D.C. Located directly across from the Vietnam Veterans Memorial, the bronze statue depicts three women nurses wearing combat fatigues, one holding a wounded soldier, another kneeling in shock over the horror of the war, and a third looking upward for a Medevac helicopter.

Nevertheless, progress for women in the military proved uneven and sometimes upsetting. For instance, the U.S. Navy established an admirable early record regarding women. After Congress lifted quotas on women in the military in 1967, the Navy recruited women; by the early 1980s, women made up nearly 7 percent of Navy forces. Unfortunately, the Tailhook scandal of 1990 blemished the Navy's public image regarding its treatment of women. After a rowdy party in Las Vegas, Nevada, in which a group of Navy personnel sexually harassed several women in the halls of their hotel, male Navy officers who had been present underwent interrogation. As it turned out, some of these men had forced Navy women to observe the lewd events. These and other men saw their careers ruined by Tailhook. But even as the onus of Tailhook hung over the Navy through the 1990s, women continued to enlist. By the early 1990s, women accounted for 11 percent of Navy personnel.

In 1993, Navy officials took a giant step forward by establishing a plan to integrate women into all aspects of Navy actions, including combat. The following year, the fatal crash of Kara Hultgreen, the first woman to fly a F-

14 Tomcat, raised questions whether the Navy had been too hasty in its efforts to promote women. Although the Navy had never investigated the crashes of male pilots, it was necessary to do so in Hultgreen's case. After a four-month study, the Navy declared Hultgreen innocent of pilot error; a technical malfunction had caused the crash that ended her life.

In 1994, Congress adopted a Defense Authorization Act that abolished legal restrictions on women's military assignments. As a result, the Army opened 32,000 ground jobs to women and the Marine Corps opened 48,000. The Navy had 9,500 billets available for women, and the Air Force reported the highest percentage of women of all the armed forces.

In 1995, the groundbreaking for the Women in Military Service for America Memorial occurred at the entrance to Arlington National Cemetery in the nation's capital. The memorial committee had collected approximately 100,000 names of women who served in United States wars, conflicts, and peacekeeping missions. According to the Defense Manpower Data Center, this figure included more than 1,000 women who served in Somalia between 1992 and 1994, more than 1,200 women who were dispatched to Haiti in 1995, and more than 5,000 women deployed to Bosnia. In addition, during the mid-1990s, women composed about 10 percent of the National Guard, more than 35,000 troops.

By the time the memorial was dedicated in 1997, the total of identified women in military service had risen to 1.8 million. The memorial's Hall of Honor recognized women who had served with special achievement or sacrifice. Women who received military awards, were prisoners of war, or who died in service were memorialized there.

During the late 1990s, every branch of the armed services established guidelines regarding women's enlistment, terms of service, and assignment to combat situations. Other policies concerned fraternization, pregnancy, and women as prisoners of war. As the United States entered the twenty-first century, not all problems relating to women in the military had been solved. Deaths of military women still made headlines. In 1998, a twenty-nine-year-old Air Force jet pilot became that branch's first female pilot fatality. Other women died as well. In 1999, a female member of the Military Police Company who placed herself between an armed gunman and three soldiers posthumously received the Soldiers Medal for heroism.

During the 2000s, growing numbers of women joined the military. In early 2005, National Public Radio reported that 350,000 women currently served, comprising 15 percent of active-duty personnel. In the war in Iraq, women accounted for one in every seven troops. Thirty-five women had died and 261 were wounded in instances ranging from combat to ambushes and car bombings. Despite these grim statistics, the number of U.S. military women continues to rise.

Daily Life

Perhaps feminism's most noticeable influence was on women's day-to-day lives. In dress, women expressed themselves in many ways. In the 1960s, 1970s, and 1980s women's outfits had ranged from long dresses to ripped jeans to "mini" skirts; during the late 1990s and early 2000s, long skirts once again appeared on store racks. In reinventing fashion with each season of the year, designers had hoped to cash in as women continuously deserted their old wardrobes and purchased new ones. Most women, however, bought some of the new fashions and incorporated them with older styles of clothing.

Meanwhile, trends in hairstyles were every bit as flexible. Women chose to wear long hair, short hair, or even a female version of the traditional men's crew-cut. They also highlighted, streaked, or colored their hair to fit their moods. In addition, they might choose to leave their hair straight or permanent-wave it into curly clusters.

While young women usually knew what was "in" at any given moment, older women were not always so sure. Thanks to feminist reform, however, many women no longer cared; all the rules their mothers had taught them regarding white gloves, matching purses and shoes, and avoiding wearing blue with green were discarded. Rather than following the dictates of fashion, modern women dressed to please themselves.

Women also felt freer from domestic duties. They cooked less, bought more prepared foods and, if they could afford to do so, ate out more frequently. Nor did women sew as much. Even women who had repaired family clothing themselves discarded torn shirts and worn-through socks in favor of purchasing new ones. Some women were fortunate enough to give away clothes of which they were tired. Thanks to the proliferation of resale shops, even poor women could dress to resemble those with more money.

Despite these changes, women's greatest daily challenge was reconciling household chores with work responsibilities. Although employed women drew on husbands, older children, kin, and friends for help, they often put in a "double-day," meaning women worked all day at work, only to work most of the night and during days off inside the home. Some coped with these unreasonable demands by relaxing their standards; it was difficult to have a tidy house, perfect children, and career advancement all at the same time. In other cases, husbands and fathers took over, sometimes choosing to stay at home full time while their wives worked or pursued careers.

For many women, the gains they enjoyed more than compensated for their stress-filled lives. In the western states, new opportunities also existed for women. During the 1980s and 1990s, women interested in ranching were no longer committed to taking over family lands and herds. Instead, they might be found running sales barns and auctions, practicing veterinary medicine, or researching herd health and reproductive technology. They entered show rings in greater numbers than ever, not only as contestants but as judges. And they worked as agricultural brokers and "futures" analysts. Undoubtedly, the western cattle industry had revolutionized, but so had conceptions of women's careers. Putting the two changes together created a wide-open situation for ambitious women.

Women made strides in professional sports as well. In 2005, driver Danica Patrick was named Indy Racing League Rookie of the Year and became the first woman to take the lead in the historic race, in which she took fourth place. And in 2006, sixteen-year-old Korean American golfer Michelle Wie was named in a *Time* magazine article, "One of the 100 people who shape our world." She was especially noted for her long drives and the interest in golf she has fostered in girls and young women.

As young women watched their mothers, they often concluded that the feminist movement had achieved its objectives. All that was left for them to do, they assumed, was to enjoy the entitlements their mothers had earned for them. Some women even declared feminism dead, no longer needed. Other women, however, determined that feminism had a long way to go, that women had much yet to achieve. This group spoke in terms of a third wave of feminism that would protect gains and establish future agendas. These wise ones also spoke of feminism's benefits not only for women, but for men as well.

Persistence of Regionalism after 1985

After 1985, American culture flattened and homogenized to an unprecedented degree. It is unclear how that homogenization has affected the American woman, for scholars have yet to conduct the comparative research and studies that will reveal whether women of various regions are more different from each other than they are similar.

Certainly, similarities existed. For instance, the black civil rights movement occurred in every region of the country. Although many do not think of African Americans as being westerners, sizeable black populations resided in urban areas like Phoenix, Seattle, and Los Angeles. One of the most violent civil rights protests had taken place in the Watts neighborhood of Los Angeles. Yet western blacks had slightly different goals than did African Americans in other regions. Unlike southern blacks, they fought job discrimination, housing restrictions, and school segregation in fact if not in law.

Other differences existed. As one example, throughout the 1990s, northeastern women divorced at a lower rate than did those in the South, who, in turn divorced at a lower rate than did women in the West, where they divorced at the highest rate in the nation, and thus in the world.

Each region also gave its own twist to reform movements. In the South, the Equal Rights Amendment had generated more opposition than support. Although Kentucky, Maryland, Tennessee, and Texas ratified the measure during the 1970s, nine other southern states did not. Rather than as a measure to protect southern women, the ERA was often seen as a threat to the family that would make women act like men. One southern white woman said, "A few women want to be men" but "don't force all of us to be one. Please." According to one poll, the majority of southern black women supported the ERA. Meanwhile, patterns of support and opposition to the ERA developed differently in the Northeast and the West.

Each region also had its own racial and ethnic problems. The West experienced a tremendous migration of Hispanics. Many of these newcomers were illegal aliens, which led to a government campaign to post guards and erect fences along the U.S.-Mexican border. Many westerners wondered if national identification cards would be the next step toward trying to separate "legal" Americans from illegal migrants. During the 1990s, the flow of immigration included growing proportions of women and children. Many of these were women-headed households in need of welfare assistance. By the early 2000s, westerners heatedly debated such questions as whether Spanish should become the nation's second "official" language.

Also in the West, Native Americans had recouped earlier population losses. Of the 325 distinct groups of Indian peoples living in the United States, the vast majority of them were located in the West. Although Indians increased in number during the 1990s, they experienced the highest rate of infant mortality of all races. Among Indian women, the rate of fetal alcohol syndrome was three to six times higher than the national average. In 1988, a Cheyenne woman told the U.S. Civil Rights Commission that Indians suffered high rates of unemployment, alcoholism, and increased teenage suicide resulting from being "mocked, dehumanized, cartooned, stereotyped."

Turn of the Twenty-first Century

Although it is tempting to view the turn of a century as the beginning of a new era, such is not the case. The year 2000 was simply a bridge between 1999 and 2001. During the twenty-first century, old problems persist; new ones appear. Former solutions are tried; new ones are suggested. Pluses offset minuses. Hope lightens despair.

All this is true for women's history. One case concerns the progress of black women. On the one hand, equality in their communities eludes them. Factors like physical abuse, rape, sexual harassment, and even demeaning rap and hip-hop lyrics keep them subordinated and fearful. In the workplace, black women and Chicanas are farther from achieving equality with men than are white women. In the business world, black women executives are relatively few, and their struggles are different from those of white women executives. The invisible glass ceiling that limits them is thicker and more impenetrable than that restraining the advancement of white women.

On the other hand, two of the most powerful people in the United States are the television personality Oprah Winfrey and Secretary of State Condoleeza Rice. These achievers provide a model for other black women and prove that change is possible. The moral is that perhaps emphasis on gender reform must be balanced by race reform, that the intersection of gender and race must be considered for further changes to take place in the twenty-first century.

Another seeming contradiction comes from the increasingly global nature of feminism. Although it is remarkable that a majority of the world's people recognize the need for change in women's lives, there are millions of women's lives that need changing. Yet American women do not hold back. When, in 1995, the United Nations sponsored the Fourth World Conference on Women in Beijing, China, 35,000 women participated, 7,000 of them from the United States. One commentator remarked that Beijing "was a city of female people. Turbans, caftans, saris, abayas, sarongs, kente cloth, blue jeans, T-shirts" blended together behind "banners, posters, buttons."

Since then, American women have joined the campaign to place on the world agenda such improvements for women as human rights, political involvement, economic development, and the end of sexual exploitation. They found organizations, make speeches and write books, and send monetary donations and experts to help. Not yet done with their own fight, they take the field on behalf of others.

Hilary Clinton provides yet another conflicted picture. As First Lady of Arkansas for twelve years beginning in 1978 and of the United States for eight years beginning in 1993, Clinton worked for health care reform and women's rights. She was criticized by some, idolized by others. During the presidency of her husband, Bill, Hilary gave up much of her activism; people thought she would disappear from the political scene at the end of her husband's second term as president. Instead, in 2000 she was elected a U.S. senator from New York and, some say, may run for president in 2008, at which time, health care reform and children's rights may yet be major national issues of the twenty-first century.

One thing is clear: the decline of the *invented* American woman. In the early twenty-first century, women face an array of choices. They can be homemakers or paid employees or both. Women compose approximately half the work force and practice in every field, including government. Sandra Day O'Connor and Ruth Bader Ginsberg were the first women on the Supreme Court, Madeleine Albright the first female secretary of state.

The ideal American woman is no longer expected to feign helplessness and act submissive.

The costs are many, the issues innumerable. What will become of marriage? Will lesbians be able to marry? Will legal abortion persist or perish? When will formalized daycare for the children of working parents finally appear in the United States, the most industrialized nation in the world but the only one without daycare? Will male students, as *Newsweek* reported early in 2006, continue to fall behind females at every level of education? In general, will American men and women draw closer or move farther apart?

Anyone who believes feminism is unneeded or dead is mistaken. Agreed, there is little unity to the story of American women. Patterns appear. Continuity vies with change, and innovation meets resistance. But, in the early twenty-first century, the story remains open-ended and unfinished. What qualities will characterize the history of women in the future? The answer will be determined not just by American women but by all Americans.

Study Guide

Checklist of important names, terms, phrases, and dates in Chapter 10. Think about what or who each was and why she, he, or it was significant.

National Organization for Women (NOW)
equality with men
Equal Rights Amendment (ERA)
Women's Equity Action League (WEAL)
feminist publications
Ms. magazine
androgyny
the "happy housewife"
Coretta Scott King
abortion on demand
Roe v. *Wade*
Women's Studies
International Women's Year Conference, 1977
Clara Pueblo v. *Martinez*
Women of All Red Nations (WARN)
Jessie Lopez de la Cruz
Black Women Organized for Action (BWOA)
National Black Feminist Organization (NBFO)
Rita Mae Brown
lesbian separatism
Adrienne Rich

Mary Daly
Angela Davis
female migrant farm workers
the "Second Wave" of feminism
Women's History Month
Dolores Huerta
comparable-worth suits
Barbara Walters
Connie Chung
Oprah Winfrey
Billie Jean King
The Dinner Party
Leontyne Price
Madonna
Maya Angelou
Alice Walker
Maxine Hong Kingston
Nicholasa Mohr
Sylvia Plath
Shirley Chisholm
Barbara Jordan
Nancy L. Kassebaum
the gender gap
Geraldine Ferraro

Loving v. *Virginia*
the feminization of poverty
no-fault divorce
displaced homemakers
eating disorders
1985
Sally K. Ride
Dr. Mae C. Jemison
Ellen Ochoa, Ph.D.
Toni Morrison

sexual harassment
menopausal women
ecofeminism
Rhonda Cornum
Vietnam Women's Memorial
Kara Hultgreen
Women in Military Service for America
    Memorial
the "double-day"
regionalism

Chapter 10 issues to think about and discuss:

* Can men and women ever be truly equal in the workplace? Before the law? In social roles? What are the advantages and disadvantages of equality?

* Should abortion remain legal in the United States? Why or why not?

* If you had had a choice, would you have been born female or male? Why?

* How did Native American, Hispanic, African American, and Asian American women's lives overlap?

* Should homosexual couples be allowed to marry legally? Why or why not?

* Should a woman be elected as President of the United States? Why hasn't this happened as of yet?

* Why did federal and state governments play such a strong role in bringing about feminist reforms?

* Why were the armed forces a last bastion of feminist change? What institutions were even more resistant to such change?

* Describe some of the problems and pitfalls in researching and studying women's history. Explain the benefits and rewards to present-day women and men of studying women's history.

* Should women's history be a required course offering in high schools, colleges, and universities? Should women's history be offered as a separate course or integrated into all other history courses?

* Do you consider yourself a feminist? Why or why not?

* What would be your top three feminist reforms in the twenty-first century?

Suggestions for Further Reading

The Feminist Movement, 1965–1985

Anderson, Karen, *Changing Woman: A History of Racial Ethnic Women in Modern America* (New York: Oxford University Press, 1996).

Baehr, Nina, "Women Making a Choice: The Long Quest for Reproductive Rights," *Radical America* 22 (1989): 44–48.

Baer, Judith A., *Women in American Law: The Struggle toward Equality from the New Deal to the Present* (New York: Holmes & Meier, 1991).

Bataille, Gretchen M., and Charles L. P. Silet, eds., *The Pretend Indians: Images of Native Americans in the Movies* (Ames: Iowa State University Press, 1980).

Berch, Bettina, *The Endless Day: The Political Economy of Women and Work* (New York: Harcourt Brace Jovanovich, Inc., 1982).

Berry, Mary Frances, *The Politics of Parenthood: Child Care, Women's Rights, and the Myth of the Good Mother* (New York: Viking Press, 1993).

Binion, Gayle, "Toward a Feminist Regrounding of Constitutional Law," *Social Science Quarterly* 72 (June 1991): 207–20.

Calderón, Roberto, and Emilio Zamora, Jr., "Manuela Solís Sanger and Emma Tenayuca: A Tribute," in *Chicana Voices: Intersections of Class, Race, and Gender,* edited by Teresa Cordóva, et al. (Austin: Center for Mexican American Studies, University of Texas at Austin, 1986).

Cantarow, Ellen, "Jessie López de la Cruz," 94–151, in *Moving the Mountain: Women Working for Social Change,* edited by Ellen Cantarow (Old Westbury, NY: Feminist Press, 1980).

Caraway, Nancie E., "The Challenge and Theory of Feminist Identity Politics: Working on Racism," *Frontiers* 12 (1991): 109–29.

———, *Segregated Sisterhood: Racism and the Politics of American Feminism* (Knoxville: University of Tennessee Press, 1991).

Cohen, Steve Martin, "American Jewish Feminism: A Study in Conflicts and Compromises," *American Behavioral Scientist* 23 (March/April 1980): 519–58.

Cook, Elizabeth Adell, "Feminist Consciousness and Candidate Preference among American Women, 1972–1988," *Political Behavior* 15 (September 1993): 227–46.

Davis, Flora, *Moving the Mountain: The Women's Movement in America since 1960* (Champaign: University of Illinois Press, 1999).

Dill, Bonnie Thornton, "The Dialectics of Black Womanhood," *Signs* 4 (Spring 1979): 543–55).

Echols, Alice, *Daring to be Bad: Radical Feminism in America* (Minneapolis: University of Minnesota Press, 1989).

Enloe, Cynthia, *The Morning After: Sexual Politics at the End of the Cold War* (Berkeley: University of California Press, 1993).

Epstein, Cynthia Fuchs, "Ten Years Later: Perspectives on the Woman's Movement," *Dissent* 22 (Spring 1975): 169–76.

Farrell, Amy Erdman, *Yours in Sisterhood: Ms. Magazine and the Promise of Popular Feminism* (Chapel Hill: University of North Carolina Press, 1999).

Foster, Martha Harroun, "Of Baggage and Bondage: Gender and Status Among Hidatsa and Crow Women," *American Indian Culture and Research Journal* 17 (1993): 121–53.

Fout, John C., and Maura Shaw Tantillo, *American Sexual Politics: Sex, Gender, and Race since the Civil War* (Chicago: University of Chicago Press, 1993).

Fox-Genovese, Elizabeth, *Feminism Without Illusions: A Critique of Individualism* (Chapel Hill: University of North Carolina Press, 1991).

Franzen, Trisha, "Differences and Identities: Feminism and the Albuquerque Lesbian Community," *Signs* 18 (Summer 1993): 891–906.

García, Alma M., "The Development of Chicana Feminist Discourse, 1970–1980," *Gender and Society* 3 (1989): 217–38.

Garrow, David J., *Liberty and Sexuality: The Right to Privacy and the Making of Roe vs. Wade* (Berkeley: University of California Press, 1998).

Harrison, Cynthia E., "A 'New Frontier' for Women: The Public Policy of the Kennedy Administration," *Journal of American History* 67 (December 1980): 630–46.

Hernández, Patricia, "Lives of Chicana Activists: The Chicano Student Movement," 17–26, in *Mexican Women in the United States: Struggle Past and Present,* edited by Magdalena Mora and Adelaida R. del Castillo (Los Angeles: Chicano Studies Research Center, University of California, Los Angeles, 1980).

Herrera-Sobek, María, ed., *Chicana Creativity and Criticism: Charting New Frontiers in American Literature* (Houston: Arte Publico Press, University of Houston, 1988).

———, *The Mexican Corrido: A Feminist Analysis* (Bloomington: Indiana University Press, 1990).

Hondagneu-Sotelo, Pierrette, "New Perspectives on Latina Women," *Feminist Studies* 19 (Spring 1993): 193–207.

Howe, Louise Kapp, *Pink Collar Workers: Inside the World of Women's Work* (New York: G. P. Putnam's Sons, 1977).

Katzenstein, Mary Fainsod, "Feminism and the Meaning of the Vote," *Signs* 10 (Autumn 1984): 4–26.

Kibria, Nazli, "Power, Patriarchy, and Gender Conflict in the Vietnamese Immigrant Community," *Gender & Society* 4 (1990): 9–24.

Kidwell, Clara Sue, "Indian Women as Cultural Mediators," *Ethnohistory* 39 (1992): 97–107.

King-Kok, Cheung, *Articulate Silences: Hisaye Yamamoto, Maxine Hong Kingston, Joy Kogawa* (Ithaca, NY: Cornell University Press, 1993).

Klein, Ethel, *Gender Politics* (Cambridge, MA: Harvard University Press, 1984).

Klein, Laura F., and Lillian A. Ackerman, eds., *Women and Power in Native North America* (Norman: University of Oklahoma Press, 1995).

Knack, Martha E., "Contemporary Southern Paiute Women and the Measurement of Women's Economic and Political Status," *Ethnology* 2 (1989): 233–48.

Lewis, Diane K., "A Response to Inequality: Black Women, Racism, and Sexism," *Signs* 3 (Winter 1977): 339–61.

Lynch, Robert N., "Women in Northern Paiute Politics," *Signs* 11 (1986): 352–66.

Margolis, Maxine L., *Mothers and Such: Views of American Women and Why They Changed* (Berkeley: University of California Press, 1984).

Mirandé, Alfredo, and Evangelina Enríquez, *La Chicana: The Mexican-American Woman* (Chicago: University of Chicago Press, 1979).

Mora, Magdalena, and Adelaida R. del Castillo, eds., *Mexican Women in the United States: Struggles Past and Present*, Occasional Paper No. 2 (Chicano Studies Research Center Publications: University of California: Los Angeles, 1980).

Moraga, Cherríe, and Gloria Anzaldúa, *The Bridge Called My Back: Writings by Radical Women of Color* (New York: Kitchen Table, Women of Color Press, 1981).

Rogow, Faith, *"Gone to Another Meeting": The National Council of Jewish Women, 1893–1993* (Tuscaloosa: University of Alabama Press, 1993).

Rowbotham, Sheila, *The Past Is Before Us: Feminism in Action Since the 1960s* (Winchester, MA: Pandora Press, 1989).

Ruiz, Vicki, ed., "Las Obreras: The Politics of Work and Family," Special Edition, *Aztlan* 20 (Spring/Fall 1991).

Ryan, Barbara, *Feminism and the Women's Movement: Dynamics of Change in Social Movement, Ideology, and Activism* (New York: Routledge, 1992).

Sánchez, Marta, *Chicana Poetry: A Critical Approach to an Emerging Literature* (Berkeley: University of California Press, 1985).

Sánchez, Rosaura, and Rosa Martinez Cruz, *Essays on La Mujer* (Los Angeles: University of California Chicano Studies Center Publications, 1977).

Singleton, Carrie Jane, "Race and Gender in Feminist Theory," *Sage* 6 (Summer 1989): 12–17.

Sommer, Laurie Kay, "Inventing Latinismo: The Creation of 'Hispanic' Panethnicity in the United States," *Journal of American Folklore* 104 (Winter 1991): 32–53.

Ybarra, Lea, "When Wives Work: The Impact on the Chicano Family," *Journal of Marriage and Family* 44 (February 1982): 169–78.

Zavella, Patricia, "'Abnormal Intimacy': The Varying Work Networks of Chicana Cannery Workers," *Feminist Studies* 11 (Fall 1985): 541–57.

———, "Reflections on Diversity among Chicanas," *Frontiers* 12 (1991): 73–85.

Assessing Gains and Losses, 1965–1985

Ammer, Christine, *Unsung: A History of Women in American Music* (Westport, CT: Greenwood Press, 1980).

Anderson, Lisa, *Mammies No More: The Changing Image of Black Women on Stage and Screen* (Lanham, MD: Rowman & Littlefield, 1997).

Bao, Xiaolan, and Roger Daniels, *Holding Up More Than Half the Sky: Chinese Women Garment Workers in New York City, 1948–92* (Champaign-Urbana: University of Illinois Press, 2001).

Bashevkin, Sylvia B., *Women on the Defensive: Living Through Conservative Times* (Chicago: University of Chicago Press, 1998).

Bloom, Harold, and William Golding, *Asian-American Women Writers* (Peabody, MS: Chelsea House Publishers, 1997).

Christian, Barbara, *Black Women Novelists: The Development of a Tradition, 1892–1976* (Westport, CT: Greenwood Press, 1980).

Collins, Lisa Gail, *Art of History: African American Women Artists Engage the Past* (New Brunswick, NJ: Rutgers University Press, 2002).

Davis, Flora, *Moving the Mountain: The Women's Movement in America since 1960* (Champaign-Urbana: University of Illinois Press, 1999).

De Alba, Alicia Gaspar, "Tortillerismo: Work by Chicana Lesbians," *Signs* 18 (Summer 1993): 956–63.

Degler, Carl N., *At Odds: Women and the Family in America from the Revolution to the Present* (New York: Oxford University Press, 1980).

Del Castillo, Adelaida R., ed., *Between Borders: Essays on Mexicana/Chicana History* (Encino, CA: Floricanto Press, 1990).

Epstein, Lee, and Joseph F. Kobylka, *The Supreme Court and Legal Change: Abortion and the Death Penalty* (Chapel Hill: University of North Carolina Press, 1992).

Etter-Lewis, Gwendolyn, *My Soul is My Own: Oral Narrative of African American Women in the Professions* (New York: Routledge, 1993).

Ferree, Myra Marx, "A Woman for President? Changing Responses: 1958–1972," *Public Opinion Quarterly* 38 (Fall 1974): 390–99.

———, "Employment Without Liberation: Cuban Women in the United States," *Social Science Quarterly* 60 (January 1979): 35–50.

Fink, Deborah, *Cutting into the Meatpacking Line: Workers and Change in the Rural Midwest* (Chapel Hill: University of North Carolina Press, 1998).

Foner, Philip S., *Women and the American Labor Movement: From World War I to the Present* (New York: Free Press, 1980).

García, María Cristina, "Adapting to Exile: Cuban Women in the United States, 1959–1973," *Latino Studies Journal* (Spring 1991): 17–33.

Green, Rayna, ed., *That's What She Said: Contemporary Poetry and Fiction by Native American Women* (Bloomington: Indiana University Press, 1984).

Groneman, Carol, and Mary Beth Norton, eds., *"To Toil the Livelong Day": America's Women at Work, 1780–1980* (Ithaca, NY: Cornell University Press, 1987).

Gustafson, Melanie, Kristie Miller, and Elisabeth Israels Perry, eds., *We Have Come to Stay: American Women and Political Parties* (Albuquerque: University of New Mexico Press, 1999).

Halper, Donna L., *Invisible Stars: A Social History of Women in American Broadcasting* (Armonk, NY: M. E. Sharpe, Inc., 2001).

Hollrah, Patrice E., *"The Old Lady Trill, the Victory Yell": The Power of Women in Native American Literature* (Philadelphia: Taylor and Francis, Inc., 2003).

Huang, Fung-Yea, *Asian and Hispanic Immigrant Women in the Work Force: Implications of the United States Immigration Policies since 1965* (Philadelphia: Taylor and Francis, 1996).

Kennedy, Elizabeth Lapovsky, and Madeline D. Davis, *Boots of Leather, Slippers of Gold: The History of a Lesbian Community* (New York: Penguin USA, 1993).

Kennedy, Susan Estabrook, *If All We Did Was to Weep at Home: A History of White Working-Class Women in America* (Bloomington: Indiana University Press, 1979).

Kessler-Harris, Alice, *Out to Work: A History of Wage-Earning Women in the United States* (New York: Oxford University Press, 1982).

———, *A Woman's Wage: Historical Meanings and Social Consequences* (Lexington: University Press of Kentucky, 1990).

Kim, Elaine H., with Janie Otani, *With Silk Wings: Asian American Women at Work* (San Francisco: Asian Women of California, 1983).

Kubitschek, Missy Dehn, *Claiming the Heritage: Afro-American Women Novelists and History* (Jackson: University Press of Mississippi, 1991).

Lamphere, Louise, "Bringing the Family to Work: Women's Culture on the Shop Floor," *Feminist Studies* 11 (Fall 1985): 518–40.

Ling, Huping, *Surviving on the Gold Mountain: A History of Chinese American Women and Their Lives* (New York: State University of New York Press, 1998).

Litoff, Judy Barrett, *American Midwives: 1860 to the Present* (Westport, CT: Greenwood Press, 1978).

Loza, Steven, *Barrio Rhythm: Mexican American Music in Los Angeles* (Urbana: University of Illinois Press, 1993).

Melosh, Barbara, *"The Physicians' Hand": Work, Culture, and Conflict in American Nursing* (Philadelphia: Temple University Press, 1982).

———, ed., *Gender and American History since 1890* (New York: Routledge, 1993).

Melville, Margarita, ed., *Twice a Minority* (St. Louis: C. V. Mosby, 1980).

Powers, Marla N., *Oglala Women: Myth, Ritual, and Reality* (Chicago: University of Chicago Press, 1986).

Prieto, Yolanda, "Cuban Women in the U.S. Labor Force: Perspectives on the Nature of Change," *Cuban Studies* 17 (1987): 73–91.

———, "Cuban Women in New Jersey: Gender Relations and Change," 185–202, in *Seeking Common Ground: Multidisciplinary Studies of Immigrant Women in the United States,* edited by Donna Gabaccia (Westport, CT: Greenwood Press, 1992).

Rebolledo, Tey Diana, Erlinda Gonzales-Berry, and Teresa Márquez, eds., *Las Mujeres Hablan: An Anthology of Nuevo Mexicana Writers* (Albuquerque: El Norte Publications, 1988).

Richmond, Marie La Liberté, *Immigrant Adaptation and Family Structure Among Cubans in Miami, Florida* (New York: Arno Press, 1980).

Robinson, Donald Allen, "Two Movements in Pursuit of Equal Employment Opportunity," *Signs* 4 (Spring 1979): 413–33.

Rogers, Mary Beth, *Barbara Jordan: American Hero* (New York: Bantam, 1998).

Romero, Mary, *Maid in the U.S.A.* (New York: Routledge, 1992).

Scott, Joan Wallach, "The Mechanization of Women's Work," *Scientific American* 247 (September 1982): 166–87.

Senese, Guy, "Promise and Practice: Important Developments in Wartime and Post-War Indian Education Policy, 1940–1975," *Journal of Thought* 19 (Fall 1984): 11–30.

Thornton, Arland, and Deborah Freedman, "Changes in the Sex Role Attitudes of Women, 1962–1977: Evidence from a Panel Study," *American Sociological Review* 44 (October 1979): 831–42.

Walker-Hill, Helen, *From Spirituals to Symphonies: African-American Women Composers and Their Music* (Westport, CT: Greenwood Publishing Group, Inc., 2002).

Wandersee, Winifred D., *On the Move: American Women in the 1970s* (New York: Twayne Publishers, 1988).

Witt, Linda, Karen M. Paget, and Glenna Matthews, *Running as a Woman: Gender and Power in American Politics* (Free Press, 1995).

Since 1985

Anzaldua, Gloria, *Borderlands/La Frontera: The New Mestiza* (San Francisco: Spinsters/ Aunt Lute Book Co., 1987).

Arendell, Terry J., "Women and the Economics of Divorce in the Contemporary United States," *Signs* 13 (Autumn 1987): 121–35.

Attebury, Lt. Col. Mary Ann, USAFR, "Women and Their Wartime Roles," *Minerva: Quarterly Report on Women and the Military* 8 (Spring 1990): 11–28.

Booher, Alice A., "American Military Women: Prisoners of War," *Minerva: Quarterly Report on Women and the Military* 11 (Spring 1993): 17–22.

Campbell, D'Ann, "Combating the Gender Gulf," *Temple Political and Civil Rights Law Review* 2 (Fall 1992): 63–91.

Chan, Sucheng, Douglas Henry Daniels, Mario T. García, and Terry P. Wilson, eds., *Peoples of Color in the American West* (Lexington, MA: D.C. Heath, 1994).

Copeland, Peter, *The Rhonda Cornum Story* (Thorndike, MN: G. K. Hall, 1992).

Del Mar Peterson, David, *What Trouble I Have Seen: A History of Violence Against Women* (Cambridge: Harvard University Press, 1996).

Delli Capini, Michael X., and Esther R. Fuchs, "The Year of the Woman? Candidates, Voters, and the 1992 Elections," *Political Science Quarterly* 108 (Spring 1993): 29–36.

Fletcher, Jean W., Joyce S, McMahon, and Aline O. Quester, "Tradition, Technology, and the Changing Roles of Women in the Navy," *Minerva* 11 (Fall/Winter 1993): 57–85.

Francke, Linda Bird, *Ground Zero: The Gender Wars in the Military* (New York: Simon & Schuster, 1997).

Garrison, Becky, "Too Many Women? What Gender–neutral Recruiting Means to Today's Navy," *Navy Times*, March 27, 1995: 10.

Gold, Victor, Sharon H. Ringe, Burton H. Throckmorton, Barbara Withers, Susan Brooks Thislethwaite, and Thomas L. Hoyt, eds., *The New Testament and Psalms: An Inclusive Version* (New York: Oxford University Press, 1995).

Golden, Stephanie, *The Women Outside: Meanings and Myths of Homelessness* (Berkeley: University of California Press, 1992).

Haynsworth, Leslie, and David Toomey, *Amelia Earhart's Daughters: The Wild and Glorious Story of American Women Aviators from World War II to the Dawn of the Space Age* (New York: William Morrow, 1998).

Herbert, Mellisa S., "From Crinoline to Camouflage: Initial Entry Training and the Marginalization of Women in the Military," *Minerva: Quarterly Report on Women and the Military* 11 (Spring 1993): 41–57.

Hirschman, Loree Draude, and Dave Hirschman, *She's Just Another Navy Pilot: An Aviator's Sea Journal* (Annapolis: Naval Institute Press, 1999).

Huyck, Heather, "Beyond John Wayne: Using Historic Sites to Interpret Women's History," 303–30, in *Western Women: Their Land, Their Lives,* edited by Lillian Schlissel, Vicki L. Ruiz, and Janice Monk (Albuquerque: University of New Mexico Press, 1988).

Katz, Michael B., Mark J. Stern, and Jamie J. Fader, "Women and the Paradox of Economic Inequality in the Twentieth-Century," *Journal of Social History* 39 (Fall 2005): 65–88.

Kidwell, Claudia Brush, and Valerie Steele, *Men and Women: Dressing the Part, History of Fashion* (Washington, DC: Smithsonian Institution Press, 1989).

Lamphere, Louise, Patricia Zavella, and Felipe Gonzales, *Sunbelt Working Mothers: Reconciling Family and Factory* (Ithaca, NY: Cornell University Press, 1993).

Maret, Elizabeth, *Women of the Range: Women's Role in the Texas Beef Cattle Industry* (College Station: Texas A&M University Press, 1993).

Mason, Mary Ann, *From Father's Property to Children's Rights: The History of Child Custody in the United States* (New York: Columbia University Press, 1994).

Medicine, Beatrice, "North American Indigenous Women and Cultural Domination," *American Indian Culture and Research Journal* 17 (1993): 121–30.

Miller, Page Putnam, ed., *Reclaiming the Past: Landmarks of Women's History* (Bloomington: Indiana University Press, 1992).

———, "Women's History Landmark Project: Policy and Research," *The Public Historian* 15 (Fall 1993): 82–88.

Musick, Judith S., *Young, Poor, and Pregnant: The Psychology of Teenage Motherhood* (New Haven, CT: Yale University Press, 1993).

Paige, Joy, *Ellen Ochoa: The First Hispanic Women in Space*, Young Adult title (New York: Rosen Publishing Group, Inc., 2004).

Ruiz, Vicki L., and Susan Tiano, eds., *Women on the U.S.-Mexico Border: Responses to Change* (Boulder, CO: Westview Press, 1991).

Sanders, Marlene, and Marcia Rock, *Waiting for Prime Time: The Women of Television News* (Urbana: University of Illinois Press, 1994).

Smith, M. Dwayne, and Ellen S. Kuchta, "Trends in Violent Crime Against Women, 1973–1989," *Social Science Quarterly* 74 (March 1993): 28–45.

Spears, Sally, *Call Sign Revlon: The Life and Death of Navy Fighter Pilot Kara Hultgreen* (Annapolis: Naval Institute Press, 1999).

Stiehm, Judith Hicks, ed., *It's Our Military, Too! Women and the U.S. Military* (Philadelphia: Temple University Press, 1996).

Stoddard, Ellwyn R., "Female Participation in the U.S. Military: Gender Trends by Branch, Rank, and Racial Categories," *Minerva: Quarterly Report on Women and the Military* 11 (Spring 1993): 23–40.

Strasser, Susan, *Never Done: A History of American Housework* (New York: Pantheon Books, 1981).

Tucker, Sherrie, "'Where the Blues and the Truth Lay Hiding': Rememory of Jazz in Black Women's Fiction," *Frontiers* 13 (1993): 26–44.

Zimmerman, Jean, *Tail Spin: Women at War in the Wake of Tailhook* (New York: Doubleday, 1995).

Turn of the Twenty-first Century

Cole, Johnnetta B., and Beverly Guy-Sheftall, *Gender Talk: The Struggle for Women's Equality in African American Communities* (New York: Random House, 2003).

Bell, Ella L., and Stella M. Nkomo, *Our Separate Ways: Black and White Women and the Struggle for Personal Identity* (Cambridge, MA: Harvard Business School Publishing, 2003).

Browne, Irene, ed., *Latinas and African American Women at Work: Race, Gender and Economic Inequality* (New York: Russell Sage Foundation, 2000).

Collier-Thomas, Bettye, and V. P. Franklin, *Sisters in the Struggle: African American Women in the Civil Rights–Black Power Movement* (New York: New York University Press, 2001).

Creatsas, George, ed., *Young Women at the Rise of the 21st Century: Gynecologic and Reproductive Issues in Health and Disease* (New York: New York Academy of Sciences, 2001).

Evans, Sara M., *Tidal Wave: How Women Changed America at Century's End* (New York: Free Press, 2003).

Hunter, Margaret, *The Lighter the Berry: Race, Color and Gender in the Lives of African American and Mexican Women* (Philadelphia: Taylor and Francis, Inc., 2005).

Manatu, Norma, and Kwyn Bader, *African American Women and Sexuality in the Cinema* (Jefferson, NC: McFarland and Co., Inc., 2002).

Rosen, Ruth, *The World Split Open: How the Modern Women's Movement Changed America* (New York: Penguin Books, 2000).

Taylor, Quintard, and Shirley Ann Wilson Moore, *African American Women Confront the West, 1600–2000* (Norman: University of Oklahoma Press, 2003).

Conclusion

Looking toward the Future

Unlike members of numerous other cultures, Americans typically have believed that change equates with progress, that progress is always positive, and that the United States achieves progress in a linear fashion. Traditionally, American history courses have reinforced these notions, teaching that the colonists who migrated to the shores of North America launched a democratic experiment, and that subsequent generations enlarged and perfected that endeavor, reaping power and prosperity as their rewards.

In the early twenty-first century, however, most Americans realize that the historical trajectory is far more complicated. Change can move a nation forward or backward. Progress can be destructive as well as constructive. Continuity can exert at least as powerful a force as change. Thus, change has consisted of cycles, which often lack clear direction and include conflict, dissension, and uncertainty. At the same time, only some people enjoyed the rewards of power and prosperity, while others paid the costs, enduring loss, poverty, and relative powerlessness.

The survey of American women's history presented here has revealed similar patterns. Between 1607 and the mid-1800s, expectations of American women changed in many ways, even though their overall configuration stayed much the same. Between the mid-nineteenth century and the early 2000s, customary gender expectations and social constructs came under attack from every side yet continued to resist destruction.

During the latter period, numerous people argued for the expansion of women's participation in American society. Female and male reformers exerted pressure on all levels of society to become more egalitarian. Through voluntary associations, these people worked for social and gender reforms. Those who advocated woman suffrage argued particularly for women's right to the ballot.

When the United States finally granted the right of suffrage to its female citizens in 1920, it became clear that the vote was not a panacea. Years earlier, Elizabeth Cady Stanton had dismissed the right to vote as "not even half a loaf . . . only a crust, a crumb." Following the achievement of suffrage, women's rights advocates realized that Stanton had been prophetic. The right of suffrage barely scratched the surface of necessary reform.

During the Great Depression and World War II, additional factors encouraged scrutiny of the customary model of American womanhood. Economic collapse, war, industrialization, urbanization, and energetic reform movements led to a general rethinking of women's roles and responsibilities. Were women to be limited only to wife- and motherhood? Or were there other roles that they might happily and effectively play in addition to these? Was the nation squandering a crucial resource in restricting women to customary, domestic lifestyles?

At the same time, the national determination to see American women as domestic, docile, cheerful, simple, and submissive beings enjoyed periods of rejuvenation, especially during the Great Depression and the back-to-the-home movement that followed the conclusion of World War II. Apparently, many Americans felt reluctant to surrender the traditional view of women as properly relegated to, and fulfilled by, the world of home and family.

Throughout each of these eras, women of color and such others as employed, lesbian, and single women received less attention and assistance than so-called mainstream women. In the 1960s, the need for a renewed feminist movement seemed apparent to women from a wide variety of backgrounds. The resulting contemporary feminist movement of that decade appealed to people of all races, classes, and types. It proved the largest ever in membership and the most widely based in constituencies, platforms, and programs.

Since then, American society experienced basic and pervasive modifications in the structure of American institutions, the fabric of American culture, and Americans' interpersonal relations. Still, the traditional pattern persevered. By the 1980s, backlash and resistance developed. The struggle between the model of womanhood and the reality of women's lives exhibited more complexity than ever before, while women of color and other groups of women often endured isolation.

At the beginning of the twenty-first century, the situation is uneven and diverse. Although the current climate may be uncertain, it does offer American women and men many opportunities to participate in fashioning their future and that of American society.

Important questions remain. How does one bring about change? How significant a role can such factors as human agency and women's distinctive culture play? Or will such social, economic, and political forces as depression and war determine the future?

If anything, the lesson of this review of women's history has been that human will and women's culture had great weight in the development of American women's history. For instance, in the face of economic and political pressures that eroded Indian women's traditions, their status as producers and traders, and their power within their tribes, they refused to allow themselves to collapse. Instead, they adapted to the market economy by producing new goods that white people and others would purchase. They also formed women's associations to fight discriminatory policies and actions. Outside forces battered them, yet they resisted and endured.

Hundreds of other women whose names have appeared herein also defied the demands of dominant institutions. African American women resisted slavery and, when urbanization later overwhelmed them, they created the blues, jazz, and a rich literature. Hispanas developed ways to protest labor injustices, then used them as a foundation to demand civil rights, urban reform, and revisions in the family structure. White women protested gender expectations based on domesticity. From Anne Bradstreet to Elizabeth Cady Stanton to Betty Friedan, they fought back. Asian American women turned Chinatowns and Little Tokyos into bases from which they learned to preserve their own customs, yet adapt to the larger American culture.

Looking at women from a perspective other than their racial or ethnic backgrounds produces similar observations. Lesbian women withstood social pressures by creating "Boston Marriages," and later such groups as Radicalesbians. Hearing-impaired women took their act on the road with such groups as the National Theatre of the Deaf and Gallaudet College Dancers. Religiously oriented women formed the Leadership Conference of Women Religious, Hadassah, and the Center for Women and Religion to achieve their ends. Radical women joined the Socialist and Communist parties, and rural women participated in such organizations as the Farmers' Alliance and the Populist party.

Today, these women provide a model and an inspiration. Although numerous Americans fear the future, most recognize that rather than signaling the necessity to quit and turn backward, anxiety only indicates a need to proceed with deliberation and care. Like the hundreds of forerunners who appear in this book, contemporary Americans must confront and resolve the issues that face them.

For instance, more women than men now obtain a college education, while such fields as law and English literature are feminizing. What do such changes mean for coming generations of Americans? How can the United States prepare its youth to accept growing numbers of women in positions of leadership and authority? How can women fortify themselves to avoid the mistakes that men of power sometimes committed? Can they avoid them?

Undertaking to answer these and other questions will benefit not only women but men as well. Clearly, people of both genders must participate. This venture also requires the participation of all types of women and men—those of Native American, Hispanic, white, African, and Asian heritage; gay and lesbian; working class and professional—for they must inhabit together the increasingly globalized world they are shaping.

Index

Inventing the American Woman: An Inclusive History, in Two Volumes, *Volume I, To 1877,* and *Volume II, Since 1877,* Fourth Edition
Developmental editor and Copy editor: Andrew J. Davidson
Production editor: Lucy Herz
Proofreader: Claudia Siler
Indexer: Pat Rimmer
Cover designer: Christopher Calvetti, c2itgraphics
Printer: Versa Press, Inc.